MRS. E. F. L. ELLET.

TAKEN IN 1850

Engraved by H.B Hall N.Y.

THE

PIONEER WOMEN

OF THE

WEST

by

Mrs. Elizabeth F. Ellet

AUTHOR OF "THE QUEENS OF AMERICAN SOCIETY,"
"THE WOMEN OF THE AMERICAN REVOLUTION," ETC.

HERITAGE BOOKS
2008

HERITAGE BOOKS
AN IMPRINT OF HERITAGE BOOKS, INC.

Books, CDs, and more—Worldwide

For our listing of thousands of titles see our website
at
www.HeritageBooks.com

A Facsimile Reprint
Published 2008 by
HERITAGE BOOKS, INC.
Publishing Division
100 Railroad Ave. #104
Westminster, Maryland 21157

Originally published
Philadelphia:
Porter & Coates
1873

— Publisher's Notice —
In reprints such as this, it is often not possible to remove blemishes from
the original. We feel the contents of this book warrant its reissue despite
these blemishes and hope you will agree and read it with pleasure.

International Standard Book Numbers
Paperbound: 978-0-7884-2126-6
Clothbound: 978-0-7884-7589-4

PREFACE.

An appropriate supplement to the memoirs of the "Women of the American Revolution," is the story of the wives and mothers who ventured into the western wilds, and bore their part in the struggles and labors of the early pioneers. Indeed, so obvious a consequence of the Revolution was the diffusion of the spirit of emigration, that the one work naturally calls for the other, the domestic history of the period being incomplete without it. To supply this want, very little published material existed, and that little in the shape of brief anecdotes, scattered through historical collections made in several Western States, and scarcely known in other parts of the Union. But a vast store might be yielded from the records of private families, and the still vivid recollections of individuals who had passed through the experiences of frontier and forest life, and it was not yet too late to save from oblivion much that would be the more interesting and valuable, as the memory of those primitive times receded into the past.

Application has been made, accordingly, to the proper sources throughout the Western States, and the result enables me to offer such a series of authentic sketches as will not only exhibit the character of many pioneer matrons—characters that would pass for strongly marked originals in any fiction—but will afford a picture of the times in the progressive settlement of the whole country, from Tennessee to Michigan. To render this picture as complete as possible, descriptions of the domestic life and manners of the pioneers, and illustrative anecdotes from reliable sources, have been interwoven with the memoirs, and notice has been taken of such political events as had an influence on the condition of the country.

All the biographies, except those of Mrs. Boone and Mary Moore, have been prepared from private records, furnished by relatives or friends, and in two or three instances by the subjects. I do not except those of Mrs. Williams and Mrs. Rouse, for which I am indebted to the courtesy of Dr. S. P. Hildreth, though they appeared in a more extended form many years since, in a Western periodical of limited circulation. My grateful acknowl edgments are due to Mr. Milton A. Haynes, of Tennessee, for the memoirs of Mrs. Bledsoe, Mrs. Brown and Mrs. Shelby, written for this work; and also to Mr. A. W. Putnam, of Nashville, Tennessee, for those of Mrs. Sevier and Mrs. Sparks. Both in Tennessee and Ohio I had access to valuable manuscripts belonging to the Historical Societies, and to letters in the possession of individuals. For most of the sketches illustrative of Michigan, included in those of Mrs. Clark, Mrs. Bryan, Mrs. Rumsey and Mrs. Noble, I have pleasure in acknowledging my obligations to an accomplished friend—Miss Mary H. Clark of Ann Arbor, Michigan. The published works from which extracts have been made, are generally mentioned, and a repetition of authorities would be unnecessary. Flint's Life of Boone, Dr. Hildreth's Notes on the Pioneer History of Ohio, Howe's Historical Collections of Ohio, and Lanman's History of Michigan, have chiefly aided me, though a vast number of other books have been consulted.

A word may be permitted here as to the proprietorship of memoirs prepared from original materials derived from private sources. It seems reasonable that the exclusive right should belong to the one who procures and works up such materials; and that no other person can, without a violation of the principles of common justice, make use of the memoirs to such an extent as to inter

fere with the interests of the original work. This remark
is called forth by the fact that a volume was published in
Buffalo, in 1851, entitled "Noble Deeds of American
Women, with Biographical Sketches of some of the more
prominent"—in which thirty-eight sketches prepared
entirely from original manuscripts, (the subjects not even
named in any other published work,) were taken from the
volumes of "The Women of the American Revolution,"
twenty-six of them being appropriated, in an abridged
form, without the slightest acknowledgment.

E. F. E.

CONTENTS.

THE PIONEER WOMEN OF THE WEST.

I.

MARY BLEDSOE.

> " Men's due deserts each reader may recite,
> For men of men do make a goodly show ;
> But women's works can seldom come to light,
> No mortal man their famous acts may know ;
> Few writers will a little time bestow,
> The worthy acts of women to repeat ;
> Though their renown and the deserts be great."

THE poet's complaint might be made with peculiar justice in the case of American women who followed the earliest adventurers into the unknown forests of the West. One of their own number often said—" A good Providence sent such men and women into the world together. They were made to match." Such a race will probably never again live in this country. The progress of improvement, art, and luxury, has a tendency to change the female character, so that even a return of the perils of war, or the necessity for exertion, would hardly develop in it the strength which belonged to the matrons who nursed the infancy of the Republic. They were formed by early training in habits of energetic industry, and familiarity with privation and danger, to take their part in subduing the wilderness for the advance of civilization. Though their descendants cannot emulate their heroic deeds, it will be a pleasing task to call up recollections of them ; to observe their patient endurance of hardship, and to compare their homely but honest exterior with the accomplishment and graces of the sex in modern days.

A large portion of the history of the early settlers of the West has never been recorded in any published work. It is full of personal adventure, and no power of imagination could create materials more replete with romantic interest than their simple experience afforded. The training of those hardy pioneers in their frontier life ; the daring with which they penetrated the wilderness, plunging into trackless forests, and encountering the savage tribes whose hunting grounds they had invaded, and the sturdy perseverance with which they overcame all difficulties, compel our wondering admiration. It has been truly said of them, " The greater part of mankind might derive advantage from the contemplation of their humble virtues, hospitable homes, and spirits patient, noble, proud, and free ; their self-respect, grafted on innocent thoughts ; their days of health and nights of sleep ; their toils by danger dignified, yet guiltless ; their hopes of a cheerful old age and a quiet grave."

But less attention has been given to their exploits and sufferings than they deserve, because the accounts read are too vague and general ; the picture not being brought near, nor exhibited with lifelike proportions and coloring. A collection of memoirs of women must of necessity include some reliable account of the domestic and daily life of those heroic adventurers, and may perhaps supply the deficiency. Commencing with the first colonists of Tennessee, which claims priority of settlement, we light upon a name associated with its early annals, and distinguished among pioneers—that of Bledsoe. But before entering on a sketch of this family, a brief view may be given of the general state of the country.

Until the year 1700, the territory of North Carolina and Tennessee, and an indefinite region extending south-west and north-west, in the language of the royal British charters, to the South Seas, was known as " our county of Albemarle, in Carolina." Even as late as

1750, the country lying west of the Apalachian mountains was wholly unknown to the people of the Carolinas and Virginia. When, a few years later, the British army under Braddock crossed the mountains from Maryland and Pennsylvania, and marched to Fort Du Quesne, that march was described by the writers of the times as an advance into the deep recesses and fastnesses of a savage wilderness. At that time the French owned all the Canadas, the valley of the Ohio and all its tributaries, and claimed the rest of the continent to the confines of Mexico, westward from the Ohio and Mississippi rivers. The old French maps of that period, and the journals and letters of French traders and hunters, together with the traditions of the Indians, afford the only reliable information in relation to the then condition of the country now composing Kentucky and Tennessee. In the French maps of those times, the Kentucky, Holston, Tennessee, and Ohio are laid down. The Kentucky is called Cataway, the Holston the Cherokee, and the Little Tennessee the Tanasees. This river, after the junction of the Holston and Tennessee, is called Ho-go-hegee, and the only Indian town marked on its banks is at the mouth of Bear Creek, near the north-west corner of Alabama. There were forts which were little more than trading posts, at several points on the Ohio and Mississippi; Fort Du Quesne, where Pittsburg now stands, and one at the mouth of the Kenhawa river; another at the mouth of the Kentucky, and Fort Vincennes, near the mouth of the Oubach, or Wabash; Fort Massac, half way between the mouth of the Ohio and the Tennessee, on the Illinois side, and another on the Tennessee, twelve miles above its mouth. They also had a fort where Memphis now stands, called Prud'homme; another at the mouth of the Arkansas, called Ackensâ; another near Natchez, and one at the junction of the Coosa and Tallapoosa, called Halabamas. South of these last forts, the Spaniards had possession in Florida, Louisiana, and Texas. The greater part of Kentucky, Tennessee, and Western Virginia, was represented on these maps as wholly uninhabited. Certain it is that not more than a dozen years afterwards, when the pioneers of Tennessee and Kentucky first explored that region, they found the banks of the Watauga, Cumberland, and Kentucky, with their tributaries, in this state. It was all one vast wilderness, into which hunting parties of Indians from its distant borders entered and roamed in pursuit of game, but in which they made no permanent lodgment. Numerous warlike nations lived south, west, and north of this wilderness, and hither it was that the lion-hearted pioneers of the Cumberland and Watauga came, with axe and rifle, to subdue at once the savage and the forest.

In 1758, Col. Bird, of the British army, established Fort Chissel in Wyth county, Virginia, to protect the frontiers, and, advancing into what is now Sullivan county, Tennessee, built a fort near Long Island, on the Holston or Watauga. There was not then a single white man living in the borders of Tennessee. The year before, Governor Dobbs of North Carolina had, at the request of the Cherokee Indians, built Fort Lowdon, and the Indians agreed to make grants of land to all artisans who would settle among them. Fort Lowdon was on the Little Tennessee, near the mouth of Tel lico river, in the centre of the Cherokee nation, and about one hundred miles south of the fort at Long Island. Between these forts were the first settlements, which struggled for several years against the fearful ravages of Indian wars, before the beginning of the Revolution.

At irregular intervals from 1765 to 1769, came pioneer parties from Virginia and North Carolina, forming " camps," " settlements," and " stations." Some of the earliest emigrants were from Raleigh and Salisbury, and settled upon the Watauga. The first settlement attempted on the spot where Nashville now stands, is said to have been in 1778, the " French Lick," as the locality was named, having been discovered, according to Haywood, in 1769 or 1770, by a party of adventurers, who were descending the Cumberland on their way to Natchez, to dispose of articles which they had, and purchase others which they wanted. They saw an immense number of buffaloes and wild game. The lick and adjoining lands were crowded with them, and their bellowing resounded from the hills and forest. The place had previously been visited by French hunters and trappers from the north. The surrounding hills were then covered with cedars, whose foliage deeply shaded the rocky soil from which they sprung, and there was no appearance of former cultivation. No prospect spread before the eye but woods and cane, inhabited by buffaloes, elks, wolves, foxes, and other wild animals. Not deterred by the neighborhood of these, or fiercer savages, the new comers here erected cabins, constructed a stockade fort, and maintained possession against several attacks by the Indians.

Two brothers of the name of Bledsoe—Englishmen by birth,—were living in 1769 at Fort Chissel, then upon the extreme border of civilization. It was not long before they removed further into the wild, and they were among the earliest pioneers in the valley of the Holston. This portion of country, now Sullivan county, was at that time supposed to be within the limits of Virginia. The Bled-soes, with the Shelbys, settled themselves about twelve miles above the Island Flats. The beauty of that mountainous region attracted others, who, impelled by the same spirit of adventure and pride in being the first to explore the wilderness, came to join them in establishing the colony. They cheerfully ventured their property and lives, and endured the severest privations in taking possession of their new homes, influenced by the love of independence and equality. The most dearly prized rights of man had been threatened in the oppressive system adopted by Great Britain towards her colonies ; her agents and the colonial magistrates manifested all the insolence of authority ; and individuals who had suffered from their aggressions bethought themselves of a country beyond the mountains, in the midst of primeval forests, where no laws existed save the law of nature—no magistrate, except those selected by themselves ; where full liberty of conscience, of speech, and of action prevailed. Yet almost in the first year they formed a written code of regulations by which they agreed to be governed ; each man signing his name thereto. These settlements formed by parties of emigrants from neighboring provinces were not, in their constitution, unlike those of New Haven and Hartford ; but among them was no godly Hooker, no learned and heavenly-minded

Haynes. As, however, from the first they were exposed to the continual depredations and assaults of their savage neighbors, who looked with jealous eyes upon the approach of the white men, it was perhaps well that there were among them few men of letters. The rifle and the axe, their only weapons of civilization, suited better the perils they encountered from the fierce and marauding Shawnees, Chickamangas, Creeks, and Cherokees, than would the brotherly address of William Penn, or the pious discourses of Roger Williams.

During the first year, not more than fifty families had crossed the mountains; but others came with each revolving season to reinforce the little settlement, until its population swelled to hundreds   During the Revolutionary struggle, that region became the refuge of many patriots driven by British invasion from Virginia, the Carolinas, and Georgia, some of the best families seeking homes there. Patriotic republicans who had sacrificed everything for their country, hoped to find in the secluded vales and thick forests of the West that peace and quiet which they had not found amidst the din of civil and foreign war. But they soon experienced the horrors of savage warfare, which swept away their property, and often robbed them of their wives and children, either by a barbarous death or slavery as captives dragged into the wild recesses of the Indian borders. They took up their residence, for mutual aid and protection, in clusters around different stations, within a short distance of one another, and many lived in the forts. Notwithstanding the frequent and terrible inroads upon their numbers, they increased to thousands within ten or fifteen years.

Not long after the Bledsoes established themselves upon the banks of the Holston, Col. Anthony Bledsoe, who was an excellent surveyor, was appointed clerk to the commissioners who ran the line dividing Virginia and North Carolina. Bledsoe had before this ascertained that Sullivan County was comprised within the boundaries of the latter province. In June, 1776, he was chosen by the inhabitants of the county to the command of the militia. The office imposed on him the dangerous duty of repelling the savages and defending the frontier. He had often to call out the militia and lead them to meet their Indian assailants, whom they would pursue to their villages through the recesses of the forest. In this month more than seven hundred Indian warriors advanced upon the settlements on the Holston, with the avowed object of exterminating the white race through all their borders. The battle of Long Island, fought a few miles below Bledsoe's station, near the Island Flats, was one of the earliest and hardest fought battles known in the traditionary history of Tennessee. Col. Bledsoe, at the head of the militia, marched to meet the enemy, and in the conflict which ensued was completely victorious ; the Indians being routed, and leaving forty dead upon the field. This disastrous defeat for a time held them in check ; but the spirit of savage hostility was invincible, and in the years following there was a constant succession of Indian troubles, in which Col. Bledsoe was conspicuous for his bravery and services.

In 1779, Sullivan County having been recognized as a part of North Carolina, Governor Caswell appointed Anthony Bledsoe colonel, and Isaac Shelby lieutenant-colonel, of its military company. About the beginning of July of the following year, General Charles McDowell, who commanded a district east of the mountains, sent to Bledsoe a dispatch, giving him an account of the condition of the country. The surrender of Charleston had brought the State of South Carolina under British power; the people had been summoned to return to their allegiance, and resistance was ventured only by a few resolute spirits, determined to brave death rather than submit to the invader. The whigs had fled into North Carolina, whence they returned as soon as they were able to oppose the enemy. Colonels Tarleton and Ferguson had advanced towards North Carolina at the head of their soldiery ; and McDowell ordered Col. Bledsoe to rally the militia of his county, and come forward in readiness to assist in repelling the invader's approach. Similar dispatches were sent to Col. Sevier and other officers, and the patriots were not slow in obeying the summons.

While the British Colonel Ferguson, under the orders of Cornwallis, was sweeping the country near the frontier, gathering the loyalists under his standard and driving back the whigs, against whom fortune seemed to have decided, a resolute band was assembled for their succor far up among the mountains.   From a population of five or six thousand, not more than twelve hundred of them fighting men, a body of near five hundred mountaineers, armed with rifles and clad in leathern hunting-shirts, was gathered.   The anger of these sons of liberty had been stirred up by an insolent message received from Col. Ferguson, that " if they did not instantly lay down their arms, he would come over the mountains and whip their republicanism out of them ;" and they were eager for an opportunity of showing what regard they paid to his threats.

    At this juncture, Col. Isaac Shelby returned from Kentucky, where he had been surveying land for the great company of land speculators headed by Henderson, Hart, and others.   The young officer was betrothed to Miss Susan Hart, a belle celebrated among the western settlements at that period, and it was shrewdly suspected that his sudden return from the wilds of Kentucky was to be attributed to the attractions of that young lady ; notwithstanding that due credit is given to the patriot, in recent biographical sketches, for an ardent wish to aid his countrymen in their struggle for liberty by his active services at the scene of conflict.   On his arrival at Bledsoe's, it was a matter of choice with the colonel whether he should himself go forth and march at the head of the advancing army of volunteers, or yield the command to Shelby.   It was necessary for one to remain behind, for the danger to the defenceless inhabitants of the country was even greater from the Indians than the British ; and it was obvious that the ruthless savage would take immediate advantage of the departure of a large body of fighting men, to fall upon the enfeebled frontier.   Shelby on his part insisted that it was the duty of Bledsoe, whose family, relatives, and defenceless neighbors looked to him for protection, to stay with the troops at home for the purpose of repelling the expected Indian assault. For himself, he urged, he had no family to guard, or who might mourn his loss, and it was better that he should advance with the troops to join McDowell. No one could tell where might be the post of danger and honor, at home or on the other side of the mountains. The arguments he used no doubt corresponded with his friend's own convictions, his sense of duty to his family, and of true regard to the welfare of his country; and the deliberation resulted in his relinquishment of the command to his junior officer. It was thus that the conscientious, though not ambitious patriot, lost the honor of commanding in one of the most distinguished actions of the Revolutionary war.

Col. Shelby took the command of those gallant mountaineers who encountered the forces of Ferguson at King's Mountain on the 7th October, 1780. Three days after that splendid victory, Bledsoe received from him an official dispatch giving an account of the battle. The daughter of Col. Bledsoe well remembered having heard this dispatch read by her father, though it has probably long since shared the fate of other valuable family papers.

When the hero of King's Mountain, wearing the victor's wreath, returned to his friends, he found that his betrothed had departed with her father for Kentucky, leaving for him no request to follow. Sarah, the above mentioned daughter of Col. Bledsoe, often rallied the young officer, who spent considerable time at her father's, upon this cruel desertion. He would reply by expressing much indignation at the treatment he had received at the hands of the fair coquette, and protesting that he would not follow her to Kentucky, nor ask her of her father; he would wait for little Sarah Bledsoe, a far prettier bird, he would aver, than the one that had flown away. The maiden, then some twelve or thirteen years of age, would laughingly return his bantering by saying he "had better wait, indeed, and see if *he* could win Miss Bledsoe who could not win Miss Hart." The arch damsel was not wholly in jest; for a youthful kinsman of the colonel—David Shelby, a lad of seventeen or eighteen, who had fought by his side at King's Mountain—had already gained her youthful affections. She remained true to this early love, though her lover was only a private soldier. And it may be well to record that the gallant colonel, who thus threatened infidelity to his, did

actually, notwithstanding his protestations, go to Kentucky the fol
lowing year, and was married to Miss Susan Hart, who made him a
faithful and excellent wife.

During the whole of the trying period that intervened between
the first settlement of east Tennessee and the close of the Revolutionary struggle, Col. Bledsoe, with his brother and kinsmen, was
almost incessantly engaged in the strife with their Indian foes, as
well as in the laborious enterprise of subduing the forest, and con-
verting the tangled wilds into the husbandman's fields of plenty. In
these varied scenes of trouble and trial, of toil and danger, the men
were aided and encouraged by the women. Mary Bledsoe, the
colonel's wife, was a woman of remarkable energy, and noted for her
independence both of thought and action. She never hesitated to
expose herself to danger whenever she thought it her duty to brave
it; and when Indian hostilities were most fierce, when their homes
were frequently invaded by the murderous savage, and females
struck down by the tomahawk or carried into captivity, she was
foremost in urging her husband and friends to go forth and meet the
foe, instead of striving to detain them for the protection of her own
household. During this time of peril and watchfulness, little attention could have been given to books, even had the pioneers possessed
them; but the Bible, the Confession of Faith, and a few such works
as Baxter's Call, Bunyan's Pilgrim's Progress, etc., were generally to
be found in the library of every resident on the frontier.

About the close of the year 1779, Col. Bledsoe and his brothers,
with a few friends, crossed the Cumberland mountains, descended
into the valley of Cumberland River, and explored the beautiful
region on its banks. Delighted with its shady woods, its herds of
buffaloes, its rich and genial soil, and its salubrious climate, their report on their return induced many of the inhabitants of East Tennessee to resolve on seeking a new home in the Cumberland Valley.
The Bledsoes did not remove their families thither until three years
afterwards; but the idea of settling the valley originated with them;
they were the first to explore it, and it was in consequence of their
report and advice that the expedition was fitted out, under the direc-

tion of Captain (afterwards General) Robertson and Col. John Donaldson, to establish the earliest colony in that part of the country.*

The daughter of Col. Bledsoe has in her possession letters that passed between her father and Gen. Robertson, in which repeated allusions are made to the fact that to his suggestions and counsel was owing the first thought of emigration to the valley. In 1784, Anthony Bledsoe removed with his family to the new settlement of which he had thus been one of the founders. His brother, Col. Isaac Bledsoe, had gone the year before. They took up their residence in what is now Sumner County, and established a fort or station at " Bledsoe's Lick "—now known as the Castalian Springs. The families being thus united, and the eldest daughter of Anthony married to David Shelby, the station became a rallying point for an extensive district surrounding it. The Bledsoes were used to fighting with the Indians ; they were men of well known energy and courage, and their fort was the place to which the settlers looked for protection—the colonels being the acknowledged leaders of the pioneers in their neighborhood, and the terror, far and near, of the savage marauders. Anthony was also a member of the North Carolina Legislature from Sumner County.

From 1780 to 1795, a continual warfare was kept up by the Creeks and Cherokees against the inhabitants of the valley. The history of this time would be a fearful record of scenes of bloody strife and atrocious barbarity. Several hundred persons fell victims to the ruthless foe, who spared neither age nor sex ; and many women and children were carried far from their friends into hopeless captivity. The settlers were frequently robbed and their negro slaves taken away ; in the course of a few years two thousand horses were stolen ; their cattle and hogs were destroyed, their houses and barns burned, and their plantations laid waste. In consequence of these incursions, many of the inhabitants gathered together at the stations on the frontier, and established themselves under military rule for the pro-

* For an account of this expedition, and the planting of the settlement, see the memoir of Sarah Buchanan,—*Women of the American Revolution* Vol. iii. p. 310.

tection of the interior settlements. During this desperate period, the pursuits of the farmer could not be abandoned; lands were to be surveyed and marked, and fields cleared and cultivated, by men who could not venture beyond their own doors without arms in their hands. The labors of those active and vigilant leaders, the Bledsoes, in supporting and defending the colony, were indefatigable. Nor was the heroic matron—the subject of this sketch—less active in her appropriate sphere of action. Her family consisted of seven daughters and five sons, the eldest of whom, Sarah Shelby, was not more than eighteen when they came to Sumner. Mrs. Bledsoe was almost the only instructor of these children, the family being left to her sole charge while her husband was engaged in his toilsome duties, or harassed with the cares incident to an uninterrupted border warfare.

Too soon was this devoted wife and mother called upon to suffer a far deeper calamity than any she had yet experienced. Anthony Bledsoe had removed his family into his brother Isaac's fort at Bledsoe's Lick. On the night of the 20th of July, 1788, a number of Indians approached, and placed themselves in ambush about forty yards in front of a passage dividing the log houses occupied by the two families. To draw the men out, they then sent some of their party to cause an alarm by riding rapidly through a lane passing near. Roused by the noise, Col. Anthony Bledsoe rose and went to the gate. As he opened it, he was shot down, the same shot killing an Irish servant, named Campbell, who had been long devotedly attached to him. The colonel did not expire immediately, but was carried back into the house, while preparations were made for defence by Gen. William Hall, and the portholes manned till break of day. The wife of Isaac Bledsoe suggested to her husband, and afterwards to her brother-in-law, in view of the near approach of death, that it was proper to make provision for his daughters. He had surveyed large tracts of land, and had secured grants for several thousand acres, which constituted nearly his whole property. The law of North Carolina at that time gave all the lands to the sons, to the exclusion of the daughters. In consequence, should the colonel die without a will, his seven young daughters would be left destitute. In this hour of bitter trial, Mrs. Bledsoe's thoughts too were not alone of her own sufferings, and the deadly peril that hung over them, but of the provision necessary for the helpless ones dependent on her care. Writing materials were procured, and having called Clendening to draw up the will, he being too much agitated to write, Isaac Bledsoe supported his dying brother while affixing his signature. Thus a portion of land was assigned to each of the daughters, who in after life had reason to remember with gratitude the presence of mind and affectionate care of their aunt.

Mrs. Bledsoe's sufferings from Indian hostility were not terminated by this overwhelming stroke. A brief list of those who fell victims, among her family and kinsmen, may afford some idea of the trials she endured, and of the strength of character which enabled her to bear up, and to support others, under such terrible experiences. In January, 1793, her son Anthony, then seventeen years of age, while passing near the present site of Nashville, was shot through the body, and severely wounded, by a party of Indians in ambush. He was pursued to the gates of a neighboring fort. Not a month afterwards, her eldest son, Thomas, was also desperately wounded by the savages, and escaped with difficulty from their hands. Early in the following April, he was shot dead near his mother's-house, and scalped by the murderous Indians. On the same day, Col. Isaac Bledsoe was killed and scalped by a party of about twenty Creek Indians, who beset him in the field, and cut off his retreat to his station near at hand.

In April, 1794, Anthony, the son of Mrs. Bledsoe, and his cousin of the same name, were shot by a party of Indians, near the house of Gen. Smith, on Drake Creek, ten miles from Gallatin. The lads were going to school, and were then on their way to visit Mrs. Sarah Shelby, the sister of Anthony, who lived on Station Camp Creek.

Some time afterwards, Mrs. Bledsoe was on the road from Bledsoe's Lick to the above mentioned station, where the court of Sumner County was at that time held. Her object was to attend to some business connected with the estate of her late husband. She was escorted on her way by the celebrated Thomas Sharp Spencer, and Robert Jones. The party was waylaid and fired upon by a large body of Indians. Jones was severely wounded, and turning, rode rapidly back for about two miles; after which, he fell dead from his horse. The savages advanced boldly upon the others, intending to take them prisoners.

It was not consistent with Spencer's chivalrous character to attempt to save himself by leaving his companion to the mercy of the foe. Bidding her retreat as fast as possible and encouraging her to keep her seat firmly, he protected her by following more slowly in her rear, with his trusty rifle in his hand. When the Indians in pursuit came too near, he would raise his weapon, as if to fire; and as he was known to be an excellent marksman, the savages were not willing to encounter him, but hastened to the shelter of trees, while he continued his retreat. In this manner he kept them at bay for some miles, not firing a single shot—for he knew that his threatening had more effect—until Mrs. Bledsoe reached a station. Her life and his own were on this occasion saved by his prudence and presence of mind; for both would have been lost had he yielded to the temptation to fire.

This Spencer—for his gallantry and reckless daring named " the Chevalier Bayard of Cumberland Valley,"—was famed for his encounters with the Indians, by whom he had often been shot at, and wounded on more than one occasion. His proportions and strength were those of a giant, and the wonder-loving people were accustomed to tell marvellous stories concerning him. It was said that at one time, being unarmed when attacked by Indians, he reached into a tree, and wrenching off a hugh bough by main force, drove back his assailants with it. He lived for some years alone in Cumberland Valley—it is said from 1776 to 1779—before a single white man had taken up his abode there; his dwelling being a large hollow tree, the roots of which still remain near Bledsoe's Lick. For one year—the tradition is—a man by the name of Holiday shared his retreat; but the hollow being not sufficiently spacious to accommodate two lodgers, they were under the necessity of separating, and Holiday departed to seek a home in the valley of the Kentucky River. But one difficulty arose ; those dwellers in the primeval forest had but one knife between them ! What was to be done ? for a knife was an article of indispensable necessity ; it belonged to Spencer, and it would have been madness in the owner of such an article to part with it. He resolved to accompany Holiday part of the way on his journey, and went as far as Big Barren River. When about to turn back, Spencer's heart relented ; he broke the blade of his knife in two, gave half to his friend, and with a light heart returned to his hollow tree. Not long after his gallant rescue of Mrs. Bledsoe, he was killed by a party of Indians, on the road from Nashville to Knoxville. For nearly twenty years he had been exposed to every variety of danger, and escaped them all ; but his hour came at last, and the dust of the hermit and renowned warrior of Cumberland Valley now reposes on " Spencer's Hill," near the Crab Orchard, on the road between Nashville and Knoxville.

Bereaved of her husband, sons, and brother-in-law by the murderous savages, Mrs. Bledsoe was obliged alone to undertake, not only the charge of her husband's estate, but the care of the children, and their education and settlement in life. These duties were discharged with unwavering energy and Christian patience. Her religion had taught her fortitude under her unexampled distresses ; and through all this trying period of her life, she exhibited a decision and firmness of character, which bespoke no ordinary powers of intellect. Her mind, indeed, was of masculine strength, and she was remarkable for independence of thought and opinion. In person she was attractive, being neither tall nor large until advanced in life. Her hair was brown, her eyes gray, and her complexion fair. Her useful life was closed in the autumn of 1808. The record of her worth, and of what she did and suffered, may win little attention from the careless many, who regard not the memory of our " pilgrim mothers :" but the recollection of her gentle virtues has not yet faded from the hearts of her descendants ; and those to whom they tell the story of her life will acknowledge her the worthy companion of those noble men to whom belongs the praise of having originated a new colony and built up a goodly state in the bosom of the forest.   Their patriotic labors, their struggles with the surrounding savages, their efforts in the maintenance of the community they had founded—sealed, as they finally were, with their own blood, and the blood of their sons and relatives— will never be forgotten while the apprehension of what is noble, generous, and good survives in the hearts of their countrymen.

II.

CATHARINE SEVIER.

In one of the pioneer parties from the banks of the Yadkin, in North Carolina, who crossed the rugged mountains to seek new homes in the valley of the Watauga, came Samuel Sherrill, with his family consisting of several sons and two daughters. One of these daughters, Susan, married Col. Taylor, a gentleman of considerable distinction; the other, Catharine, became the second wife of Gen. Sevier. Mr. Sherrill's residence was finally upon the Nola Chucka, and known as the Daisy Fields. He was a tiller of the soil, a hard-working man, "well to do in the world" for an emigrant of that day, and he was skilled in the use of the rifle, so that it was said, "Sherrill can make as much out of the grounds and the woods as any other man. He has a hand and eye to his work; a hand, an eye, and an ear for the Indian and the game."

Buffalo, deer, and wild turkeys came around the tents and cabins of those first emigrants. A providence was in this that some of them recognized with thankfulness. These settlements encroached upon the rights and hunting-grounds of the natives; and although some had been established and permitted to remain undisturbed for several years, yet when Capt. James Robertson arrived from Virginia, in 1772, with a large party of emigrants, and selected lands on the Watauga, he endeavored to secure an occupation with the approbation of the Indians; therefore he effected a "lease" from the Cherokees of all the lands on the river and its tributaries for eight years.

Jacob Brown, with his family and friends, arrived from North Carolina about the same time with the Sherrills, and these two families became connected by intermarriage with the Seviers, and ever remained faithful to each other through all the hostile and civil commotions of subsequent years. The family of Seviers came among the very earliest emigrants from Virginia, and aided in the erection of the first fort on the Watauga.*

With few exceptions, these emigrants had in view the acquisition of rich lands for cultivation and inheritance. Some indeed were there, or came, who were absconding debtors or refugees from justice, and from this class were the tories of North Carolina mostly enlisted.

The spirit of the hunter and pioneer cannot well content itself in a permanent location, especially when the crack of a neighbor's rifle, or the blast of his hunting-horn may be heard by his quick ear; therefore did these advanced guards often change their homes when others crowded them at a mile's distance. It must be remembered that these advances into the wilderness could only be made by degrees, step by step, through years of tedious waiting and toilsome preparation. And thus, though they had a lease from the Indians, a foothold in the soil, stations of defence, and evidently had taken a bond of fate, assuring them in the prospect of rich inheritances for their children, they could not all abide while the great West and greater Future invited onward. Richer lands, larger herds of buffaloes, more deer, and withal as many Indians were in the distance, upon the Cumberland and Kentucky Rivers. The emigrants advanced, and they took no steps backwards. In a few

* Valentine Zavier (the original family name), the father of John Sevier, was a descendant from an ancient family in France, but born in London; emigrated to America; settled on the Shenandoah, Va.; removed thence to Watauga, N. C.; and finally settled on the Nola Chucka, at Plum Grove.

years they were found organizing "provisional governments upon "the dark and bloody ground" of Kentucky, and at the Bluffs, the site of the beautiful capital of Tennessee. And these Watauga and Nola Chucka pioneers were the leading spirits throughout.

Lord Dunmore, in fitting out the expedition against the Indian tribes, which ended with the memorable battle of Point Pleasant, gave John Sevier the commission of captain.

In the first Cherokee war of 1776, the early settlements were in great danger of being destroyed. The prowling savages picked off the emigrants in detail, and being somewhat successful resolved to attack the settlements and stations at different points on the same day—in June, 1776. But they were so defeated in the battles of Long Island and at the Island Flats, on the Holston, and in their attack and siege of the Watauga Fort, that a happy change was wrought, and hopes of quiet were encouraged. The attack on the latter station was conducted by an experienced Indian chief, Old Abraham, of the Chilhowee Mountain region. It was a fierce attack, but the fort fortunately held within it two of the most resolute men who have ever touched the soil of Tennessee, and to whom East and Middle Tennessee were subsequently more indebted than to any other men who have ever lived—James Robertson and John Sevier—they having then no higher titles than captains. Some thirty men were under their command or direction.

The approach of the Indians had been stealthy, and the first alarm was given by the flight and screams of some females, who were closely pursued by the savages in large force. One of the women was killed, and one or two captured. In this party of females was Miss Catharine Sherrill, daughter of Samuel Sherrill, who had removed into the fort only the day previous.

Miss Sherrill was already somewhat distinguished for nerve, action, and fleetness. It was said "she could outrun or outleap any woman; walk more erect, and ride more gracefully and skilfully than any other female in all the mountains round about, or on the continent at large." Although at other times she proved herself to know no fear, and could remain unmoved when danger threatened, yet on this occasion she admits that she did run, and "run her best." She was very tall and erect, and her whole appearance such as to attract the especial notice and pursuit of the Indians; and as they intercepted the direct path to the gate of the fort, she made a circuit to reach the enclosure on another side, resolved, as she said, to scale the walls or palisades. In this effort, some person within the defences attempted to aid, but his foot slipped, or the object on which he was standing gave way, and both fell to the ground on opposite sides of the enclosure. The savages were coming with all speed, and firing and shooting arrows repeatedly. Indeed, she said, "the bullets and arrows came like hail. It was now—leap the wall or die! for I would not live a captive." She recovered from the fall, and in a moment was over and within the defences, and "by the side of one *in uniform*."

This was none other than Capt. John Sevier, and the first time she ever saw him. This was the beginning of an acquaintance destined in a few years to ripen into a happy union, to endure in this life for near forty years. "The way she run and jumped on that occasion was often the subject of remark, commendation, and laughter." In after life she looked upon this introduction, and the manner of it, as a providential indication of their adaptation to each other—that they were destined to be of mutual help in future dangers, and to overcome obstacles in time to come. And she always deemed herself safe when by his side. Many a time did she say: "I could gladly undergo that peril and effort again to fall into his arms, and feel *so out of danger*. But then," she would add, "it was all of God's good providence." Capt. Sevier was then a married man, his wife and younger children not having yet arrived from Virginia. His wife's name was Susan Hawkins, and she was a native of Virginia, where she died.

In 1777, Capt. Sevier received a commission from the State of North Carolina, and was thus decidedly enlisted in the cause of American independence; and not long after this, he was honored with the commission of colonel, bearing the signature of George Washington. In 1779, his wife died, leaving him ten children.

Several of the eldest were sons, who had come with their father to gain and improve a home in the wilderness. They were trained to arms and to labor. He had selected land on the Watauga and Nola Chucka, his chosen residence being on the latter stream, and for many years known as Plum Grove. In the year 1780, he and Miss Sherrill were married, and she devoted herself earnestly to all the duties of her station, and to meet the exigencies of the times. It may well be supposed that females spun, wove, and made up most of the clothes worn by these backwoods people. Girls were as well skilled in these arts as were the boys in such as more appropriately belonged to their sphere and strength.

Not long after the marriage, Col. Sevier was called to the duty of raising troops to meet the invasion of the interior of North Carolina, under Tarleton, Ferguson, and other British officers. Preparations were hastily made, and the various forces assembled which fought the important battle of King's Mountain. Col. Sevier had three sons and one brother in that engagement. His favorite brother, Joseph, was killed, and one son wounded. These sons were between the ages of sixteen and twenty-one. Boys were early taught to use the rifle with skill. This was the formidable weapon in pursuit of game, and in all the Indian wars.

It was always a source of much gratification to Mrs. Sevier, and one of which she fondly boasted, that among the first work she did after her marriage, was to make the clothes which her husband and three sons wore the day they were in the memorable battle of King's Mountain. And she would say, " Had his ten children been sons, and large enough to have served in that expedition, I could have fitted them out."*

In the course of years, Mrs. Sevier became the mother of eight children, three sons and five daughters; and thus Col. Sevier was

* The private orderly, or memorandum-book of Col. De Poister, on whom the command devolved after Ferguson was killed on King's Mountain, and who ordered the surrender, was, with other papers, handed to Col. Sevier This book was presented to the writer of this memoir by Mrs. Gen Sevier and her son, G. W. S., after the writer's marriage into the family.

the father of eighteen children, all of whom maintained good char acters, were " given to hospitality," and lived comfortably and use-fully, although none of them acquired great wealth.   Mrs. Sevier was often left alone to manage domestic affairs, not only within doors, but without.   The life of the Colonel was one of incessant action, adventure, and contest.   The calls of his fellow-citizens, and the necessities of the times, withdrew him frequently from home. The history of the Indian wars of East Tennessee, of the settlement of the country, and of the organization of the State Government, is the record of the deeds of his life.   No commander was more fre-quently engaged in conflicts with the Indians with equal success and such small loss of his men.   And yet it is a notable fact that he enjoyed, to a remarkable extent, the respect of the tribes and chiefs with whom he contended.   It is a known historical fact that in 1781 he had taken to his own home, on the Chucka, a number of Indian prisoners, it is said thirty, where they were treated with so much kind-ness by his wife and family that several of them remained for years, although they performed very little work, and this wholly at their option.   The influence of Mrs. Sevier was intentionally and happily exerted upon these captives, that it might tell, as it did, upon their friends within " the nation ;" and the family, no doubt, enjoyed more protection than otherwise they could have expected.

Col. Sevier acquired a sobriquet among the Indians, which was some evidence of their familiarity with and attachment to him, ard probably of advantage.   As long as he lived they called him " Chucka Jack."   He was afterwards called the " Treaty-maker." They had a name for Mrs. Sevier also, which is now not remembered. The tories were the worst enemies, and perpetrated more damage to Col. Sevier's property than did ever the Indians ; and from them Mrs. Sevier had repeatedly to hide most of her small stock of house-hold articles.   She usually remained at the farm, and never would consent to be shut up in a blockhouse, always saying—

> " The wife of John Sevier
> Knows no fear."

" I neither skulk from duty nor from danger."

And we believe this was emphatically true. We have seen her in advanced age—tall in stature, erect in person, stately in walk, with small, piercing blue eyes, raven locks, a Roman nose, and firmness unmistakable in her mouth and every feature. She was able to teach her children in the exercises conducive to health and usefulness, to strength of nerve and to action. None could, with equal grace and facility, placing the hand upon the mane of a spirited horse, and standing by his side, seat herself upon his back or in the saddle. She had the appearance and used the language of independence, haughtiness, and authority, and she never entirely laid these aside. Yet was not her pride offensive, nor her words or demeanor intended heedlessly to wound. It could be said of her without any question, that she " reverenced her husband," and she instilled the same Scriptural sentiment into the minds of his children. The very high respect and deference which one of her dignified appearance ever paid to him, no doubt had a favorable influence upon others ; for though he was a man of remarkable elegance of person, air and address, and of popular attraction, yet it must be confessed that she contributed much to all these traits, and to his usefulness and zeal in public service. She relieved him of his cares at home, and applauded his devotion to the service of the people.

Her reply to those who urged her "to fort," or to take protection in one of the stations, was, " I would as soon die by the tomahawk and scalping-knife as by famine ! I put my trust in that Power who rules the armies of Heaven, and among men on the earth. I know my husband has an eye and an arm for the Indians and the tories who would harm us, and though he is gone often, and for weeks at a time, he comes home when I least expect him, and always covered with laurels. * * If God protects him whom duty calls into danger, so will He those who trust in him and stand at their post. * * Who would stay out if his family forted ?"

This was the spirit of the heroine—this was the spirit of Catharine Sevier. Neither she nor her husband seemed to think there could be danger or loss when they could encourage or aid others to daring, to duty, and to usefulness. Col. Sevier at one time advised her to go into the fort, but yielded to her respectful remonstrance. At one time the tories came to her house and demanded her husband's whereabouts, and finally avowed that their intention was to hang him on the highest tree in front of his house; but that if she would tell them where he was, she and her children should be safe. Of course she refused to give them the information. One man drew a pistol and threatened to blow out her brains if she did not tell or at least give up all the money she had.

"Shoot! shoot!" was her answer. "I am not afraid to die! But remember, while there is a Sevier on the earth, my blood will not be unavenged!"

He dared not—he did not shoot. The leader of the gang told the man to put up his pistols, saying, "such a woman is too brave to die." She knew some of the party, and that they were noted thieves and tories.

At another time they came to her smokehouse to carry off meat. She took down the gun, which her husband always left with her in good order, and said to them: "The first one who takes down a piece of meat is a dead man!" They could not mistake her resolution. Her tone, manner, and appearance avowed clearly enough that she uttered no vain warning; that she knew her rights and dared maintain them. They left without taking anything. In the fall of 1780, a noted loyalist by the name of Dykes planned the seizure of Sevier, but the plot was discovered to Mrs. Sevier by his wife, as she stood by the smokehouse with her apron held out to receive meal and a slice of meat from the Colonel's lady.*

Some of their negroes were stolen and never all recovered, being taken into the Indian nation by the tories, and thence to Savannah or Charleston while in possession of the British. There was a mortal enmity between some of the active tories and the Seviers, resulting in the hanging of some of the former on two occasions.

* See Wheeler's North Carolina.

It fell to the lot of Mrs. Sevier to do acts of hospitality and kindness to some of this set and their descendants many years after the war. And these kindnesses she performed, although she acknowledged that she felt at the same time the spirit of re- venge rankling in her bosom. "Some of them," she would say " and perhaps all their children, may make worthy people and good citizens if they are not kept continually ashamed and mortified by being reminded of their bad conduct or of their tory origin."

The sick and wounded soldier ever found a welcome and nursing at the home of Sevier. The supplies for many of the Colonel's Indian expeditions were from his own private means. His wife, sons, and servants were remarkably successful in raising corn and hogs, and cheerfully were these given to the furtherance of the great ob- jects in hand.*

All her life long was Mrs. Sevier distinguished for her kindness and liberality to the poor. Towards children she was gentle, though she had an appearance and manner which prevented them from giving that annoyance they are apt to do to the aged. It was usual with her to keep a supply of maple-sugar and cinnamon-bark in her spice-box, from which she would gratify them, and then wave them kindly away. This motion of her hand was expressive, and easily understood.

In 1784 occurred the scenes of the "State of Frankland." The people of East Tennessee, becoming dissatisfied with the con- dition of affairs under North Carolina, and impelled, as they urged, by the necessity of self-protection, organized a separate and indepen- dent government, giving that name to the new State. John Sevier was its first and last Governor. The establishment of this little re-

* When the paper currency of North Carolina was so depreciated that a $100 bill would rarely buy " a pone of corn-bread and slice of ham," and many persons would not take it at all in exchange for provisions or other property, the *soldier* could always purchase an ample supply at a fair estimate at Plum Grove, and thus by sales of lands, personal property, and perhaps in satisfaction for his military and public services, did the "old Continental currency" accumulate in the desk of Gen. Sevier to sums of between $200,000 and $300,000, which, with his papers, were left in the hands of his son, the late Col. G. W. S., of Tennessee.

public was declared by the Governor of North Carolina to be no less than revolt, and all concerned in it were commanded to return to their duty and allegiance, and to refuse obedience to any self-created authority, unsanctioned by the legislature of North Carolina. Notwithstanding this remonstrance, the new government proceeded in the exercise of sovereignty. In the conflict of authorities and the civil and personal contests which grew out of this state of things in the revolted territory, the prudent and judicious conduct of Mrs. Sevier added to her husband's reputation as well as her own. His house became the place of general resort. It was proclaimed open and free to all the friends of the rights of self-defence and independence, and the impressive dignity and noble bearing of Mrs. Sevier made a deep and lasting impression upon all who resorted to that home for counsel, aid, or hospitality.

The supporters of the new State were obliged in time, however, to enter into measures of adjustment. When the Governor was seized by its enemies and spirited away into the interior of North Carolina, Mrs. Sevier, with the promptness, energy, and daring which qualify for any occasion of utmost moment, aroused his friends, and would have gone, as a fearless leader, " to conquer or to die." But seeing that her relatives, his relatives, sons and friends were resolved upon his release and restoration, she little doubted his speedy return, and she was not disappointed.

And when a returning sense of justice, and the revulsion of public sentiment and power of popular gratitude, produced a repeal of " the odious acts of exclusion" of North Carolina, placing him " in lone conspicuity," and the people called him, by unanimous voice, again and again, and yet again, to preside as Governor of Tennessee, and to a Seat in Congress of the United States, then did her great heart swell with thankfulness to God and her fellow-citizens. Then did she acknowledge that her husband had not endured peril, toil, and sacrifice in vain, though far short of the reward to which she thought him justly entitled. And we doubt not posterity will coincide in this judgment.

During the twelve years in which he officiated as Governor of

Tennessee, his wife made his home delightful to him and his children. It was the rest of the weary, the asylum of the afflicted, well
known as " the hospitable mansion of the first Governor, the people's
favorite."

The education of Mrs. Sevier, in respect of literature and the
embellishments of dress and music, was such as she acquired chiefly
from reading the Bible, hearing the wild birds sing, and the Indians'
pow-wow. " I picked up a good deal," she was accustomed to say,
"from observation of men and their acts—for that was a business
with us in the early settlements—and we examined the works of
nature to some advantage ; but as to school education, we had pre-
cious little of that except at our mothers' knees."

She embraced the religious sentiments of the Presbyterians, and
her life throughout was exemplary and useful. In this faith she
lived and died. A favorite expression of hers was : " I always trust
in Providence." And she taught her children that " trust in God,
with a pure heart, is to be rich enough ; if you are lazy, your blood
will stagnate in your veins, and your trust die." She would never
be idle. Knitting often engaged her fingers, while her mind and
tongue were occupied in thought and conversation. She always
wore at her side a bunch of very bright keys.

After the death of Gov. Sevier on the Tallapoosa, in 1815, where
he had gone to cement peace and establish the boundary with the
Creek Indians, Mrs. Sevier removed to Overton County, in Middle
Tennessee, where most of her children resided. She selected a most
romantic and secluded spot for her own retired residence. It was
upon a high *bench*, or spur of one of the mountains of that county,
a few miles from Obeds River, with higher mountains on either side.
There were some ten or fifteen acres of tillable land, and a bold
never-failing spring issuing from near the surface of the level tract,
which cast its pure cold waters down the side of the mountain
hundreds of feet into the narrow valley. In a dense wood near that
spring, and miles distant from any other habitation, did her sons erect
her log cabins for bedroom, dining-room, and kitchen, and others
for stable and crib. She resided for years at " The Dale," with the

General's aged body-servant, Toby (who had accompanied him in all his Indian campaigns), his wife, Rachel, and a favorite female servant and boy. Seldom did she come down from her eyrie in the mountain. The aged eagle had lost her mate. She made her nest among the lofty oaks upon the mountain heights, where she breathed the air and drank the water untainted and undisturbed, fresh and pure, and nearest to the heavens.

We have visited her in that chosen spot. "The Governor's widow" could never be looked upon as an ordinary countrywoman. Whoever saw her could not be satisfied with a single glance—he must look again. And if she stood erect, and her penetrating eye caught the beholder's, he judged at once there was in that mind a consciousness of worth and an acquaintance with notable events. He would wish to converse with her. She used language of much expressiveness and point. She never forgot that she was the widow of Gov. and Gen. Sevier; that he had given forty years of his life to the service of his country, and in the most arduous and perilous exposure, contributing from his own means far more than he ever received from the public treasury; and yet he never reproached that country for injustice, neither would she murmur nor repine.

At times she was disposed to sociable cheerfulness and humor, as one in youthful days, and then would she relate interesting anecdotes and incidents of the early settlement of the country, the manners and habits of the people, of the "barefoot and moccasin dance" and "spice-wood tea-parties." Her woman's pride, or some other feminine feeling, induced her to preserve with the utmost care an imported or bought carpet, of about twelve by fifteen feet in size, which had been presented to her as the "first Governor's wife," and as the first article of the kind ever laid upon a "puncheon," or split-log floor west of the Alleghany Mountains. Whenever she expected company upon her own invitation, or persons of character to pay their respects to her, the Scotch carpet was sure to be spread out, about the size of a modern bedquilt. But as soon as company departed, the ever-present and faithful servants, Suzy and Jeff, incontinently commenced dusting and fo'ding, and it was soon again boxed up. Three times were we permitted the honorable privilege of placing our well cleaned boots upon this dear relic from the household of the first Governor of Tennessee, and of admiring the pair of ancient and decrepit branch-candlesticks as they stood on the board over the fireplace.

The bucket of cool water was ever on the shelf at the batten-door, which stood wide open, swung back upon its wooden hinges; and there hung the sweet water-gourd; and from very love of everything around, we repeatedly helped ourselves. The floors, the doors, the chairs, the dishes on the shelves—yea, everything seemed to have been scoured. There was a lovely cleanness and order, and we believe, " godliness with contentment."

She was remarkably neat in her person, tidy, and particular, and uniform in her dress, which might be called half-mourning—a white cap with black trimmings. She had a hearth-rug, the accompaniment of the favorite carpet, which was usually laid before the fireplace in her own room, and there she commonly was seated, erect as a statue—no stooping of the figure, so often acquired by indolence and careless habit, or from infirm old age—but with her feet placed upon her rug, her work-stand near her side, the Bible ever thereon or in her lap, the Governor's hat upon the wall—such were the striking features of that mountain hermitage.

There was resignation and good cheer—there was hospitality and worth in that plain cottage; and had not the prospect of better fortune, and attachment to children married and settled at a distance, induced her own sons to remove from her vicinity, she ought never to have been urged to come down from that " lodge in the wilderness." But her last son having resolved to remove to Alabama, she consented to go with him and pass her few remaining days in his family.

She departed this life on the 2d October, 1836, at Russelville, in the State of Alabama, aged about eighty-two.

III.

REBECCA BOONE.

In the rural cemetery near Frankfort, upon a hill overlooking the river, under the shadow of protecting trees, are two green mounds, unmarked by slab or stone informing the stranger that the remains of two honored pioneers—Daniel Boone and his wife, rest beneath. The beauty of the locality is unrivalled, and it is not far from the magnificent monument erected by Kentucky to her brave officers fallen on the field of battle; the splendid shaft inscribed with their names, and surmounted by a figure of Victory holding crowns in her hands. It is hoped that ere long the State will do justice to the memory of those whose arduous efforts won a victory not less glorious over the untamed wilderness, and opened the way to others as bold and persevering.

It will be remembered that the father of Daniel Boone had his residence on the borders of the Yadkin in North Carolina, at no great distance from the eastern slope of the Alleghanies; then a frontier country, and the greater part of it unbroken forest. Near the farm here opened, was another owned by Mr. Bryan, comprising about a hundred acres beautifully situated on a gentle swell of ground; the eminence crested with laurels and yellow poplars, which half concealed the farmer's dwelling. A wild mountain stream ran along the base of the hill. This Joseph Bryan was the oldest son of Morgan Pryan, of Virginia, the head of a very respectable family. His daughter, Rebecca, was born near Winchester, in Virginia.

Flint's "Life of Boone," contains the following account of his first meeting with his future wife, referred to as authentic by other biographers :

"Young Boone was one night engaged in a fire hunt with a young friend. Their course led them to the deeply timbered bottom which skirted the stream that wound round Bryan's pleasant plantation. That the reader may have an idea what sort of a pursuit it was that young Boone was engaged in, during an event so decisive of his future fortunes, we present a brief sketch of a night fire hunt. Two persons are indispensable to it. The horseman that precedes, bears on his shoulder what is called a *fire pan*, full of blazing pine knots, which casts a bright and flickering glare far through the forest. The second follows at some distance with his rifle prepared for action. No spectacle is more impressive than this of pairs of hunters thus kindling the forest into a glare. The deer, reposing quietly in his thicket, is awakened by the approaching cavalcade, and instead of flying from the portentous brilliance, remains stupidly gazing upon it, as if charmed to the spot. The animal is betrayed to its doom by the gleaming of its fixed and innocent eyes. This cruel mode of securing a fatal shot is called in hunters' phrase—*shining the eyes.*

"The two young men reached a corner of the farmer's field at an early hour in the evening. Young Boone gave the customary signal to his mounted companion preceding him, to stop; an indication that he had *shined the eyes* of a deer. Boone dismounted and fastened his horse to a tree. Ascertaining that his rifle was in order he advanced cautiously behind a covert of bushes, to rest the right distance for a shot. The deer is remarkable for the beauty of its eyes when thus shined. The mild brilliance of the two orbs was distinctly visible. Whether warned by a presentiment, or arrested by a palpitation and strange feelings within, at noting a new expression in the blue and dewy lights that gleamed to his heart, we

say not. But the unerring rifle fell, and a rustling told him the
game had fled. Something whispered him it was not a deer ; and
yet the fleet step, as the game bounded away, might easily be mistaken for that of the light-footed animal. A second thought im
pelled him to pursue the rapidly retreating game ; and he sprang
away in the direction of the sound, leaving his companion to occupy
himself as he might. The fugitive had the advantage of a considerable advance of him, and apparently a better knowledge of the
localities of the place. But the hunter was perfect in all his field
exercises, and scarcely less fleet-footed than a deer, and he gained
rapidly on the object of his pursuit, which advanced a little distance
parallel with the field fence, and then, as if endowed with the
utmost accomplishment of gymnastics, cleared the fence at a leap.
The hunter, embarrassed with his rifle and accoutrements, was driven
to the slow and humiliating expedient of climbing it. But an outline of the form of the fugitive, fleeting through the shades in the
direction of the house, assured him that he had mistaken the species
of the game. His heart throbbed from an hundred sensations, and
among them an apprehension of the consequences of what would
have resulted from discharging his rifle, when he had first shined
those liquid blue eyes. Seeing that the fleet game made straight
in the direction of the house, he said to himself: 'I will see the
pet deer in its lair,' and he directed his steps to the same place.
Half a score of dogs opened their barking upon him as he approached the house, and advertised the master that a stranger
was approaching. Having hushed the dogs, and learned the name
of his visitant, he introduced him to his family as the son of their
neighbor Boone.

   " Scarce had the first words of introduction been uttered, before the
opposite door opened, and a boy apparently of seven, and a girl of
sixteen, rushed in, panting for breath, and seeming in affright.

   " ' Sister went down to the river and a *painter* chased her, and she
is almost scared to death,' exclaimed the boy.

   " The ruddy, flaxen-haired girl stood full in view of her terrible
pursuer, leaning upon his rifle, and surveying her with the most

eager admiration. 'Rebecca, this is young Boone, son of our neighbor,' was the laconic introduction. Both were young, beautiful, and at the period when the affections exercise their most energetic influence. The circumstances of the introduction were favorable to the result, and the young hunter felt that the eyes had *shined* his bosom as fatally as his rifle shot had ever the innocent deer of the thickets. She too, when she saw the light, open, bold forehead, the clear, keen, yet gentle and affectionate eye, the firm front, and the visible impress of decision and fearlessness of the hunter— when she interpreted a look which said as distinctly as looks could say it, 'how terrible it would have been to have fired!' can hardly be supposed to have regarded him with indifference. Nor can it be wondered at that she saw in him her beau ideal of excellence and beauty. The inhabitants of cities, who live in mansions, and read novels stored with unreal pictures of life and the heart, are apt to imagine that love, with all its golden illusions, is reserved exclusively for them. It is a most egregious mistake. A model of ideal beauty and perfection is woven in almost every youthful heart, of the brightest and most brilliant threads that compose the web of existence. It may not be said that this forest maiden was deeply and foolishly smitten at first sight. All reasonable time and space were granted to the claims of maidenly modesty. As for Boone, he was remarkable for the backwoods attribute of never being beaten out of his track, and he ceased not to woo, until he gained the heart of Rebecca Bryan. In a word, he courted her successfully, and they were married."

Boone's first step after his marriage was to find a suitable place where he might cultivate his farm, and hunt to the greatest advantage. His wife remained at home, while he went to explore the unsettled regions of North Carolina. When he had selected a locality near the head waters of the Yadkin, Rebecca, with the same resolute spirit of enterprise which afterwards led her to the wilds of Kentucky, bade farewell to her friends, and followed her adventurous husband. In a few months her home had assumed a pleasant aspect; a neat cabin stood on a pleasant eminence near the river, surrounded by an enclosed field; the farm was well stocked and with the abundance of game in the woods, the settlers had no lack of means for comfort and enjoyment. The rude dwelling frequently offered the traveller shelter ; and by a cheerful fire and table loaded with the finest game, with the enhancing blessing of a hospitable welcome, was many a tale of adventure narrated, while as yet the surrounding forest was untouched by an axe. For some years the young couple lived in this sylvan retirement, till the fields of other emigrants opened wide clearings, and dwellings rose so thickly in the neighborhood as to form villages ; when Boone made up his mind to remove to some wilder spot.

The country west of the Cumberland Mountains was almost unknown in 1760. Some few hardy adventurers had struck into the pathless forests which extended along the frontier settlements, but the Alleghanies had proved an insurmountable barrier to the families of settlers. The stories told by adventurers, meanwhile, who had ventured into the skirts of the wilderness, kindled the imagination of enterprising hunters. In 1767, Finley went still further, and penetrated through a portion of Tennessee. " There is nothing," says the biographer of Boone, " grand or imposing in scenery, nothing striking or picturesque in the ascent and precipitous declivity of mountains covered with woods; nothing romantic or delightful in deep and sheltered valleys through which wind clear streams—that was not found in this region. Mountains stretch along in continuous ridges, and now and then shoot up into elevated peaks. On the summit of some spread plateaus, which afford the most romantic prospects, and offer every advantage for cultivation, with the purest and most bracing atmosphere. No words can picture the secluded beauty of some of the vales bordering the small streams, which fling their spray, transparent as air, over moss-covered and time-worn rocks, walled in by precipitous mountains, down which pour numerous waterfalls."

The rich soil and inviting aspect of this country gave large ideas of its advantages ; and as the wanderer penetrated into Kentucky, the luxuriant beauty of its plains, its rich cane-brakes and flower-covered forests promised everything desirable in a new home. The forest abounded with deer, elk, and buffaloes, and more savage wild beasts had their lair in its depths and in the thick tangles of the green cane ; while pheasants, partridges, wild turkeys, &c., were as plenty as domestic fowls upon a farm. The report of Finley determined Boone to go westward, and others having been induced to join him in an exploring expedition, six assembled at his house on the first of May, 1769—all the neighbors being gathered to witness their departure. Mrs. Boone parted with her husband, who left his house laden with his rifle, hunter's bag of ammunition, and light knapsack—the only luggage taken by the adventurers. Their expedition across the Alleghanies into the boundless forests of the Ohio valley, where the buffalo roamed like herds of cattle, has been elsewhere described. The land appeared the very paradise of hunters, and Boone could not imagine how any one who could fix his home in such a region, would stay among the barren pine-hills of North Carolina. The exploring party divided, to take different routes, and Boone and Stewart were taken prisoners by wandering Indians.

They managed, however, to escape, and Boone joined his elder brother, while Stewart and another of their number were killed. The brothers were soon in want of ammunition, and the elder Boone returned to North Carolina, while Daniel, regardless of danger, remained alone in the rough cabin he had built, from the first of May to the 27th of July, 1770, at which time his brother came back with cheering news from his family. Having finished their survey, both returned to report to their neighbors what they had seen, and form a company of such persons as were willing to join the families of the Boones in their pioneer settlement. Their descriptions of the luxuriance of the country—its cane-brakes, clover plains, limestone springs, maple orchards, streams and forests filled with game and wild-fowl, were matched by fearful accounts from others of the depredations and cruelties of Indians, dangers of wild beasts, and diseases peculiar to a wild country ; so that it was two years before preparations were completed for the expedition. The party commenced the march the 26th September, 1773, and were

joined by forty persons in "Powell's valley," a settlement some
distance westward; numbering about eighty in all.   They crossed
the wild and rugged range of mountains by the course the brothers
had traced on their return, but they were not destined to proceed
much further.   As they descended the west side of Walden's ridge,
along a narrow defile, they were suddenly startled by the yells of
Indians, and a fierce affray ensued, in which six men were killed,
and some of the stock scattered and lost.   In the general distress,
the company decided unanimously on giving up the attempt to form
a settlement in Kentucky, and returning to Clinch River, forty
miles in the rear, where a number of families had already located
themselves.   It may be supposed that Mrs. Boone, whose eldest son
had been slain in the encounter, had lost all spirit for the enterprise,
and her husband was obliged to submit to the decision of the rest.
Their new home, accordingly, was for some time on the banks of
Clinch River.   In June, 1774, Boone was required by Governor
Dunmore of Virginia, to conduct a party of surveyors to the falls of
Ohio.   In 1775, he superintended the erection of a fort on the
Kentucky River, afterwards called Boonesborough.   The fort consisted of one block-house and several cabins, surrounded by palisades.
This work was accomplished amidst troubles from the Indians, and
when it was finished Boone returned for his family.   They took up
their abode at the earliest military station—except the house built by
Harrod in 1774 in Kentucky—Mrs. Boone and her daughters being
the first white women who had ever stood on the banks of Kentucky river.

It was the close of summer, and at this time the spot selected for
their residence appeared in its best aspect.   The early autumn was
mild and beautiful, and arrangements were made for the cultivation
of the land as soon as spring should open.   Winter came, and
passed with little discomfort.   Their cabins were thoroughly daubed
with clay; they had abundance of fuel, and were at no loss for
game and provisions.   Those who went out to fell trees, however,
were constrained to be on their guard against attacks from Indians,
who might aim at them from some covert in the woods, and the

men never left home without carrying their rifles and knives. The women occasionally ventured a short distance without the palisades in the day-time, but never out of sight of the fort.

The months thus passed without monotony or want of excitement; spring opened, the trees to be felled were girdled, the brush cut down and burned, preparations made for ploughing the field, and a garden spot marked off, which, when the virgin earth had been thrown up, was given in charge to Mrs. Boone and her daughters. They had brought out a stock of seeds from the old settlements, and went out every bright day to plant them. The little party of women was reinforced, among others, by the daughters of Col. Calloway, a friend of Boone, who had brought his family to the station. Their fondness for possessing themselves of the spoils of the forest, led to a romantic instance of the peril of the times.

A little daughter of Boone, with Calloway's two, was captured by Indians the 7th of July. Flint says they were gathering flowers in the woods when the savages rushed upon them ; and that they were not missed till some time after they had been carried off. I copy the account given of the pursuit of Boone, and the recovery of the captives, by Col. Floyd, an actor in the scene—in preference to other narratives. He says the girls were taken out of a canoe in the river, within sight of Boonesborough. " The affair happened late in the afternoon, and the spoilers left the canoe on the opposite side of the river from us, which prevented our getting over for some time to pursue them. Next morning by daylight we were on the track, but found they had totally prevented our following them by walking some distance apart, through the thickest cane they could find. We observed their course, and on which side we had left their sign, and travelled upwards of thirty miles. We then imagined that they would be less cautious in travelling, made a turn in order to cross their trace, and had not gone but a few miles before we found their tracks in a buffalo path ; pursued and overtook them on going about ten miles, just as they were kindling a fire to cook. Our study had been more to get the prisoners without giving the

3

Indians time to murder them after they discovered us, than to kill
the savages. We discovered each other nearly at the same time.
Four of us fired, and all rushed on them, which prevented their carrying anything away, except one shot gun without ammunition.
Mr. Boone and myself had a pretty fair shot just as they began to
move off. I am well convinced I shot one through, and the one he
shot dropped his gun; mine had none. The place was very thick
with cane, and being so much elated on recovering the three little
broken-hearted girls, prevented our making any further search. We
sent them off without their moccasins, and not one of them so much
as a knife or a tomahawk."*

With the commencement of the war of the Revolution, the
ravages of Indian warfare along the whole line of border settlements became more extensive and violent; British influence and
resources securing the savages as their allies along the frontier, from
the north-eastern part of Vermont and New York to the Mississippi.
The story of Boone's life is interwoven with the scenes of plunder,
captivity, burning and massacre, which swept and in many instances
desolated the infant colonies of the north and west. Yet new emigrants came, many of them of respectable standing, and some noted
in the history of the time. Mrs. McGary, Mrs. Hogan, and Mrs.
Denton, had taken up their residence in the fort at Boonseborough.
At the same time hordes of savages crossed the Ohio with the design
of extirpating these germs of social establishments in the Indian's
favorite hunting-ground, and in numerous detachments spread in
every direction through the forest.

But the increase of danger did not drive back the pioneers, or
prevent still further reinforcements. Those who first ventured into
Kentucky and Tennessee, had come in small parties, but on their
return to the old settlements they gathered companies of their friends
and connections, old and young, with their wives and children,
flocks and herds, resolved on emigration, and pledged by mutual

---

* See Butler's History of Kentucky. Some of the biographies of Boone
state that he went alone on the expedition. Flint gives a beautiful romance
which unfortunately has been contradicted on reliable authority.

necessity to stand by each other in life and death. There was among them none of the jealousy and want of unity which prevail, more or less, among their descendants; yet were not these primitive hunters assimilated to savages in their habits, but possessing keen and strong intellects as well as powerful frames, and every qualification for social life. The first care on reaching their destination was to select a spot for the new dwelling, usually chosen on a gently elevated ground of exuberant fertility, where trees were sparse, and there was no underbrush to prevent the hunter's riding at full speed. The growth of cane, wild clover, and *pawpaw* marked the best soil. Cabins being put up for immediate use, the little settlement was converted into a station. For this purpose it was necessary to enclose a spring or well, near a salt lick or sugar orchard if practicable ; then a wide space must be cl ared, so that the enemy could not approach close under the shelter of the woods. The station was to overlook, moreover, as much of the country as possible. It included from half an acre to an acre of ground, and the trench was usually dug four or five feet deep and planted with large and close pickets, forming a compact wall ten or twelve feet above the surface of the earth. The pickets were of hard timber and about a foot in diameter, and the soil around them was rammed into great solidity. At the angles were small projecting squares called *flunkers*, with oblique port-holes, from which the fire of sentinels within could rake the external front of the station ; and in front and rear two folding gates swung on enormous wooden hinges. The gates were barred every night, and sentinels posted alternately, one being stationed on the roof in time of peculiar danger. These fortified places in the wilderness had their clean turfed area for dancing, wrestling, or other athletic exercises ; the inmates of the fort passed their evenings sociably together, cheerful fires blazing within the enclosure, and suppers of venison and wild turkeys, wild fruits and maple beer were enjoyed with double relish amid the distant howling of wolves, or the Indian warwhoop, heard like the roar of the dying storm. Such was Bryants station in 1782, the nucleus of the earliest settlements in the rich and lovely country

of which Lexington is the centre—and such were others built at
that period.

The captivity of Boone, his escape and return to Boonesborough,
and the Indian siege of that station in 1778—the last it sustained—
belong to the biography of the renowned woodsman, not to this
memoir.   When during a long interval no information concerning
Boone could be obtained, he was supposed by the people at the
garrison and his family to have fallen a victim to savage vengeance.
Mrs. Boone, believing herself widowed, at length resolved, with her
children, to leave the western forests, and return to the banks of the
Yadkin.   Kentucky, she said, had indeed been to her a " dark and
bloody ground."   The family returned to their friends in North
Carolina, nearly five years having elapsed since they had started
with the first party of emigrants for Kentucky.   The friends from
whom she then parted had heard afterwards of their disastrous
encounter with the Indians, their return to Clinch River, and subsequent residence at Boonesborough ; but knew nothing of their further
trials.   When about the close of the summer of 1778, these pilgrims returning from the western wilds were seen approaching on
pack-horses, the sight caused no little surprise and wonder among
the dwellers on the banks of the Yadkin.   The mother wore deep
mourning, and her dejected countenance showed the grief that had
worn her strong spirit ; the same melancholy was evident in the
faces of her eldest surviving son, and the daughter who had been
captured ; the other children being too young to feel trial or change.
The travellers were clad in skins, and the primitive habiliments of
the wilderness, and as the cavalcade stopped at Mr. Bryan's house,
the neighbors collected to learn what had happened, and listen with
deep interest to Mrs. Boone's relation of her adventures and
sorrows.

After having driven the enemy from Boonesborough, Col.
Boone set out to cross the Alleghanies in pursuit of his wife and
children ; surmounting with iron strength of endurance the difficulties of the way.   It may be imagined how joyfully his return was
hailed by those who had so long believed him dead.   They returned

in the following summer to Boonesborough, which enjoyed tranquillity as the country became more thickly settled. Many incidents of interest after this re-union, in which Boone was prominent, are recorded in the history of Kentucky, but do not pertain to this sketch. One connected with another pioneer, may be mentioned as illustrative.

Benjamin Logan, who had brought his family from the Holston to Logan's Fort, in March, 1776, was obliged afterwards to remove them for safety to Harrodsburgh. Before the attack on Harrodsburgh in the winter of 1777, he returned with six families to the cabins he had built, and commenced palisading the station. " On the 20th of May, while the females of the establishment were milking their cows, sustained by a guard of their husbands and fathers, the whole party was suddenly assailed by a large body of Indians, concealed in a canebrake. One man was killed and two wounded, one mortally, the other severely. The remainder reached the interior of the palisades in safety. The number in all was thirty, half of whom were women and children. A circumstance was now discovered exceedingly trying to such a benevolent spirit as that of Logan. While the Indians were still firing, and the inmates exulting in their safety while others mourned over their dead and wounded, it was perceived that one of the wounded, by the name of Harrison, was still alive, and exposed every moment to be scalped. All this his wife and family could discover from within. It is not difficult to imagine their agonized condition and piercing lamentations. Logan displayed on this occasion the same tender compassion and insensibility to danger, that characterised his friend Boone in similar circumstances. He endeavored to rally a few of the male inmates of the place to join him, rush out, and bring the wounded man within the palisades. But so obvious was the danger, so forlorn appeared the enterprise, that no one could be found disposed to volunteer his aid, except a single individual by the name of John Martin. When he had reached the gate, the wounded man raised himself partly erect and made a movement as if trying to reach the fort himself. On this Martin desisted from the enterprise and left Logan to attempt it alone. He rushed forward to the wounded man, who made some effort to crawl onward by his aid ; but weakened by the loss of blood, and the anguish of his wounds, he fainted, and Logan taking him in his arms, bore him towards the fort. A shower of bullets was discharged at them, many of which struck the palisades close to Logan's head, as he brought the wounded man safe within the gate, and deposited him in the care of his family.

"The station, at this juncture, was destitute both of powder and ball, and there was no chance of supplies nearer than Holston ; all intercourse between station and station was cut off. Without ammunition the fort could not be defended against the Indians, and the question was how to obtain a supply in this pressing emergency. Capt. Logan, selecting two trusty companions, left the fort by night, evading the besieging Indians, reached the woods, made his way in safety to Holston, procured the necessary supplies of ammunition, and packed it under their care on horseback, giving them directions how to proceed. He then left them, and traversing the forest by a shorter route on foot, reached the fort in safety ten days after his departure. The Indians still kept up the siege with unabated perseverance, and the hopes of the diminished garrison had given way to despondency. The return of Logan inspired them however with renewed confidence."

We select another narrative in detail, to convey an idea of Indian hostility on the one hand, and the manner in which it was met on the other. "A family lived on Cooper's run, in Bourbon county, consisting of a mother, two sons of mature age, a widowed daughter with an infant in her arms, two grown daughters, and a daughter ten years old. The house was a double cabin. The two grown daughters and the smaller girl were in one division, and the rest of the family in the other. At night a knocking was heard at the door of the latter division, asking in good English and the customary Western phrase : 'Who keeps house ?' As the sons went to open the door, the mother forbade them, affirming that the persons claiming admission were Indians. The young men sprang to their guns ; and the Indians finding themselves refused admittance at the door, made an effort at the opposite one. That door they soon beat open with a rail, and endeavored to take the three girls prisoners. The little girl sprang away, and might have escaped in the darkness and the woods, but the foolish child under a natural impulse ran to the other door and cried for help. The brothers within it may be supposed would wish to go forth and protect the feeble and terrified wailer. The mother taking a broader view of duty, forbade them. The savages soon hushed the cries of the distressed child by the merciless tomahawk. While some of the Indians were engaged in murdering this child, another was binding one of the grown girls whom he had captured, the other young woman defending herself with a knife which she had been using at a loom at the moment of attack. The intrepidity she displayed was unavailing. She killed one Indian and was herself dispatched by another. The savages meanwhile having obtained possession of one half the house, fired it. The persons shut up in the other half had now no other alternative than to be consumed in the flames rapidly spreading towards them, or to go forth and expose themselves to the murderous tomahawks that had already laid three of the family in their blood. The Indians stationed themselves in the dark angles of the fence, where, by the bright glare of the flames, they could see everything, and yet remain themselves unseen. Here they could make a sure mark of all that should escape from within. One of the sons took charge of his aged and infirm mother, and the other of his widowed sister and her infant. The brothers emerged from the burning ruins, separated and endeavored to spring over the fence. The mother was shot dead as her son was piously helping her over, the other brother being killed as he was gallantly defending his sister. The widowed sister, her infant and one of the brothers escaped the massacre and alarmed the settlement. Thirty men, commanded by Col. Edwards, arrived next day to witness the appalling spectacle presented around the smoking ruins of this cabin. Considerable snow had fallen, and the Indians were obliged to leave a trail which easily indicated their path. In the evening of that day, they came upon the expiring body of the young woman, apparently murdered but a few moments before their arrival; the Indians having been premonished of their pursuit by the barking of a dog that followed them. The white men overtook and killed two of the savages that had strayed behind, apparently as voluntary victims to secure the retreat of the rest."

After numerous perils and escapes, and great services to the country, Boone had the privilege of rejoicing in the peace that followed the defeat of the northern tribes of Indians by General Wayne His perseverance had triumphed over all obstacles, and the kindred spirit of his wife had aided and encouraged him in his various adventures, whether descending the Alleghanies, tracing the course of the Cumberland and Tennessee, roaming through the forests of Kentucky, wandering a captive through the wilderness to the great lakes, or following the waters of the Wabash, Miamis, and Scioto. When the tide of emigration had poured into the country, and disputes and litigation arose as to the ownership of land, the band of primitive pioneers was dispersed, and Boone moved his family to the woods on the banks of the Great Kanawha, having heard that deer and buffaloes were to be found on the unsettled lands near that river. Their home was for some years near Point Pleasant; but game was not so abundant as could be desired, and the report of adventurers returned from the vast prairies and unexplored forests of the Missouri, determined Boone once more to flee from the encroaching advance of civilization. Taking up his rifle and light luggage, he set out with the faithful companion of his wanderings and their children, driving their stock before them, and passed through Cincinnati in 1798. They settled in St. Charles County, about forty miles above St. Louis. After Missouri had come under the government of the United States, the tide of emigration and enterprise again swept by the dwelling of our pioneers, driving off the game, and changing the hunting grounds into farms. A follower too, even more sure to overtake them, came on apace ; old age with its consequent infirmities. Mrs. Boone died in March 1813 A most faithful and efficient helpmeet had she proved to the pioneer, possessing the same energy, heroism, and firmness which he had shown in all the vicissitudes of his eventful career, with the gentler qualities by which woman, as the centre of the domestic system, diffuses happiness and trains her children to become useful and honored in after life. Having shared willingly in the hardships, labors and dangers of those adventurers whose names live in grateful remembrance, she is entitled to some portion of the renown that has embalmed them.

An anecdote or two illustrative of the insecurity of families in those days, and of the horrors undescribed in most cases, may not be inappropriate before closing this memoir. In the spring of 1780, Alexander McConnel, who lived at Lexington, then a small cluster of cabins, having killed a buck in the woods, went home for a horse, and returning, was seized and carried off by five Indians. After several days' travel, when they reached the banks of the Ohio, they omitted the precaution of binding him closely one night, merely tying the buffalo tug around his wrists, and fastening it to their bodies ; and he resolved on making his escape. About midnight, casting his eyes in the direction of his feet, they fell on the glittering blade of a knife which had escaped its sheath, and was lying near the feet of one of the Indians. He could not reach it with his hands, but with some difficulty grasped the blade between his toes, and drew it within reach. He then cut his cords, and silently extricated himself from his captors; but he knew it would be necessary to kill them, to avoid pursuit and certain death. After anxious reflection, his plan was formed, and carefully removing the guns of the Indians, which were stacked near the fire, and hiding them in the woods, he took two, and returning to the spot where his enemies were still sleeping, he placed the muzzles of each on a log within six feet of his victims, and pulled both triggers. Both shots were fatal ; he then ran to secure one of the other rifles, and fired at two of the savages, standing in a line, killing one and wounding the other, who limped off into the forest. The fifth darted off like a deer, with a yell of astonishment and terror. McConnel not wishing to fight any more such battles, selected his own rifle from the stack, and made the best of his way to Lexington. A Mrs. Dunlap, who had been several months a prisoner among the Indians on Mad River, soon afterwards came to the same place, having

3*

made her escape, and reported that the survivor had returned to his tribe with a lamentable tale of an attack by a large party of white men, who had killed the poor bound prisoners, as well as his companions !*

An adventure of a different kind befel McKinley, a school teacher, in the following year. While sitting alone at his desk, he heard a slight noise at the door, and saw an enormous wild cat. He rose to snatch up a cylindrical rule to defend himself, but the creature darted upon him, tore his clothes from his side, and buried her claws and teeth in his flesh. He threw himself on the edge of the table, and pressed the assailant against its sharp corner with all his force. Her cries, mingled with his own, now alarmed the neighbors, and after a few moments the dead animal was disengaged from her prey, though her tusks were dislodged with some difficulty from between his ribs.

In the beginning of 1794, a party of Indians killed George Mason, on Flat Creek, twelve miles from Knoxville. In the night he heard a noise in his stable, and stepped out ; was intercepted before he could return, by the savages, and fled, but was fired upon and wounded. He reached a cave, from which he was dragged out and murdered, and the Indians returned to the house to despatch his wife and children. Mrs. Mason heard them talking as they approached, and hoped her neighbors, aroused by the firing, had come to her assistance. But perceiving that the conversation was neither in English nor German, she knew they were enemies. She had that very morning learned how to set the double trigger of a rifle. Fortunately the children were not awakened, and she took care not to disturb them. She had shut the door, barred it with benches and tables, and taking down her husband's well charged rifle, placed herself directly opposite the opening which would be made by forcing the door. Her husband came not, and she was but too well convinced he had been slain. She was alone in darkness, and the yelling savages were pressing on the house. Pushing with great violence, they gradually opened the door wide enough to attempt an entrance, and

* McClung's Sketches of Western Adventure.

the body of one was thrust into the opening and filled it, two or three more urging him forward. Mrs. Mason set the trigger of the rifle, put the muzzle near the body of the foremost, and fired. The first Indian fell; the next uttered the scream of mortal agony. The intrepid woman observed profound silence, and the savages were led to believe that armed men were in the house. They withdrew, took three horses from the stable, and set it on fire. It was afterwards ascertained that this high-minded woman had saved herself and children from the attack of twenty-five assailants.

The opportunity seems favorable to notice the spirit and manners of those primitive times of Kentucky history. After the period of the attack on Bryant's Station, and the disastrous battle of the Blue Licks, which took place on the 18th of August, 1782, notwithstanding the dangers which surrounded the settlements, they began to have more of the aspect of communities. The proportion of women, which had hitherto been so small, became larger, and a license to marry is said to have been the first process issued by the clerks of the new counties. The first settlers having generally been composed of those who had braved the perils of settling the frontiers of the adjacent states, their helpmates were accustomed to labor and hardship. The duties of the household were discharged by the females.

"They milked the cows, prepared the meats, spun and wove the garments of their husbands and children; while the men hunted the game of the woods, cleared the land, and planted the grain. To grind the Indian corn into meal on the rude and laborious handmill, or to pound it into hominy in a mortar, was occasionally the work of either sex. The defence of the country, the building of forts and cabins, fell most properly to the share of the men; though in those hardy times, it was not at all uncommon for females, during a siege, to run bullets and neck them for the rifle. Deer skins were extensively used for dress, to compose the hunting shirt, the long overalls, the leggins, and the soft and pliable moccasins; the buffalo and bear furnished the principal covering for the night. Handkerchiefs tied round the head, often supplied the place of hats; strips of buffalo hide were used for ropes. Stores or shops were unknown:

wooden vessels either prepared by the *turner*, the *cooper*, or their
rude representatives in the woods, were the common substitutes for
table furniture.   A tin cup was an article of delicate luxury almost
as rare as an iron fork.   Every hunter carried a knife, too aptly
called a *scalping knife*, in the hands of the white man as well as
in those of the Indian; and one or two knives would compose the
cutlery of families.   The furniture of the cabin was appropriate to
the habitation; the table was made of a slab, or thick, flat piece of
timber, split and roughly hewn with the axe, with legs prepared in
the same manner.   This latter instrument was the principal tool in
all mechanical operations, and with the adze, the auger, and above
all, the *rifle*, composed the richest mechanical assortment of Kentucky.   Stools of the same material and manufacture, filled the
place of chairs.   When some one more curiously nice than his
neighbors, chose to elevate his bed above the floor (often the naked
ground), it was placed on slabs laid across poles which were again
supported by forks driven into the floor.   If, however, the floor
happened to be so luxurious as to be made of puncheons (another
larger sort of slabs), the bedstead became hewed pieces, let into the
sides of the cabin by auger holes in the logs.   The cradle of these
times was a small rolling trough, much like what is called the sugar
trough, used to receive the sap of the sugar maple.   Still the food
in these rude habitations, and with this rough and inartificial furniture, was the richest milk and finest butter furnished by the luxuriant pasture of the woods, covered with the rich pea vine and the
luscious cane.   The game of the country, it has been already seen,
struck the experienced eye of even Boone as profuse beyond measure; it was the theme of admiration to every hunter; nor did the
abundance afford slight assistance to the whites in their conquest of
the land.   The enemy would never have permitted provisions to
have been transported, or to have grown by the slow and peaceable
processes of farming; and the consequence must have been that
the stations would have been starved into surrender, but for the providential supply of the deer, the buffalo, and the bear.   These were
to be obtained by every gallant rifleman; and this so abundantly

that the buffalo has often been shot in order to enjoy either its hump or its tongue. The hospitality of these times was much less a merit than an enjoyment; often a protection to both parties. The fare was rough, but heartily and generously divided with every fellow-woodsman."*

Generosity, hardihood, bravery, and endurance of suffering, were prominent and undeniable features in the character of these first settlers. But the female sex, though certainly an object of more regard than among the Indians, had to endure much hardship, and occupy a rank inferior to the male partner, among the *earliest* emigrants, the state of society exercising high physical qualities rather than mental or artificial endowments.

ANNA INNIS, widow of Hon. Henry Innis, and mother of Mrs. J. J. Crittenden, died at Cedar Hill, near Frankfort, Kentucky, May 12th, 1851. This lady was one of the pioneers of Kentucky, and has been the pride of her State and an ornament to the country. Her early days were spent in the wilderness, and yet in the society of such men as Clarke, Wayne, Shelby, Scott, Boone, Henderson, Logan, Hart, Nicholas, Murray, Allen, Breckenridge, and all the great and heroic spirits of the West. She saw Washington as he led his broken army through the Jerseys, and as he returned in triumph from Yorktown. Of this remarkable woman the *Frankfort Commonwealth* says :

" Her tenacious memory retained all she had seen, and she became the chronicler of her own times, and interwove her narrative with traditions of the past. Providence had been kind in all his dealings with her. He had blest her with a strong mind and constitution, and with great cheerfulness and courage. He had blessed her in her ' basket and her store.' He had blessed her in her children, and at last when the message came, having borne all the trials of a long and eventful life with heroic firmness, she died in the full communion and fellowship of the Presbyterian Church, of which she had been long an exemplary member."

* Butler's Kentucky.

Another of the eminent daughters of Kentucky was the mother of Gen. Leslie Combs, whose maiden name was Sarah Richardson. She was of a respectable Quaker family of Maryland, connected by blood with the Thomases and Snowdens. Leslie, the youngest of twelve children, was just eighteen when he started as a volunteer to join the Kentucky troops ordered to the northern frontier, under Gen. Winchester, in 1812. Two of his elder brothers had previously entered the service, and with earnest entreaties he prevailed on his parents to let him go, setting forward alone a few weeks after the army had marched. "I shall never forget," were his words in after years, "the parting scene with my beloved and venerated mother, in which she reminded me of my father's history, and her own trials and dangers in the early settlement of Kentucky, and closed by saying to me ' as I had resolved to become a soldier, I must never disgrace my parents by running from danger; but die rather than fail to do my duty.' This injunction was ever present to me afterwards in the midst of dangers and difficulties of which I had then formed no idea, and stimulated me to deeds I might otherwise, perhaps, have hesitated to undertake or perform."

The residence of Mrs. Combs, after her removal from the picketed station where she first lived in Kentucky, was on a farm about six miles from Boonesborough. The family suffered much from the depredations of the Indians who then infested the country from the Ohio to the Tennessee. Mrs. Combs' riding horse was shot down under her eldest son while he and his father were on a trapping excursion within two or three miles of home. They did not return as soon as expected, and the mother was left alone in the cabin with two or three little children, a prey to the most agonizing apprehensions. It was through her industry and energy that her children were enabled to obtain a better education than was usual in the country in those days. This fact is mentioned in the inscription on her tombstone, which stands on the farm where they lived and died, alongside of that inscribed with the name of her husband, recorded as " a Revolutionary officer and a Hunter of Kentucky."

NOTE.—See page 428.

IV.

CHARLOTTE ROBERTSON.

CHARLOTTE REEVES was the second daughter of George Reeves and Mary Jordan, and was born in Northampton County, N. C., in January 1751. Her parents were poor in worldly possessions, and were able to give their children only a limited education ; but they trained them to labor and habits of systematic industry, and in those strict principles which guided and preserved their parents through life, and made their example useful. Soon after the marriage of Charlotte with James Robertson, the young couple crossed the mountains and fixed their abode in one of the new settlements on the Watauga or Holston River.

In 1779, Robertson went with some others to explore the Cumberland Valley, leaving his family behind. They explored the country to the neighborhood of the spot where Nashville now stands, planted there a field of corn, and leaving three of the party to keep the buffaloes out of the corn, returned to East Tennessee for their families. The fame of the fertile Cumberland lands, the salubrity of the air, the excellence of the water, and the abundance of game of all sorts, was soon diffused through all the frontier settlements, and many took the resolution of emigrating to this land of plenty. Companies came and built cabins and block houses and in the latter part of February or first of March 1780.

Mrs. Robertson left her home at the mouth of Big Creek on the
Holston, for the purpose of joining her husband. Her party consisted of herself and four small children, her brother William
Reeves, Charles Robertson her husband's brother, her sister-in-law,
and three little nieces, with two white men servants, a negro woman
and her infant. These voyagers were conveyed in two of the small
and frail flat-boats appointed to convey the families of emigrants to
their new homes in the wilderness. Capt. James Robertson was to
head the party travelling by land through Kentucky to the same
point of destination, and driving the cattle belonging to the little
colony ; and had left home some weeks previously, with his eldest
son, fourteen years of age. Those who went by water descended
the north fork of the Holston, and proceeded down Tennessee
River. The various difficulties they encountered, the perils and
fatigues of this tedious and dangerous trip, were more numerous
that it is now possible to detail. At the mouth of Duck River they
expected to land and make their way through the wilderness to the
" Cumberland County," but the guides failing to meet them, they
continued their voyage to the mouth of the Tennessee. At this
point their difficulties were fearfully increased. The ice was just
broken up in the Ohio, the water was rising, and the aspect of things
appeared so discouraging to their pilot. that he abandoned the enterprise in despair, and left the company to make their way in the best
manner possible up the river, having to ascend against a rapid current, with clumsy and scarcely manageable boats, some two hundred
miles. The emigrants were worn out and disheartened with the
toil of the voyage already accomplished, the men were strangers to
the navigation of the Ohio, which flowed for the most part
through an unbroken forest, infested on either side with wild
beasts and more merciless Indians ; their lives seemed endan-
gered at every step, and so dreary was the prospect, that about
one half the company decided against pursuing the enterprise,
bade adieu to their companions, and shoving their boats into
the smooth current of the Ohio, sought homes for their families in
Natchez. The others turned their bows up the river. Of Mrs.

Robertson's party only two men were left, her brother and brother-in-law. They lashed the two boats together; Mrs. Johnson, the widowed sister of Capt. Robertson, undertook to serve as pilot, and managed the steering oar, while Mrs. Robertson and Hagar, the African woman, worked at the side oars alternately with Reeves and Robertson. By this tedious and laborious progress, they made their way up the Ohio to the mouth of the Cumberland, and up the Cumberland to the point of destination, landing in the beginning of April at the site of Nashville.

Haywood, in his history of Tennessee, describes the voyage made by "The Adventure" and other boats, which, leaving the fort on the Holston the 22d of December, 1779, did not reach the "Big Salt Lick" till the latter part of April. An extract may give an idea of the perils of the expedition. In passing Indian villages on the Tennessee, the voyagers had been accosted by many of the savages with professions of friendship, designed to cover a hostile purpose.

"In a short time the crew came in sight of another town, situated on the north side of the river, nearly opposite a small island. Here also the Indians invited those on board to come on shore, calling them brothers, and seeing the boats standing to the opposite side, told the passengers that their side was the best for the boats to pass the island on. A young man on board the boat of Capt. John Blackmore, approaching too near the shore, was shot in the boat from the shore. Mr. Stewart had set off in a boat on board which were blacks and whites to the number of twenty-eight. His family being diseased with the small pox, it was agreed that he should keep at some distance in the rear. He was to be informed each night where the others lay by the sound of a horn. The foremost boats having passed the town, the Indians collected in considerable numbers. Seeing him far behind, they intercepted him in their canoes, and killed and made prisoners the whole crew. The crews of the other boats were not able to relieve him, being alarmed for their own safety, for they perceived large bodies of Indians marching on foot down the river, keeping pace with the boats, till the Cumberland mountain covered them from view. The boats were

now arrived at the place called the Whirl or Suck, where the river
is compressed into less than half its common width, by the Cumberland mountain jutting into it on both sides.   In passing through
the upper part of these narrows, at a place termed the Boiling Pot,
a man of the name of John Cotton was descending the river in a
canoe with a small family, and had attached it to Robert Cart-
wright's boat, into which he and his family had entered for safety.
The canoe was here overturned, and the little cargo lost.   The movers
pitying his distress, concluded to land and assist him in recovering
his property.   Having landed on the north shore at a level spot
they began to go towards the place where the misfortune had happened, when the Indians, to their astonishment, appeared on the
opposite cliffs, and commenced firing down upon them.   The Indians
continued their fire from heights upon the boats.   In the boat of
Mr. Gower was his daughter Nancy.   When the crew were thrown
into disorder and dismay, she took the helm, and steered the boat,
exposed to all the fire of the enemy.   A ball passed through her
clothes, and penetrated the upper part of her thigh, going out on
the opposite side.   It was not discovered that she was wounded by
any complaint she made, or a word she uttered, but after the danger was over, her mother discovered the blood flowing through her
clothes."

Reaching the mouth of the Tennessee the 20th of March, they
parted with their companions who were discouraged from proceeding, and the Adventure, with the boats which accompanied her, went
up the Ohio.   "They made but little way on that day, and encamped on the south bank of the Ohio, suffering on that and the
two following days much uneasiness from hunger and fatigue.   On
the 24th of March, they came to the mouth of Cumberland River,
but its size was so much less than they had expected to find it, that
some would not believe it to be the Cumberland.   It flowed in a
gentle current ; they had heard of no river on the south side of the
Ohio, between the Tennessee and Cumberland, and they determined
to go up this as the Cumberland, and did so.   On the 25th, the
river seemed to grow wider ; the current was very gentle, and they

were now convinced it was the Cumberland. The crews were now without bread, and were obliged to hunt the buffalo, and feed on his flesh. On the 24th of April, 1780, they came to the Big Salt Lick, where they found Capt. James Robertson and his company, and where they were gratified at meeting those friends whom, but a little before, it was doubtful whether they should ever see again. They also found a few log cabins, erected by Capt. Robertson and his associates, on a cedar bluff, on the south side of the river, at some distance from the Salt Spring."

For years after their removal the families of the settlement suffered many privations, and were compelled to live most of the time within the shelter of the forts, being subjected to ferocious attacks by the Indians. Two of Mrs. Robertson's sons were murdered by the savages. It was indeed a constant scene of anxiety and danger to the close of the Indian war in 1794, and the frequent alarms, and incidents of persons being killed or wounded at or near the fort occupied by our heroine, gave her full experience of all the horrors of war. At one time she had the agony of seeing brought in from the adjoining woods the headless body of a beloved son ; and it cannot be wondered at that she was heard to say in after life—she would not live those years over again to be insured the possession of the world.

" In the year 1782, and for several years afterwards, the common custom of the country was, for one or two persons to stand as watchmen or sentinels, whilst others labored in the field ; and even whilst one went to a spring to drink, another stood on the watch with his gun ready to give him protection by shooting a creeping Indian, or one rising from the thicket of canes and brush, that covered him from view ; and wherever four or five were assembled together at a spring or other place where business required them to be, they held their guns in their hands, and with their backs turned to each other, one faced the north, another the south, another the west, watching in all directions for a lurking or creeping enemy. While the people were so much harassed and galled by the Indians that they could not plant and cultivate their corn-fields, a proposition was made in a council of the inhabitants of the bluff, to break up the settlement and go off. Capt. Robertson pertinaciously resisted this proposition; it was then impossible to get to Kentucky; the Indians were in force upon all the roads and passages which led thither; for the same reason it was equally impracticable to remove to the settlements on the Holston. No other means of escape remained but that of going down the river in boats, and making good their retreat to the Illinois; and to this plan great obstacles were opposed, for how was the wood to be obtained with which to make the boats? The Indians were every day in the skirts of the bluff, lying concealed among the shrubs, privy and cedar trees, ready to inflict death upon whoever should attempt to go to the woods to procure timber for building a boat. These difficulties were all stated by Capt. Robertson; he held out the dangers attendant on the attempt on the one hand; the fine country they were about to possess themselves of on the other; the probability of new acquisitions of numbers from the interior settlements, and the certainty of being able, by a careful attention to circumstances, to defend themselves till succor could arrive. Finally, their apprehensions were quieted, and gradually they relinquished the design of evacuating the positions they occupied."*

The following extract from a "Talk" from "The Glass," a Cherokee chief, to Gov. Blount, dated "Look-out Mountain," Sept. 10th, 1792, may show something of the state of feeling prevalent between the hostile parties.

"Codeatoy returned here from the treaty at Nashville, and tells us that Col. Robertson said there had been a great deal of blood spilled in his settlement, and that he would come and sweep it clean with our blood. This caused our young warriors to assemble together to meet him, as he told Codeatoy that the first mischief that should be done, he would come; and we knew of course it would not be long before something might happen, as there are Creeks daily going to that settlement; and as they expect to suffer for the doings of others, they resolved they would meet him, or go to the

* Haywood

settlements and do mischief, as they were to be the sufferers, do it who would. But with the assistance of Bloody Fellow, John Watts, and some other head men, we have sent them to their different homes, and to mind their hunting, in hopes you will not suffer any of your people to send any more threatening talks. We took pity upon the innocent that might suffer on both sides, which undoubtedly would have been the case. As I have always listened to your talks, I hope you will listen to mine, and have peace."*

Gov. Blount writes to Gen. Robertson, March 8th, 1794 :

"Your letter of 6th Feb., sent express by James Russell, was handed to me much stained with his blood by Mr. Shannon, who accompanied him. Russell was wounded by a party of Indians who ambuscaded him about eighteen miles from South West Point, which he with difficulty reached, and was obliged to continue there for several days before he could be removed. He is now in the hands of a skilful surgeon, and it is hoped will recover. His fifty dollars have been dearly earned ; but instead of complaining, he may rejoice that he has so often escaped."†

In a letter from John McKee to " The Glass" and other chiefs of the lower towns of the Cherokee nation, he speaks of an expectation on their part that he would meet them on the middle ground for a " ball play." This was a national game, by which parties sometimes decided their claims to disputed land. It was a manly sport often witnessed by assembled thousands.

The following description of the game is furnished by a gentleman of Nashville, who has lived among the Indians.

The contending parties always consist of twelve on a side— twenty-four in all, selected from among the most athletic men in the station. Each side is headed by one who is captain, or principal man. The ball used on such occasions was generally made of the common punk, obtained from the knots of trees, or some soft dry root, and is always covered with dressed buckskin, and about the size of a walnut. The ball is never to be touched with

* Copied from MS. letter in the Historical Collection at Nashville.
† MS. Letter.

the hands, but is caught, held, and thrown with a set of sticks made expressly for the purpose. The ball stick is made of a piece of tough wood, about six feet in length, and the thickness of a small walking-stick, reduced one half in the middle, for about ten inches. The piece of wood is then bent till the ends are brought together, forming a bowl something like the bowl of a spoon, while the two strips of wood are wrapped together from the bowl to the ends with a leathern string, to make the handle; the bowl being finished with buckskin strings, fastened to the wood on all sides, and crossing each other, forming meshes like a fine seine, and left loose so as to bag a little. The ball-stick, when finished, was a spoon with a bowl about as large as a man's hand, and a handle some three feet long. Each man is furnished with two sticks, which together would hold as much as a quart measure.

The playground is generally laid off east and west, and the two poles are placed from a quarter to half a mile from each other. The poles are two stakes put up about twenty yards apart, and the ball has to pass between these two stakes in order to count one in the game. Halfway between the poles a line is drawn ; those who wish the ball to pass through the western pole, take their stand about twenty yards east of the centre line, and those in favor of the eastern pole take their position about the same distance on the west of the line. While the two captains take their stand at the division line, the ball is laid upon the ground, on the centre line. One of the captains takes it up with his sticks, and throws it up some thirty or forty feet ; and then the game begins. The two captains, one in favor of the western, the other of the eastern pole, as the ball descends, contend for it, leaping as high as they can, while the sticks rattle and crash together ; should these two be of equal strength and expertness in the game, the contention may be long and fierce, and it sometimes so happens that they struggle until perfectly exhausted, without the ball taking a start for either pole. At other times the ball is caught in its descent, and hurled with great rapidity towards one of the poles ; but whatever direction it takes, it meets the opposition of eleven persons who have taken their stand in that direction, by some of whom it is sure to be caught and hurled in a different direction. I have seen the ball hurled back and forward in this way for minutes together. At other times I have seen the whole twenty-four contend pell-mell together for several seconds, while a spectator could not tell where the ball was. Again, I have seen the whole party take a right angular direction to the poles, in consequence of the hand being interrupted at the moment of throwing the ball, and thus work away entirely without the limits of the playground, until recalled by the judges.

There is no time for breathing, from the moment the ball is thrown up at the centre line, until it passes through one of the poles, unless the judges should call them off for the purpose of recess ; and never have I seen human beings so much fatigued as at the end of one of these strains.

One thing which I have observed extremely objectionable in these plays, is this ; any one of the party is allowed to *double up* his antagonist, notwithstanding they are not permitted to strike, scratch, or bruise each other. The *doubling* is done in the following manner : One will catch his antagonist, throw him upon his back, take him by the feet, elevate them, and press his head and shoulders upon the ground until the poor fellow is disabled in the back. This practice results sometimes in rendering the individual so helpless, that he has to be carried off the ground.

The only clothing carried into a ball-play, is the belt, with a piece of some kind of cloth about eighteen inches square, appended in front ; but they generally come out of these plays, as far as clothing is concerned, about as they came into the world. There is always the same number in reserve that are engaged in the play, so that when one is disabled, another supplies his place, in order that the number, twenty-four, may be kept up. There are two sets of judges ; six for and six against the western pole, take their position there ; and in like manner at the eastern pole. The ball has to pass twelve times between the same pole, or stakes, before the game ends.

In 1794, Mrs. Robertson went on horseback into South Carolina accompanied by her eldest son, to bring out her aged parents, who had removed to that State with some of their children. They returned to Tennessee with their daughter, who was now able to offer them a comfortable home, and under her roof the remainder of their days passed in peace and comfort. Both lived beyond the eightieth year of their life, and had the passage to the grave smoothed by the devoted attentions of an affectionate daughter, and her equally devoted children.

At the period of most imminent danger to the settlement, Mrs. Robertson was often deprived of the support which kept the other women from despondency. Her husband was looked upon as the special protector of the infant colony, and had laborious duties to perform for its security and comfort. He was obliged every year to take the long and hazardous journey through the wilderness to North Carolina, for the purpose of attending the sessions of the Legislature, and using his utmost endeavors to have the aid of that body extended to the feeble and distant settlement on the Cumberland. This was done by Gen. Robertson for eight or ten years in succession, and while thus absent from home a great part of his time, he and his family were exposed to perils of various kinds, and obliged to remain ignorant for long intervals of each other's condition. For fourteen years these trials, endured by Mrs. Robertson and her family, called for their utmost fortitude and energy to bear up under them, and under harassing anxiety for the fate of their absent guardian, exposed unprotected to the attacks of savage enemies.

On one occasion, Gen. Robertson and his eldest son, Jonathan, then nearly grown to manhood, went into the surrounding woods to see after some horses that had gone astray. The General had a led horse, and did not take his gun. They had scarcely entered the woods when they were fired on by five or six Indians who lay in ambush near the path. A ball passed through the young man's thigh and entered his horse's side ; the father also received two balls, one fracturing the bones of his left arm just above the wrist, the other passing through the flesh of his right arm without injuring the bone. Jonathan's horse, maddened by fright and the wound, became unmanageable, and plunged so violently, that fearing the animal might fall with him, and entangle him beyond escape, he raised himself in his stirrups and leaped to the ground, alighting on his feet. He then turned on the Indians, who rushed towards him, and prepared to fire, while the savages ran to the shelter of trees to protect themselves. One was behind a tree not large enough to screen his body, and young Robertson taking aim, fired at him ; then hastened after his father, whose horse, released for the moment from the control of the bridle by the disabling of the rider's hands, had dashed off furiously in a different direction from the fort. When the General heard his son shouting to him, he checked the animal, and the young man sprung on the back of the led horse, which had followed close on the heels of the other. The whole scene occurred within the hearing of the inmates of the fort, and as the fugitives were compelled to take a circuitous route to reach a place of safety, it may be imagined what were the feelings of the wife and mother during a prolonged period of fearful suspense, when the probabilities that her husband and son were murdered or captive, increased with every passing moment. The Indian Jonathan had shot, was found afterwards so badly wounded that he died in a few days. His gun and shot-bag were found secreted under a log near the tree, the bark of which had been scalped by the bullet.

A short time after Jonathan's marriage, he determined on making a settlement on some land he had purchased, a mile or so from his father's fort. He built a cabin, and commenced clearing the land ; but was prevented by other occupations from continuing his work, and hired a man by the name of Hiland to carry it on. This laborer went to the place alone ; but had been employed only a few days, when returning one evening from his work, he cut a large bundle of green cane, and was carrying it on his shoulder to his house ; the rustling of this cane afforded a party of Indians a fair opportunity of coming up behind him without being perceived, and as he was in the act of throwing the cane over the fence, they shot him down and scalped him. Gen. Robertson, hearing of the occur-

4

rence, determined, if possible, to insure future security to the settlers by pursuing and cutting off these marauding parties, and issued an order to Capt. Thomas Murray, to raise a company of volunteers and overtake the Indians, or pursue them into the very heart of the nation. A detachment was raised ; the settlers, anxious to strike a blow for their own security, joining in large numbers, and the pursuit was commenced with a hundred and ten mounted men. After a few days, the spies reported the Indians encamped on the Tennessee at the Muscle Shoals ; the company attacked the camp, and several of the savages were killed, some making their escape, and two squaws being captured.

Young Robertson, meanwhile, was not discouraged from prosecuting his enterprise, but removed to his new place with his wife, and a negro named Ephraim. Determined to persevere in preparing the land and making a home for his family, he engaged two of his wife's cousins, named Cowen, to assist him in his labors. They were all at work one day in the clearing, and were as usual summoned to dinner by a call from the house. They had stacked their arms against a large tree some fifty yards from the edge of the clearing, and between that and the house. It had been settled between them that in case of an attack by Indians, they should rush instantly to seize their arms, each take a tree, and make a stand against the enemy. On hearing the call to dinner, the men laid down their working implements, and stopped to push up the brush which had not been consumed into the brush-piles, not perceiving that several Indians had crept along under cover of the woods, and approached very near them. The moment they discovered the enemy, they sprang forward to secure their arms, while the savages, who had reached the edge of the clearing by the time the white men gained their weapons, rushed in pursuit. The directions previously agreed upon were observed, and each pioneer snatched his gun and sprang behind a tree. At the moment Robertson raised his gun, he perceived an Indian partly concealed behind another tree, and preparing to fire. His body projected far enough beyond the cover to afford a fair chance of hitting him ; Robertson fired, and at the same instant the Cowens did also. This spirited defence alarmed the Indians; they began to retreat, and had disappeared in the cane before their foes could reload. Meanwhile poor Ephraim, who had a terror of gunpowder, could not stand his ground with the rest of the party, but hastened with all his speed towards the house; and when, after the flight of the enemy, the white men raised the Indian yell by way of a triumph note, the affrighted negro, rushing into the cabin, gave the inmates reason to suppose that all their friends were killed and scalped. This horrible fear, however, was soon dissipated by the appearance of the victorious settlers returning to the house. One of the Cowens was slightly wounded in the hand, and the rim of Robertson's hat on one side was nearly severed from the crown by an Indian bullet, but no other injury had been received. This incident is worthy of notice, as the only instance during the period of the Indian troubles in which white men, fired on while at work in the field, made a stand, and succeeded in driving off the assailants. It was afterwards ascertained from the Indians that five of their number had been either killed or wounded so desperately that they died before reaching home. It should be mentioned that one of the pioneers used a British musket loaded with rifle bullets, and fired at a number of Indians together as they rushed into the thin cane bordering the clearing. It was believed the party of savages had numbered fifteen.

An instance of female heroism which occurred at a station some six miles west of Nashville, may be here related. Mrs. Dunham, the wife of one of the pioneers, while sitting in her house at work—her little children playing in the yard—heard them scream out suddenly, and rushing to the door, saw them running from several Indians. One of the savages was in the act of clutching her daughter, six or seven years of age, and succeeded in laying hold of the child, a few yards from the door. There were no men on the premises; but the mother seized a hoe standing against the house near the door, and rushed at the Indian with the uplifted weapon. Before she came near enough to strike him with it, however, he let go the child, who ran into the house, the mother following. The

Indian pursued them closely, and pushed his gun into the door before it could be closed, to shoot Mrs. Dunham. She kept her hold of the door, and slammed it to violently, catching the gun between it and the door-post, and holding it with all her force, while the savage tried in vain to get the weapon released. She then, with singular presence of mind, called aloud as if to some person within, " Bring me that gun !" The Indian understood enough of English to know her meaning, and believing there were other persons in the house, he left his gun and made off. The other children had found shelter in the house, and were thus preserved from massacre by their mother's energy and self-possession.

Mrs. Dunham's oldest son, Daniel—a boy nine or ten years of age—had a remarkable escape. He was out playing one day with two or three other boys a little larger than himself, and the youthful party carelessly wandered a short distance out of gunshot of the fort. They were observed by some Indians who resolved to take them prisoners. This was a more profitable business than killing them, as they could make useful servants of the captives, or obtain a large ransom for them from their bereaved friends. With this object, the savages left their guns, and crept stealthily as near the boys as the nature of the ground permitted them to do without being seen. As they rose upon their feet to spring forward and seize their prey, the boys saw them, gave a cry of alarm, and instantly started in a life and death race for the fort. Young Dunham, the smallest lad, was the hindmost, but he fled with the speed of a frightened fawn, closely pursued, however, his enemy gaining ground upon him, till just as he came within the range of protection from the fort, the Indian overtook him, and laid hold of his flannel hunting shirt. Throwing his arms back suddenly, the nimble boy slipped out of the garment and ran on, leaving the disappointed savage holding his trophy, for he dared not pursue the fugitive any further.

Through a multitude of such trials Mrs. Robertson was preserved. She was the mother of eleven children, and lived to an advanced age, leaving a number of descendants, useful and prosperous citizens in the valley to which she came as a pioneer. She witnessed the gradual growth of the place selected as her home from a wilderness to a rude settlement, and thence to a town of importance. In 1805 Nashville boasted but one brick house, although Market-street and a few others were laid out. There was a log schoolhouse, and the wild forest encircled the future capital. There was difficulty at that time in procuring supplies of provisions; it took three or four months to go to and from New Orleans in the flat-bottomed boats, which always started as soon as the waters rose, and returned in the spring laden with groceries, grain, and various articles for provision and clothing. Furs were procured of the Indians. There were at that period no good schools in the valley, and pupils were sent to Carolina and the Eastern States to be educated, by parents who were able to afford the expense. Stores for use or trading purposes were sometimes brought in wagons from Baltimore and Philadelphia, through the eastern portion of Tennessee; but pack-horses had been generally used. Two men could manage ten or fifteen horses, carrying each about two hundred pounds, by tying one to the other in single file, one man taking charge of the leading, the other of the hindmost horse, to keep an eye on the proper adjustment of the loads, and to stir up any that appeared to lag. Bells were indispensable accompaniments to the horses, by which they could be found in the morning when hunting up preparatory to a start. Grass or leaves were inserted in the bells to prevent the clapper from moving during the travel of the day. The first wagon-load of merchandize brought over the mountains on the southern route, is said to have been in 1789, when it was nearly a month making a trip of one hundred and forty miles.

"The water-craft used in descending the Ohio in those primitive times, were flat boats made of green oak plank, fastened by wooden pins to a frame of timber, and caulked with tow or any other pliant substance that could be procured. Boats similarly constructed on the northern waters, were called "arks," but on the Western rivers they were denominated Kentucky boats. The materials of which they were composed were found useful in constructing temporary buildings for safety and protection against the inclemency of the weather, after they had arrived at their destination."*

In early life Mrs. Robertson became a member of the Methodist Episcopal Church, and with her husband joined the first society of that denomination organized in the country, under the preaching of Wilson Lee. The class met to hear the word preached and for social communion, about three miles west of Nashville. She continued an exemplary member of this Church to her death.

In all the relations of life she was faithful, and strict in the performance of every duty. Her manners were modest, unassuming and gentle; she was kind and affectionate in her family, a most devoted and loving mother, and a careful, though indulgent mistress. She was ever open-hearted and benevolent, soothing the ills she had no power to remove. Her industrious habits and self-denying virtues were an example to all who knew her, and she was esteemed and beloved by a large circle of friends and acquaintances. In person she was rather above the medium size, with a symmetrical form, and regular, interesting, and expressive features. She retained to the close of life the faculties of mind and body in uncommon vigor; and in the full expectation of a glorious immortality calmly closed her eyes on the scenes of earth in her ninety-third year, June 11th, 1843, at the house of her son-in-law, John B. Craighead, three miles west of Nashville.

General Robertson was engaged during the greater part of his life in public service. In his latter years he was appointed Indian agent in the Choctaw nation, where he died in 1814. His bones were removed some years since from the Indian lands, and deposited in the burial ground at Nashville. The sons murdered by the Indians were Peyton Henderson, eleven years of age, and James Randolph, about twenty. With the exception of these, and an infant daughter, the children of Mrs. Robertson lived to marry and have families of their own. Three daughters and two sons are living at this date, and Dr. Robertson, one of the sons, is one of the most highly esteemed citizens of Nashville.

* Burnet's Notes.

V.

JANE BROWN.

MANY fearful tales of the individual suffering which marked the early history of Tennessee, are only known to a few as family traditions, and remembered by the descendants of those who bore a part, as stories of the nursery and not as chapters in the great historic record of the past. Yet the experience and conduct of a single individual may often better illustrate the condition, progress, and character of a people, than whole chapters devoted to the details of a campaign.

The traditional recollections detailed in the following sketch of the family of James Brown, connected as they were intimately with some of the most important political events of that period, cannot fail to throw new light upon the pioneer history of the country, and inspire our hearts with renewed gratitude to those hardy, but wise men and women, who built up so goodly a State amidst so many troubles, in the dark and bloody valleys of the Shauvanon, Tanasees, and Ho-go-hegee.

Jane Gillespie was born in Pennsylvania about the year 1740. Her father was a pioneer in the settlement of North Carolina. Her family was one of the most respectable as well as the most worthy in the county of Guilford, where they resided during the Revolutionary war. Two of her brothers, Col. and Maj. Gillespie, were distinguished for their gallantry and devotion to the cause of liberty, and were honored as brave officers. Herself and most of her fam ily were members of the Rev. David Caldwell's church at Guilford, and ardently espoused his political and religious principles.

About the year 1761 or 1762, Miss Gillespie became the wife of James Brown, a native of Ireland, whose family had settled in Guilford some years before. At the beginning of the Revolution, Mrs. Brown had a large family of small children, but she freely gave up her husband when his country demanded his services. During the masterly retreat of General Greene, in the winter of 1781, on Dan and Deep rivers, Brown was the pilot and guide of Colonels Lee and Washington, and by his intimate knowledge of the couutry, its by-paths and fords, contributed not a little to the successful countermarches of the American army, by which they were enabled to elude and break the spirit of the army of Lord Cornwallis. When the Americans assumed the offensive, and, from a retreating, suddenly became a pursuing army, Brown pressed eagerly into the fight witL the bold troopers of Lee and Washington.

Being in moderate circumstances, and pressed by the cares of a large and increasing family, Brown's ardent temperament was not satisfied with the prospect of a plodding life of toil in Guilford. For nis Revolutionary services he had received from the State of North Carolina land-warrants, which entitled him to locate a large quantity of land in the wilderness beyond the mountains. His neighbors had made him sheriff of his county, and a justice of the County Court, and he was rapidly rising in the estimation of his countrymen for his patriotism, integrity, and many other virtues of a good citizen. But he readily saw the advantages which he might secure to his rising family by striking out into the deep forests, and securing for them the choicest homes in the Tennessee and Cumberland valleys. He could command only a trifle in money for his land scrip, but by exposing himself to a few years of hardship and danger, he could secure independent estates for his numerous children. With him, to be convinced was to act : his decision and his action went together. Tearing himself from the bosom of his family and all the endearments of a happy home circle, he set out on his journey to explore the valley of the Cumberland. The whole of Tennessee was then a wilderness, except a small spot on the Holston or Watauga, on the east, and a small spot around Nashville and Bledsoe's Lick, on the west of the Cumberland Mountains. Taking with him his two eldest sons, William and John, and a few tried friends, he explored the Cumberland valley. He secured lands on the Cumberland river below Nashville, at the place now known as Hyde's Ferry. He also explored the wilderness south, as far as Duck river, and located a large body of land south of Duck river, near Columbia. The whole country was then almost untrodden by the foot of the white man. It was the hunting-ground of the Chickasaws, Creeks, and Cherokees, and was full of deer, elk, bears, and buffaloes. The rich uplands, as well as the alluvial bottoms of the rivers, were covered with cane-brakes, which were almost impervious to man. Whoever penetrated these regions, did so with knife and hatchet to cut away the cane, and with rifle to oppose the savage beasts and savage men who sheltered in its deep fastnesses. But Brown's heart was a bold one, and his hopes for the future animated him to perseverance. Having located by actual survey several fine tracts of land, he determined to return to Guilford, and remove his family to their new home in the West. Leaving William as a deputy surveyor under Col. Polk, and John to open and cultivate a small field, and build some cabins at the mouth of White's Creek, he returned to North Carolina.

In the winter of 1787–8, Brown and his family, having disposed of their property, found themselves on the banks of the French Broad in what is now Hawkins county, Tennessee, waiting the opening of the spring, before beginning their journey across the mountains to the Cumberland valley.

In 1785, the treaty of Hopewell had been concluded with the Cherokees, guaranteeing reciprocal friendship between that nation and the Americans. At the time Brown arrived on the banks of the French Broad, there was apparent acquiescence in the terms of this treaty, and the Cherokee and the white man seemed, for a

4*

time, to have smoked the pipe of peace, and buried the tomahawk for ever.

There were two routes to the Cumberland Valley at this time, the one by land, the other by water. The land route was a long and tedious one, through the Cumberland Gap, across the head waters of the Cumberland, Green, and Barren rivers in Kentucky, to Bledsoe's Lick, or Nashville. The other route was easier of accomplishment, and more desirable; because, being by the descent of the river, it admitted of the transportation of goods and aged persons. Brown, on his recent visit to Cumberland, had heard of Col. Donaldson's voyage down the Tennessee, up the Ohio and Cumberland, to Nashville, and of one or two other parties who had succeeded in making the same voyage. As he had women and small children, and packages of valuable goods, which he was taking to the West, he resolved to hazard the descent of the Tennessee river.

He was not ignorant of the fact that there were many populous Indian towns on the Tennessee river, of both the Cherokee and Chickasaw nations, and that marauding parties of Creeks and Shawanees were often on its shores and in the towns. He knew the danger of the voyage, on account of the hostile Indians; and he also knew its numerous shoals, rapids and eddies, rendered its navigation perilous to such frail open boats as could then be constructed. But he trusted in the honest disposition of the Cherokees to conform to the treaty of Hopewell, and judged that the marauding Creeks and Shawanees would prove less dangerous on the water than on the circuitous land route to the Cumberland. Having been habitually exposed to danger for many years, it is probable he rather sought the most perilous route, feeling a sort of manly desire to meet and overcome it.

Having built a boat in the style of a common flatboat, modeled as much as possible after Noah's ark, except that it was open at the top, he prepared to adventure the fearful voyage. About the 1st of May, 1788, having taken on board a large amount of goods suitable for traffic among the Indians and the pioneers in Cumberland, his party embarked upon the bosom of French Broad. The party was a small and weak one, considering the dangers it had to encounter, and the valuable cargo it had to defend. It consisted of Brown, two grown sons, three hired men and a negro man ; in all, seven grown men ; Mrs. Brown, three small sons and four small daughters ; an aged woman, the mother of one of the hired men, and two or three negro women, the property of Brown.

To make up for the weakness of his party, Brown had mounted a small cannon upon the prow of his boat, and no doubt relied as much for his security upon the known terror which such guns inspired in the savages, as upon any damage which he expected to inflict upon them with it. Thus appointed and thus equipped, this happy family began its eventful descent of the river. All was gladness, all was sunshine. The land of their fathers, of their loved friends and pastor, was behind them ; beneath their oars flashed the bright waters of a lovely stream, whose winding channel would soon bear them to their new home in the valley of the fairy Cumberland. As they passed rapidly along, the father sat in the midst of his little children, hopefully describing their new home in the deep forests of the West.

They thus descended the French Broad to the Tennessee, and went on merrily down its waters to Chickamauga, a considerable town of Cherokee Indians, not far from the present site of Chattanooga. Here the Indians appeared friendly ; the principal chief went on board the boat, and made inquiry for various articles of goods, proposed to trade, and finally took his leave, with many professions of kindness. Our voyagers continued their descent, rejoicing in the happy omen which the friendship of the Chickamauga chieftain opened for their future. The next day, the 9th of May, the solitary pirogue or flatboat had passed several Indian villages, and had come in view of the towns of Running Water and Nickajack, the last Cherokee towns where there was any considerable body of Indians. The voyagers began to rejoice in their happy deliverance from the principal dangers which had threatened their journey. They would in a few hours be through the mountain passes, on the wide bosom of a noble river, where they would be comparatively free from the ambuscades of lurking savages.

Suddenly four canoes, with white flags raised, and naked savages kneeling in them as rowers, glided out into the river, and rapidly approached; fearing some mischief, Brown immediately turned his cannon upon the approaching canoes, and with lighted match, bade them keep off at the peril of their lives.

Struck with astonishment at the bold threat, they paused, and pulled their frail canoes a little out of the range of the big gun. A man by the name of John Vaun, a well-known half-breed, who spoke good English, was the leader of the party. He spoke to Brown, and said that his party came in friendship; as an evidence of that they had raised a white flag; they came as his friends to trade with him. Brown, who was a bold and fearless man, and dared to face a thousand savages, still kept them off; but at last, confiding in the assurances of Vaun that he was a white man, and that the Indians would respect the persons and property of his party, in an unguarded moment he consented that several of the Indians might come on board. A dozen Indians now came on board, and lashed their canoes to the side of the boat. As they came near the town, hundreds dashed out into the river in their canoes, and came alongside of the boat. Having thus secured possession, the leading men, especially Vann, assured Brown that no harm was intended. In the mean time, each Indian seized upon whatever he fancied and threw it into his canoe. In this way several boxes and trunks were instantly rifled. Vann pretended to order his followers to abstain, but they paid no attention to him. A bold warrior now demanded of Brown the key to a large chest, that contained his most valuable stores, which he refused to give, telling the Indian that Mrs. Brown had it. The Indian demanded it of Mrs. Brown, but she boldly refused to give it up. He then split the top of the chest open with his tomahawk, and his example was immediately followed by the other Indians, who broke open and rifled every box and package on the boat. While this was going on, a savage rudely took hold of Joseph Brown, a lad fifteen years old, but was forced by the father to let the boy go. An instant after, the Indian seized a sword lying in the boat, and while Brown's back was turned to him, struck him on the back of the neck, almost severing his head from his body. Brown turned in the agony of death and seized the Indian, and in the struggle was thrown into the river, where he sank to rise no more. The boat was now turned into the mouth of a little creek, in the town of Nickajack, and the whole party taken on shore, in the midst of several hundred warriors, women and children. In the mean time, Vann continued to tell the sons of Brown that all this was a violation of the treaty of Hopewell, and that Breath, the chief of Nickajack and Running Water, who was expected there that night, would punish the marauders, restore their goods, and send them on their voyage. Several leading warriors of the upper town had seized Brown's negroes as lawful spoil, and had dispatched them in canoes to their several homes. Whatever may have been Vann's true motives, his interference on this occasion had the effect to place the whole party at the mercy of the Indians, without resistance. If he acted in good faith, he was shamefully deceived by his followers; but if he only used his address to disarm the voyagers, that they might the more easily fall victims to savage ferocity, his conduct exhibits the climax of perfidy.

A party of Creek braves, who were engaged with the men of Nickajack and Running Water in this outrage, having seized upon their share of the plunder, and having taken possession of Mrs. Brown, her son George, ten years old, and three small daughters, immediately began their march to their own nation. While the Cherokees were deliberating upon the fate of the prisoners and a division of the spoils, they adroitly withdrew from the council, on the plea that this all belonged to the head men of Nickajack. Thus, in one short hour deprived of husband, sons, friends, liberty and all, this devoted woman, with her five smallest children, began her sad journey on foot along the rugged, flinty trails that led to the Creek towns on the Tallapoosa river.

At the time of this outrage, there was living at or near Nickajack, a French trader, named Thomas Tunbridge, married to a white woman, who had been taken prisoner near Mobile, when an infant, and raised by the Indians.   After she was grown, she was exchanged, but refused to leave the Indians, distrusting her ability to adapt her habits to civilized life.   She had been married to an Indian brave, by whom she had a son, now twenty-two years old, who was one of the boldest warriors of the Cherokee towns.   He had already killed six white men in his forays to the Cumberland settlement. Having all the versatility of his mother's race, as well as the ferocity and courage of his father, he was fast rising into distinction as a warrior, and bade fair to reach the first honors of his nation.   His praises for daring and chivalry were in the mouths of all.

His mother was now growing old, and having no young children, her son desired to present to her some bright-eyed boy as a slave ; for according to the savage code of the times, each captive became a slave to his captor.   This woman's son, whose name was Kiachat-alee, was one of the leaders of the marauding party who had seized upon Brown's boat, and from the first knew the fate of the party. Before the boat landed, he tried to induce Joseph to get into his canoe, with the intention of withdrawing him from the general massacre that was soon to take place, but the boy would not go with him.   When the boat landed, Kiachatalee took Joseph to his step-father, Tunbridge, who in good English told the boy he lived a mile out of the town, and invited him to go and spend the night with him.   This the boy did, after asking the consent of his elder brothers.   Tunbridge seized the boy by the hand and hurried him away. They had scarcely gone out of the town before they heard the rifles of the savage braves, who were murdering his brothers and friends. What were the feelings of the poor boy at this moment !   His father slain ; his brothers and friends weltering in their blood, amidst the yells of savage assassins ; and his mother, brother and sisters borne off, he knew not whither, by a band of lawless Creek marauders ! To add to his agony at such a moment, an aged Indian woman, with hair disheveled, and her round, fat face discolored with excitement, followed them to the trader's house, calling upon Tunbridge to produce the white man, exclaiming, with a fiendish air of triumph, " All the rest are killed, and he must die also !"

The trader calmly replied to her, "He's ou'y a little boy. It s a shame to kill children. He shall not be killed."

The old hag was excited, and vowed that the boy should be killed. She said, "He was too large to allow him to live. In two or three years he would be a man; he would learn the country, its towns and its rivers; would make his escape and come back with an army of white men to destroy us all." She said her son, Cutty-a-toy, was a brave chief, and that he would be there in a few minutes to kill the boy.

In a few minutes Cutty-a-toy, followed by many armed warriors, rushed upon the trader's house, and demanded the white boy, saying that he was too large, that he would be grown, would make his escape, and bring back an army to destroy their town.

The trader stood, with cool courage, in the door of his lodge, and refused to surrender the prisoner, saying it was not right to kill children, and also warning the angry chief that the boy was the prisoner of Kiachatalee, his son, and if he was injured or slain, Kiachatalee would be revenged for it. As Kiachatalee was only a young warrior, and Cutty-a-toy a chief and a gray-beard, this threat of revenge greatly incensed him. In an instant he raised his tomahawk, and, with the air of a man who intends a deed of murder, demanded of the trader, "And are you the friend of the Virginian?"

Answering the look rather than the words, the trader stepped out of his door, and said to the bloody brave, "Take him."

Cutty-a-toy then rushed into the trader's lodge, seized the boy by the throat, and was about to brain him with his tomahawk, when the wife of Tunbridge interposed in a tone of supplication which at once succeeded.

"Will the brave chieftain kill the boy in my house? Let not the boy's blood stain my floor."

The appeal of the woman reached the savage's heart. He dropped his weapon, and slowly dragged the boy out of the lodge into the midst of a crowd of savages, who waved their knives and hatchets in the poor lad's face, in order to enjoy his terror.

In the path which led from the house, the boy fell upon his knees, while the savages were tearing off his clothes, and asked the trader to request the Indians to give him one half hour to pray. The trader roughly replied, " Boy, it's not worth while ; they'll kill you." As he stood in momentary expectation of his fate, the trader's wife again interposed, and begged the savage chief not to kill the boy in her yard, or in the path along which she had to carry water, but to take him out into the mountains, where the birds and wolves might eat up his flesh, where she could not see his blood !

The appeal of the woman was again heard, and giving the boy his pantaloons, they held a short talk, and agreed to take him down to Running Water, saying to the trader's wife, " We will not spill this boy's blood near your house; but we will take him to Running Water, where we will have a frolic knocking him in the head."

Having gone about three hundred yards, they halted and formed a circle around the victim. He again fell upon his knees, and with his face upturned towards heaven, and his hands firmly clasped on his breast, remained in prayer, expecting at each moment the fatal blow. At this dreadful moment he thought of Stephen, to whose vision the heavens were opened at the moment of his death, and was happy. As the savage braves stood around him, young Brown saw their stern aspect of revenge suddenly relax, and a smile of sympathy and pity succeed. They called the trader, told him to take the boy, that they would not kill him ; and Cutty-a-toy said he loved the boy, and would come back in three weeks and make friends with him. It was afterwards ascertained that Cutty-a-toy had taken some of Brown's negroes, and claimed them as his prisoners, and that his fear lest Kiatchatalee might retaliate by killing his negro prisoners, was the thought which suddenly turned him to mercy and pity. So thought his own followers ; for when he said he *loved* the boy, and would not kill him, his savage followers replied :

" No, no, he does not love the boy; it's the boy's negroes he loves."

When Cutty-a-toy's mother saw that the boy's life would not be taken, she seemed displeased ; went up to him and cut off his scalp lock, and kicked him so rudely in the side as almost to kill him, exclaiming, " I've got the Virginian's scalp."

The Tuskegee chief, Cutty-a-toy, led his party away, leaving Joseph in the hands of the trader and his wife. In two or three days he was taken into Nickajack, and the kind old chief, Breath, who greatly regretted what had taken place in his absence, took him by the hand, calmly heard a narrative of his situation from the trader's wife, and then told the boy that he must be adopted into his tribe, and become an Indian if he would save his life; that there was no other way in which his life could be saved. To that end, the chief adopted him into his own family, and told Joseph that he was his uncle, and that Kiatchatalee was his brother. His head was then shaved, leaving only a fillet of hair on the top, in which a bunch of feathers was tied, his ears pierced for rings, and his clothes taken off; the flap substituted for trowsers, and a short shirt for a coat, shirt, and vest, his nether vestments consisting of a pair of deer-skin moccasins. In this condition he was pronounced an Indian, with the exception of a slit in each ear, which the kindness of the chief deferred making until cold weather.

The trader's wife took him to see his two sisters, Jane, aged ten, and Polly, aged five years, who had just been brought back to Nickajack; a party of Cherokees having pursued the Creek braves, and recaptured from them these two small girls, after they had been taken some distance towards the Creek towns. From his sister Jane, Joseph learned the destination of the party who had carried off his mother, his brother George, and sister Elizabeth. The children were now in the same town, adopted into different families, and it was a source of consolation to them to be allowed to see each other occasionally. In the various toils which were imposed upon the little captives, such as carrying water and wood, pounding hominy, and working corn in the fields, and on the part of the boy, looking after the stock, nearly a year passed, without many incidents worthy of note. Hostile parties of savages came and went, and tales of barbarous deeds done by them on the distant frontiers were often told in the hearing of the children; but none brought deliverance for them.   Yet in but few instances did the savage neighbors of these captive children treat them unkindly.   Three or four times Joseph's life was in danger from lawless braves, whose bloodthirsty natures panted for the blood of the white man.   The good old chief, Breath, hearing of these things, caused young Brown to be armed, and declared that it should be lawful for him to slay any Indian who should maltreat him.

In a few months Joseph was allowed a rifle and a horse, and permitted to go into the woods to hunt.   He might often have availed himself of the kindness of his savage friends, and made his escape to the frontiers, but he loved his little sisters, and his love for them restrained his desire for freedom, lest his escape might add to the rigors of their slavery, or perhaps for ever prevent their deliverance.

In the meantime open war had been going on between the Indians and the people of Cumberland and East Tennessee.   Two thousand warriors, principally Cherokees, of whom four or five hundred were horsemen dressed as white men, made an irruption into East Tennessee, killing everything before them.   Generals Sevier and Martin, with a large body of pioneers, had marched into their territory, laying waste their fields and villages.   When their chief, Big Tassel, came to Sevier's camp with a flag to hold a talk, he was killed by a soldier named Kirk, whose family had been murdered by his warriors.   This outrage added new flames to the rage of the Cherokees, who no longer sought peace.   In their revengeful foray, they stormed Fort Gillespie, eight miles from Knoxville, and butchered men, women and children, carrying off Mrs. Glass, the sister of Capt. Gillespie.

These savages were not wholly illiterate: many of their leaders could speak and even write English, and they well understood the sacred character of a white flag and of treaties.   The following proclamation, written at Fort Gillespie after the massacre, by Watts, or some of his half-breed followers, is curious and illustrative.   It is signed by Bloody Fellow, Categisky, John Watts, and The Glass.

Oct. 15th,* 1798.

To Mr. JOHN SEVIER *and* JOSEPH MARTIN, *and to* You, *the Inhabitants of the New State.*

" We would wish to inform you of the accidents that happened at Gillespie's Fort, concerning the women and children that were killed in the battle.

" The Bloody Fellow's talk is, that he is now here upon his own ground. He is not like you are, for you kill women and children and he does not. He had orders to do it, and to order them off the land, and he came and ordered them to surrender, and they should not be hurt, and they would not. And he stormed it and took it.

" For you, you beguiled the head man (Big Tassel), who was your friend, and wanted to keep peace.

" But you began it, and this is what you get for it. When you move off the land, then he will make peace, and give up the women and children.

" And you must march off in thirty days.

" Five thousand is our number !"

In the spring of 1789, an exchange of prisoners was agreed upon at a talk held with Gen. Sevier. It was agreed that the Cherokees should make an absolute surrender of all the white persons within their borders, and runners were sent to each of the head men, to send their captives to the Little Turkey for an exchange. When these runners came to Nickajack, young Brown was on a trading trip down the river with his Indian brother Kiachatalee, and did not return until Mrs. Glass and all the other prisoners had gone up to Running Water, where the chief was awaiting their arrival.

When young Brown got home, he was sent with one of his sisters to Running Water, in order to he sent up to the treaty-grounds to be exchanged. His little sister would not leave her Indian mother, who had ever treated her kindly, but wept and clung to her neck, declaring that it would break her Indian mother's

* Haywood gives the date of the taking of the fort as the 10th September, but in his appendix the 15th.

heart if she left her. This tender feeling was a tribute to savage kindness, but young Brown finally took his sister in his arms, and carried her some distance, before he could reconcile her to go with him. His eldest sister belonged to a trader, who said he had bought her with his money, and would not let her go. Joseph had to leave her behind, being wholly unable to redeem her.

At Running Water, young Brown heard Turkey, the head chief, stating to his chiefs around him the terms of the treaty he had made: and in doing so, his followers upbraided him for agreeing to deliver so many prisoners without any ransom. To this the chief replied, " Little John (meaning Sevier) would have it so ; he is a very mean man—a dog ; but he has my daughter a prisoner, and he knew I would have to agree to any terms, to get her back."

The next morning, when the Indian chief was about to start his prisoners forward, young Brown refused to go, and was taken to the chief to give his reasons. He then stated that one of his sisters was left in Nickajack, and that he never would consent to be set at liberty without her. The savage chief immediately sent for the girl, and after some delay, Col. Bench, the chief of the mounted regiment of Indians, went himself, and brought the girl to Running Water. Thus, about the first of May, 1789, young Brown and his two sisters were once more restored to liberty. Being reduced to poverty, these now orphan children were sent into South Carolina, to sojourn with some relatives until their elder brother, who was in Cumberland, could go after them, or until their mother should be released from her captivity amongst the Creeks.

We must now return to the 9th of May, 1788, and continue the narrative of Mrs. Brown's captivity. Having seen her husband fall by the hands of savages, she was hurried away by her captors, and took the road southward, just as she heard the yells and rifles of the cruel savages who murdered her sons and their companions. What must have been the feelings of horror and agony of this poor woman, herself a prisoner in the hands of she knew not whom, and borne she knew not whither ! To add to the horror of her situation, she soon saw two of her sweet little daughters torn from her side by a party of Cherokees, and borne back, she knew not whither, nor for what end

Driven forward on foot for many days and nights, she continued to bear up under the bodily fatigues and mental anguish by which she was tortured, her feet blistered and swollen, and driven before the pack-horses along a flinty path, every moment expecting death if she failed, and every moment expecting to fail! She yet accomplished many days' travel, and finally reached one of the upper Creek towns on the Tallapoosa, far down in the wilderness. Arrived at the town of her captor, she found herself a slave, doomed to bear wood and water, pound hominy, and do all servile offices for her savage mistress. To add to her distress, her son, nine years old, and her daughter, seven, were taken to different towns, and she was left indeed alone in her sorrow.

At the period of Mrs. Brown's captivity, Alexander M'Gillevray, a half-breed Creek, of Scotch descent, was the head chief of the Muscogee Indians, and assumed the title of Commander-in-chief of the Upper and Lower Creeks and the Seminoles; being the military as well as the civil governor of all the Indians of Florida, Alabama, and Lower Georgia. He was a man of keen sagacity, forest-born and forest-bred, combining the shrewdness of the savage with the learning of the civilized man. Fortunately for Mrs. Brown, her cruel captor took her to a town in which lived a sister of M'Gillevray, who was the wife of a French trader by the name of Durant. Her age and dignified bearing under the toils imposed upon her, excited the sympathy and compassion of this kind-hearted Indian woman. Several weeks passed before she found an opportunity, but when Mrs. Brown's savage master was absent, the wife of Durant spoke to her kindly, told her that she pitied her sorrow, and would, if she could, relieve her. She said her brother, the chief of the Creeks, did not approve of his people's making slaves of the white women, and that he was a liberal, high-minded man, who had a soul of honor, and would never turn away from a helpless woman who came to him for succor. "Why do you not fly to him?" asked the simple-hearted woman.

Mrs. Brown explained to her her total ignorance of the country, and her inability to reach the residence of Col. McGillevray. The Indian woman listened to her, and then said, " It is true : but if you will, there is my horse, and there is my saddle. You are welcome to them ; but you must take them. I cannot give them, but my husband shall never pursue. You can take them without danger." It was arranged. On a certain morning the Indian woman sent an aged Indian, who was to act as the guide of Mrs. Brown, as far as a trader's house ; from which point the trader was to procure a guide and a horse.

At the appointed time, Mrs. Brown, mounted upon her friend's horse and saddle, started in pursuit of her Indian guide, who travelled on as though entirely unconscious of her existence. She arrived in safety at the trader's lodge, and was by him furnished with a guide and horse to the chieftain's residence. Full of gratitude for intended kindness, she yet approached the Creek chieftain with many feelings of doubt and misgiving. He received her kindly, heard her story attentively, and after considering it well, gave Mrs. Brown a cordial welcome to his house, and bade her stay with his wife, as a member of his family. He explained to her that, according to the usage of his people, she belonged to her captor, and that he had no right to take her from him.

He said, however, that he could no doubt reconcile her master by some presents, when he should follow, as he no doubt would before long. He told her she could make shirts or other garments for the traders, and soon provide herself with everything necessary for her comfort. In the meantime, he would furnish her with whatever she needed. Mrs. Brown accepted the savage chieftain's proffered protection, and took shelter under his roof. She had been there but a few days when she was startled by the appearance of her savage master, who had followed her to her place of refuge. Fortunately for her, the chieftain was at home, and himself met her pursuer. The Indian gruffly demanded of his chieftain the white woman, his prisoner.

Col. McGillevray at once informed him that she was in his

house, and that he had promised to protect her. The savage merely replied, " Well, if you do not give me back my prisoner, I'll kill her." The wily chieftain knew his man, and humoring his temper, replied,. " That is true. She is your prisoner, and you can kill her, if you choose. I know she is a weak woman, and you are a brave warrior. Would you tie the scalp of a squaw about your neck ?"

" But she can carry water, and hoe corn, and pound hominy for my wife," said the Creek warrior; " and she's mine; she's my prisoner."

" That's true," said the chieftain ; " but if you kill her, will she carry any more water ? Can the dead work ? If you will consent to leave her with me, so that I can send her back to her people, I will send your wife a new dress, and will give you a rifle, some powder and lead, and some beads and paints; and when you go back to your wife, she will not see the blood of a woman upon your hands !"

Savage cupidity overcame savage revenge, and Mrs. Brown became the ransomed captive of the brave and generous McGillevray ; a noble instance of chivalry on the part of a savage chieftain, which reflects more honor on his name than the glory of a hundred battles fought by his people during his chieftaincy. For several months she plied her needle in his lodge, and by her experience in the craft of needle-work soon rendered herself useful to her Indian friends, and by her dignity and energy commanded their respect.

The chieftain on his next visit to the upper Creek towns, found Mrs. Brown's daughter, Elizabeth, aged about seven years, generously purchased her from her master, and upon his return home had the pleasure of restoring the sweet child to her distressed mother : a grateful duty, nobly performed ! He also informed Mrs. Brown that he had seen her son George, and tried to induce his master to part with him, but that he was so much attached to the boy he would not part from him on any terms. But he assured her he would not fail, as soon as possible, to ransom her son, and restore him also to her arms.

In November, 1789, Col. McGillevray had appointed to meet commissioners to arrange terms of peace, at Rock Landing, Georgia. On his departure for the treaty grounds, he took Mrs. Brown and her daughter, and there delivered them to her son William, who came from South Carolina, and had gone thither in hopes that he might be enabled to hear something of her and her long lost children.

Thus, in November, 1789, after eighteen months' captivity, she was at last united with her surviving children. They spent a short time in South Carolina with some relatives, and returned to Guilford, N. C., at last restored to her friends, whom she had left but two short years before. But what a change had taken place in her destiny since she had started westward with her husband, sons, and neighbors, so full of life and hope! All her captive children were now restored to her, except George, who was in one of the upper Creek villages, doomed to a still longer captivity.

Mrs. Brown had two sons who were in the Cumberland Valley on the 9th of May, 1788; William the surveyor, and Daniel, aged twelve years, who went over the land route with some stock, to the Cumberland Valley. During her short stay in Guilford, her benefactor, the Creek chieftain, passed through Guilford Court House, and sent word to Mrs. Brown that he was there. She immediately went with her brother, Col. Gillespie, Rev. Dr. Caldwell, and her son William, and thanked him with them. In addition, her brother offered to pay Col. McGillevray any sum he might think proper to demand, as the ransom of Mrs. Brown and her daughter, but the generous Creek refused any compensation whatever. He said he owed it to humanity and honor to do as he had done, and that to receive pay for it would deprive him both of the real pleasure and real honor of such a deed. He assured Mrs. Brown he would not fail to use his best efforts to restore her son, and she might rely upon his finding out some means to accomplish so good an object.

Mrs. Brown, with the remnant of her family, again turned her face westward, seeking the new home which the foresight of her husband had prepared for her and her children, and to which he was so boldly conducting them when he perished. And now at last, in 1791, this devoted woman and all her surviving children but one, found themselves at their new home, at the mouth of White's creek, near Nashville. About this time her son Joseph, while travelling with a small party of friends, was shot through the arm by a party of savages in ambush; a severe wound, from which he did not recover for some time.

In 1792, a formidable body of Creeks, Cherokees, and Shawanees invaded Cumberland Valley, attacked Buchanan's Station, and were repulsed with great loss. Joseph Brown came the next morning, with a large party of friends, to the assistance of Buchanan, but the Indians had retreated Upon approaching the scene of action, what was young Brown's astonishment at finding his Indian brother, Kiachatalee, lying cold in death upon the field, near the walls of the fort against which he had so gallantly led the assault! The next year, Joseph attended a treaty at Tellico, in East Tennessee, where he met a nephew of Kiachatalee, named Charles Butler, with whom he had been well acquainted while a prisoner at Nickajack. Butler gave him the Indian version of the attack on Buchanan's Station, and also the story of Kiachatalee's heroic death. He said the assault was led by Kiachatalee; that he attempted to set fire to the block-house, and was actually blowing it into a flame, when he was mortally wounded. He continued, after receiving his mortal wound, to blow the fire, and to cheer his followers to the assault, calling upon them to fight like brave men, and never give up till they had taken the fort.*

There were many incidents of frontier life, such as Mrs. Brown's was now, which would be interesting to the present generation, but the length of this sketch will necessarily exclude many of them. On one occasion, her eldest son, William, while in pursuit of a party of

* For the incidents connected with the attack on Buchanan's Station, see *Women of the American Revolution*, vol. iii., Memoir of SARAH BUCHANAN, which should be read in connection with the Tennessee Sketches in this volume. In it the Shawanee chief is represented as performing the heroic part really performed by Kiachatalee.

Indians near Nashville, was severely wounded in the arm, so that almost every member of her family had been captured, wounded, or slain by the hands of the Indians. These were trials hard to bear; yet amidst all her troubles Mrs. Brown bore herself as an humble Christian, devoutly grateful to the Giver of all good, that He had watched over her and guided her footsteps aright, in the midst of so many sorrows.

In the year 1794, such had been the continued outrages of the savages from the lower Cherokee towns, in conjunction with marauding Creeks and Shawanees, upon the Cumberland settlements, that the principal pioneers resolved to fit out an expedition at their own expense, march to Nickajack and Running Water, and punish those lawless people with fire and sword. The national administration had, by its Commissioners, made treaty after treaty with the Cherokees, but still the people of these lower towns continued their depredations, against the wishes of the upper Cherokees; and it was impossible to induce the national government to take the decided steps which these bold pioneers knew were so absolutely necessary to check the marauding spirit of the lower Cherokee towns. These towns were far down the Tennessee, in the midst of mountain fastnesses, which the foot of white man had never trod. They felt secure from all aggression, and reposed in full confidence that whoever might suffer on account of their incursions into Cumberland, their towns were unapproachable.

At this time Joseph Brown was living near Nashville with his mother, and had recently gone with Gen. Robertson to attend an Indian council at Tellico block-house. The intimate knowledge young Brown had obtained of these lower towns and their people by his residence there, enabled him to communicate a good idea of the country and the people from whom the Cumberland settlements had so long suffered. The death of Kiachatalee at Buchanan's Station, on the 30th September, 1792, his warlike character, so well known to Brown, and his leadership as a warrior among the men of Nickajack and Running Water, all pointed out these towns as the hives from which came forth such swarms of marauding Indians.

Despairing of succor from the national government, Gen. Robertson wrote to Col. Whitley, of Kentucky, who was a well-known partisan, to be at Nashville about the 1st September, 1794, with as many trusty riflemen as he could bring with him. About the same time Col. Mansco, Gen. Johnson of Robertson, Col. Montgomery of Clarksville, and Gen. Robertson, each quietly raised a few trusty men. Maj. Ore at that time commanded a squadron of mounted men, who were in the employ of the United States as rangers, to protect the frontiers of Cumberland. At the request of Gen. Robertson, Maj. Ore arrived at Buchanan's Station just in time to join the expedition.

In the meantime, boats were made of hides, and tried in the Cumberland river, to ascertain their capability of transporting the troops across the Tennessee. These boats were made each of two raw hides, as large as could be got, sewed together, and each was found capable of carrying about fifty guns, and one or two men. They were capable of being rolled up and packed on mules or horses, and could in a few moments be fully equipped and launched.

All the parties being assembled, it was ascertained that there were about six hundred, including Maj. Ore's Rangers. As all but his command were volunteers, who came out without any authority, it was resolved to give Ore the nominal command of the whole party, which would give color of authority to the party to make the campaign, and would save them from the odium of making a lawless invasion of the Indian country. Col. Whitley and Col. Mansco were, however, the prime movers of the campaign, and had most of the responsibility of its conduct. With the troops were more than a dozen leading partisan officers, who had been distinguished in many an Indian battle.

On the 7th September, 1794, this formidable army of invasion set out for Nickajack; and although the route had been unexplored, and the mountains and river lay between them and their enemies, they had counted the cost, fitted out their boats, and had resolved to strike a blow that would teach the lawless Indians a severe lesson.

The troops made a forced march, reached the Tennessee river just

after dark on the fourth day, and in thirty minutes had their raw-
hide boats afloat in the river, ready to bear over the arms. They
immediately began to cross the river, landing a short distance below
the town of Nickajack. Most of the men swam over in perfect
silence, their arms and clothes being conveyed in the boats, and on
rafts rudely constructed of bundles of canes. In order to guide the
swimmers, a very small fire was kindled at the water's edge, by the
party which first crossed. Out of six hundred, only two hundred
and thirty could be induced to cross over ; some holding back because they could not swim, and others because they were subject to
the cramp ; while others, no doubt, reflecting upon the number of
the enemy, and the difficulty of a retreat when once across so wide a
river, did not feel quite willing " to stand the hazard of the die."
But in the face of appalling dangers, some men showed a stout-
heartedness which might have done honor to the bravest of the
brave. A young man by the name of Joseph B. Porter, who could
not swim at all, tied an armful of dry canes together, and nothing
daunted, plunged into the rapid river, and kicked himself over in
safety. Young Brown, although still lame in one arm, from the
wound he had received in the Indian ambuscade, plunged into the
river, and swam safely over. At daylight there were two hundred
and thirty on the south bank of the Tennessee, within half a mile of
Nickajack, and yet they were undiscovered. Leaving Brown, with
twenty picked men, to guard the crossing of the creek, at the lower
end of the town, with instructions to meet them in the centre of the
town as soon as he heard their fire, the main body turned towards
the town, and came down upon it from above.

Although Nickajack contained about three hundred warriors, they
were so completely surprised that they made little resistance ; but
flying precipitately, took to their canoes, and attempted to cross the
river. Some fled to Running Water, and others secreted themselves
in the thickets. The whole town ran with blood. About seventy
warriors were slain, and a large number of women and children were
taken prisoners. Young Brown carried the lower end of the town
manfully, killing several warriors, and taking some prisoners. In

one instance, he killed an Indian warrior in single combat, and carried away his scalp.

As soon as Nickajack was taken, a detachment was sent to destroy Running Water. On the way, the Indians met them, and after an obstinate resistance, gave way, but not till they had wounded three Americans, one of them, Joshua Thomas, mortally. Running Water was also taken, and both towns immediately reduced to ashes. Among the dead, Brown recognized the body of Breath, the generous chief who had adopted him into his family when he was a prisoner. In the towns, many articles of stolen property, which were recognized as belonging to men who had been killed in Cumberland Valley, were found. In addition to these, fresh scalps were found in Nickajack, as well as a number of letters, taken by the Indians from the mail-bags, after having killed the rider. They also found a quantity of powder and lead, recently sent by the Spanish government to these Indians.

Never was a visitation of this kind so justly merited as it was by these towns. They were the principal crossing-places for the war-parties of Creeks, Shawnees, and Cherokees, who went to harass the Cumberland and Kentucky settlements. But two days before their destruction, a war dance was held there, at which were several Cherokee chiefs, as well as Creeks, who had resolved to wage a still more relentless war on the frontiers.

While Brown could not but feel that the hand of Providence had signally punished these towns for their outrage on his family, his exultation was prevented by the death of his brother-in-law, Joshua Thomas, a brave soldier and a kind, generous friend, who was the only one slain by the enemy on this occasion.

The prisoners recognized young Brown, and alarmed for their safety, pleaded with him to save their lives, saying that his life had once been spared by them. He assured them that they were in no danger; that the white people never killed prisoners, women and children.

This blow was so unexpected and successful, that it inspired the Cherokees with a sincere desire for peace, which they soon after concluded, and never again violated. Soon after this affair, young George Brown was liberated by the Creeks. Joseph returned home and lived some years with his mother. He was devoted to business, and of most exemplary conduct in every relation of life. He soon attached himself to Rev. Thomas B. Craighead's congregation, near Hayesboro', and was made an elder in the church.

For several years, he and his mother and brothers memorialized the Congress of the United States to reimburse them for the goods and slaves taken from them in violation of the treaty of Hopewell. But their claims were still unregarded, and still delayed, year after year. In 1806, a treaty was finally concluded with the Indians which opened all the lands on Duck river to the occupation of those who had located their warrants there. Thus Mrs. Brown and her children came into possession of a large and splendid tract of land south of Columbia, to which she soon after removed with her son Joseph.

During the Creek war of 1812, a large number of Cherokee Indians offered their services to Gen. Jackson against their red brethren. Gen. Jackson immediately wrote to Joseph Brown, who had lately been elected colonel by his neighbors, requesting him to consent to command a regiment of Cherokee Indians. This he promptly agreed to do, and started to join the army for that purpose. He however, never took charge of the Indians, but served with the army, as aid to Gen. Robards, as well as interpreter and guide.

He was thus a participant in the battle of Talladega, and had the honor of leading and conducting a charge upon the most hotly contested part of the Indian lines. During this campaign Brown again met Charles Butler, the nephew of Kiachatalee, and learned from him that the old Tuskegee chief, Cutty-a-toy, was still alive. He learned also that he was then living on an island in the Tennessee river, near the mouth of Elle river, and that he had with him several negroes, the descendants of the woman taken by him at Nickajack, on the 9th of May, 1788.

Col. Brown had at that time a claim before Congress for the

value of those negroes, but had always been put off by reason of some defect in the proof as to their value, or some other matter of form. He now determined that, as his negroes were still in the hands of the original wrong-doer, the Tuskegee chief, he would get possession of them, and carry them home. He stated to General Jackson the facts of the case, demanded of him and obtained an order appointing a mixed commission of American and Cherokee officers, to value the negroes of Cutty-a-toy. The Cherokees had long been at peace with the whites, and were now in alliance with them against the Creeks, and under such circumstances there was friendly intercourse between them.

With ten picked men, Brown proceeded to the island, went to the head man's lodge, exhibited to him Gen. Jackson's order, and demanded that Cutty-a-toy's slaves should be immediately sent over to Fort Hampton, to be valued, in pursuance of said order. The head man sent for Cutty-a-toy, and it was immediately agreed that all would go to the fort the next morning.

The next morning, the negroes, Cutty-a-toy, his wife, and some friends, went with Col. Brown to the Fort. In crossing the river Brown and his men took up the negroes and Cutty-a-toy's wife behind them, to carry over the water, while the Indian men crossed on a raft higher up.

When he reached the fort he directed his men to proceed with the negroes towards Ditto's landing, while he turned into the fort with Cutty-a-toy's wife, to await the arrival of the Indians. He immediately called on the commandant of the fort, Col. Williams, stated the history of the case, the order of Gen. Jackson, the failure of Congress to pay for the slaves, and the fact that they were now in his possession; and frankly asked him what course he would pursue, under the circumstances. "Take the negroes home with you," said the Colonel; "and if you wish to do it, and have not men enough, I will give you more."

Upon the arrival of Cutty-a-toy and his followers, they were invited into the fort, and Col. Brown made known to him that he had sent the negroes off, but was willing for the commissioners to proceed to value them. The Indian became enraged. At last, in the midst of the garrison, officers and men, and the Indians, Col. Brown gave a brief narrative of the murder of his father by Cutty-a-toy's party, the murder of his brothers, and the captivity of his mother, small brother and sisters; of the capture of the slaves by Cutty-a-toy, and his attempt on the life of Col. Brown himself, then a boy at the house of the French trader; of his being saved at the intercession of the trader's wife, and the Indian's desire to save the life of his captive negro woman. "It is now," said Col. Brown, " nearly twenty-five years, and yet during all that time you have had the negro and her children as your slaves, and they have worked for you; and yet you got them by the murder of my father and brothers! You made me an orphan and a beggar, when but for you, I had begun the world with the smiles of a father, and the comforts of a home provided by his care. For this wrong, this crime, Cutty-a-toy, you deserve to die !"

Here Cutty-a-toy hung his head, and said, " It is all true: do with me as you please."

The soldiers who stood around, many of them the neighbors of Col. Brown, said, " Kill him ! he ought to die." But Brown was now a Christian, and had long since ceased to cherish feelings of revenge against the savage murderer of his father.

"No, no, Cutty-a-toy," he proceeded, " although you deserve to die, and at my hands, yet I will not kill you. If I did not worship the Great Spirit who rules all things, I would slay you; but vengeance is his, and I will leave you to answer to him for your crimes ! I will not stain my hands with your blood ; you are now old, and must soon go down to the grave, and answer to that Great Spirit for the life you have led. Live and repent."

Here Cutty-a-toy assumed a bolder front, and said, by certain treaties made in 1794, this property was guaranteed to him, and that he would sue Brown in the Federal Courts, as some other Indians named by him had done, in similar cases ; but he finally agreed, if Brown would give him a young negro fellow, he might take the rest, including two women and some children, which was generously done.

Thus the fortunes of war, controlled by the steady perseverance of her son, at length restored to Mrs. Brown a part of her long-lost property. Many years afterwards, when Gen. Jackson became President, Col. Brown finally obtained an allowance from Congress for a part of the property lost by his father in 1788. In 1810, he became a member of the Cumberland Presbyterian Church, and in 1823, a regular ordained minister of that Church.

Having lived to the advanced age of ninety, and never having re-married, but always making her home with her son Joseph, Mrs. Brown left this world of vexation and sorrow, for such it had been to her, at her son's residence in Maury County, Tennessee. Hers was a most eventful life, full of trials almost beyond human endurance; yet she did not murmur, but tried to see in all her afflictions the kind guidance of a wise Providence.

George, soon after his release from captivity, emigrated to the South, and after nearly fifty years' honorable citizenship near Wood-ville, Mississippi, died in the bosom of his family. The captive daughter, Jane, whose release was due to the manly courage of her youthful brother, was married to a Mr. Collingsworth, and became with him a citizen of Texas as early as 1819, where her children yet reside.

The history possesses all the attractions of a romance; yet it is but a plain sad story of trials and sufferings incident to the period and to border life. The only survivor of that pioneer family is the Rev. Joseph Brown, of Maury County, better known as Col. Brown. From notes and memoranda furnished by him, the principal details of this narrative have been written. It cannot fail to be useful to the future historian of Tennessee, yet Haywood, in his history of five hundred pages, only makes the following allusion to the facts contained in this narrative. Speaking of the treaty of peace made at Tellico, October 20, 1795, between the people of Tennessee, and the Creeks and Cherokees, they (the Creeks,) says the historian, "at this time delivered up Brown, son of Mrs. Brown,

5*

formerly a prisoner in the Creek nation." How inadequate is
such a notice to do justice either to the sufferings of Mrs. Brown
and her children, or to the generous protection of the Creek
chieftain to whom they were indebted for their deliverance! For
notwithstanding the "obloquy which both history and tradition
have thrown upon the characters of the Creek and Cherokee warriors, some bright gleams occasionally break through, which throw
a melancholy lustre over their memories." But a large portion of
the pioneer history of Tennessee has never been written. Replete
with incidents and heroic deeds which might challenge the admiration of the world, yet all that has been written by Haywood and
others would scarcely serve as a thread to guide the future historian
through the labyrinth of events which crowded upon the infant
colonies of the Holston and the Cumberland.

In 1792 the family of Joseph Wilson, who was a pioneer in the
Cumberland Valley, from Carolina, was living at Zeigler's Station in
what is now Sumner County, Tennessee. This station was near
Cumberland River, a few miles from Bledsoe's Lick, but being
nearer the frontier, was more exposed to the incursions of the Indians.
It was only a small picketted fort, with a blockhouse, and contained but thirteen men, including a son of Wilson, not yet grown.
Near the fort was a small farm which was cultivated by the inmates
of the station. In the afternoon of the 26th of June, 1792, a large
party of Creek Indians assaulted the station, but after a severe contest in which several of the defenders were killed and wounded, the
savages were repulsed. There being no surgeon in the party, a
messenger was despatched to a neighboring station for a physician
to attend the wounded, and for aid to repel any new assault which
might be made. Before either surgeon or aid arrived, however, the
Indians renewed the assault, and night coming on, they succeeded
in setting fire to the buildings, which spread with such rapidity, that
the assailed were compelled to decide between instant destruction by

the flames and a cruel and lingering death by the hands of the savages. Five of the defenders were already slain, and four others wounded. In this moment of extreme peril, Mrs. Wilson urged her husband to attempt to break through the lines of the savages, and make his escape. It was probable they would spare her life, and those of her young children, but for him death was certain, unless he could make his escape by a sudden sortie from the blockhouse. Wilson hesitated, and feeling the horror of his situation, seemed to prefer death with his family, to leaving his wife and children to the cruelty of the foe; but his heroic wife urged him for her sake to leave her, saying that she would be safer in the hands of the Indians without him than with him. The same appeal was made to another man who was unhurt, but he refused to leave the fort. But a few minutes remained; the flames were sweeping over the roof of the block-house, and the assailants stood around with rifles and their hatchets to strike down any one who attempted to escape. In this dreadful moment Wilson yielded to his wife's entreaties, bade his son, a lad fifteen or sixteen years of age follow, and dashing boldly out of the flaming building, was followed by his son. Several shots were instantly fired, one of which took effect in Wilson's foot, but father and son passed beyond the lines of the assailants, pursued by yelling savages as they fled. Becoming sick from the loss of blood, Wilson secreted himself in a clump of bushes in the field, while his son went on to obtain a horse from a neighboring field. As he lay thus concealed some pursuing savages passed within a few feet of his hiding-place, but fortunately missed him. The lurid flames of the burning block-house, meanwhile, revealed, as he thought, the fate of his wife and children.

As soon as her son and husband had disappeared, Mrs. Wilson, with an infant in her arms, and followed by five small children, the eldest a lovely girl about ten years old, walked slowly out of the block-house, expecting each instant to receive the fatal blow; but yielding to a generous impulse and perhaps not unwilling to obtain captives, who might be made slaves, the Indian warriors spared her life, and made her and her children prisoners. All the rest of the inmates of the fort were killed or burned, except the man who had been dispatched for succor and a surgeon, both of which failed to arrive till the station was in ashes, and the assailants had retreated towards their nation with their prisoners. Capt. Alfred Wilson, a relation of Joseph Wilson, came with a party of friends to the help of the besieged, but came only in time to discover the blackened and charred bones of those who were burned.

In the meantime, young Wilson obtained horses, returned to the place of his father's concealment, and after having with difficulty placed him on one of the horses, conveyed him to Bledsoe's Station. A party of the soldiers hastily assembled, pursued, but did not overtake the retreating savages, and ti as Mrs. Wilson and her children were carried, as captives, into the White Grounds, in the Upper Creek Nation.

In a few weeks Gov. Blount arrived at Nashville, and called into service three hundred men, in order to defend the frontiers, but the many women and children who were captives in the Creek Towns were left to languish in a barbarous country.

Mrs. Wilson was the sister of Col. White of Knoxville, and through his interposition, after more than twelve months' captivity, was, with all her children (except her eldest daughter,) restored to her home. Few persons can now imagine the painful suspense in which Wilson and his wife spent that year of separation. An aged pioneer matron,* who resided near Bledsoe's Lick during this period, has said that Wilson seemed to her to have been the most unhappy man in the world, during the year of his wife's captivity.

Although the family was now again restored to a happy reunion, yet their home circle lacked one bright-eyed prattler, yet in slavery and exile among her savage captors. It was not until after the destruction of Nickajack and Running Water, that young Sally Wilson was restored to the arms of her parents. And then how changed! During her captivity, she had forgotten her own language and her people, and for several months sighed for her forest home! But soon regaining her language, with it came also the

* Mrs. Shelby.

remembrance of home and friends, and the home circle was again complete.

Mr. and Mrs. Wilson lived many years after this terrible experience of pioneer life, and reared their children to usefulness and honor. Many of their descendants yet reside in Tennessee, while not a few, seeking a better home in the far West, have adventured, like their sires, into the deep solitudes of the wilderness, where they too may yet experience some of the dark trials of their ancestors.

VI.

MARY MOORE.

BEFORE proceeding to sketches illustrating a later period, it will be proper to take a view of the early condition of that portion of Virginia, which, lying on the sunset side of the great range of mountains, belonged to the West. De Hass, in his History of the Indian Wars of Western Virginia, says that before 1749, the country was untrodden by foot of white man, except occasional traders who may have ventured on the heads of some of the tributary streams rising in the Alleghany mountains. It is said that in this year a lunatic wandered into the wilderness of the Greenbriar country, and on returning home, told his friends he had discovered rivers flowing in a westward direction. His report induced two pioneers to enter the mountain wild, where they were found in 1751 by the agent for the Greenbriar company. Further attempts to colonize the country were not made for some years. The first permanent settlements by Zane and Tomlinson, were at or near Wheeling; hardy emigrants followed, and pushed into the fine regions along the Upper Monongahela. When it became known that outposts were established on the confines of civilization, hundreds pressed forward to join the adventurous settlers, and secure homes in the forest domain.

" The escape of Mrs. Denis, who had been taken captive in the

James river settlement, in 1761, presents a parallel to narratives of female captives in the early history of the settlement of New England. Her husband having been slain, after being taken captive, the Indians took her over the mountains and through the forests to the Chilicothe towns north of the Ohio. There she seemed to conform to their ways, painted and dressed herself, and lived as a squaw. Added to this, she gained fame by attending to the sick, both as a nurse and a physician; and became so celebrated for her cures, as to obtain from that superstitious people the reputation of being a necromancer, and the honor paid to a person supposed to have power with the Great Spirit.

" In 1763 she left them, under the pretext of obtaining medicinal herbs, as she had often done before. Not returning at night, her object was suspected, and she was pursued. To avoid leaving traces of her path, she crossed the Scioto three times, and was making her fourth crossing forty miles below the towns, when she was discovered, and fired upon without effect. But in the speed of her flight, she wounded her foot with a sharp stone, so as to be unable to proceed. The Indians had crossed the river, and were just behind her. She eluded their pursuit by hiding in a hollow sycamore log. They frequently stepped on the log that concealed her, and encamped near it for the night. Next morning they proceeded in their pursuit of her; and she started in another direction as fast as her lameness would permit, but was obliged to remain near that place three days. She then set off for the Ohio, over which she rafted herself at the mouth of the Great Kanawha, on a drift log; travelling only by night through fear of discovery, and subsisting only on roots, wild fruits, and the river shell-fish. She reached the Green Briar, having passed forests, rivers, and mountains, for more than three hundred miles. Here she sank down exhausted, and resigned herself to die, when providentially she was discovered by some of the people of that settlement, and hospitably treated at one of their habitations."*

The settlement was made to suffer severely for this hospitable act.

* Flint—Indian Wars of the West.

" A party of fifty or sixty Shawanese, coming under the garb of friendship, suddenly fell upon the men, butchering every one of them, and made captives of the women and children. They next visited the Levels, where Archibald Clendenin had erected a rude block-house, and where were gathered quite a number of families— and were here again entertained with hospitality. Mr. Clendenin had just brought in three fine elk, upon which the savages feasted sumptuously. One of the inmates was a decrepid old woman, with an ulcerated limb; she undressed the member, and asked the Indian if he could cure it. ' Yes,' he replied ; and immediately sunk his tomahawk into her head. This was the signal, and in-stantly every man in the house was put to death.

" The cries of the women and children alarmed a man in the yard, who escaped and reported the circumstances to the settlement at Jackson's river. The people were loth to believe him, but were soon convinced, for the savages appeared, and many of the flying families were massacred without mercy. The prisoners were then marched off in the direction of the Ohio. Mrs. Clendenin proved herself in that trying moment a woman fit to be one of the mothers of the West. Indignant at the treachery and cowardly conduct of the wretches, she did not fail to abuse them from the chief down, in the most unmeasured manner. The savages, to intimidate her, would flap the bloody scalp of her dead husband against her face, and significantly twirl their tomahawks above her head, but still the courageous woman talked to them like one who felt her injuries and resolved to express the feeling. On the day after her captivity, she had an opportunity to escape, and giving her infant to a woman, slipped unobserved into a thicket. The child soon beginning to cry, one of the Indians inquired concerning the mother; but getting no satisfactory reply, swore he would ' bring the cow to the calf,' and taking the infant by the heels dashed out its brains against a tree. Mrs. Clendenin returned to her desolate home, and secured the remains of her husband from the rapacious jaws of the wild animals with which the woods abounded. It is stated that a black woman, in escaping from Clendenin's house, killed her own child to prevent its cries attracting the attention of the savages. Such were some of the horrid realities endured by the first settlers of Western Virginia."*

Early in 1778, an attack was made on a block-house in the country of the Upper Monongahela. The children allowed to play outside, discovered Indians, and running in, gave the alarm. " John Murphy stepped to the door, when one of the Indians, turning the corner of the house, fired at him. The ball took effect, and Murphy fell into the house. The Indian springing in, was grappled by Harbert, and thrown on the floor. A shot from without wounded Harbert, yet he continued to maintain his advantage over the prostrate savage, striking him as effectually as he could with his tomahawk, when another gun was fired from without, the ball passing through his head. His antagonist then slipped out at the door, badly wounded in the encounter.

" Just after the first Indian entered, an active young warrior, holding a tomahawk with a long spike at the end, came in. Edward Cunningham instantly drew up his gun, but it flashed, and they closed in doubtful strife. Both were active and athletic ; each put forth his strength, and strained every nerve to gain the ascendency. For awhile the issue seemed doubtful. At length, by great exertion, Cunningham wrenched the tomahawk from the hand of the Indian, and buried the spike end to the handle in his back. Mrs. Cunningham closed the contest. Seeing her husband struggling with the savage, she struck at him with an axe. The edge wounding his face severely, he loosened his hold, and made his way out of the house. The third Indian who had entered before the door was closed, presented an appearance almost as frightful as the object he had in view. He wore a cap made of the unshorn front of a buffalo, with the ears and horn still attached, and hanging loosely about his head. On entering the room, this hideous monster aimed a blow with his tomahawk at Miss Reece, which inflicted a severe wound on her hand. The mother, seeing the uplifted weapon about to descend on her daughter, seized the

* See De Hass for this and following anecdotes.

monster by the horns; but his false head coming off, she did not succeed in changing the direction of the weapon.   The father then caught hold of him; but far inferior in strength, he was thrown on the floor, and would have been killed, but for the interference of Cunningham, who having cleared the house of one Indian, wheeled and struck his tomahawk into the head of the other.   During all this time, the door was kept secure by the women.   The Indians from without endeavored several times to force it, and would at one time have succeeded; but just as it was yielding, the Indian who had been wounded by Cunningham and his wife, squeezed out, causing a momentary relaxation of their efforts, and enabled the women again to close it.

"On the 11th of April some Indians visited the house of William Morgan, on Dunker's bottom.   They killed his mother and two or three others, and took the wife and her child prisoners.   On their way home, coming near Pricket's fort, they bound Mrs Morgan to a bush, and went in quest of a horse for her to ride, leaving the child with her.   She succeeded in untying with her teeth the bands which confined her, and wandered all that day and part of the next, before she came within sight of the fort.   Here she was kindly treated, and in a few days sent home."

Early in March, 1781, a party of Indians came to the house of Capt. John Thomas, on one of the branches of the Monongahela. He was a pious man, and was engaged in family worship, surrounded by his wife and seven children, when the Indians approached his cabin.   Anticipating no attack, he had not secured his house so well as was his custom, for the season had not advanced sufficiently to cause alarm.   He had just repeated a line of the hymn

"Go worship at Immanuel's feet,"

when the savages fired; the Christian father fell dead, and the murderers forcing the door, entered and commenced the work of death. Mrs. Thomas implored their mercy, but the tomahawk did its work, till the mother and six children lay weltering in blood by the side of the slaughtered father. They then proceeded to scalp the fallen and plunder the house, and departed, taking with them one little boy, a prisoner.

" Elizabeth Juggins, whose father had been murdered the preceding year in that neighborhood, was at the house when the Indians came; but as soon as she heard the report of the gun and saw Capt. Thomas fall, she threw herself under the bed, and escaped the observation of the savages. After they had completed the work of blood and left the house, fearing that they might be lingering near, she remained in that concealment till the house was found to be on fire. When she crawled forth from her asylum, Mrs. Thomas was still alive, though unable to move, and casting a pitying glance towards her murdered infant, asked that it might be handed to her. On seeing Miss Juggins about to leave the house, she exclaimed ' Oh Betsey, don't leave us!' Still anxious for her own safety, the girl rushed out, and taking refuge for the night between two logs, in the morning early spread the alarm. When the scene of these enormities was visited, Mrs. Thomas was found in the yard, much mangled by the tomahawk and considerably torn by hogs; she had perhaps, in the struggle of death, thrown herself out at the door. The house, with Capt. Thomas and the children, was a heap of ashes."

On the 29th of June, 1785, the house of Mr. Scott, a citizen of Washington County, Virginia, was attacked, and he and four children butchered on the spot. He and the family had retired, except Mrs. Scott, who was undressing, when the painted savages rushed in and commenced the work of death. " Scott being awake, jumped up, but was immediately fired at; he forced his way through the midst of the enemy and got out of the door, but fell; an Indian seized Mrs. Scott, and ordered her not to move from a particular spot; others stabbed and cut the throats of the three younger children in their bed, and afterwards lifting them up, dashed them upon the floor, near the mother. The eldest, a beautiful girl eight years old, sprang out of bed, ran to her parent, and in the most plaintive accents cried ' O, mamma, mamma! save me!' The mother, in the deepest anguish of spirit, and with a flood of tears, entreated the

savages to spare her child; but with brutal ferocity they toma-
nawked and stabbed her in the mother's arms. Near Scott's dwelling lived another family of the name of Ball: the Indians attacked
them at the same time; the door being shut, they fired into the
house through an opening between two logs, and killed a young
lad; they then tried to force the door, but a surviving brother fired
through and drove them off; the rest of the family ran out of the
house and escaped. In Scott's house were four good rifles, well
loaded, and a good deal of clothing and furniture, part of which
belonged to people that had left it on their way to Kentucky. The
Indians, thirteen in number, loaded themselves with the plunder,
then speedily made off, and continued travelling all night. Next
morning their chief allotted to each man his share, and detached nine
of the party to steal horses from the inhabitants at Clinch river.

" The eleventh day after Mrs. Scott's captivity, the four Indians who
had her in charge stopped at a place of rendezvous to hunt. Three
went out, and the chief being an old man, was left to take care of
the prisoner, who by this time expressed a willingness to proceed to
the Indian towns, which seemed to have the desired effect of loosen-
ing her keeper's vigilance. In the daytime, as the old man was
graning a deer skin, the captive, pondering on her situation, and
anxiously looking for an opportunity to make her escape, took the
resolution, and went to the Indian carelessly, asking liberty to go a
small distance to a stream of water, to wash the blood off her apron,
which had remained besmeared since the fatal night of the murder
of her little daughter. He said in English—' Go along;' she then
passed by him, his face being in a contrary direction from that she
was going, and he very busy. After getting to the water, she went
on without delay towards a high, barren mountain, and travelled
until late in the evening, when she came down into the valley in
search of the track she had been taken along, hoping thereby to find
the way back without the risk of being lost and perishing with
hunger in uninhabited parts. That night she made herself a bed
with leaves, and the next day resumed her wanderings. Thus did
the poor woman continue, from day to day, and week to week,

wandering in the trackless wilderness. Finally, on the eleventh of August, she reached a settlement on Clinch River known as New Garden.

" Mrs. Scott related, that during her wanderings from the 10th of July to the 11th of August, she had no other means of subsistence than chewing and swallowing the juice of young cane, sassafras, and some plants she did not know the name of; that on her journey she saw buffaloes, elk, deer, and frequently bears and wolves, not one of which, although some passed very near, offered to do her the least harm. One day a bear came near her with a young fawn in his mouth, and on discovering her, dropped his prey and ran off. Hunger prompted her to try and eat the flesh, but on reflection, she desisted, thinking the bear might return and devour her ; besides, she had an aversion to raw meat. She long continued in a low state of health, and remained inconsolable for the loss of her family, particularly bewailing the cruel death of her little daughter."

One of the most melancholy occurrences on Wheeling Creek was the murder of two sisters—the Misses Crow. Three of them left their parents' house for an evening walk along the shaded banks of a beautiful stream—the Dunkard, or lower fork of the Creek. " Their walk extended over a mile, and they were just turning back, when suddenly several Indians sprang from behind a ledge of rock, and seized all three of the sisters. They led the captives a short distance up a bank, when a halt was called, and a parley took place. It seems that some of the Indians were in favor of immediate slaughter, while others were disposed to carry them into permanent captivity. Unfortunately the arm of mercy was powerless. Without a moment's warning, a fierce looking savage stepped from the group with elevated tomahawk, and commenced the work of death. This Indian, said the surviving sister, ' began to tomahawk Susan ; she dodged her head to one side, the weapon taking effect in her neck, cutting the large neck vein ; the blood gushing out a yard's length. The Indian who had her by the hand jumped back to avoid the blood. The other Indian then began the work of death on my sister Mary. I gave a sudden jerk and got loose from the one that held me, ran with all speed and took up a steep bank, gaining the top safely. Just as I caught hold of a bush to help myself up, the Indian fired, and the ball passed through the clump of hair on my head, slightly breaking the skin ; the Indian taking round to meet me as I would strike the path that led homeward. But I ran right from home, and hid myself in the bushes near the top of the hill. Presently I saw an Indian passing along the hill below me ; I lay still until he was out of sight, and then made for home.' " This third sister was Christina, afterwards Mrs. John McBride, of Carlisle, Monroe County, Ohio.

" Early on the morning of the 27th of March, 1789, two Indians appeared on the premises of Mr. Glass, residing a few miles back of the present town of Wellsburgh. Mrs. Glass was alone in the house, except an infant and a small black girl ; was engaged in spinning, and had sent her negro woman to the woods for sugar water. In a few moments she returned, screaming at the top of her voice, 'Indians! Indians!' Mrs Glass jumped up, and running first to the window and then to the door, attempted to escape ; but an Indian met her and presented his gun ; she caught hold of the muzzle, turned it aside, and begged him not to kill her. The other Indian in the meantime caught the negro woman and brought her into the house. They then opened a chest and took out a small box and some articles of clothing, and without doing any further damage, departed with their prisoners. After proceeding about a mile and a half, they halted and held a consultation, as she supposed, to kill the children ; this she understood to be the subject by their gestures. To one of the Indians who could speak English, she held out her little boy and begged him not to kill him, as he would make a fine chief after a while. The Indian made a motion for her to walk on with the child. The other Indian then struck the negro child with the pipe end of his tomahawk, which knocked it down, and then, by a blow with the edge across the back of the neck, despatched it. About four o'clock they reached the river, a mile above the creek, and carried a canoe which had been thrown up in some drift wood, into the river. They got into this canoe and worked it down to the mouth of ush run, about five miles; pulled the canoe into the mouth of the stream as far as they could, and going up the run about a mile, encamped for the night. The Indians gave the prisoners all their own clothes for covering, and one of them added his own blanket; shortly before daylight the Indians got up, and put another blanket over them. The black woman complained much on account of the loss of her child, and they threatened if she did not desist, to kill her.

" About sunrise they commenced their march up a very steep hill and at two o'clock halted on Short creek, about twenty miles from the place whence they set out in the morning. The spot had been an encampment shortly before as well as a place of deposit for the plunder which they had recently taken from the house of Mr. Vanmeter, whose family had been killed. The plunder was deposited in a sycamore tree. They had tapped some sugar trees when there before, and now kindled a fire and put on a brass kettle, with a turkey which they had killed on the way, to boil in sugar water.

" Mr. Glass was working with a hired man in a field about a quarter of a mile from the house, when his wife and family were taken, but knew nothing of the event till noon. After searching about the place, and going to several families in quest of his family, he went to Well's Fort, collected ten men, and that night lodged in a cabin, on the bottom on which the town of Wellsburg now stands. Next morning they discovered the place where the Indians had taken the canoe from the drift, and their tracks at the place of embarkation. Mr. Glass could distinguish the track of his wife by the print of the high heel of her shoe. They crossed the river and went down on the other side until they came near the mouth of Rush run; but discovering no tracks of the Indians, most of the men concluded they would go to the mouth of the Muskingum by water, and therefore wished to turn back. Mr. Glass begged them to go as far as the mouth of Short Creek, which was only two or three miles; and to this they agreed. When they got to the mouth of Rush run, they found the canoe of the Indians. This was identified by a proof which shows the presence of mind of Mrs.

Glass. While passing down the river, one of the Indians threw into the water several papers which he had taken out of Mr. Glass's trunk ; some of these she carelessly picked up, and under pretence of giving them to the child dropped them into the bottom of the canoe. These left no doubt. The trail of the Indians and their prisoners up the run to their camp, and then up the river hill, was soon discovered.

"About an hour after the Indians had halted, Glass and his men came in sight of their camp. The object then was to save the lives of the prisoners by attacking the Indians so unexpectedly as not to allow time to kill them. With this view they crept along till they got within one hundred yards of the camp. Fortunately, Mrs. Glass's little son had gone to a sugar tree, but not being able to get the water, his mother had stepped out to get it for him. The negro woman was sitting some distance from the two Indians, who were looking attentively at a scarlet jacket which they had taken some time before. On a sudden they dropped the jacket, and turned their eyes towards the men, who, supposing they were discovered, immediately discharged several guns and rushed upon them at full speed, with an Indian yell. One of the Indians, it was supposed, was wounded the first fire, as he fell and dropped his gun and shot pouch. After running about one hundred yards, a second shot was fired after him, which brought him to his hands and knees ; but there was no time for pursuit, as the Indians had informed Mrs. Glass that there was another encampment close by. The other Indian at the first fire, ran a short distance beyond Mrs. Glass, so that she was in a right line between him and the white men ; this artful manœuvre no doubt saved his life, as his pursuers could not shoot at him without risking the life of the white woman."

The party reached Beach Bottom fort that night. Mrs. Glass subsequently married a Mr. Brown, and was long a resident of Brooke County.

" In the burying-ground of New Providence, in Rockbridge
County, Virginia, there is a grave, surpassing in interest all surrounding graves. It is by the side of the resting-place of the
pastor of the people who worshipped in the neighboring church.
ts inhabitant once walked by his side a cherished one.* His
deep blue, sunken eye, that flashed so fiercely in moments of indignation, always beamed sweetly into her full, jet-black orbs, that
could do nothing but smile or weep. But those smiles and tears
charmed equally the savages in the wilderness, and Christian people
of Providence.

" The maiden name of this woman was Mary Moore. The
melancholy romance of her early days, and the Christian excellence
of her mature and closing years, make her memory immortal. The
history of the destruction of the retired dwelling of her father—his
murder, with that of two brothers and a sister on a fair summer's
morning—the captivity of her mother and herself, with a brother
and two sisters, and a hired girl, the murder of the brother and one
sister on the way to the wigwam homes of their captors—the
death by fire and torture of her mother and remaining sister—the
rescue of herself and the hired girl, together with a brother, the
captive of a former year, and their return to their relatives in
Virginia—combines in one story all the events impending over the
emigrant families taking possession of the rivers and valleys of
Western Virginia."

James Moore, whose father, of Scottish ancestry, had emigrated
from Ireland to Pennsylvania, and thence to Virginia, married
Martha Poage, and Mary, his second daughter, was born in his new
home in a valley on the waters of the Blue Stone, a branch of New
River. It was called " Apps' Valley," from Absalom Looney, a
hunter, " supposed to be the first white man who disturbed the
solitude, or beheld the beauty of the narrow low grounds luxuriating

* This memoir is taken from " Sketches of Virginia, Historical and
Biographical," by Rev. William Henry Foote, D.D., portions being abridged.
The authentic materials were obtained by him from Rev. James Morrison
the son-in-law and successor to Rev. Samuel Brown.

in the pea vine and sweet myrrh. The surrounding and distant
scenery partook both of the grand and the beautiful. To Mr.
Moore, the valley was enchanting; and being out of the track of
the savages in their war incursions eastward, it seemed secure
equally from the vexations of the civilized and the savage.

" Mr. Looney, the hunter, built his cabin a mile lower down the
creek ; John Poage about two and a half miles above ; and a number of cabins were scattered about as convenience or fancy dictated.
Mr. Moore's highest expectations in raising stock were realized.
Assisted by Simpson, he soon became possessor of a hundred head
of horses, and a large number of horned cattle, which found pastur-
age sufficient for both summer and winter, with little aid or care
from man. His dream of safety was broken. The wily savage
discovered the white man's track, and the white man's cabin west of
those Alleghanies, which they resolved should be an everlasting barrier
between their homes in Ohio to which they had fled, and the hated
whites who held the corn-fields and hunting-grounds of their
fathers and their race, between those great mountains and the
Atlantic shores.

" To revenge this encroachment, the savages commenced their
depredations, and compelled isolated families, summer after summer,
to betake themselves to forts and stockades for their mutual
defence.   On one occasion a number of men being at the house
of Mr. John Poage, one of them, on stepping out after nightfall,
observed to his companions that a good look-out ought to be kept
for Indians that night, for he heard an unusual noise, as of the hoot-
ing of owls, which he supposed to be the signal of Indians approaching the house from different quarters. About midnight the house
was surrounded by savages ; but finding the doors secured and the
inmates on the watch, the Indians retired without committing any
depredations.   One of the party in the house seized a gun, not his
own, unaware that it was double triggered, pressed the muzzle
through the cracks of the cabin against the body of a savage who
was slily examining the state of things within, and in his eagerness
to discharge the piece broke both the triggers, and the savage

escaped All was stillness both within and without the house; such was the nature of savage warfare. Mr. Poage and most of the families now retired from this advanced position to the more secure neighborhoods in Rockbridge, Botetourt and Montgomery, while Mr. Moore and a few others remained.

" Mr. Moore was a man of courage; he loved the solitude and sweetness of the valley, and would not retreat through any fear of the hostile Indians. Five children were added to his family in this valley, making the number nine. Of these Mary, the fifth, was born in the year 1777, and passed the first nine years of her life in alternate solitude and alarms. On the 7th of September, 1784, James, then fourteen years of age, was sent to Poage's deserted settlement to procure a horse for the purpose of going to the mill about twelve miles distant, through a dreary wilderness. He did not return, and the anxious search discovered trails of savages. In time the hope he had hidden in the woods or fled to some distant habitation, gave way to the sad conviction that his fate for life or death had been committed to the hands of barbarians. This bereavement grieved, but did not subdue the heart of the father, who resolutely, almost stubbornly, maintained his position. After some time, a letter was received from Kentucky, giving him information of his lost son, then supposed to be in or near Detroit. Before any effective steps could be taken for his recovery, another and more mournful scene was enacted in Apps' Valley, awfully contrasting with the grandeur and beauty of surrounding nature, and the domestic peace and piety of Moore's dwelling.

" The morning of the 14th July, 1786, a party of Indians came up Sandy River, crossed over to the head of Clinch, passed near where Tazewell Court-house now is, murdered a Mr. Davison and wife, and burned their dwelling, and passed on hastily to Apps' Valley, before any alarm could be given. A little spur puts out from the mountain, and gradually sloping towards the creek, about three hundred yards before it sinks into the low grounds, divides; at the extremity of one division stood Moore's house, and near the other the trough at which he was accustomed to salt his horses. At the time of the greatest peril all seemed most secure. It was harvest time; and there were two men assisting Mr. Moore in his harvest. The guns were discharged on the preceding evening, to be reloaded some time in the morning. Simpson lay sick in the loft; the men had repaired early to the wheat-field, to reap till breakfast time; Moore was engaged in salting his horses; his wife busied in her domestic concerns, and two of the children at the spring. Suddenly the savage yell was heard, and two parties rushed from their hiding-places on the ridge, the one down the slope to the house, and the other towards Mr. Moore. Two children, Rebecca and William, were shot dead near the salt block, on their return from the spring, and the third, Alexander, near the house. Mary rushed in, and the door was shut and barred against the approaching savages by Mrs. Moore and Martha Ivans, a member of the family, just in time to prevent their entrance. Mr. Moore finding himself intercepted by the Indians at the house, ran on through the small lot that surrounded it, and on climbing the fence, paused and turned, and in a moment was pierced with seven bullets. Springing from the fence, he ran a few paces, fell and expired. The two men in the harvest-field, seeing the house surrounded by a large company of savages, fled and escaped unharmed. Martha Ivans seized two of the guns, and ran upstairs to the sick man, Simpson, calling on him to shoot through the crevices; but the poor man had already received his death-wound from a bullet aimed from without. Two stout dogs defended the door most courageously, till the fiercest was shot. Martha Ivans and Mary Moore secreted themselves under a part of the floor, taking with them the infant Margaret; but the sobbings of the alarmed child forbade concealment. Should Mary place the child upon the floor, and conceal herself? or share its fate? She could not abandon her little sister even in that perilous moment, and left her hiding-place and her companion. The Indians were now cutting at the door and threatening fire. Mrs. Moore perceiving that her faithful sentinels were silenced, Simpson expiring, and her husband dead, collected her four children, and kneeling down, committed them to God; then rose, and unbarred the door.

" After all resistance had ceased, the Indians, satisfied with the blood that had been shed, took Mrs. Moore and her four children, John, Jane, Mary, and Margaret, prisoners ; and having plundered to their satisfaction, set fire to the dwelling.   Martha Ivans crept from the approaching flames, and again concealed herself beneath a log that lay across the little stream near the dwelling.   While catching a few of the horses, one of the Indians crossed the log under which she was secreted, and sat down upon the end of it. The girl seeing him handle the lock of his gun, and supposing he had discovered and was about to fire upon her, came out, to the great surprise of the savage—for he had not seen her, and to his great apparent joy delivered herself a captive.   In a short time the Indians were on their march with their captives to their Shawnee towns in Ohio.   The two men who escaped, hastened to the nearest family, a distance of six miles, and as soon as possible spread the alarm among the settlements ; but before the armed men could reach the spot, the ruin was complete, and the depredators far on their way to Ohio.

" After the horrible events of the morning, perhaps the mother wept not when the captors, dissatisfied with the delicate appearance and slow travelling of her weak-minded and feeble-bodied son John, despatched him at a blow, and hid him from the sight of pursuers.   The hours of night passed slowly and sorrowfully as the four captives, all females, lay upon the ground, each tied to a war-rior, who slept tomahawk in hand, to prevent a re-capture, should they be overtaken by the pursuing whites.   On the third day a new cup of sorrow was put into the mother's hand.   The infant Margaret, whom Mary could not part with, had been spared to the mother ; the Indians even assisting in carrying it.   On the third day it became very fretful from a wound it had received on its cheek ; irritated by its crying, a savage seized it, and dashing its head against a tree, tossed it into the bushes.   The company moved on in silence ; the sisters dared not, the mother would not, lament the fate of the helpless loved one.

"After some twenty days of wearisome travel down the Sandy

and Ohio Rivers, they came to the Scioto ; here the Indians showed
Mrs. Moore some hieroglyphics on the trees representing three
Indians and a captive white boy ; this boy, they told her, was her
son whom they had captured in their expedition two years before,
who had been here with them, and was still a captive. The
prisoners were then taken to their towns, near where Chilicothe now
stands, and were kindly received.   After a few days a council was
called, and an aged Indian made a long speech dissuading from war ;
the warriors shook their heads and retired.   This old man took
Mary Moore to his wigwam, treated her with great kindness, and
appeared to commiserate her condition.   In a short time a party of
Cherokees, who had made an unsuccessful expedition in the western
part of Pennsylvania, on their return home passed by the Shawnee
towns, and stopped where Mrs. Moore and her daughter Jane were.
Irritated at their ill success, and the loss of some of their warriors,
the sight of these prisoners excited an irresistible thirst for revenge.
While the Shawnees were revelling with liquor, the Cherokees
seized the mother and daughter, and condemned them to the torture by fire and death at the stake.   Their sufferings were protracted through three days of agony.   The uncomplaining mother
comforted her poor dying child with gospel truth and exhortation,
and died with a meekness that astounded the savages.   The
Shawnees never approved of this gratuitous act of cruelty, and
always expressed unwillingness to converse about it.

" When Mrs. Moore and her children, as captives, left their habitation in App's Valley, Mary took two New Testaments which she
carried through all her wearisome journey to the Scioto ; one of
them was taken from her by the young savages, and the other was
her companion through the days of her bondage.   The old Indian
who showed her kindness on arriving at the towns, would often call
her to his side and make her read to him, that he might hear 'the
book speak ;' and when any of the young Indians attempted to
hide it from her, as they often did, he interposed with sternness and
compelled them to restore it.

" The two girls remained with the Shawnees till the fall of the year 1788, being kept as property of value without any definite object. Contentions sometimes arose among the Indians about the right of ownership; and in times of intoxication, death was threatened as the only means of ending the quarrel. Whenever these threats were made, some of the sober Indians gave the girls the alarm in time for their secreting themselves. While free from the influence of drink, the Indians expressed great fondness for the girls, particularly the little black-eyed, golden-haired Mary.

" The Shawnees continuing to be very troublesome to the frontiers, in the fall of 1788 an expedition was fitted out to destroy their towns on the Scioto. The Indians were informed by the traders of the design and departure of the expedition, and watched its progress. On its near approach they deserted their towns, secreting their little property, and carrying their wives and children and aged ones beyond the reach of the enemy. Mary Moore revolved in her mind the probable chances of concealing herself in the forests until the arrival of the forces, and thus obtaining her liberty; and was deterred from the attempt by the reflection that the season was late, and possibly the forces might not arrive before winter. Late in November the American forces reached the Scioto, burned the Shawnee towns, destroyed their winter provisions as far as they could be found, and immediately returned home. After the departure of the forces the Indians returned to their ruined towns, and winter setting upon them, deprived of shelter, their extreme sufferings compelled them to seek for aid in Canada. On the journey to Detroit they endured the extremes of hunger and cold. Martha Ivans and Mary Moore with few garments, traversed the forests with deer-skin moccasins, the only covering for their feet in the deep snows. Not unfrequently they awoke in the morning covered with the snow that had fallen during the night; once the depth of their snowy covering was twelve or fourteen inches, their only bed or protection, besides the bushes heaped together, being their single blanket. On reaching Detroit the Indians gave themselves to riotous drinking, and to indulge this appetite sold their young captives Mary was purchased for half a gallon of rum, by a person named

Stogwell, who lived at Frenchtown; Martha by a man in the neighborhood of Detroit. Being soon after released she took up her resi dence with a wealthy and worthy English family by the name of Donaldson, and received wages for her services. The purchaser of Mary neither liberated her, nor expressed any kindness for her, but employed her as a servant, with poor clothing and scanty fare. The circumstances of her redemption and return to her friends in Virginia, are related by her brother James Moore, in the narrative of his own captivity and redemption." This presents so faithful a picture of Indian captivity, that we shall extract part of it before resuming the history of Mary.

" My father sent me to a waste plantation about two miles and a quarter up the valley, to get a horse to go to mill. I came within a few paces of the field, when suddenly the Indians sprang out from behind a large log; and being before alarmed, I screamed with all my might. The Indian that took me, laid his hand on the top of my head and bade me hush. There were only three Indians in the company. Their leader, Black Wolf, a middle-aged man, of the most stern countenance I ever beheld, about six feet high, having a long black beard, was the one who caught hold of me.

" In a few moments we started on our journey. The Indians went up into the thicket where their kettle and blankets were hid, covered up in the leaves, and took them. We travelled down a creek called Tugg, the north fork of Sandy, that afternoon about eight miles. The walking was very laborious on account of the high weeds, green briers, logs, and the mountainous character of the country. At night we lay down in a laurel thicket without fire or anything to eat. The night was rainy. I lay beside Black Wolf, with a leading halter round my neck tied very tight, and the other end wrapped round his hands, so as to make it very secure, and so that I could not get away without waking him. He had also searched me very carefully to see that I had no knife. During the afternoon the two young Indians walked before; I next to them, and old Wolf followed; and if any sign was made he would remove it with his tomahawk, so that there might be no marks or traces of the way we had gone. I frequently broke busnes, which he discovered and shook his tomahawk over my head, giving me to understand that if I did not desist he would strike me with it. I then would scratch the ground with my feet; this he also discovered and made me desist; and showed me how to set my feet flat so as not to make any special marks. It then became necessary for me to cease any efforts to make a trail for others to follow. About sun-down Old Wolf gave a tremendous warwhoop, and another the next morning at sunrise. This was repeated every evening at sun-down, and every morning at sunrise, during our whole journey. It was long, loud, and shrill, signifying that he had one prisoner. The custom is to repeat it as frequently as the number of prisoners. This whoop is different from the one they make when they have scalps.

"In the evening of September 9th, we encamped for the night under a projecting cliff, and here for the first time kindled a fire. Old Wolf took the precaution of cutting a number of bushes and bending them outward from our encampment so as to embarrass any one approaching us, if we had been pursued. The next day they killed a lean bear, but so very lean they would not eat of it; so we were still without food. Several times during the days of our fasting, the Indians went to the north side of a poplar, and cut off some of the bark near the root, pounded it, and put it in the kettle and put water on it; this we drank occasionally, which seemed to have a salutary effect in relieving the sufferings of hunger.

"We killed buffalo and deer as we stood in need, till we arrived (Sept. 29th) at the towns over the Ohio, on the head waters of Mud River, which took us about twenty-two days' travelling. I travelled the whole route barefooted, and frequently walked over large rattlesnakes, but was not suffered to kill or interrupt them, the Indians considering them their friends.

"We crossed the Ohio, between the mouths of Guyandotte and Big Sandy, on a raft made of dry logs tied together with grape vines. On the banks of the Scioto we lay by one day, and the Indians made pictures on the trees of three Indians and of me; intended as hieroglyphics to represent themselves and me as their prisoner.

6*

These they afterwards showed to my sister.   Near this, Old Wolf went off and procured some bullets which he had secreted.

"When we were within a short distance of the towns, the Indians blacked themselves, but not me.   I was taken to the residence of Wolf's half-sister, to whom he had sold me for an old grey horse. Shortly after I was sold, my mistress left me in her wigwam for several days entirely alone, leaving a kettle of hominy for me to eat. In this solitary situation I first began earnestly to pray and call upon God for mercy and deliverance, and found great relief in prayer.   I now found the benefit of the religious instruction and examples I had enjoyed."   *   *

"In about two weeks after I had been sold, the woman who bought me sent me out in company with her half-brother and others, on a winter's hunting excursion.   We were very unsuccessful.   My sufferings from hunger and cold were very great.   I had scarcely any clothing; the snow was knee-deep ; my blanket was too short to cover me.   Often after having lain down and drawn up my feet to get them underneath my blanket, I was so benumbed that I could not, without considerable exertion, get my legs stretched out again. Early in the morning the old Indian would build a large fire, and send me and all the young Indians and make us plunge all over in cold water, which I think was a very great benefit to me, and pre-vented me from catching cold, as is usual under circumstances of so much exposure."

The husband of James's mistress one day came home from a meeting of the Powwow Society, and informed her that an apparition sent by the Great Spirit, had reproved the Indians for their sins, their idleness and want of brotherly kindness, and had predicted the de-struction of their towns.   These predictions were literally fulfilled in the course of three years, in the invasion of Logan from Kentucky. In the mean time a French trader from Detroit, named Baptiste Ariome, took a fancy to young Moore on account of his resemblance to one of his sons, and bought him for fifty dollars' worth of brooches, crapes, and other commodities.   James also met with a trader from Kentucky, whom he requested to write a letter to his father, and give it to a young man he had rescued from the Indians, to convey to Mr. Moore. At the house of Ariome James was treated like a son, and worked on the farm, occasionally assisting in trading expeditions. On one of these he heard of the destruction of his father's family, from a Shawanee Indian who was one of the party of assailants. The information was given the latter part of the same summer in which the massacre was perpetrated. In the winter following, James heard that his sister Mary was purchased by Mr. Stogwell, and that she was ill-treated in his family. In the spring Stogwell moved into the neighborhood where he lived; young Moore immediately went to see his sister, and found her in an abject condition, clothed in a few dirty rags. Being advised to apply to the commanding officer at Detroit, he went with Simon Girty to Col. McKee, superintendent for the Indians, who had Stogwell brought to trial to answer the complaint against him; and though the poor girl was not taken from her inhuman master, it was decided that when an opportunity offered for her return home, she should be released without remuneration. This was brought about through the efforts of Thomas Ivans, the brother of Martha, who had determined to seek his lost sister, and the members of Mr. Moore's family who might be living. Clothing himself in skins, and securing some money about his person, with rifle in hand, he proceeded to the tribes in whose possession the captives had been, and traced their wanderings to their several places of abode. His sister was living at Mr. Donaldson's; Mary Moore was delivered up by Mr. Stogwell, and James by Mr. Ariome. "All being at liberty," says Moore, "we immediately prepared to go to our distant friends, and as well as I can remember, set out some time in October, 1789; it being about five years from the time I had been taken prisoner by the Indians, and a little more than three from the captivity of my sister. A trading-boat coming down the lakes, we obtained a passage in it for myself and sister Polly to the Moravian towns, a distance of about two hundred miles, which was on our way to Pittsburgh. There, according to appointment, the day after our arrival, Thomas Ivans and his sister Martha met us. We then prepared immediately for our journey to Pittsburgh. Here Mr. Ivans got his shoulder dislocated, in consequence of which we stayed a part of the winter in the vicinity, with an uncle and aunt of his, until he became able to travel. Having expended all his money with the doctor and in travelling, he left his sister Martha, and proceeded with Polly and myself to the house of an uncle about ten miles south-west of Staunton, and having received from an uncle, the administrator of his father's estate, compensation for his services, he afterwards returned and brought his sister Martha.

" A day or two after we set out, having called at a public house for breakfast, while it was preparing, my sister took out her Testament and was engaged in reading. Being called to breakfast, she laid down her Testament, and when we resumed our journey she forgot it. After we had proceeded several miles she thought of her Testament, and strongly insisted on turning back; but such were the dangers of the way, and such the necessity of speeding our journey, that we could not."

Martha Ivans married a man by the name of Hummer, removed to Indiana, and reared a large family, so that she is included in the list of pioneer mothers. Two of her sons became Presbyterian clergymen. Shortly after her return to Rockbridge, Mary Moore went to live with her uncle, Joseph Walker, about six miles south of Lexington, and in mature years became the wife of Rev. Samuel Brown, pastor of New Providence. She became the mother of eleven children, nine of whom survived her; and through life retained a strong attachment for the wild people of the forest, which no memory of wrong could obliterate. The self-reliance, patience, and self-denial she acquired, in part, in her captivity, were eminent through life. She was blessed with children as dutiful and pious as she had proved in her childhood, and saw, in her success in training her household, the influence of her own force of character developed by such strange circumstances, and the power of a Christian example.

Some idea of the difficulties of travel in those days may be given by the following extract from a description of a journey westward in 1784.* "Pack-horses were the only means of transportation then, and for years after. We were provided with three horses, on one of which my mother rode carrying her infant with all the table furniture and cooking utensils. On another were packed the stores of provisions, the plough irons, and other agricultural tools. The third horse was rigged out with a pack saddle and two large creels, made of hickory withs in the fashion of a crate, one over each side, in which were stowed the beds and bedding, and the wearing apparel of the family. In the centre of these creels there was an aperture prepared for myself and little sister, and the top was well secured by lacing to keep us in our places, so that only our heads appeared above. Each family was supplied with one or more cows; their milk furnished the morning and evening meal for the children, and the surplus was carried in canteens for use during the day.

"When the caravan reached the mountains, the road was found to be hardly passable for loaded horses. In many places the path lay along the edge of a precipice, where, if the horse had stumbled or lost his balance, he would have been precipitated several hundred feet below. The path was crossed by many streams raised by the melting snow and spring rains, and running with rapid current in deep ravines; most of these had to be forded, and for many successive days, hair-breadth escapes were continually occurring; sometimes horses falling, at others carried away by the current, and the women and children with difficulty saved from drowning. Sometimes in ascending steep acclivities, the lashing of the creels would give way, both creels and children tumble to the ground and roll down the steep, unless arrested by some traveller of the company. The men who had been inured to the hardships of war, could endure the fatigues of the journey; it was the mothers who suffered; they could not, after the toils of the day, enjoy the rest so much needed at night. The wants of their suffering children must be attended to. After preparing their simple meal, they lay down with scanty covering in a miserable cabin, or, as it sometimes happened, in the open air, and often unrefreshed, were obliged to rise early to encounter the fatigues and dangers of another day."

"The division lines between those whose lands adjoined, were generally made in an amicable manner, before any survey of them was made by the parties concerned. In doing this, they were guided mainly by the tops of ridges and water courses, but particularly the former. Hence the greater number of farms in the western parts of Pennsylvania and Virginia bear a striking resemblance to an amphitheatre; the tops of the surrounding hills being the boundaries of the tract to which the family mansion belongs."

Besides the exposure of the emigrants to Indian depredations and massacres, " they had other trials to endure which at the present day cannot be appreciated. One of the most vexatious was the running away of their horses. As soon as the fly season commenced the horses seemed resolved on leaving the country and crossing the mountains. They swam the Monongahela, and often proceeded a hundred and fifty miles before they were taken up. During the husband's absence in pursuit of them, the wife was left alone with her children in their unfinished cabin, surrounded by forests, in which the howl of wolves was heard from every hill. If want of provisions, or other causes, made a visit to a neighbor's necessary, she must either take her children with her through the woods, or leave them unprotected, under the most fearful apprehension that some mischief might befal them before her return. As bread and meat were scarce, milk was the principal dependence for the support of the family. One cow of each family was provided with a bell, which could be heard from half a mile to a mile. The matron on rising in the morning listened for her cow-bell, which she knew well enough to detect, even amidst a clamor of others. If her children were small, she tied them in bed to prevent their wandering, and guard them from danger of fire and snakes; and guided by the tinkling of the bell, made her way through the tall weeds and across the ravines until she found the objects of her search. Happy on her return to find her children unharmed, and regardless of a thorough wetting from the dew, she hastened to prepare their breakfast of milk boiled with a little meal or hominy ; or in the protracted absence of her husband, it was often reduced to milk alone. Occasionally venison and turkeys were obtained from hunters."

An anecdote is related in the "American Pioneer," of Gov. McArthur, on his first visit to the West, which throws light on the situation of the early settlers. He stopped some time at Baker's Station, about twenty miles below Wheeling. There was war with the Indians, and the settlers about Fish Creek were occupying the station for security ; so long, however, had the enemy been absent from that section of country, that the inmates went and came when they pleased. A young lady of great beauty, who lived at the place, had acquired proficiency in the art of shooting with the rifle. " I think her name was Scott, but it may have been Baker. Early one morning she went to the run, some fifty or sixty yards above the post, to wash linen, taking her gun along, and young McArthur accompanied her to stand guard while she was employed at the wash tub. Before long a small dog that was with them commenced barking, and gave such manifestations of alarm that the young lady desired her companion to make a hasty reconnoissance of the adjacent grounds. The motions of the dog had awakened fear that Indians might be lurking close by, but McArthur discovered nothing to confirm the suspicion. The washing was resumed and in due course completed ; after which they both returned to the station. Just as they were about to enter the gate, a tall athletic looking Indian sprang from behind a tree not more than thirty paces beyond the spot where they had been washing, and darted off rapidly into the woods. Pursuit was instantly made, but he was not overtaken. He must have posted himself behind the tree during the previous night, with the intention of shooting the first person that ventured out of the works in the morning. The appearance of two disconcerted his plan. McArthur's gallantry on this occasion was the means of saving the young lady's life."

De Hass describes a station as a parallelogram of cabins united by palisades, so as to present a continued wall on the outer sides, the cabin doors opening into a common square on the inner side. A fort was generally a stockade enclosure, embracing cabins, etc., for the accommodation of several families. Doddridge says, " a range of cabins commonly formed at least one side, separated by divisions or partitions of logs. The walls on the outside were ten or twelve feet high, with a roof sloping inward. Some of the cabins had puncheon floors, but the greater part were earthen.

" The blockhouses were built at the angles of the fort, and projected about two feet beyond the outer walls of the cabins and stockades. Their upper stories were about eighteen inches or two feet every way larger than the under one, leaving an opening at the commencement of the second story, to prevent the enemy from making a lodgment under their walls. In some forts, instead of blockhouses, the angles were furnished with bastions. A large folding gate, made of thick slabs, nearest the spring, closed the fort. The stockades, bastions, cabins, and blockhouse walls were furnished with portholes at proper heights and distances. The whole of the outside was made completely bullet proof. The families belonging to these forts were so attached to their own cabins on their farms, that they seldom moved into the fort in the spring until compelled by some alarm ; that is, when it was announced by some murder that Indians were in the settlement."

Butler describes the dwellings of the first settlers of the West as composed of the trunks of trees, bared of their branches, notched at the ends and fitted upon one another in a quadrangular shape, to the desired height. Openings through the logs left room for doors and shutters. A capacious opening, nearly the whole width of the cabin, made the fire-place. By this ample width economy of labor in cutting fire-wood, as well as comfort in houses, was consulted.

" The furniture of the table, for several years after the settlement of the country, consisted of a few pewter dishes, plates and spoons; but mostly of wooden bowls, trenchers and noggins. If these last were scarce, gourds and hard-shelled squashes made up the deficiency. The iron pots, knives and forks were brought from the East, with the salt and iron, on pack-horses. These articles of furniture corresponded very well with the articles of diet. 'Hog and hominy' was a dish of proverbial celebrity. Johnny-cake or pone was at the outset of the settlements the only form of bread in use for breakfast and dinner; at supper, milk and mush was the standard dish. When milk was scarce, hominy supplied its place, and mush was frequently eaten with sweetened water, molasses, bear's oil, or the gravy of fried meat.

" In our display of furniture, delf, china and silver were unknown. The introduction of delf ware was considered by many of the backwoods people as a wasteful innovation. It was too easily broken, and the plates dulled their scalping and clasp knives. Tea and coffee, in the phrase of the day, 'did not stick by the ribs.' The idea then prevalent was, that they were only designed for people of quality, who did not labor, or for the rich. A genuine backwoodsman would have thought himself disgraced by showing a fondness for such 'slops.'

" On the frontier and particularly among hunters in the habit of going on campaigns, the dress of the men was partly Indian. The hunting-shirt universally worn was a kind of loose frock, reaching half way down the thighs, with large sleeves, open before, and so wide as to lap over a foot or more when belted. The cape was large, and sometimes fringed with a ravelled piece of cloth, of different color from the hunting-shirt. The bosom of this dress served as a wallet to hold bread, cakes, jerk, tow for wiping the barrel of the rifle, or any other necessary for the hunter or warrior. The belt, always tied behind, answered several purposes; in cold weather the mittens, and sometimes the bullet-bag, occupied its front part; on the right side was suspended the tomahawk, on the left the scalping knife in its leathern sheath. The hunting-shirt was generally made of linsey, sometimes of coarse linen, and a few of dressed deer-skin; these last very cold and uncomfortable in wet weather. The shirt and jacket were of the common fashion. A pair of drawers, or breeches and leggins, were the dress of the thighs and legs; a pair

of moccasins answered for the feet much better than shoes. These
were made of dressed deer-skin, and were mostly of a single piece,
with a seam along the top of the foot, and another from the bottom
of the heel, as high or a little higher than the ancle joint. Flaps
were left on each side, to reach some distance up the legs. These
were nicely adapted to the ancles and lower part of the leg by
thongs of deerskin, so that no dust, gravel, or snow could get within
the moccasin. In cold weather this was well stuffed with deer's hair
or dried leaves, to keep the feet comfortably warm; but in wet
weather it was usually said that wearing moccasins was 'a decent
way of going barefoot;' and such was the fact, owing to the spongy
texture of the leather of which they were made. Owing to this de-
fective covering of the feet, many of our hunters and warriors were
afflicted with rheumatism in their limbs. Of this disease they were
all apprehensive in cold or wet weather, and therefore always slept
with their feet to the fire, to prevent or cure it as well as they could.
This practice unquestionably had a very salutary effect, and prevented many of them from becoming confirmed cripples in early
life.

"In the latter years of the Indian war, our young men became
more enamored of the Indian dress. The drawers were laid aside,
and the leggins made longer, so as to reach the upper part of the
thigh. The Indian breech cloth was adopted. This was a piece of
linen or cloth, nearly a yard long, and eight or nine inches broad,
passing under the belt, before and behind, leaving the ends for flaps
hanging before and behind over the belt, sometimes ornamented
with coarse embroidery. To the same belt which secured the breech
cloth, strings, supporting the long leggins, were attached. When this
belt, as was often the case, passed over the hunting-shirt, the upper
part of the thighs and part of the hips were naked. The young
warrior, instead of being abashed by this, was proud of his Indian
dress. In some few instances I have seen them go into places of
public worship in this dress." De Hass adds, that old hunters have
said it was the most comfortable, convenient, and desirable that could

have been invented for the times in which it was used. Linsey coats and gowns were the universal dress of the women in early times.

A description of a wedding among the pioneers may serve to illustrate their manners. The following is taken from Doddridge's Notes:

" In the first years of the settlement, a wedding engaged the attention of a whole neighborhood, and the frolic was anticipated by old and young with eager expectation. This will not be wondered at, as a wedding was almost the only gathering unaccompanied with the labor of reaping, log-rolling, building a cabin, or planning some warlike expedition.

" On the morning of the wedding day, the groom and his attendants assembled at the house of his father, for the purpose of reaching the home of his bride by noon, the usual time for celebrating the nuptials. Let the reader imagine an assemblage of people, without a store, tailor, or mantuamaker within a hundred miles ; and an assemblage of horses, without a blacksmith or saddler within an equal distance ; the gentlemen dressed in shoepacks, moccasins, leather breeches, leggins, linsey hunting-shirts, and all home-made ; the ladies in linsey petticoats and linsey or linen bedgowns, coarse shoes, stockings, handkerchiefs, and buckskin gloves, if any. If there were any buckles, rings, buttons. or ruffles, they were the relics of olden times, family pieces from parents or grandparents. The horses were caparisoned with old saddles, old bridles or halters, and pack-saddles, with a bag or blanket thrown over them ; a rope or string as often constituted the girth as a piece of leather. The march, in double file, was often interrupted by the narrowness and obstructions of the horse-paths, for there were no roads ; and these difficulties were often increased by fallen trees and grape vines tied across the way. Sometimes an ambuscade was formed by the wayside, and an unexpected discharge of several guns took place, so as to cover the wedding company with smoke. Let the reader imagine the scene that followed this discharge ; the sudden spring of the horses, the shrieks of the girls, and the chivalrous bustle of their partners to save them from falling. If a wrist, elbow, or ancle happened to be sprained, it was tied with a handkerchief, and little more was thought or said about it.

"The ceremony of the marriage preceded the dinner, which was a substantial backwoods feast of beef, pork, fowls, and sometimes venison and bear meat roasted and boiled, with plenty of potatoes, cabbage, and other vegetables. During the dinner the greatest hilarity always prevailed, although the table might be a large slab of timber hewed out with a broad axe, supported by four sticks set in auger holes; and the furniture, some old pewter dishes and plates, eked out with wooden bowls and trenchers. A few pewter spoons, much battered about the edges, were seen at some tables; the rest were made of horn. If knives were scarce, the deficiency was made up by the scalping knives which every man carried in sheaths suspended to the belt of the hunting-shirt. After dinner the dancing commenced, and generally lasted till the next morning. The figures of the dances were three and four-handed reels and jigs. The commencement was always a square four, which was followed by what was called 'jigging it off;' that is, two of the four would single out for a jig, and be followed by the remaining couple. The jigs were often accompanied with what was called 'cutting out;' that is, when either of the parties became tired of the dance, on intimation, the place was supplied by some one of the company, without any interruption to the dance. In this way it was often continued till the musician was heartily tired of his situation. Towards the latter part of the night, if any of the company, through weariness, attempted to conceal themselves for the purpose of sleeping, they were hunted up, paraded on the floor, and the fiddler ordered to play 'Hang out till to-morrow morning.'

"About nine or ten o'clock a deputation of the young ladies stole off the bride and put her to bed. In doing this it frequently happened that they had to ascend a ladder instead of stairs, leading from the dining and ball-room to a loft, the floor of which was made of clapboards lying loose. This ascent, one might think, would put the bride and her attendants to the blush; but as the foot of the ladder was commonly behind the door, purposely opened for the occasion, and its rounds at the inner ends were well hung with hunting-shirts, dresses, and other articles of clothing—the candles being on the opposite side of the house, the exit of the bride was noticed but by few. This done, a deputation of young men, in like manner, stole off the groom, while the dance still continued, and late at night refreshment in the shape of 'black Betty'—the bottle—was sent up the ladder, with sometimes substantial accompaniments of bread, beef, pork and cabbage. The feasting and dancing often lasted several days, at the end of which the whole company were so exhausted with loss of sleep, that many days' rest was requisite to fit them to return to their ordinary labors."

Sometimes it happened that neighbors or relations not asked to the wedding, took offence, and revenged themselves by cutting off the manes, foretops and tails of horses belonging to the wedding company.

The same writer thus describes the usual manner of settling a young couple in the world:—" A spot was selected on a piece of land belonging to one of the parents, for their habitation, and a day appointed shortly after their marriage, to commence the work of building their cabin. The materials were prepared on the first day, and sometimes the foundation laid in the evening. The second day was allotted for the raising. The cabin being furnished, the ceremony of housewarming took place before the young couple were permitted to move into it. The house-warming was a dance of a whole night's continuance, made up of the relations of the bridegroom and their neighbors. On the day following, the young couple took possession of their new premises.

" Many of the sports of the early settlers of this country were imitative of the exercises and stratagems of hunting and war. Boys were taught the use of the bow and arrow at an early age ; but although they acquired considerable adroitness, so as to kill a bird or squirrel, yet it appears to me that in the hands of the white people, the bow and arrow could never be depended on for warfare or hunting. One important pastime of the boys—that of imitating the noise of every bird and beast in the woods—was a necessary

part of education on account of its utility under certain circumstances. Imitating the gobbling and other sounds of the wild
turkey, often brought those ever watchful tenants of the forest
within reach of the rifle. The bleating of the fawn brought its dam
to her death in the same way. The hunter often collected a company of mopish owls to the trees about his camp, and amused
himself with their hoarse screaming. His howl would raise and
obtain responses from a pack of wolves, so as to inform him of their
whereabouts, as well as to guard him against their depredations.

" This imitative faculty was sometimes requisite as a measure of
precaution in war.   The Indians, when scattered about in a neighborhood, often collected together by imitating turkeys by day and
wolves or owls by night. In similar situations our people did the
same.   I have often witnessed the consternation of a whole neighborhood in consequence of the screeching of owls.   An early and
correct use of this imitative faculty was considered as an indication
that its possessor would become in due time a good hunter and a
valiant warrior.

" Throwing the tomahawk was another boyish sport in which
many acquired considerable skill.   The tomahawk, with its handle
of a certain length, will make a given number of turns within a
certain distance ; say in five steps it will strike with the edge, the
handle downwards—at the distance of seven and a half it will
strike with the edge, the handle upwards, and so on. A little
experience enabled the boy to measure the distance with his eye
when walking through the wood, and to strike a tree with his toma
hawk in any way he chose. A well grown boy at the age of twelve
or thirteen, was furnished with a small rifle and shot pouch.   He
then became a foot soldier, and had his port-hole assigned him.
Hunting squirrels, turkeys, and racoons, soon made him expert in
the use of his gun.

" The athletic sports of running, jumping, and wrestling, were the
pastimes of boys in common with men.   Dramatic narrations,
chiefly concerning Jack and the Giant, furnished our young people
with another source of amusement during their leisure hours.   The

different incidents of the narration were easily committed to memory, and have been handed down from generation to generation." The singing of the first settlers was rude enough. " Robin Hood furnished a number of our songs ; the balance were mostly tragical ; these were denominated ' love songs about murder.' As to cards, dice, backgammon, and other games of chance, we knew nothing about them. They are among the blessed gifts of civilization !

" Hunting was an important part of the employment of the early settlers. For some years the woods supplied them with the greater amount of their subsistence, and it was no uncommon thing for families to live several months without a mouthful of bread. It frequently happened that there was no breakfast till it was obtained from the woods. Fur constituted the people's money ; they had nothing else to give in exchange for rifles, salt, and iron, on the other side of the mountains. The fall and early part of the winter was the season for hunting the deer, and the whole of the winter, including part of the spring, for bears and fur-skinned animals. It was a customary saying, that fur is good during every month in the name of which the letter R occurs.

" As soon as the leaves were pretty well down, and the weather became rainy, accompanied with light snows, these men, after acting the part of husbandmen as far as the state of warfare permitted, began to feel that they were hunters, and became uneasy at home, their minds being wholly occupied with the camp and chase. Hunting was not a mere ramble in pursuit of game, in which there was nothing of skill and calculation ; on the contrary, the hunter before he set out in the morning, was informed by the state of the weather where he might reasonably expect to find his game, whether on the bottom, the sides, or tops of the hills. In stormy weather the deer always seek the most sheltered places, and the leeward side of the hills. In rainy weather, when there is not much wind, they keep in the open woods on the high ground. In every situation it was requisite for the hunter to ascertain the course of the wind, so as to get the leeward of the game. As it was necessary, too, to know the cardinal points, he had to observe the trees to ascertain them.   The bark of an aged tree is thicker and much rougher on the north than the south side ; and the same may be said of the moss.   From morning till night the hunter was on the alert to gain the wind of his game, and approach them without being discovered.   If he succeeded in killing a deer, he skinned 't and hung it up out of the reach of the wolves, and immediately resumed the chase till the close of the evening, when he bent his course towards his camp ; when arrived there he kindled up his fire, and together with his fellow hunter, cooked his supper.   The supper finished, the adventures of the day furnished tales for the evening, in which the spike-buck, the two and three pronged buck, the doe and barren doe, figured to great advantage."*

" A place for a camp was selected as near water as convenient, and a fire was kindled by the side of the largest suitable log that could be procured.   The ground was preferred to be rather sideling, that the hunters might lie with the feet to the fire, and the head up hill.   The common mode of preparing a repast was by sharpening a stick at both ends, and sticking one end in the ground before the fire, and their meat on the other end.   This stick could be turned round, or the meat on it, as occasion required.   Sweeter roast meat than was prepared in this manner no European epicure ever tasted. Bread, when they had flour to make it of, was either baked under the ashes, or the dough rolled in long rolls, and wound round a stick like that prepared for roasting meat, and managed in the same way.   Scarce any one who has not tried it, can imagine the sweetness of such a meal, in such a place, at such a time.   French mustard, or the various condiments used as a substitute for an appetite, are nothing to this."†

* Doddridge's Notes.   † American Pioneer.

VII.

ANN HAYNES.

IT is mentioned in " The Women of the American Revolution,"[*] that on the approach of Cornwallis to Charlotte, the family of Mr Brown sought refuge at the house of James Haynes, who lived upon the road leading north of Cowan's Ford on the Catawba River. While they remained here, the British in pursuit of Morgan stopped at the house, plundered it, and made the owner a prisoner. Mrs. Haynes, despoiled of everything in the way of provision, herself conducted family worship that night, and praying for the restoration of her captive husband, entreated earnestly the interposition of Providence to protect *the right.* This pious and exemplary matron, whose heart bled for the woes of her oppressed country, and who encouraged her sons to struggle bravely in its defence, was little aware of the extent of the beneficent influence her noble character was to exercise on succeeding generations. The death-bed gift she received from her father—a copy of the Westminster Confession of Faith printed at Edinburgh in 1707—was bequeathed by her as sacredly to her son, John Haynes, and is kept as a venerated relic in his family. Eight of the descendants of Mrs. Haynes are now ministers in the Presbyterian church, devoted to the exposition and extension of the true and simple doctrines of the gospel,

[*] Memoir of Jane Gaston, Vol. III. page 229

7

while others are engaged in the same good work in other denomina-
tions—all carrying out and exemplifying the sterling principles
derived from their independent ancestors of the era of Cromwell's
Protectorate.

One of Mrs. Haynes' descendants has favored me with some
notices of the matron and her family, from the recollections of her
widowed daughter-in-law, Margaret Haynes, who was for some
years a resident of Cornersville, in Tennessee. Her maiden name
was Ann Huggins. She was the daughter of John Huggins, a
Scotch Presbyterian, who emigrated from the north of Ireland to
America about 1730. She married James Haynes about 1748.
In a catalogue of the Pioneer Women of the West, her name may
well find a place. After her marriage, she settled upon the verge
of civilization, in the county of Dauphin, Pennsylvania, where she
was exposed to the frontier troubles of that colony, but stronger
attractions soon drew her family to the South.

In 1752, James Haynes and two brothers, and many kinsmen
with their families, ventured out to the then Far West, in the valley
of the Catawba, in the colony of North Carolina. Here, upon the
very borders of the hostile Cherokees and Catawbas, they established
themselves, building a fort as a defence against Indian incursions,
and maintained their position by the strength of their arms. For
several years, cooped up within the limits of a frontier station, they
courageously opposed the marauding parties of the hostile tribes in
their neighborhood. It was in this year that the settlement of the
upper country, both of North and South Carolina, began. At that
time the frontiers of Pennsylvania were east of the mountains; and
Fort Duquesne was a French trading post. The settlements in
Virginia were still confined to the Atlantic slope, and it was several
years later, when Col. Bird of the British army, advanced into
the wilderness, and established Fort Chissel, as a protection to
the advancing settlements. Still later, Gov. Dobbs, of North
Carolina, succeeded in establishing Fort Loudon, in the midst of the
Cherokee nation. Notwithstanding its exposed situation, the
settlement grew rapidly, so that in a few years the entire valley of

the Catawba was occupied. At this time there were so many buffaloes in this region, that a good hunter could easily kill enough in a few days, to supply his family for the year. Wild turkeys, bears, deer, wolves, and panthers, were also abundant. Every little mountain stream abounded with otters, beavers, and musk-rats. Each pioneer could raise as many head of cattle as he thought proper; the profusion of canes and grasses, rendering stock-raising so easy, that the means of plentiful living was almost to be had without labor. A few skins usually sufficed to purchase upon the seaboard all the necessary supplies of iron, salt, etc., for the year.

This kind of life, requiring the daily use of the rifle, and much exercise on horseback, and exposure to the open air in the woods, made these hardy men the best of soldiers, and enabled them to cope with the wild warriors of the savage tribes who dwelt on their borders. The axe, and the rifle, and the horse, were their constant companions. Each settler sought a home near some clear spring or stream, convenient to the *range* and susceptible of defence against the Indians. In such a settlement the means of education were limited, and but for the religious zeal and pious labors of a few educated ministers who cast their fortunes with the colonists, would have been unattainable. The Rev. Hezekiah Balch, afterwards a signer of the Mecklenburg Declaration of Independence, was one of them.

In all the trials and disorders of the transition state of society peculiar to the frontiers of the West, these pioneers never forgot the principles, nor gave up the practice of those Christian virtues which they had received from their ancestors. Here, in the midst of the solitudes of their deep pine forests, they reared their sons and daughters in the fear of God and in the love of liberty, and when the storm of civil war burst forth, and they were called upon to sustain the cause of an oppressed people, they did not hesitate to send their sons forth to battle for " the right."

An aged citizen of Marshall County, Tennessee, often described the appearance of his own father and James Haynes, both prisoners in the hands of the British the night after Gen. Davidson's death at

Cowan's Ford.   He saw these aged men and many other prisoners driven like sheep into a corn-crib, the door of which was filled with rails, and a sentinel placed over it; and thus without blanket or fire, they passed a long winter night in 1781.

The venerable Mrs. Haynes survived her husband but a short time.   True to the principles of her faith, upon her dying bed she gave to each of her children her parting words of advice with one of the religious books contained in her library.   To her son John, she gave the Westminster Confession of Faith; to another, Bunyan's Pilgrim's Progress; to a third, Flavel, etc., works usually found in that day in the library of every Christian.   She died about the year 1790.

Her husband was no less stern and inflexible in his religious principles.   When the question of the introduction of the new version of the Psalms was agitated in the Church at Centre Meeting-House, after much debate, it was put to the vote, and Haynes was left alone as the advocate of the old version.   His brethren tauntingly asked him if he was going to stand out alone.   He replied, " yes, as long as the world stands; " and so he did to the end of his life.

A rude and humble stone now marks the last resting place of both, at their own home, near Centre Meeting-House, Iredell County, N. C., where, more than a century ago, they sat down amidst the dim solitudes of the western wilderness.   The old homestead is now the residence of James Sloan, a relative of the family.

The three sons, Joseph, John and James, and the son-in-law, Capt. Scott, bore arms against the Cherokees, and against the British and loyalists.   They were brave young men, of active habits, and accustomed to hard service; rode much about the country, and were always ready for any enterprise requiring toil and exposure, or skill and daring.   In proportion as they made themselves useful to the whig party, they were of course persecuted by the loyalists.   Their irregular life in military service never caused them to do aught contrary to the strict principles of their faith;   they never travelled, except when rigid necessity required it, on the Sabbath, being Puritans enough to look upon profanity and Sabbath-breaking with as much abhorrence as upon horse stealing. They served—John bearing a prominent part—in the first battle fought in North Carolina in which the whigs were victorious, after the suspension of hostilities succeeding the fall of Charleston; that of Ramsour's Mill, in Lincoln County.*

Capt. Scott, the son-in-law of Mrs. Haynes, was killed at Cowan's Ford, at the same time with Gen. Davidson, who had been stationed there by Gen. Greene, with a small force, to delay the passage of the British army across the Catawba. Joseph Haynes barely escaped with his life in this action. Soon after, the British passing, as already mentioned, near the house of the elder James Haynes, stopped and plundered it, took him prisoner, and boasted in the hearing of his family, that they had killed his son-in-law at the Ford, hinting that his sons also were either killed or captured. The old man was over sixty, and in feeble health; his venerable appearance and Quaker habiliments should have secured their respect, but the crime of sending so many brave sons to battle was not to be forgiven. Family tradition, confirmed by the recollection of his daughter-in-law, states that they pulled off his coat, overcoat, and silver knee and shoe-buckles, and made him dismount and walk on through mud and water, urged forward by the prick of bayonets; also that the news of his capture and the pillaging of his house was carried to his sons by his daughter Hannah, who made her way through bypaths for forty miles, eluding the marauding parties scattered through the country, to the American army. Her brothers immediately set off in pursuit, found their father at length by the roadside, watched over by a wounded American soldier, and conveyed him home.

Another adventure is remembered, in which John Haynes figured, during that memorable retreat of Gen. Greene. He was sent as a scout, with three others, to give notice of the approach of Tarleton's dragoons. While posted on a hill they were suddenly startled by the appearance of a squadron of his light horse turning round a clump of trees close at hand, with the design of cutting off their

---

* A description of this battle, communicated by a southern gentleman, has been rendered superfluous by the very full and graphic account contained in Mr. Wheeler's excellent *History of North Carolina*, recently published.

retreat. The only point left open was a lane, a mile or so long, through a wide plantation. The four whigs instantly commenced the race, closely pursued by the British dragoons with their drawn sabres, the parties near enough to hear each other's voices—the royalists calling upon the rebel squad to surrender, and now and then discharging a pistol to enforce the order. The hindmost fugitive, one George Locke, was at length cut down by a sabre-stroke, and killed ; the others, hotly pursued, reached the end of the lane, and instantly turned into the thick woods, where they could ride with ease, being practised woodsmen, while the progress of the heavy-armed dragoons of Tarleton was retarded. As they dashed into the cover, they discharged their pistols over their shoulders, killing the leading horseman, a subaltern, who had the moment before cut down their companion, and was almost in the act of performing the same office for them. Fearing an ambuscade, the party hastily retreated, leaving the body of the subaltern where he fell. His uniform was taken off by a negro, and often worn by him after the close of the war.

In his advanced age John Haynes often amused his friends by recounting this and other anecdotes of races with the British troopers. On one occasion he was alone, hemmed in by pursuing horsemen, and driven to the banks of Candle Creek, at a point where the height of the banks and the width of the channel seemed to preclude all hope of escape. Being well mounted and a fearless rider, he dashed to the stream, his enemies close upon him with drawn sabres, cleared the creek at a bound, and was safe from his pursuers who dared not make the leap.

The two other sons, Joseph and James, were with Gates and Greene, and in many of the most trying scenes of the war. Joseph was one of the first who broke the cane and hunted the buffalo in the valley of Duck River, Tennessee. He was a brave soldier and an ardent patriot. It was his boast, that of all his kinsmen who were able to bear arms, there was not one who did not fight on the side of the Republic. He survived most of them who served with him, and after a long and useful life in the land to which he had gone as a pioneer, he died in July 1845, at his residence on Silver Creek, Maury County, Tennessee, in the 96th year of his age.

His brother John was born in a fort or station in the valley of the Catawba, where his family had taken shelter from the incursions of the Cherokee Indians in 1759. All three brothers with their families emigrated to Tennessee in the beginning of the present century, and established themselves in the southern part of Middle Tennessee.

John Haynes and his sons opened the road from the north side of Duck River, near Cany Spring, to the south side of Elk-ridge, where Cornersville now stands. Here father and sons opened farms, aided in erecting churches and school-houses, and soon found themselves surrounded by crowds of emigrants from Carolina and Virginia. They never forgot the precepts of their venerable ancestor, nor neglected their duty to pander to the taste of a less rigidly moral population. John lived to the age of seventy-seven, and kept his character for rapid riding to the last. It was often averred by his friends that he never rode in a walk, but always in a gallop. He died in 1838, but his widow, Margaret Haynes, survived him many years, dying the 3rd July, 1851, at the residence of her son, James S. Haynes, Esq., in her 88th year. Even at that advanced age, she retained her physical and intellectual faculties so perfectly, as to render her reminiscences of the times of peril and bloodshed both reliable and interesting. She remembered to have heard Rev. James McCree preach the funeral of Gen. Davidson at Centre meeting-house soon after the war, at which were present more than a dozen widows of those who had fallen in defence of their country. Her chief employment was reading religious books and studying the Scriptures. She gave food to the hungry and clothing to the needy, encouraging, reproving, and admonishing those around her, and diligently following every good work.

There were other children, daughters of James and Ann Haynes, who married worthy men in Rowan and Mecklenburg, North Carolina, where most of them continued to live. Their descendants are now widely scattered through the West and South, probably numbering three or four hundred, and many of them have been active in the service of their country. Several were engaged in the war of 1812 ; others subsequently in the Florida or Seminole war, and in the recent war with Mexico; Milton A. Haynes being a subaltern in the Florida war, and a Captain of Tennessee Volunteers in the Mexican war, and two of his brothers serving as subalterns. One of them lost his life in the service. The Rev. Cyrus Haynes, of Illinois, and the Rev. John Haynes of Mississippi, are the grandsons, and several other respectable clergymen of different States are descendants of the subject of this sketch.

VIII.

RUTH SPARKS.

Ruth Sevier was the second daughter of Gen. John Sevier, by his second marriage with Catharine Sherrill. She was born—the precise date is not known—at Plum Grove, their residence on the Nolachucka in that part of North Carolina now known as East Tennessee those settlements then forming the extreme borders of the country inhabited by civilized Americans.

During some five and twenty years, the greater part of the time from 1769 to 1796, the settlers—as it has been seen—were troubled more or less every year by Indian depredators, and murders and bloody battles were common occurrences. It cannot be wondered at that females born and reared in the midst of such perils should be imbued with a sturdy courage, and a self-reliance acquired only by familiar acquaintance with danger and hardship. Boldness and force of character might be expected, with the occasional manifestation of a daring more than feminine, and a love of wild and romantic adventure; while the cultivation of the gentler graces, and the refinement which is such an ornament to womanhood, might be supposed to be frequently neglected. It will not be rational, therefore, for modern judgment to condemn too rigidly what in the manners of that period did not accord with the ideas of etiquette in vogue at the present day The heart and the morals of our ancestors were

7*

uncorrupted, and we should not mark for disapproval their non-observance of external properties. "Times change, and we change with them," is an admitted truth; whether for the better or not, perhaps it would not be easy to decide.

Throughout Western Virginia and North Carolina but few opportunities or advantages were then offered for the education of children, and the duty of instructing them, particularly daughters, devolved chiefly upon the mothers among the frontier settlers. This duty was in general attended to as diligently as circumstances permitted, and women who had themselves enjoyed in a very limited degree the privilege of schooling, but had graduated under the rough but thorough tutoring of hard experience, did not often fail to impart to their little ones, with a portion of their own energy, perseverance, and spirit of enterprise, such a knowledge of practical matters at least, as proved sufficient for all purposes of life. Often too, they incited their children to avail themselves of opportunities presented to acquire even what might be termed learning. Such training had the parents of our heroine, and such they gave her; and thus without any regular schooling, she made rapid attainments, having been gifted by nature with a powerful and active mind, a ready apprehension, and great energy and strength of purpose. The condition of society in those unsettled and eventful times, and the stirring incidents in which her parents and their associates were continually forced to participate, had also much effect in forming her character, imparting a force, decision, and promptness which she might not otherwise have possessed.

During the Indian wars in which Gen. Sevier commanded the troops and was the leader in so many expeditions and successful encounters, being acknowledged as "the friend and protector of the exposed settlements," Ruth evinced a strong interest in the history and character of those warlike tribes. She learned not only the names of the chiefs, but of many of the common warriors. Some of them she saw at her father's house in the intervals of peace, and availed herself of the opportunity to become well acquainted with .hem, and acquire a knowledge of their manners and customs. She manifested a particular curiosity to learn as much as possible of their mode of living and domestic habits. All the information she sought was readily communicated to her by the Indians, who were influenced by grateful feelings towards her father for his generous kindness to the friendly savages who had visited him, and to some thirty prisoners whom he brought to his house and took care of liberally at his own expense. These had been selected from about one hundred captives taken in the year 1781. Ten of these thirty remained for three years at the residence of Gen. Sevier. Ruth was a great favorite with them all, and not only learned the Cherokee language, but so completely won the regard of every one of them, that on their return to the nation they named her to the chiefs and warriors with such expressions of commendation as amounted to a pledge of safety to the family, in case of any future difficulty, to be considered more sacred than the guarantee extended to other settlers. The kindness shown by " Nolachucka Jack " and his wife to the captives and other Indians, was mentioned the more frequently, as it gave occasion to speak of " Chucka's Rutha." " She will be chief's wife some day," was the prediction of many.

Mrs. Sevier had been accustomed to place much confidence in her friends among the children of the forest, which she never found betrayed. While the captives were at her house she permitted the Indian girls to play with Ruth and accompany her in errands and visits to the neighbors. The watchful solicitude they manifested at all times for her safety, and their desire to please her by any little service in their power, convinced the mother that the little girl was entirely secure in their company, while the unlimited trust she placed in the savages was returned on their part by gratitude, and a determination to merit her kindly regard. Thus, prisoners as they were, they lived contented and happy, bound to their host more strongly than bonds or imprisonment could have fettered them. The effect of these mutual good offices was seen long afterwards, and repeatedly acknowledged in various negotiations and treaties, where the presence and " talks" of Gen. Sevier exercised a decisive influence in persuading the savages to accede to the wishes of the whites for the extension of boundaries and the promotion of peace.

Many instances are mentioned which caused alarm to the family of Gen. Sevier and the settlers living on the Nolachucka, in which Ruth's courage and spirit were of service. Once she gave notice of the approach of tories in time for her mother to have the most valuable articles removed from the house, and concealed in an old lime-kiln. On another occasion, while playing or bathing in the stream with one of the captive Indian girls, she fancied she saw enemies lurking near the banks, and hastened to give warning. Once an attempt to cross the river with the same or another Indian maiden, had nearly proved a fatal experiment, when two young men of the same band of Cherokee captives, came unexpectedly to their relief. Ruth learned in her earliest childhood to shoot well with the musket and rifle, and could take a surer aim than many an ordinary huntsman.

The prediction of the Indians that " Chucka's Rutha" would become the wife of a chief was fulfilled singularly enough, as we proceed to explain. In the early settlement of Kentucky, when violent and destructive attacks were made on the settlements—during frequent incursions by the tribes living north of the Ohio river, a number of children had been captured, and for the most part carried off to the Indian villages near the Lakes. Among others thus taken, was a child four years of age, who was either captured or purchased by one of the principal chiefs of the Shawanese, upon the head waters of the Scioto River. This Indian had two sons nearly of the same age with the youthful captive, who was adopted as a third son, and immediately placed with them as a companion and brother, rather than as a slave, being treated with unusual kindness and indulgence. He received a new name on his adoption—Shawtunte—a cognomen which was changed after his release for that of Richard Sparks ; though whether the latter was his true and original name or not, we have no means of ascertaining. His Indian playmates were Tecumseh, and his elder brother the Prophet. Both these were afterwards well known as chiefs of power and influence, and as resolute and dangerous enemies of the United States. Tecumseh was ambitious, bold and energetic, and withal of a more amiable disposition than his brother ; but neither of them was deficient in the qualities necessary to form the brave and successful warrior. By their enterprise and exertions the plan was organized for an extensive combination among the tribes of the West and Northwest, including some of the Southwest, for the purpose of a general war upon the Americans. This mischievous conspiracy among the tribes was got up chiefly through the influence of agents of the British government, and threatened a vast amount of misery and bloodshed to the extensive and exposed American settlements on the frontier. The confederacy was broken up by the victories gained by Gen. Harrison at the battle of Tippecanoe, Nov. 6th, 1811, and upon the Miami River, followed by that of the Thames, Oct. 5th, 1813. The British Government had conferred upon Tecumseh the commission of a Major General. He lost his life in the battle of the Thames.

To return to Shawtunte. He remained in the family of Tecumseh about twelve years, till he was sixteen years old, acquiring the habits of the Indians, and becoming a proficient in their language ; for he had, indeed, little knowledge of any other. Some time before the victories of Gen. Wayne over the Indians on the Miamies, gained in 1794, he was exchanged or released, and having bid adieu to his Indian friends, returned to Kentucky. Thence he proceeded to the settlements on the Holston and Nolachucka. His relatives did not recognize him, particularly as he could not speak English. His mother only knew him by a mark she remembered.

Having heard of Gen. Sevier, and being inspired with profound respect for one who had obtained so high a reputation as a military officer, he ventured at length to seek his acquaintance. The General became deeply interested in the history of the young man, and was anxious to obtain from him some account that could be depended on, of the numbers and disposition of the northern tribes of Indians. He desired also an accurate description of the country stretching between the Ohio and the Lakes, over much of which Shawtunte had passed in his various travels while domesticated among the savages. He was quite willing to gratify his friend by stories of Indian life and adventure, and his accounts of the perils and hardships he had encountered in his sojourn in the wilderness, awakened the lively sympathy of his auditor. It may be supposed that the General was not the only listener on such occasions, to these tales of adventure wilder than romance, as he had without hesitation admitted Shawtunte to the acquaintance and hospitality of his fam ily. The interest expressed in fair faces at his narration, could not fail to encourage vivid details of " most disastrous chances,

> Of moving accidents by flood and field,"

such as might well enchain the hearing of those who had seen enough of Indian life to take an interest in all that concerned their savage neighbors. As an evidence of his regard, Gen. Sevier promised to exert his influence in procuring him a military appointment; and did so with such good effect that he was honored with a captain's commission. He performed service as a spy, and it is said was very useful in Gen. Wayne's army ; also, that he stood high as an officer and a gentleman. Meanwhile he had been aiming at a conquest of another sort in the family of the Governor-General, having become deeply enamored of his fair daughter, Ruth. Her appearance at this time is described as being very prepossessing. In symmetry of form and grace of attitude she was unrivalled. It was said, "she was never in the least awkward ; she never sat, stood, or walked, but with a natural ease and grace that was perfect; and she was always a figure for a painter." She had regular and delicate features, with a complexion extremely fair, blue eyes, and a chiselled mouth, expressive of intelligence and lively humor. Her personal attractions were enhanced by a cheerful and sociable disposition, a self-possessed and unembarrassed manner, and a faculty of accommodating herself to any situation or circumstances, with powers of entertaining conversation which made her society sought eagerly by both sexes. It will not be wondered at that she never failed to make an impression, or that she was an acknowledged centre of attraction ; yet as she was entirely free from vanity or arrogance, and seemed animated not so much by a love of display as by a cheerful and kindly spirit, and a desire to enjoy and contribute to the enjoyment of others, she was not so much envied as loved.

It may seem strange enough that the affections of a creature so lovely and accomplished, should be bestowed on one as untutored as the wild Indian; but so it was, notwithstanding the difference between them in education and manners, station and prospects in life. At the time of his marriage with the Governor's daughter, the liberated captive was wholly unlettered, not knowing how to read or write. His youthful and charming bride became his teacher, and he soon made such proficiency, that " he might have passed tolerably in an examination of boys in the spelling-book." His attainments, however, were not such as to enable him to spell or read with perfect correctness, or to write with elegance, when he was promoted to the rank of colonel in the United States army, and was ordered to Fort Pickering, on the Mississippi. Here he was stationed in 1801–2. This military station, now the beautiful and flourishing city of Memphis, was established on the borders of the territory of the Chickasaw Indians, as a link in the chain of military defences on the waters of the great river, for the purpose of preserving peace with the savage nation, and protecting emigration. The purchase of Louisiana followed soon after, and Col. Sparks proceeded with his regiment to New Orleans when the country was given into the possession of the American government. After this he was stationed for a short time at Baton Rouge, and for a longer period at Fort Adams, in the Mississippi territory. Mrs. Sparks accompanied her husband to each of these places, and remained as long as it was his duty to stay at the post. She always performed the duty of his secretary, keeping his accounts, writing his letters, and making out his reports to superior officers and the War Department.

In Natchez and other towns where there was anything that could

be called society, the claims of Mrs. Sparks to the respect and admiration of social circles, did not fail to be recognized ; she was, indeed,
" the cynosure of neighboring eyes," and her influence became very
extensive.   During her residence in Louisiana and at Fort Adams,
several of the Choctaws were in the habit of calling almost daily at
her house, to bring venison and wild turkeys or ducks, receiving in
recompense some token of remembrance from the " tyke (wife) of
Shawtunte," for they had learned the history of Col. Sparks, and
knew his Indian name ; also that Mrs. Sparks was the daughter of
a warrior whose deeds were well known, and whose bravery was
highly esteemed by the southern tribes of Indians.

After a residence of some ten years in the Southern military District, the health of Col. Sparks became so infirm, that he was induced,
by the earnest advice of Gen. Sevier, to send an application to the
War Department, in consequence of which he was permitted to
return to Tennessee.   Thence he proceeded to Staunton, in Virginia,
at which place, or in its vicinity, he died, about 1815.   During this
last visit to Tennessee, he passed through Nashville and Gallatin,
remaining some days, and recounted some of the events of his captivity to persons who called upon him and Mrs. Sparks.   Among
these was Thomas Washington, Esq., who is still living in Nashville,
and remembers many incidents.   The gentleman to whom I am indebted for this memoir, obtained many of the particulars from Mrs.
Sparks herself, and from her brother, who was from early youth an
officer in the army ; while her sister, the widow of Maj. William
M'Clelland, of the United States' army, who now resides at Van
Buren, in Arkansas, confirms every statement.   Some of the records
pertaining to this portion of the family history, are in the Historical
Society library at Nashville.

The father of Mrs. Sparks has been mentioned as " the Governor,"
although the period alluded to was before the organization of the
State of Tennessee.   This honorable title had been appropriated to
him as governor of the " State of Frankland," from the year 1784 to
1788.   When Tennessee was admitted into the Union, he became

her first governor, holding that office, with an interval of only two years, for more than eleven years.

Mrs. Sparks entered into a second marriage with an intelligent and wealthy planter of Mississippi. Her residence was a beautiful and highly improved country seat, within view of the town of Port Gibson, in Mississippi, and the splendid hospitality so remarkable on these secluded plantations, was duly exercised at " Burlington," where there was a continual succession of visitors. The fair mistress of this stately abode was distinguished by the same cheerfulness, genial kindness and attention to her guests as in her more youthful years. She was a model housewife, and everything about her establishment was always in perfect order. In the summer of 1824, while on a visit to some friends at Maysville, Kentucky, her useful life was terminated, her faith in the Redeemer growing brighter as the final scene approached. She never had any children, but was at all times extremely fond of them, and particularly pleased with the society of young persons, who always manifested a strong attachment for her.

IX

SARAH SHELBY.

SARAH, already mentioned as the eldest daughter of Mrs. Bledsoe, was born in the first year of the first settlement of Tennessee. She was very young when her family removed from Fort Chissel, Virginia, to East Tennessee. Their residence was then on the frontier, near the island flats, in what is now Sullivan County. Her early education was excellent, considering the circumstances of location and the want of the advantages of instruction which could be enjoyed in older communities. She attended the first and only lessons in dancing, given in 1784, not long before her marriage, at the house of Mr. Harris, twelve miles from Col. Bledsoe's residence. The teacher was Capt. Barrett, an English officer who had served under the royal banner in the war of the Revolution, and then left the service, determined to cast his lot for the rest of his days with the brave republicans against whose liberties he had fought. It was among the singular vicissitudes of life, that a loyal captain who in all probability had served under Col. Ferguson at the battle of King's Mountain, battling to the death against the Tennessee mountaineers, should be found afterwards in the wilderness giving lessons to their daughters in this graceful accomplishment! The gentleman who furnishes this memoir quaintly observes, that " not being able to make the fathers run, he was content with making the daughters dance."

While the family still lived in Sullivan County, Miss Bledsoe was married, in 1784, to David Shelby. Soon after, the young couple, with Col. Bledsoe and his family, came and fixed their homes in the midst of the wilderness of the Cumberland Valley, which Bledsoe and his brother had explored in 1779. The journey by land at that time from East Tennessee was a difficult and perilous one, across mountains and through forests and canebrakes, where it was impossible to force a wagon. Every article carried had to be packed on horses.

The families who formed this pioneer settlement in the Cumberland Valley were not destitute of means to live comfortably in a region where the necessaries and comforts of life could be procured, but isolated as they were from all advantages of communication or interchange with the friends they had left, they were thrown entirely upon the resources of their own labor and ingenuity. Their dwellings were rude cabins made of logs, sometimes rough and sometimes hewn. For protection against the Indians a number of these cabins were surrounded by pickets bullet-proof, and several families, usually related to each other, or attached as old neighbors, lived within the fenced space. Sometimes the pioneers resided in the blockhouses, built in the salient points of these picketed enclosures. The upper story of these blockhouses projected over the lower one, with portholes in the floor, so that persons within might shoot an assailant who approached too near under cover of the projection. The term "station," in the frontier vocabulary of those times, meant a blockhouse, picketed so as to shelter several families. It was usually called by the name of the builder or the owner of the land—as "Buchanan's Station," &c. Some, however, were known by more fanciful designations, as "Bledsoe's Lick," "French Lick," etc.

It has been already stated that at the time of Col. Bledsoe's exploration of the Cumberland Valley, no white man lived within the limits of Tennessee, west of the mountains, except a few French traders who had become naturalized among the Indians. After the removal of the family they suffered many hardships, which pressed most heavily upon the women, while shut up within military defences in the midst of the forest. No supplies of groceries or dry goods could be obtained in the valley, and all the clothing worn by the pioneers, male and female, was of home manufacture. Not one of the females was exempted from this labor; all learned how to spin and weave, and it was the pride and glory of these stout-hearted dames to prepare the material and make up with their own hands the clothes worn by themselves, their husbands and children. Col. Bledsoe was attired in a full suit manufactured by his wife and daughters, when he represented the Cumberland Valley in the Legislature of North Carolina.

All articles of consumption which could not be procured in the woods or raised on their plantations, were very scarce. Salt could only be obtained by tedious and dangerous journeys to the Kanawha salt works in Virginia, or to some French salt works in Illinois, then a part of Louisiana. Imported sugar, coffee and tea were almost excluded from use among the families in the valley, by the expense and difficulty of procuring them. For the first two or three years, before the dangers in the midst of which they lived, permitted them to cultivate the soil to any extent, even bread was scarcely to be had. The rifle of the pioneer procured for his family venison, bear's meat and wild turkeys, as well as protected them from Indian marauders. A little sugar was made every spring from the maple trees, which grew in great abundance in the untrodden forest. For this purpose large parties of old and young, male and female, when they had fixed upon a convenient location, assembled and bivouacked, or "camped," to use their own phrase, in the woods near the grove of maples, which were soon notched and pierced. The sap was caught in small troughs dug out with an axe, and carried to the camp, where it was boiled down in large pots. In two or three days thus spent, sugar enough was often produced to furnish a year's supply for a family, and the occasion did not fail to afford opportunity for a rustic re-union for all the young people of the neighborhood.

Nothing was known at that time of the culture of cotton. Flax was grown, however, and the prettiest girls in the valley hatchelled, spun and wove it ; the forest trees and shrubs yielding ample materials for dye-stuffs, by which a variety of colors might be furnished for ball or bridal costume for the fairest demoiselles of the new colony. A beautiful scarlet was produced from sassafras and sumach, and the walnut furnished a bright brown, of which color were dyed the jeans which formed full suits, elegant enough for the gentlemen's holiday wearing. This material, made in old style, is still a favorite in all the rural districts of Tennessee, the process of its manufacture having been taught, as a hereditary art, by mother to daughter, from generation to generation.

If we may rely upon tradition, the women whose time was thus passed exclusively in useful occupations, and whose labors demanded continual exercise, were superior in personal beauty to their paler and more luxurious descendants. Be that as it may, their ideas of feminine accomplishment and female merit were certainly different from those of modern days. A young woman then prided herself, not on finery purchased with the labor of others, but on the number of hanks of thread she could spin, or yards she could weave in a day on a rustic loom, made, perhaps, by her father or brother. Many a maiden whose father could reckon his acres of land in the wilderness by thousands, has appeared at church or at a country assembly dressed from head to foot in articles manufactured entirely by her self, and looking as bright and lovely in her gay colors as the proudest city dame who could lay the looms of India under contribution.

Mrs. Shelby's husband was the first merchant in Nashville, and perhaps in middle Tennessee. He established himself as such in 1790, and after two or three years, removed to Sumner County, where he was appointed to the office of clerk, the first chosen in the county. This office he continued to hold, residing in Gallatin, till his death in 1819. He maintained throughout life a high and honorable position among the settlers of the Valley, possessing qualities of mind and heart which would have commanded success and enured usefulness in the most eminent station to which a republican could have aspired, in the new State which he and his family aided in building up. But he was not ambitious, and preferred retirement in the bosom of his family, and the unostentatious discharge of the duties of an humble office, husbanding the resources he possessed for the purpose of giving his children a substantial education, and fitting them for lives of usefulness.

Mrs. Shelby has frequently mentioned incidents that occurred on different occasions when she and her husband were compelled to fly from Indians, and narrowly escaped destruction. At one time the savages came to the block-house where she lived, and attempted to shoot through a crack in the chimney. It happened that Mrs. Shelby, feeling a presentiment of danger, had stopped the crevice on the inside by a plank, which the bullets could not penetrate without having their deadly force spent. The savages were around the house during the night, as was discovered by their tracks about the place, and the finding of several articles belonging to them, such as pipes, moccasins, etc.

The day after the death of Col. Anthony Bledsoe, Mrs. Shelby went with her husband, son and servants to Bledsoe's Lick, to attend his funeral, although the distance was ten miles, and it was known the Indians were in the forest. The son, now Dr. Shelby, of Nash-ville, remembers that his father went in advance, armed with a rifle and holsters, his mother next, and that he followed with a negro, who also carried a rifle.

In 1788, while living on Station Camp Creek, in Sumner County, Mrs. Shelby was one day at home with only her little children. As usual in the early settlements, they lived in a log cabin, in which open places between the logs served the place of windows. Her husband was in the fields, some distance from the house. While seated by the fire she was startled by the appearance of an Indian warrior, fully armed, approaching her cabin. Quick as thought, she took down a loaded rifle that hung on the wall, and whispered to her son, then only six years old, to go out by the back door, and run into the field for his father, which he did quietly, but with all speed. Then placing herself near the door, she put the muzzle of the rifle through a crack in the wall, and stood, with her finger on the trigger, ready to shoot the Indian as he came near, approaching the door. Just at the moment when Mrs. Shelby was about to shoot, with deadly aim, the savage saw the gun, and with hasty strides retreated to the woods. Thus the heroism of the matron saved not only her own life, but the lives of several small children. Soon after the retreat of the Indian, Mr. Shelby and his son reached the house, to embrace the heroic wife and mother, who still stood with the rifle in her hands.

The history of Mrs. Shelby and her family, if properly given, would embrace almost the entire history of Tennessee; nor would it be possible to offer anything like an adequate sketch of the founders of the colony of Cumberland Valley, without writing in detail the history of that eventful period. This may be done by some future historian, the scope of whose work will permit him to do full justice to the patient and self-denying toil, and the heroic deeds of those enterprising pioneers. Whenever this is done, the names of Bledsoe, Shelby, Sevier, Robertson, Buchanan, Rains, and Wilson, cannot fail to shine forth prominently in the picture. These men were neither refugees from justice, nor outlaws from civilization, but belonged to a band of patriots who came, like Hooker, Haynes, or Roger Williams, to set up the altar of freedom, and find a home in primeval forests, beyond the reach of oppression, where they might live independently, and in time happily. They came not, as they knew, to an ideal paradise, or happy valley, but to a dreary wilderness, where a thousand perils environed them; beyond the paternal care of either state or federal government; harassed from time to time by a savage foe; destitute of regular supplies of provisions or munitions of war; depending for subsistence on the forest and the small patches of cornfield they were able to cultivate in the intervals of Indian campaigns; a mere handful of men, with a few helpless women and children, and equally dependent slaves; yet they kept their ground, and year by year increased in numbers and strength, till after a struggle of fifteen years against fearful odds of Indian enemies, the colony numbered from seven to eight thousand! During all this time

of trial, the armed occupation was maintained with toil and bloodshed, both of men and women, who showed, in times of emergency,
that they, too, possessed the lion will and the lion heart.   Thrilling
was the story of their adventures, with which, in after years, they
held their listeners spell-bound ; and far surpassing the wildest romance were their homely but interesting narratives, glowing in the
warm coloring of life.   They told

> " How oft at night
> Their sleep was broke by sudden fright,
> Of Indian whoop and cruel knife
> To spill the blood of babe and wife ;
> How prowling wolves and hungry bears
> Increased their dangers and their cares;
> How bold and strong these pilgrims were—
> That feared not Indian, wolf, or bear ;
> By sickness pressed, by want beset,
> Each ill they braved, each danger met ;
> 'Midst want and war their sinews grew,—etc."

Among the women of this period, remembered particularly for
the energy and cheerful self-denial with which they aided the hardy
pioneers, encouraging and animating them, while sharing in their
labors, none did her part more nobly, with more womanly grace as
well as firmness and resolution, than Mrs. Shelby.   Her memory
preserved to an advanced age every prominent incident connected
with the settlement of East Tennessee and of the Cumberland Valley.   Every part of the State, within her recollection, was a wilderness.   Having lived through the border troubles and succeeding
years of change, having survived the slaughter of her nearest relatives by the murderous Cherokees and marauding Creeks and Shawanese, she lived to see that helpless and bleeding colony of the
Watauga, increase and multiply and grow up in the midst of the
receding forest to a goodly State—it may be said, a nation.

This venerable matron died on the 11th of March, 1852, in the
eighty-sixth year of her age.   She was in her usual health, and
occupied with her needle, only three days before her death.   She

had long been a member of the Episcopal church, and gave up her spirit to God with Christian resignation, leaving an affectionate circle of her children and descendants to mourn her departure.

She had been in the habit of going to visit her relatives in the old county where she formerly resided. The fourth of July, 1851, was kept by a number of aged pioneers in Sumner, assembled to dine together, and many were the interesting recollections called up on that occasion.

After 1832, Mrs. Shelby's residence was with her son, Dr. Shelby at his beautiful country-seat, " Faderland," in the vicinity of Nashville, now almost surrounded by the new town of Edgefield. It was a pleasure to her to receive and converse with all interested in the early history of Tennessee, and she presented in her own bearing and character a noble example of the heroines of those times of trial. The laborious, painful, and perilous experiences of her life withal, never marred the harmony of her nature ; and in advanced age she had the contented and cheerful spirit of one whose days have glided away in undisturbed tranquillity. She was a deeply spiritual Christian, engaged continually, as far as her strength permitted, in the dispensation of charities, and exhibiting to those who knew her, the beauty of an humble and earnest " walk by faith."

Her husband, David Shelby, died in 1822, leaving several children, who were reared to sustain their part with usefulness in the arena of life, and in the midst of difficulties to exhibit the same energy and patience which had distinguished their parents. Judge Shelby, of Texas, was one of these children. John, the eldest son, was the first white child born in Sumner County, and is one of the oldest and worthiest citizens of Nashville. He determined in youth to study medicine, and was sent to Philadelphia to have the advantage of instruction under the celebrated Dr. Rush. He settled early in Nashville, where for many years he devoted himself successfully to the practice of his profession, being also occupied in the management of a large private business, in taking care of his town property. In 1813, he was a volunteer under Jackson, in the Creek war, and received a wound in the eye in the battle of Enotochopco

Though holding the office of surgeon in the army, he took an active part in rallying and leading the troops in this memorable action, and in acknowledgement of his services was honorably mentioned by the General.

He is now sixty-seven years of age, and after an arduous and well spent life, is still able to perform the duties of a responsible office, and to manage the business of a large farm. One of his daughters is the wife of the Hon. George Washington Barrow, late representative in Congress for the Nashville District, and during the years 1841–5, Chargé d'Affaires to the court of Portugal. Another daughter is Mrs. Priscilla Williams, now residing at Memphis, Tennessee.

X.

REBECCA WILLIAMS.

WALTER SCOTT's Rebecca the Jewess was not more celebrated for her medical skill and success in treating wounds than was Rebecca Williams among the honest borderers of the Ohio river. She was the daughter of Joseph Tomlinson, and was born the 14th of February, 1754, at Will's Creek, on the Potomac, in the province of Maryland. She married John Martin, a trader among the Indians, who was killed in 1770 on the Big Hockhocking by the Shawanees, one of her uncles being killed at the same time. In the first year of her widowhood, Mrs. Martin removed with her father's family to Grave Creek, and resided near its entrance into the Ohio, keeping house for her two brothers. She would remain alone for weeks together while they were absent on hunting excursions; for she had little knowledge of fear, and was young and sprightly in disposition.

In the spring of 1774, she paid a visit to her sister, who had married a Mr. Baker, and resided upon the banks of the Ohio, opposite Yellow Creek. It was soon after the celebrated massacre of Logan's relatives at Baker's station. Rebecca made her visit, and prepared to return home as she had come, in a canoe alone, the distance being fifty miles. She left her sister's residence in the afternoon, and paddled her canoe till dark. Then, knowing that the moon would rise at a certain hour, she neared the land, leaped on shore, and fastened her craft to some willows that drooped their boughs over the water. She sought shelter in a clump of bushes, where she lay till the moon cleared the tree tops and sent a broad stream of light over the bosom of the river. Then, unfastening her boat, she stepped a few paces into the water to get into it. But, as she reached the canoe, she trod on something cold and soft, and stooping down discovered, to her horror, that it was a human body. The pale moonlight streamed on the face of a dead Indian, not long killed, it was evident, for the body had not become stiff. The young woman recoiled at first, but uttered no scream, for the instinct of self-preservation taught her that it might be dangerous. She went round the corpse, which must have been there when she landed, stepped into her bark, and reached the mouth of Grave Creek, without further adventure, early the next morning.

In the ensuing summer, one morning while kindling the fire, blowing the coals on her knees, she heard steps in the apartment, and turning round, saw a very tall Indian standing close to her. He shook his tomahawk at her threateningly, at the same time motioning her to keep silence. He then looked around the cabin in search of plunder. Seeing her brother's rifle hanging on hooks over the fireplace, he seized it and went out. Rebecca showed no fear while he was present; but immediately on his departure, left the cabin and hid herself in the standing corn till her brother came home.

In the following year the youthful widow was united to a man of spirit congenial to her own. Isaac Williams had served as a ranger in Braddock's army, and accompanied Ebenezer and Jonathan Zane in 1769, when they explored the country about Wheeling, having before that period made several hunting excursions to the waters of the Ohio. He explored the recesses of the western wild, following the water courses of the great valley to the mouth of the Ohio, and thence along the shores of the Mississippi to the turbid waters of the Missouri; trapping the beaver on the tributaries of this river as early as 1770. His marriage with Rebecca was performed with a simplicity characteristic of the times. A travelling preacher who chanced to come into the settlement, performed the ceremony at short notice, the bridegroom presenting himself in his hunting dress and the bride in short-gown and petticoat of homespun, the common wear of the country.

In 1777, the depredations and massacres of the Indians were so frequent that the settlement at Grave Creek, consisting of several families, was broken up. It was a frontier station, and lower down the Ohio than any other above the mouth of the Great Kanawha. It was in this year that the Indians made the memorable attack on the fort at Wheeling.* Mr. Williams and his wife, with her father's family, moved to the Monongahela river, above Redstone, old fort, where they remained until the spring of 1783. They then returned to their plantations on Grave Creek, but in 1785 were obliged to remove again into the garrison at Wheeling. While there, Mrs. Williams excercised the healing art for the benefit of the soldiers, as no surgeon could be procured. With the assistance of Mrs. Zane, she dressed the wounds of one wounded in fourteen places by rifle shots while spearing fish by torchlight, and with fomentations and simple applications, not only cured his wounds, which every one thought an impossible undertaking, but saved an arm and leg that were broken. Dr. Hildreth mentions that many years afterwards, while he was attending on a man with a compound fracture of the leg, in the neighborhood of Mrs. Williams' house, she was present at one of the dressings, and related several of her cures in border times.

It has been stated that Rebecca Martin, before her marriage to Mr. Williams, acted as housekeeper for her brothers for several years. In consideration of which service, her brothers, Joseph and Samuel, made an entry of four hundred acres of land on the Virginia shore of the Ohio river, directly opposite the mouth of the Muskingum, for their sister; girdling the trees, building a cabin, and planting and fencing four acres of corn, on the high second bottom, in the

* See sketch of Elizabeth Zane. " *Women of the American Revolution.*' **Vol.** II.

spring of the year 1773. They spent the summer on the spot, occupying their time with hunting during the growth of the crop. In this time they had exhausted their small stock of salt and bread stuff, and lived for two or three months altogether on boiled turkies, which were eaten without salt. The following winter the two brothers hunted on the Big Kanawha. Some time in March, 1774, they reached the mouth of the river on their return. They were detained here a few days by a remarkably high freshet in the Ohio.

That year was long known as that of Dunmore's war, and noted for Indian depredations. The renewed and oft repeated inroads of the Indians, led Mr. Williams to turn his thoughts towards a more quiet retreat than that at Grave Creek. Fort Harmer, at the mouth of the Muskingum, having been erected in 1786, and garrisoned by United States troops, he came to the conclusion that he would now occupy the land belonging to his wife, and located by her brothers. This tract embraced a large share of rich alluvions. The piece opened by the Tomlinsons in 1773, was grown up with young saplings, but could be easily reclaimed. Having previously visited the spot and put up log cabins, Williams finally removed his family and effects thither, the twenty-sixth of March, 1787, being the year before the Ohio company took possession of their purchase at the mouth of the Muskingum.

In the January following the removal to his forest domain, his wife gave birth to a daughter, the only issue by this marriage. Soon after the Ohio company emigrants had established themselves at Marietta, a pleasing and friendly intercourse was kept up between them and Mr. Williams ; and as he had now turned his attention more especially to clearing and cultivating his farm than to hunting, he was glad to see the new openings springing up around him, and the rude forest changing into the home of civilized man. Settlements were commenced at Belprie and Waterford the year after that at Marietta ; as yet little being done in cultivating the soil, their time chiefly occupied in building cabins and clearing the land.

A brief account of the progress of this first settlement made in will be interesting, and may here be appropriately introduced

It is prepared from a large volume of Notes on Pioneer History, by Dr. S. P. Hildreth.

The country on the Ohio river was little known to the English till about 1740, after which traders went occasionally from Pennsylvania and Virginia, and at later periods attempts were made to make settlements in different localities. In 1787 the Ohio company was formed to purchase land and form settlements; funds were raised and a large number of acres contracted for, and surveyors and boat-builders were set at work. In April, 1788, a company of pioneers started in the "Adventure" galley from Simrell's Ferry, thirty miles above Pittsburgh, on the Yohiogoany, and landed at the mouth of the Muskingum. Vegetation was already advanced in the wild spot selected for their residence; the trees were in leaf, and the rich clover pastures offered abundant sustenance for their stock. Lots were surveyed, and the new town laid out on the right bank of the Ohio, at the junction of the clear waters of the Muskingum, was called Marietta, in honor of Queen Marie Antoinette, whose friendly feeling towards the American nation had, as it was well known, strongly influenced her royal consort.

The location proved fortunate in point of health as well as fertility; and game being abundant, the emigrants wanted for nothing. The ground was soon broken, and corn and vegetables planted. The temporary regulations for the government of the little community, were written out, and posted on the smooth branch of a large beech tree, near the mouth of the Muskingum. The fourth of July was celebrated by a public dinner set out in an arbor on the bank; and Gen. Varnum, one of the judges, delivered the oration, while the officers of the garrison drank and responded to the toasts. The bill of fare on this occasion, which has been recorded, presented an array of venison, bear and buffalo meat, and roast pigs; and among the fish, a pike weighing a hundred pounds, speared at the mouth of the Muskingum. On the 20th July, William Brook, of New England, preached the first sermon ever preached to white men in Ohio, Moravian missionaries having hitherto been employed to spread the truths of the Gospel among the savages. It may be interesting to know what was the text on this memorable occasion; it was in Exodus xix., 5, 6: "Now, therefore, if ye will obey my voice indeed, and keep my covenant, then ye shall be a peculiar treasure to me above all people; for all the earth is mine; and ye shall be unto me a kingdom of priests and a holy nation."

On the 20th August, the north-west blockhouse was so far completed, that a dinner was given by the directors of the company to Governor St. Clair and the officers of Fort Harmer, which the principal citizens attended, with the wives of many of the officers, and several other ladies, who had thus early ventured into the wilderness. A fine barge, rowed by twelve oars, brought the company from the fort up the Muskingum to the opposite bank, from which the appearance of the new fort was grand and imposing.

The first death is noticed as that of a child, on the 25th of August. The number of settlers this year, after a reinforcement from New England, was one hundred and thirty-two, and Marietta was at this time the only white settlement in the territory now constituting the State of Ohio. In December, about two hundred Indians came to make a treaty, and the council fire was kindled in a large log-house outside the fort. Articles were adjusted and agreed to, and the Indians departed well pleased with the settlers, whom they pronounced very different from the "long knives" and stern backwoodsmen of Kentucky. During the winter succeeding, the Ohio was filled with ice, and no boat moved up or down till March, which caused a great scarcity of provisions, for nothing could be procured but venison and bear's meat, and it was difficult to find either deer or bears in the vicinity of the town. The inhabitants were obliged to live for weeks without bread, eating boiled corn, or coarse meal ground in a hand-mill, with the little meat they could procure. As soon as the river opened, flour could be purchased from boats trading from Redstone and the country near Pittsburg, and before long a road was cut through to Alexandria. The first marriage, between the Hon. Winthrop Sargent, secretary of the North West Territory, and Miss Rowena Tupper, daughter of Gen. Tupper, was celebrated on the 6th February, 1789, by Gen. Rufus Putnam, judge of the Court of

Common Pleas for Washington, the first organized county. A public festival was appointed for the 7th April, the anniversary of the commencement of their settlement, and was observed for many years, till the country became peopled with strangers, who knew nothing of the hardships and trials encountered by the primitive settlers. It is now sometimes kept as a holiday, for picnic excursions or social parties.

Flint says he distinctly remembers the wagon that carried out a number of adventurers from Massachusetts, on the second emigration to the forests of Ohio; its large black canvass covering, and the white lettering in large capitals, "To Marietta, on the Ohio."

Belprie was a branch settlement made by the direction of the Ohio company; the name taken from "belle prairie," or beautiful meadow. After the lots were drawn, the settlers moved to their farms in April, 1789, and when their log cabins were built, commenced cutting down and girdling the trees on the rich lowlands. From the destructive effects of frost in September of this year, the crops of corn were greatly injured, and where planted late, entirely ruined. In the spring and summer of 1790, the inhabitants began to suffer from a want of food, especially wholesome bread-stuffs. The Indians were also becoming troublesome, and rendered it hazardous boating provisions from the older settlements on the Monongahela, or hunting for venison in the adjacent forests. Many families, especially at Belprie, had no other meal than that made from musty or mouldy corn; and were sometimes destitute even of this for several days in succession. This mouldy corn commanded nine shillings, or a dollar and a half a bushel; and when ground in their hand-mills and made into bread, few stomachs were able to digest it, or even to retain it for a few minutes.

During this period of want, Isaac Williams displayed his benevolent feeling for the suffering colonists. Being in the country earlier he had more ground cleared, and had raised a crop of several hundred bushels of corn. This he now distributed among the inhabitants at the low rate of three shillings, or fifty cents a bushel, when at the same time he had been urged by speculators to take a

8*

dollar for his whole crop. " I would not let them have a bushel," said the old hunter. He not only parted with his corn at this cheap rate, but prudently proportioned the number of bushels according to the number of individuals in a family. An empty purse was no bar to the needy applicant ; but his wants were equally supplied with those who had money, and credit was given until more favorable times should enable him to discharge the debt. Capt. Jonathan Devoll, hearing of Williams' corn, and the cheap rate at which he sold it, made a trip to Marietta to procure some of it ; travelling by land, and in the night, on account of the danger from Indians, a distance of twelve or four-teen miles. Williams treated him with much kindness, and after letting him have several bushels of corn at the usual price in plenti-ful years, furnished him with his only canoe to transport it home.

Like Isaac and Rebecca of old, this modern Isaac and Rebecca were given to good deeds ; and many a poor, sick, and deserted boatman has been nursed and restored to health beneath their hum-ble roof. Full of days and good deeds, and strong in the faith of a blessed immortality, Williams resigned his spirit to him who gave it, the 25th of September, 1820, aged eighty-four years, and was buried in a beautiful grove on his own plantation, surrounded by the trees he so dearly loved when living.

In spite of treaties, the Indians continued to harass the settlements in western Virginia, and in August attacked a surveying party em-ployed by the Ohio Company in running the lines of the townships. The savages seemed to hold the surveyor's chain and compass in utter detestation. In the winter of 1790, the governor of the North West Territory, St. Clair, removed his family from his plantation at " Potts' Grove," in Westmoreland County, Pennsylvania, to Marietta. One of his daughters, Louisa, was long remembered as one of the most distinguished among the ladies of that day. In strength and elasticity of frame, blooming health, energy and fearlessness, she was the ideal of a soldier's daughter, extremely fond of adventure and frolic, and ready to draw amusement from everything around her. She was a fine equestrian, and would manage the most spirited horse with perfect ease and grace, dashing at full gallop through the open woodland surrounding the " Campus Martius," and leaping over logs or any obstacle in her way. She was also expert in skating, and was rivalled by few, if any young men in the garrison, in the speed, dexterity, and grace of movement with which she exercised herself in this accomplishment. The elegance of her person, and her neat, well-fitting dress, were shown to great advantage in her rapid gyrations over the broad sheet of ice in the Muskingum, which for a few days in winter offered a fine field, close to the garrison, for this healthful sport; and loud were the plaudits from young and old, from spectators of both sexes, called forth by the performance of the governor's daughter. As a huntress she was equally distinguished, and might have served as a model for a Diana, in her rambles through the forest, had she been armed with a bow instead of a rifle, of which latter instrument she was perfect mistress, loading and firing with the accuracy of a backwoodsman, killing a squirrel on the top of the tallest tree, or cutting off the head of a partridge with wonderful precision. She was fond of roaming through the woods, and often went out alone into the forest near Marietta, fearless of the savages who often lurked in the vicinity. As active on foot as on horseback, she could walk several miles with the untiring rapidity of a practised ranger. Notwithstanding her possession of these unfeminine attainments, Miss St. Clair's refined manners would have rendered her the ornament of any drawing-room circle; she was beautiful in person, and had an intellect highly cultivated, having received a carefully finished education under the best teachers in Philadelphia. Endowed by nature with a vigorous constitution and lively animal spirits, her powers, both of body and mind, had been strengthened by such athletic exercises, to the practice of which she had been encouraged from childhood by her father. He had spent the greater part of his life in camps, and was not disposed to fetter by conventional rules his daughter's rare spirit, so admirably suited to pioneer times and manners, however like an amazon she may seem to the less independent critics of female manners at the present day. After the Indian war, Miss St. Clair returned to her early home in the romantic glens of Ligonier valley.

It is said that the first woman who came to Marietta was the w.fe of James Owen, and that she received a donation lot of one hundred acres from the Ohio company on this account. She gave shelter to a man who had been put ashore from a boat on the way to Kentucky, and took the small-pox from him, which soon spread, and most of the inhabitants were inoculated to preserve them from the terrible ravages of the disease. Hardly was this anxiety over than the great scarcity of provisions already noticed prevailed ; good corn rising to the price of two dollars a bushel, and the distress increasing as the summer approached. There were few cows and no oxen or cattle to spare ; hogs were scarce, and the woods were bare of game, the deer and buffaloes within twenty miles having been killed or driven away by the Indians. In this extremity great kindness was shown among the settlers, each sharing what he had with his neighbors, and those who had cows dividing their milk The poor obtained supplies of fish from the river. The Indians this year—1790— commenced a new species of warfare, by attacking boats in the river usually owned by emigrants on the way to Kentucky, Their principal rendezvous was near the mouth of the Scioto, and a favor- ite device to get possession of a boat, was to make a white man stand on the bank and entreat the crew to land and take him on board, saying he had just escaped from Indian slavery and if recap- tured would be put to death. By this mode of appeal to the com- passion of emigrants, the men in several boats were induced to land, when the savages lying in ambush would seize the boat or shoot down the crew from their hiding-place. The decoy was sometimes an actual prisoner, whom they forced to act his part, and sometimes a renegade white who joined them voluntarily for the sake of a share in the plunder.

In October a large company of French emigrants arrived at Marietta, coming down the Ohio in "Kentucky arks," or flatboats. Many were from Paris, and wondered not a little at the broad rivers and vast forests of the West. The distress and destitution into which they were thrown by the failure of the Scioto company to fulfil thei contracts and the substitution of lands on the Ohio below the Kanawha, are mentioned in another sketch. Gen. Rufus Putnam was commissioned by the principal men in the Scioto company to build houses and furnish provisions for these colonists, and did so at great loss, the company eventually failing and dissolving. Indian hostilities commenced in January, 1791, with an attack on the blockhouse at Big Bottom. This building stood on the first or low bottom, a few rods from the shore on the left bank of the Muskingum, four miles above the mouth of Meigs' Creek and thirty from Marietta. A few rods back, the land rose several feet to a second or higher bottom, which stretched out into a plain of half a mile in width, extending to the foot of the hills. Big Bottom was so called from its size, being four or five miles in length, and containing more fine land than any other below Duncan's falls. Excepting the small clearing round the garrison, the whole region was a forest. This settlement was made up of thirty-six young men, but little acquainted with Indian warfare or military rules. Confident in their own prudence and ability to protect themselves, they put up a blockhouse which might accommodate all in an emergency, covered it, and laid puncheon floors, stairs, &c. It was built of large beech logs, and rather open, as it was not chinked between the logs ; this job was left for a rainy day or some more convenient season. They kept no sentry, and had neglected to set pickets around the blockhouse, and their guns were lying in different places, without order, about the house. Twenty men usually encamped in the house, a part of whom were now absent, and each individual and mess cooked for themselves. One end of the building was appropriated for a fire-place, and at close of day all came in, built a large fire, and commenced cooking and eating their suppers.

A party of Indians came into a cabin occupied by a few of the men, near the blockhouse, and spoke to them in a friendly manner, partaking of their supper. Presently taking some leathern thongs and pieces of cord that had been used in packing venison, they seized the white men by their arms, and told them they were prisoners. Another party attacked the blockhouse so suddenly and unexpectedly that there was no time for defence, shooting down and

tomahawking the men. One stout Virginia woman, the wife of
Isaac Meeks, who was employed as their hunter, seized an axe and
made a blow at the head of the Indian who opened the door ; a
slight turn of the head saved his skull, and the axe passed down
through his cheek into the shoulder, leaving a huge gash that severed nearly half his face; she was instantly killed by the tomahawk
of one of his companions before she could repeat the stroke. This
was all the injury received by the Indians, as the men were killed
before they had time to seize their arms which stood in the corner
of the room. While the slaughter was going on, a young man in
the prime of life sprung up the stair-way and out upon the roof ;
while his brother, a lad of sixteen, secreted himself under some
bedding in the corner of the room. The Indians on the outside
soon discovered the former, and shot him in the act of begging them
to spare his life, " as he was the only one left."

Twelve persons were killed in this attack. The savages had
vowed that before the trees put forth leaves, the smoke of a white man's
house should not rise north-west of the waters of the Ohio. The
inhabitants assembled at the three stations at Marietta, Belprie and
Waterford, new blockhouses were built at the expense of the Ohio
company, and two hunters were employed to act as spies for each
garrison. Gen. Putnam complained to President Washington of
the danger in which the settlements stood of being entirely swept
away without a reinforcement of troops, and a military force was
sent for their defence in the ensuing summer.

The following incident is illustrative : " On a day in March,
Rogers and Henderson sallied out of the garrison at an early hour,
to scout up the Muskingum. They ranged diligently all day without seeing any Indians, or discovering signs of their being in the
neighborhood. Just at night, as they were returning to the
garrison by a cow-path, and had come within a mile of home,
two Indians rose from behind a log, fifty yards before them, and
fired. Rogers was shot through the heart, and as he fell, Henderson attempted to support him, but he told him he was a dead man,
and he must provide for his own safety. He turned to escape down the

side of the ridge, to the bottom, and two more savages who had reserved their fire, rose and discharged their rifles at him as he ran; one of the balls passing through the collar of his hunting-shirt, the other through the silk handkerchief which was bound round his head, and formed a part of a ranger's dress, barely grazing the scalp. His blanket, folded like a knapsack on his back, probably saved his life,—shielding the vital part by its numerous folds, from the passage of a bullet. The Indians well knew what a protection this would be, and therefore aimed at his head. After running a few hundred yards on the back track, he discovered that the savages had taken a shorter course and got ahead of him, and making a short turn to the right, up a ravine, he crossed the ridge and came out into the valley of Duck Creek, unmolested. While making this detour, he fell quite unexpectedly on the camp of the savages, and saw one busily engaged in kindling a fire, and so diligently occupied that he did not observe the white man. Henderson could easily have shot him, but as his pursuers had lost the direction of his course, he thought it imprudent by firing to give them notice of his whereabouts, and went on to the garrison at the point. The alarm gun was fired, and answered from Fort Harmer and Campus Martius. The story spread through the village that Rogers had been killed, and Henderson chased to the garrison by Indians, who were then besieging its gates. The darkness of night added to the confusion of the scene. The order, in case of an alarm, was for every man to repair to his alarm post, and the women and children to the blockhouses. Some idea of the proceedings of the night may be obtained from the narration of an eye-witness :

" ' The first applicant for admission to the central blockhouse was Col. Sproat, with a box of papers for safe keeping ; then came some young men with their arms ; next, a woman with her bed and her children ; and after her, old William Moultin, from Newbnry-port, with his leathern apron full of old goldsmith's tools and tobacco. His daughter, Anna, brought the china tea-pot, cups and saucers. Lydia brought the great bible ; but when all were in, 'mother' was missing. Where was mother? She must be killed by the Indians. 'No,' says Lydia, 'mother said she would not leave the house *looking so ;* she would put things a little to rights.' After a while the old lady arrived, bringing the looking-glass, knives and forks, etc.' "

From the commencement of the settlement, the Sabbath had been kept as a day of rest ; and from 1789, regular service was performed in the north-west block-house at Campus Martius. The military law required the regular muster of troops every Sunday at ten o'clock. They were paraded by beat of drum, the roll called, arms inspected, and then the procession, headed by Colonel Sproat with drawn sword, the clergyman and the civil officers, with accompaniment of fife and drum, marched into the hall appropriated for divine service. The arms of the soldiers were placed by their sides, or in some convenient place, ready for use. "One Sunday morning in the latter part of September, Peter Niswonger, one of the rangers, went to visit a field he had planted with corn and potatoes, on the east side of Duck Creek. He had some fattened hogs in a pen, one of which he found killed, and a portion of the meat cut out and carried off. Several hills of potatoes had been dug, and in the loose earth he discovered fresh moccasin tracks ; a proof that Indians had done the mischief. Peter hurried back to the garrison at the point, and gave the alarm. It was in the midst of morning service, and the inhabitants were generally assembled in the large block-house. The instant the words, 'Indians in the neighborhood,' were heard, the drummer seized his drum, and rushing out at the door, began to beat the long roll ; the well known signal for every man to hasten to his post. The place of worship, so quiet a few minutes before, was now a scene of alarm and confusion. The women caught up their little children and hastened homeward, and the place of prayer was abandoned for that day. Anxiety for the fate of their brothers and husbands, who had gone in pursuit of the dreaded enemy, banished all thoughts but the silent, fervent prayer for their safe return. A party was soon mustered of five or six of the rangers, several volunteer citizens, and soldiers from the company stationed at the point. The men went up in canoes to the mouth of Duck Creek, where they left their water-craft. The more experienced rangers soon fell upon the trail, which they traced across wide bottoms, to the Little Muskingum. At a point about half a mile below where Conner's mill now stands, the Indians forded the creek; and about a mile eastward, in a hollow between the hills, was seen the smoke of their camp fire. The rangers now divided the volunteers into two flanking parties, with one of the spies at the head of each; three of their number acting in front. By the time the 'flankers' had come within range of the camp, the Indians discovered their foes, by the noise of soldiers who lagged behind and were not so cautious in their movements, and instantly fled up the run on which they were encamped; two of their number leaving the main body, and ascending the point of a hill with a ravine on the right and left. The rangers now fired, while the Indians, each taking his tree, returned the shot. One of the two savages on the spur of the ridge was wounded by one of the spies on the right, who pushed on manfully to gain the enemy's flank. The men in front came on more slowly, and as they began to ascend the point of the ridge, Ned Henderson, who was posted on high ground, cried, ' Hence! there is an Indian behind that white oak; he will kill some of you !' One of the white men instantly sprang behind a large tree; another behind a hickory too small to cover more than half his body, while the third jumped into the ravine. At the instant the Indian fired, he looked over the edge of the bank to see the effect of the shot, and saw the man behind the hickory wiping the dust of the bark from his eyes; the ball having grazed the tree without doing him any injury except cutting his nose with the splinters. At the same time the Indian fell, pierced with several balls."

" The first Sunday school was taught by Mrs. Andrew Lake, a kind-hearted, pious old lady from New York, who had brought up a family of children herself, and therefore felt the more for others ; she took compassion on the children of the garrison, who were spending the Sabbath afternoons in frivolous amusements, and established a school in her own dwelling. After parson Story's services were finished, she regularly assembled as many of the younger children as she could persuade to attend, and taught them the Westminster catechism, and lessons from the Bible, for about a hour. Her scholars amounted to about twenty in number. She was very kind and affectionate towards them, so that they were fond of assembling to listen to her instructions. Her explanations of Scripture were so simple and childlike, that the smallest of the little ones could understand them, and were rendered very pleasant by her mild manner of speaking. The accommodations for the children were very rude and simple, consisting only of a few low stools and benches, such a thing as a chair being unknown in the garrison. One of her scholars, then a little boy of four years old, who gave me a sketch of the school, says—for lack of a seat he was one day placed by the kind old lady on the top of a bag of meal, that stood leaning against the side of the room. The seed thus charitably sown in faith and hope, was not scattered in vain; as several of her scholars became prominent members of the church."

The offer of lands for military service brought new emigrants from Pennsylvania and Virginia, and the firmness and wisdom of directors and agents, backed by the counsel of old Revolutionary officers, preserved the settlement in the midst of formidable dangers. Among other inconveniences brought by war, the mills were stopped, and it was necessary to grind the corn in hand-mills, though flour might still be procured at " head-waters."

There were but two hand-mills in the garrison, and a large coffee-mill, which had once belonged to a ship of war. The hopper held a peck of corn, and it was in great demand. After this imperfect grinding, the finest of the meal was separated with a sieve for bread, and the coarse boiled with a piece of venison or bear's meat, making a rich and nourishing diet, well suited to the tastes of the hungry pioneers.

One instance of strict honor, in the midst of privation is mentioned of the wife of an officer in the United States' service, and one of the most worthy men in the colony. During the period of the greatest distress, the mother had consented to cook for a young man who owned a lot adjoining hers, and ate his meals at his own cabin. While the bread, which was made of musty meal, was baking, she always sent her children out to play, and when baked, locked it immediately in the owner's chest, lest they should see it, and cry for a piece of what she had no right to give them. When a few kernels of corn chanced to be dropped in grinding, the children would pick them up like chickens, and eat them. A few of the inhabitants had cows, for which, in summer, the forest afforded ample provender. In the latter part of the winter, the sap of the sugar maple, boiled down with meal, made a rich and nutritious food; and the tree was so abundant, that as large quantities of sugar were made as the number of kettles in the settlement would permit. By the middle of July, the new corn was in the milk, and fit for roasting; and this, with squashes, beans, etc., put an end to fears of actual starvation. So urgent was the necessity, that these different vegetables, before they were fully formed, were gathered and boiled together, with a little meal, into a kind of soup much relished. It was even said that the dogs would get at and devour the young corn.

Under these discouraging circumstances, the inhabitants contributed all the money they could raise, and sent two active young men by land to "Red Stone," to procure supplies of salt meat and a few barrels of flour. It was a hazardous journey, on account of the inclemency of the weather—it being early in December—and danger from the Indians, who since St. Clair's defeat were more active in harassing the settlements. The young men, however, reached head waters, and made the necessary purchases, which they were about sending down the river when it was suddenly closed by ice. Nothing, meanwhile, was heard of them at home, and the winter wore away in uncertainty, some supposing the messengers had gone off with the money, and others that they had been killed by the savages. The ice broke up the last of February with a flood that inundated the ground on which the garrison was built, and early in March the young men arrived with a small Kentucky boat loaded with supplies, and entering the garrison by the upper gate, moored their ark at the door of the commandant, to the great relief and joy of the inhabitants.

The expedition of Gen. Harmar having failed of its object, the north-west territory was still a battle-ground for confederate tribes from Lakes Erie and Michigan, from the Illinois, the Wabash, and the Miamis. The famous chief, Little Turtle, was at their head. This failure having made a deep impression, there was a demand for a greater force under the command of a more experienced general ; and Arthur St. Clair was selected as most capable of restoring American affairs in the north-west. His army was assembled at Cincinnati with the object of destroying the Miami towns. Gen. St. Clair's defeat on a branch of the Wabash, November 4th, 1791, was one of the heaviest disasters in the annals of savage warfare. Its effect was to expose the whole range of frontier settlements on the Ohio, to the fury of the Indians, and spread so much alarm among the inhabitants, that many talked of leaving the country. Their final determination, however, was to stay and defend their property, and the ensuing winter, in spite of disasters, brought fresh arrivals of colonists. During the continuance of the war, the men were obliged to work their fields with arms in their hands ; parties of fifteen or twenty laboring, while three or four were posted as sentries in the edge of the woods or enclosure. Thus food for their families was obtained at the risk of the rifle or the tomahawk.

The year 1791 was more fruitful of tragic events in the vicinity of Marietta than any other. After that time the Indians were occupied in defending their own borders, or their villages, against American troops, and had little time for hostile incursions. The expenses in which the war had involved the Ohio Company, caused the failure of payment for the lands ; petitions were presented to Congress for donation lots, and those emigrants who came after the termination of Indian hostilities obtained better lands, on more favorable

terms, than those who had undergone all the privations, labors, and
sufferings which preceded the privileged season.

"The winter of 1791–2," says Spencer in his narrative, "was followed by an early and delightful spring; indeed, I have often
thought that our first western winters were much milder, our springs
earlier, and our autumns longer than they now are. On the last of
February, some of the trees were putting forth their foliage; in
March, the red-bud, the hawthorn and the dog-wood in full bloom
checkered the hills, displaying their beautiful colors of rose and lily;
and in April the ground was covered with the May apple, bloodroot,
ginseng, violets, and a great variety of herbs and flowers. Flocks of
parroquets were seen, decked in their rich plumage of green and
gold. Birds of every species and of every hue, were flitting from
tree to tree; and the beautiful redbird, and the untaught songster of
the west, made the woods vocal with their melody. Now might be
heard the plaintive wail of the dove, and now the rumbling drum of
the partridge, or the loud gobble of the turkey. Here might be
seen the clumsy bear, doggedly moving off, or urged by pursuit
into a laboring gallop, retreating to his citadel in the top of some
lofty tree; or—approached suddenly—raising himself erect in the
attitude of defence, facing his enemy and waiting his approach;
there the timid deer, watchfully resting, or cautiously feeding, or
aroused from his thicket, gracefully bounding off, then stopping,
erecting his stately head and for a moment gazing around, or snuff-
ing the air to ascertain his enemy, instantly springing off, clearing
logs and bushes at a bound, and soon distancing his pursuers. It
seemed an earthly paradise; and but for apprehension of the wily
copperhead, who lay silently coiled among the leaves, or beneath
the plants, waiting to strike his victim; the horrid rattlesnake, who
more chivalrous, however, with head erect amidst its ample folds,
prepared to dart upon his foe, generously with the loud noise of his
rattle apprised him of danger; and the still more fearful and insi-
dious savage, who, crawling upon the ground, or noiselessly approaching behind trees and thickets, sped the deadly shaft or fatal bullet,

you might have fancied you were in the confines of Eden or the borders of Elysium."

The author of "Miami County Traditions," says : " The country all around the settlement presented the most lovely appearance ; the earth was like an ash-heap, and nothing could exceed the luxuriance of primitive vegetation ; indeed, our cattle often died from excess of feeding, and it was somewhat difficult to rear them on that account. The white-weed, or bee-harvest, as it is called, so profusely spread over our bottom and woodlands, was not then seen among us ; the sweet annis, nettles, wild rye, and pea-vine, now so scarce, every where abounded ; they were almost the entire herbage of our bottoms ; the two last gave subsistence to our cattle, and the first, with our nutritious roots, were eaten by our swine with the greatest avidity. In the spring and summer months, a drove of hogs could be scented at a considerable distance, from their flavor of the annis root."

When Gen. Putnam had concluded a treaty with the Indians on the Wabash, fourteen of the chiefs came to Marietta, November 17th, 1792, under the escort of American officers. The next day a public dinner was given to them at Campus Martius, to which the officers of the garrison and the citizens of Marietta were invited. The procession was formed on the bank of the Ohio, where the boat landed, and the chiefs were conducted, with martial music, to the north-east gate of the garrison, a salute of fourteen guns being fired as soon as the head of the column appeared in sight. The procession then moved through the gate to the dining hall, a room twenty-four by forty feet large, in the hall of the north-west block-house, where the feast provided had been arranged by the ladies of the garrison. An eye-witness says : " The entertainment was very novel, and the scene peculiar and striking. Shut up in the garrison, and at war with the other tribes of the forest, shaking hands with our red guests, and passing from one to another the appellation of *brother !* It seemed to renew the scenes of the first year's settlement, and make us almost forget war was upon our border."

After the banquet and ceremonies were concluded, the chiefs were again conducted to their boats. The next day they were invited by several gentlemen of the stockade garrison at the point, to smoke the pipe of friendship; after which they proceeded on their journey.

Another of the female pioneers whose name tradition has preserved, is Sally Fleehart, who became the wife of John Warth, a noted hunter and ranger, and lived in one of the barracks. Warth learned to read and write in the intervals of his ranging tours, and after the peace settled in Virginia, and served as a magistrate, becoming a wealthy planter and owning a number of slaves. His success was attributable to the education given him by his wife, who had been brought up on the frontier, and possessed not only unusual intellectual cultivation for that class, but all the intrepidity and activity common to women at that day, in a remarkable degree. She could fire a rifle with great accuracy, and bring down a bird on the wing, or a squirrel from the tree, as readily as could the practised arm of her husband.

The women resident in the forts had but little respite from anxiety and dread, except in the depths of winter, when the Indians rarely committed depredations, or lay in watch about the settlements. As soon, however, as the wild geese, seen in flocks steering their course northward, or the frogs piping in the swamp, gave token of the approach of the more genial season, the return of the savage foe might be expected. Thus the more timid part of the community, and the elder females never welcomed the coming of spring with the hilarity it generally awakens, preferring the " melancholy days" of gloom and tempest, when they and their children were comparatively safe ; regarding the budding of trees and opening of wild flowers with sad forebodings, and listening to the song of birds as a prelude to the warcry of the relentless savage. The barking of the faithful watchdog at night was another cause of terror, associated as it was with visions of the Indian lurking in his covert ; and it was seldom heard by the timid mother without raising her head from the pillow to listen anxiously for the sound of the distant warwhoop, or the report of the sentry's rifle ; to sink again into uneasy slumber, and dream of some wild deed or fearful occurrence. Some amusing inci-

dents are related of the alarm created in a garrison by the sudden
outcry of persons who were dreaming of Indian assault. This part
of the suffering peculiar to those times, can hardly be imagined in
our days of peace and security.

One instance of the confusion created by a false alarm may be
given :—" One dark and rainy night in June, while John Wint, a
youth of eighteen, was on the watch in the tower of the middle
blockhouse, he saw by a flash of lightning a darklooking object
climbing over a log, which lay about fifty yards from the fort. A
report had been previously circulated of Indians being seen in the
neighborhood, and this appeared about the height of a man. At
the next flash John hailed and fired the same instant. All remained
quiet outside; but the report awakened every body within the garrison, and men came running from all quarters in great alarm,
thinking the savages were already upon them, for no sentinel ever
fired without good cause. The women came hurrying along with
their screaming children, and the soldiers with their guns ready for
service. In the midst of the tumult, Col. Sproat was soon on the
ground, and questioned the sentinel closely as to what he had seen
or heard. John was rather confused at the disturbance he had
raised without being able to state some more definite cause than the
dark body bearing resemblance to a man, which he had seen
standing on a log. He said he had fired at a white spot he saw
above its head by the flash of lightning, and there were many sur-
mises as to what it could be; some thinking it must be an Indian,
others protesting John had fired at nothing to see the fun of a night
alarm, as he was known to be fond of a little harmless sport. No
further signs of the enemy were discovered, as no one would venture
out in the dark to reconnoitre for savages. In the morning, after the
gates were opened, a party went to the log pointed out by John,
and found a large black dog, which belonged to one of the soldiers,
with a rifle shot through the centre of a white spot in his forehead."
The accuracy of the shot attested the sentry's excellence as a marksman, though much useless anxiety had been excited by his mistake

This is a brief notice of the earliest settlement in Ohio, the germ

whence has sprung a great and powerful State. The termination of
the Indian war, brought about by the victorious campaign of Gen.
Anthony Wayne, and the conclusion of the treaty at Greenville in
1795, restored peace to the harassed settlements ; mills were erected,
roads opened, and the inhabitants who had so long been immured
within the walls of forts, went forth to till their grounds and clear
away the forest unembarrassed by the dread of a lurking enemy.

Brickell, in his narrative of captivity among the Indians, relates a
curious anecdote of the escape of Mrs. Jane Dick. " Her husband
had concerted a plan with the captain of the vessel which brought
the presents, to steal her from the Indians. The captain concerted
a plan with a black man who cooked for McKee and Elliot, to steal
Mrs. Dick. The black man arranged it with Mrs. Dick to meet him
at midnight in a copse of underwood, which she did, and he took
her on board in a small canoe, and headed her up in an empty hogs-
head, where she remained till the day after the vessel sailed, about
thirty-six hours. I remember well that every camp and the woods
were searched for her, and that the vessel was searched ; for the
Indians immediately suspected that she was on board, but not thinking of unheading hogsheads, they could not find her." This happened the summer before Wayne's campaign.

———

MARY HECKEWELDER, the daughter of Rev. John Heckewelder,
whose early labors as a Moravian missionary among the Indians are
well known, is said to have been the first white child born in Ohio.
The following sketch was sent by her to the editor of the American
Pioneer : " I was born April 16th, 1781, in Salem, one of the
Moravian Indian towns on the Muskingum river, Ohio. Soon
after my birth, times becoming very troublesome, the settlements
were often in danger from war parties, and from an encampment of
warriors near Gnadenhutten ; and finally, in the beginning of September of the same year, we were all made prisoners. First, four
of the missionaries were seized by a party of Huron warriors, and

9

declared prisoners of war; they were then led into the camp of the Delawares, where the death-song was sung over them. Soon after they had secured them, a number of warriors marched off for Salem and Schönbrunn. About thirty savages arrived at the former place in the dusk of the evening, and broke open the mission-house. Here they took my mother and myself prisoners, and having led her into the street and placed guards over her, they plundered the house of everything they could take with them and destroyed what was left Then going to take my mother along with them, the savages were prevailed upon, through the intercession of the Indian females, to let her remain at Salem till the next morning—the night being dark and rainy, and almost impossible for her to travel so far. They consented on condition that she should be brought into the camp the next morning, which was accordingly done, and she was safely conducted by our Indians to Gnadenhutten.

"After experiencing the cruel treatment of the savages for some time, they were set at liberty again; but were obliged to leave their flourishing settlements and forced to march through a dreary wilderness to Upper Sandusky. We went by land through Goshachguenk to the Walholding, and then partly by water and partly along the banks of the river, to Sandusky creek. All the way I was carried by an Indian woman, carefully wrapped in a blanket, on her back. Our journey was exceedingly tedious and dangerous; some of the canoes sunk, and those that were in them lost all their provisions and everything they had saved. Those that went by land drove the cattle, a pretty large herd. The savages now drove us along, the missionaries with their families usually in the midst, surrounded by their Indian converts. The roads were exceedingly bad, leading through a continuation of swamps.

"Having arrived at Upper Sandusky, they built small huts of logs and bark to screen them from the cold, having neither beds nor blankets, and being reduced to the greatest poverty and want; for the savages had by degrees stolen almost everything both from the missionaries and Indians on the journey. We lived here extremely poor, often having very little or nothing to satisfy the cravings of hunger; and the poorest of the Indians were obliged to live upon their dead cattle, which died for want of pasture.

"After living in this dreary wilderness, in danger, poverty, and distress of all sorts, a written order arrived in March, 1782, sent by the governor to the half-king of the Hurons and to an English officer in his company, to bring all the missionaries and their families to Detroit, but with a strict order not to plunder nor abuse them in the least. The missionaries were overwhelmed with grief at the idea of being separated from their Indians; but there being no alternative, they were obliged to submit to this, one of the heaviest of their trials. The poor Indians came weeping to bid them farewell, and accompanied them a considerable way, some as far as Lower Sandusky. Here we were obliged to spend several nights in the open air, and suffered great cold besides other hardships. April 14th, we set out and crossed over a part of the lake, and arrived at Detroit by the straits which join Lakes Erie and Huron. We were lodged in the barracks by order of the governor. Some weeks after, we left the barracks with his consent and moved into a house at a small distance from the town.

"The Indian converts gathering around their teachers, they resolved, with the consent of the governor, to begin the building of a new settlement upon a spot about thirty miles from Detroit, on the river Huron, which they called New Gnadenhutten, and which increased considerably from time to time. Here I lived till the year 1785, when I set out with an aged missionary couple to be educated in the school at Bethlehem."

The murder of the Moravian Indians was one of the most atrocious transactions in the history of the West. They consisted chiefly of Delawares, with a few Mohicans; had been converted to Christianity through the zeal and influence of Moravian missionaries, and had lived ten years quietly in their villages of Gnadenhutten, Schönbrunn, Salem, and Lichtenau. Although in friendship with the whites, they fell under the displeasure of the border settlers, who suspected them of aiding and abetting the hostile savages; an expedition against them was undertaken in March, 1782, after some

Indian incursions, by a party of men chiefly from the Monongahela, led by Col. David Williamson; they were induced by assurances of good-will, to assemble at Guadenhutten, and there were deliberately massacred in cold blood. It is said that the number of killed was ninety-six, including women and children. Two only of the devoted Indians made their escape.

———

"RUHAMA GREENE was born and raised in Jefferson County, Virginia. In 1785, she married Charles Builderback, and with him crossed the mountains and settled at the mouth of Short Creek, on the east bank of the Ohio, a few miles above Wheeling. Her husband, a brave man, had on many occasions distinguished himself in repelling the Indians, who had often felt the aim of his unerring rifle. They therefore determined at all hazards to kill him.

"On a beautiful summer morning in June, 1789, at a time when it was thought the enemy had abandoned the western shores of the Ohio, Capt. Charles Builderback, his wife and brother, Jacob Builderback, crossed the Ohio to look after some cattle. On reaching the shore, a party of fifteen or twenty Indians rushed out from an ambush, and firing upon them, wounded Jacob in the shoulder. Charles was taken while he was running to escape. Jacob returned to the canoe and got away. In the mean time, Mrs. Builderback secreted herself in some drift-wood, near the bank of the river. As soon as the Indians had secured and tied her husband, not being able to discover her hiding-place, they compelled him, with threats of immediate death, to call her to him. With a hope of appeasing their fury, he did so. She heard him, but made no answer. Here, to use her words,—'a struggle took place in my breast, which I cannot describe. Shall I go to him and become a prisoner, or shall I remain, return to our cabin and provide for and take care of our two children?' He shouted to her a second time to come to him, saying, that if she obeyed, perhaps it would be the means of saving his life She no longer hesitated, but left her place of safety, and surrendered herself to his savage captors. All this took place in full view of their cabin, on the opposite shore, where they had left their two children, one a son about three years of age, and an infant daughter. The Indians, knowing that they would be pursued as soon as the news of their visit reached the stockade at Wheeling, commenced their retreat. Mrs. Builderback and her husband travelled together that day and the following night. The next morning, the Indians separated into two bands, one taking Builderback, and the other his wife, and continued a westward course by different routes.

"In a few days, the band having Mrs. Builderback in custody, reached the Tuscarawas river, where they encamped, and were soon rejoined by the band that had her husband in charge. Here the murderers exhibited his scalp on the top of a pole, and to convince her that they had killed him, pulled it down and threw it into her lap. She recognised it at once by the redness of his hair. She said nothing, and uttered no complaint. It was evening ; her ears pained with the terrific yells of the savages, and wearied by constant travelling, she reclined against a tree and fell into a profound sleep, and forgot all her sufferings, until morning. When she awoke, the scalp of her murdered husband was gone, and she never learned what became of it.*

" As soon as the capture of Builderback was known at Wheeling, a party of scouts set off in pursuit, and taking the trail of one of the bands, followed it until they found the body of Builderback. He had been tomahawked and scalped, and apparently suffered a lingering death.

* Her husband commanded a company at Crawford's defeat. He was a large, noble looking man, and a bold and intrepid warrior. He was in the bloody Moravian campaign, and took his share in the tragedy, by shedding the first blood on that occasion, when he shot, tomahawked and scalped Shebosh, a Moravian chief. But retributive justice was meted to him. After being taken prisoner, the Indians inquired his name. "Charles Builderback," replied he, after some little pause. At this revelation, the Indians stared at each other with malignant triumph. "Ha !" said they, "you kill many Indians—you big captain—you kill Moravians." From that moment, probably, his death was decreed.

" The Indians, on reaching their towns on the Big Miami, adopted Mrs. Builderback into a family, with whom she resided until released from captivity. She remained a prisoner about nine months, performing the labor and drudgery of squaws, such as carrying in meat from the hunting grounds, preparing and drying it, making moccasins, leggins and other clothing for the family in which she lived. After her adoption she suffered much from the rough and filthy manner of Indian living, but had no cause to complain of ill-treatment otherwise.

" In a few months after her capture, some friendly Indians informed the commandant at Fort Washington, that there was a white woman in captivity at the Miami towns. She was ransomed and brought i 'p the fort, and in a few weeks was sent up the river to her lone) .abin, and the embrace of her two orphan children. She then re   ossed the mountains, and settled in her native county.

" In 1791, Mrs. Builderback married Mr. John Greene, and in 1798, they emigrated to the Hockhocking valley, and settled about three miles west of Lancaster, where she continued to reside until the time of her death, about the year 1842. She survived her last husband about ten years."*

* Historica. Collections of Ohio.

XI.

REBECCA ROUSE.

AMONG other families who ventured on the long and perilous journey from the granite soil of New England, in the year 1788, a year never to be forgotten in the annals of Ohio, were those of John Rouse and Jonathan Devoll. Before the period of the Revolution, Mr. Rouse had followed the vocation of a whaleman and seaman, from the port of New Bedford, and was now living on a small farm in the town of Rochester, Massachusetts, near the little harbor of Mattepoisett. His family consisted of a wife and eight children. Capt. Jonathan Haskell, who also lived in Rochester, and had been an officer in the war, joined him in fitting out the expedition, and furnished a large covered wagon and two of the horses, Mr. Rouse furnishing the other two. An active young man, named Cushing, who wished to settle in the west, was employed to drive the wagon. As the journey was a long one, they took as few articles of beds, bedding, and cooking utensils, as they could possibly do with on the road. Their clothing and other goods were packed in trunks and large wooden boxes made to fit the inside of the wagon.

The parting from their old neighbors at Mattepoisett, was one of much tenderness, accompanied by many hearty adieus and sincere prayers for their welfare on the journey, and their happiness in that

far away region.   No one, at this day, can imagine with what dread
and awe a journey to the new territory west of the Ohio, was then
viewed by the simple-hearted people of New England. A party of
young ladies, on horseback, accompanied the females as far as " The
Long-plain," distant six miles.   Here they tarried for about a week
amongst their kinsfolk and former neighbors; for at this place
Rouse had lived many years, and here most of the children had been
born.

The morning they left Mattepoisett, an interesting occurrence took
place which shows the strong attachment of the female heart to
home and relatives.   A rich old farmer of that place, who had taken
a great liking to Bathsheba, the eldest daughter, and was anxious
that his son should obtain her for a wife, offered to give her by deed
a nice farm and good dwelling-house, if she would stay amongst
them and not go with the family to the West.   But her affection
for her parents, sisters, and brothers was too great to forego the pleasure of their society probably for the rest of her life, and the offer
was declined, much to the sorrow of the generous old man.   The
week flew rapidly away in social intercourse with their kindred, and
solemn and sorrowful were the greetings of the farewell hour.   The
distance was so great, and the dangers of the wilderness so many,
that they all thought the parting was to be final as to this world;
and so indeed it proved to the larger portion of them.   Capt. Haskell joined them that morning from Rochester, and early in October,
1788, they took their departure from " The Long-plain," and commenced their arduous journey to Muskingum, as the new settlement
was then called.   They reached Providence the second day, at evening—at which place they were joined by the family of Jonathan
Devoll, composed of Mrs. Devoll and five children. Mrs. Nancy
Devoll was the sister of Mrs. Rouse.   Her husband had been absent
nearly a year, attached to the party of pioneers sent by the Ohio
company the autumn previous.   He was the naval architect of the
"May-flower," which conveyed the first detachment of men from
Simrel's Ferry, on the Yohiogany, to the mouth of the Muskingum,
and one of the first who landed the 7th of April, 1788, on the soil

of the present State of Ohio. Their large covered wagon, with four horses, was fitted up in a similar style to the other, and was driven by Isaac Barker, an only brother of the married females, who had left a wife and family in Rochester, till he could return and bring them the following year.

After travelling through New England, New York, and Pennsylvania, early in November the pilgrims reached the foot of the mountain ranges, and commenced the ascent of those rocky barriers which divide the sources of the Susquehanna river from those which fall into the Ohio.

The evening after they left Carlisle, they were overtaken by an old acquaintance and neighbor, who was also with his family on his way to Muskingum. He had started about the same time with the others, with an ox team of three yokes, and by dint of steady and late driving, had managed to keep within a day's march of them, and here, by making a little extra exertion, he overtook them. Ox teams were preferred to horses by many of the early New England emigrants, in their long journeys to the new purchase. Probably one reason for this was their greater familiarity with their use as beasts of draught; another, that they were much better suited to work among stumps and logs, and were also much less likely to be stolen by the Indians. Their rate of travel was a little slower than that of the horse, but they could make about twenty miles a day where the roads were good.

The roads at that day, across the mountains, were the worst that we can imagine, cut into deep gullies on one side by mountain rains, while the other was filled with blocks of sandstone. The descents were abrupt, and often resembled the breaks in a flight of stone stairs, whose lofty steps were built for the children of Titan rather than the sons of men. As few of the emigrant wagons were provided with lock-chains for the wheels, the downward impetus was checked by a large log, or broken tree top, tied with a rope to the back of the wagon and dragged along on the ground. In other places, the road was so sideling that all the men who could be spared were required to pull at the side stays, or short ropes attached to

9*

the upper side of the wagons, to prevent their upsetting. By divid
ing their forces with Isaac, they made out to prevent any serious
accidents of this kind, although it seemed many times impossible to
prevent it. The ground, naturally moist and springy on the sides
of the mountains, was now rendered very muddy and wet by the
November rains, which had begun to fall almost daily. As they
approached the middle and higher ranges, the rain was changed to
snow and sleet, which added still more to the difficulties and dreariness of the way. From the weight of the loaded wagons and the
abrupt acclivities of the road, it fell to the lot of the women and
children to walk up all the steep ascents—it being beyond the power
of the horses to pull their additional weight up many of the sharp
pitches of the mountains. The children often stuck by the way, or
lost their shoes in the mud, occasioning a world of trouble to the
elder girls, to whose share it fell to look after the welfare of the little
ones.

After crossing the "Blue mountain," the "Middle," and the
"Tuscarora mountain," late one Saturday evening they descended into
the "Ahwick valley," and Mr. Rouse's family put up at the house
of an honest German Dunkard, named Christian Hiples ; while the
other two teams went to an old tavern stand, well known to the
early pack-horsemen and borderers of that region. This was a quiet
and tolerably fertile valley, environed by mountains. In it was
seated old "Fort Littleton," and under the protection of its walls
had sprung up, many years ago, quite a thriving settlement, with a
number of fine plantations. All this part of the country, and as far
east as Carlisle, had been, about twenty-five years before, depopu
lated by the depredations of the Indians. Many of the present
inhabitants well remembered those days of trial, and could not see
these helpless women and children moving so far away into the
wilderness as Ohio, without expressing their fears at the danger
they would incur from the deadly hate of the Indians.

They tarried over the Sabbath, and the following Monday, under
the hospitable roof of this Christian Dunkard—whose long white
beard, reaching to the waist, greatly excited the curiosity of the

children. His family consisted of several young women, who treated
the wayfaring females with great kindness; heating their huge out-
of-door oven for them, and assisting them in the baking of a
large batch of bread for the journey, with many other acts of true
Christian charity.   On Tuesday morning, when they departed, they
loaded them with potatoes and vegetables from their garden, as
many as they would venture to carry, without making any charge.
They parted from them with many prayers and good wishes
for their welfare on the road, and the happy termination of
their long and perilous journey.   The inhabitants generally treated
them kindly, and the further they advanced into the confines
of the wilderness, and left the older settlements, the more hospitality
abounded.   They received them more readily into their houses, and
more willingly assisted them with their cooking utensils, or any
other thing they possessed, or the wayfarers needed.

While the travellers in Rouse's wagon were treated so kindly,
Isaac, who was excitable and very headstrong, met with rather
rough usage from the hand of the old inn-keeper with whom
he put up. This man had been a great bruiser in his younger days,
and had lost one eye in some of these frays; a thing not at all uncommon among the early borderers. He was naturally a rough
man, and the loss of his eye added still more to his ferocious
appearance. It seems that he had placed the rounds of the rack, in
his stable, so close together it was next to impossible for the horses
to pull any of the hay through, so that, although there was
plenty before them, they were none the better for it. Isaac could
not stand quietly by and say nothing, when his hard-working
horses needed their food so much; and then to pay for that they
did not eat besides! He remonstrated with the landlord on
the matter, but received only abuse for his pains. After pay-
ing back a little of the same coin, he fell to work and broke
out every other round. The old fellow then fell upon Isaac,
determined to give him a sound beating; but in this he was sadly
mistaken, and got very roughly handled himself. The horses, however, got plenty of hay, and Isaac told him he should be back

again in the spring, and if he found the slats replaced, he would give him another and still sounder thrashing.

Three days after leaving the quiet valley, with much exertion and many narrow escapes from oversetting, they reached the little village of Bedford. During this period they had crossed " Sideling hill," forded some of the main branches of the Juniata, and threaded the narrow valleys along its borders. Every few miles, long strings of pack-horses met them on the road, bearing heavy burthens of peltry and ginseng, the two main articles of export from the regions west of the mountains. Others overtook them loaded with kegs of spirits, salt, and bales of dry goods, on their way to the traders in Pittsburgh. The fore-horse generally carried a small bell, which distinguished him as the leader. One man had the charge of ten horses, which was as many as he could manage by day, and look after at night. For many years this was the manner in which nearly all the transportation was done over the mountains. The roads were nearly impassable for wagons till near the close of the Indian war, in 1795.

One of their greatest trials was in crossing the Alleghanies. Four miles beyond Bedford, the road to the right was called the " Pittsburg road," while that to the left was called the " Glade road," and led to Simrel's ferry, on the Yohiogany river. This was the route of the emigrants, and led, as well as the other, across the Alleghany. In passing this formidable barrier, our travellers were belated ; and it was nearly midnight before they reached the house where they were to lodge. The night was excessively dark; the whole party, except the younger children, were on foot, and could only keep the path by feeling the bushes along the sides of the road. It so happened that Michael Rouse and Capt. Haskell, who was their only guide, had gone ahead with the other wagon, and was entirely beyond hail ; leaving Isaac, with Mr. Rouse and all the females, to pick their way along the miry road in the best manner they could. In the midst of all this gloom, the spirits of the former never flagged in the least ; but the more difficulties increased the louder he sang, and some of his most cheerful ditties were echoed that night from the rocky side of the Alleghany. Mr. Rouse, who had been often exposed to winds and storms, could not stand the trudging along, ancle deep, in the mud and dark, without venting his feelings in many a hearty curse on the vexations of the night. When about a mile from the house, they were unexpectedly cheered at hearing the lively whistle of Michael; and directly after, in a turn of the road, espied the light of a lantern brought by Capt. Haskell, who had returned after putting up his own team, to meet the stragglers and guide them on the way. A bright fire was blazing on the hearth of the little log inn, the warmth and sparkling of which soon restored their spirits. It was past midnight before they had cooked and eaten their suppers and spread their couches on the puncheon floor of the hut. The fatigues of the journey caused them to sleep very soundly, and they awoke the next morning with fresh courage to meet the trials of the day before them.

In descending the Alleghany, the children and girls were much delighted at seeing the side of the road covered with the vivid green leaves and bright scarlet berries of the "partridge bush," or " checkerberry." It was a common fruit at " The Longplain," and the sight of it reminded them of their home and the scenes they had left. For a while the little boys forgot the fatigues of the road at the sight of this favorite fruit, and cheered each other with joyous shouts, as fresh patches from time to time appeared by the side of the way. Even the married females were exhilarated by the cheerful spirits exhibited by the children, and partook freely of the spicy fruit which they collected in large handfuls. As they descended the western slope of the mountains, the springs of limpid water, which gushed fresh and pure from the earth along its sides, now ran babbling along to join their puny rills with those of the Ohio. This range is the dividing ridge between the eastern and the western streams, and the travellers could now see the waters which flowed towards the end of their journey.

After reaching the foot of this picturesque range, they had to cross a region called " The Glades," an elevated plateau, which, in many points, bore a strong resemblance to the prairies of the west. The soil was dark colored, thinly coated with trees, and covered with coarse grass. In crossing "Laurel ridge," which bounds the western side of the glades, and is so named from the profusion of rhododendron, or rosebay, and kalmia latifolia, or laurel, which cluster along its rocky sides, the girls and older boys had to walk the whole distance. The labor was the more difficult from the ground being covered with snow, which had fallen to the depth of several inches on the sides and top of the ridge, during the last twenty-four hours; while at the same time it had been raining in the valley, or table land, between the ranges. The bushes were bent down by the weight of the snow, and partly obstructed the path; so that long before they got over, their shoes were saturated with water, and their clothes were dribbled and wet half leg high. The "boxberries" still showed their bright scarlet faces, peeping out beneath the snow and ice, as large as common red cherries. At the western foot of the ridge, their road was crossed by a stream too deep for them to ford; and the girls being several miles ahead of the wagons, whose progress was very slow, were much rejoiced to find a cabin in which they could rest until the teams came up. The rendezvous for the night was beyond the creek, as this was the only place where they could get feed for their horses. While waiting at this spot, a stout young mountaineer, clad in his hunting-frock and leggins, came dashing along on a powerful horse, and very kindly, as well as gallantly, offered to take the girls over the stream, if they would trust themselves behind him on the horse, and conduct them safely to the house where they were to stop. But his uncouth dress and their own natural timidity made them decline the offer, choosing rather to wait the arrival of their friends. Just at dark they came up, and taking them into the wagons, they crossed the stream more to their own liking, if not more safely than under the charge of the young mountaineer.

The following day they crossed "Chesnut ridge," the last of the mountain ranges, so named from the immense forests of chesnut trees that clothe its sides and summit, for nearly the whole of its extent in Pennsylvania and part of Virginia. The soil is sandy and rocky; and so exactly adapted to the growth of this tree, that no part of the world produces it more abundantly. In fruitful years, the hogs, from a distance of twenty or thirty miles, were driven by the inhabitants, every autumn, to fatten on its fruit. Bears, wild turkeys, elk and deer, travelled from afar to this nut-producing region, and luxuriated on its bountiful crop. The congregations of wild animals, on this favored tract, made it one of the most celebrated hunting grounds, not only for the Indians, but also for the white man who succeeded him in the possession of these mountain regions. The children here loaded their little pockets with chesnuts, and for a while forgot the pinching cold of the half frozen leaves and frost covered burrs among which they were scattered. Not long after crossing this ridge they reached Simrel's ferry, on the Yohiogany river. They hailed this spot with delight, as they were to travel no further in their wagons, but finish the journey by water. They were also glad on another account; two of the horses had been failing for some days, were now near giving out, and in fact died before reaching Buffalo, a small village on the Ohio river.

It was now near the last of November, and winter fast approaching. In a short time a boat was procured, as they were kept ready made for the use of emigrants. The one they bought was about forty feet long and twelve feet wide, but without any roof, as they could not wait for it to be finished. On board of this they put their wagons, and contrived to make a temporary shelter with their linen covers. The horses were sent by land across the country to Buffalo, at the mouth of Buffalo creek, distant by this route only fifty-three miles from the ferry, but more than a hundred by water. This was a common practice with the early emigrants, as the water of the Yohiogany was too shallow in autumn to float a boat drawing over eighteen or twenty inches. In the stern of the boat was a rude fire-place for cooking, and their beds were spread on the floor of the ark.

After laying in a stock of food, they pushed merrily out into the current of the " Yoh," as it was familiarly called by the borderers of that region, and floated rapidly along, sometimes grazing on the shallows, and at others grounding on the sandbars. By dint of rowing and pushing they made out to get on; especially after falling into the larger current of the Monongahela, and reached Pittsburgh in safety on Sunday evening. They were now at the junction of these two noble streams, the Alleghany and Monongahela, and saw the waters of the charming Ohio, the object of all their toils and were, apparently, at the end of their journey. Near the point of land where the Ohio first takes its name, they landed their uncouth and unwieldy water-craft, making it fast to a stake on the bank. It was late in the afternoon, and the men went up into the town to purchase some articles needed to make the families comfortable in their downward voyage. Pittsburg then contained four or five hundred inhabitants, and several retail stores, and a small garrison of troops was kept up in Old Fort Pitt. To our travellers, who had lately seen nothing but trees and rocks, with here and there a solitary hut, it seemed to be quite a large town. The houses were chiefly built of logs, but now and then one had begun to assume the appearance of neatness and comfort.

Capt. Haskell and Mr. Rouse, for some cause now forgotten, did not return to lodge in the boat, but stayed at the tavern ; Michael, Isaac, and Cushing had gone overland with the horses, so that the women and children were left alone in the boat. In the middle of the night, one of the older boys was awakened by the water coming into his bed on the floor. He immediately raised an outcry, and in the midst of the darkness, bustle, and confusion of the moment, they found the boat was half leg deep in the water. Great was the consternation of the older females, who thought, not without reason, that they must all be drowned. It so happened that the water was not very deep where the boat was moored, and as the gunwales rested on the bottom at the depth of two or three feet, it could sink no further. This disaster was occasioned by the falling of the river during the night ; the land side of the boat rested on the shore, while the outer corner settled in the stream until the water ran through the seams in the planking above the gunwale—they being badly caulked. They hurried on shore as fast as they could. A kind-hearted man, by the name of Kilbreath, whose house stood on the bank near the boat, heard the screams of the children, and taking a light came to their assistance. He invited them all up to his house and provided them lodging by a good warm fire; he then called some men to his aid, and before morning, got the wet articles out of the boat, and assisted the females in drying them. When Mr. Rouse and Capt. Haskell came back in the morning, they were much chagrined at the accident; as had they been on board, they thought it could have been prevented. The next morning Mr. Kilbreath gave them all a nice warm breakfast, and like the good Samaritan, would take nothing but their grateful thanks for his trouble. Having baled out the boat and got her once more afloat, they reloaded their household goods, got on board a stock of provisions, and prepared to renew their voyage in the course of the day.

It so happened that there was an old trapper and hunter by the name of Bruce, who was familiar with the river, just ready to start down stream in a large canoe, or pereauger, on a trapping expedition for the winter, on some of the more southern waters; him they engaged for a pilot, as was the custom in those early days, although there was but little or no danger from the intricacy of the channel. His canoe was about forty feet long, and had on board a barrel of flour, some fat bacon, four beaver traps, a camp kettle, two tin cups, and a light axe. These, with his rifle, blanket, and ammunition, formed his stock for the winter. The canoe was lashed alongside the boat, and he came on board as pilot.

It was near the middle of the afternoon, on Monday, when they put out from Pittsburgh. The day had been cloudy and threatened rain from the south. Just at evening the wind shifted to the northwest and blew quartering across the bend of the river in which they were then floating. It soon rose to a complete gale, and knocked up such a sea, as threw the crests of the waves over the side of the boat, threatening to upset, if not sink, the unwieldy craft. In this dilemma, the pilot and all hands exerted their utmost at the oars, to bring the boat to land on the "Federal," or Pennsylvania shore ; but the wind and the waves were both adverse. The boat could have been landed on the right, or "Indian shore," but they feared to do so, lest in the night they should fall into the hands of the Indians, who although it was apparently a time of peace, robbed the boats and killed the straggling whites at every favorable opportunity. The large pereauger bounded and thumped against the side of the boat, threatening to break in the planks, and was cut loose by the hand of the pilot. In this extremity, when every fresh wave threatened to overwhelm them, Bruce cried out to his shipmates, in a voice that was easily heard above the storm, "We must put over to the Indian shore, or every man, woman and child will be lost!" Previous to this, the more feeble portion of the passengers had kept tolerably quiet, although exceedingly alarmed ; but this announcement, to the women and children, sounded like their death knell, and the boat instantly resounded with their screams of despair. Capt. Haskell, who had been accustomed to perils of various kinds, and was a man of iron nerves, did what he could to calm their terrors. Bruce, who was in fact a skilful pilot, as well as a brave man, instantly laid the bow of the boat over to the Indian shore. The wind and the waves both favored the movement, and with a little aid from the oars in a few minutes she was riding in safety under a high point of land, which sheltered them from the wind in comparatively quiet water.

The sudden transition from the jaws of death to this tranquil haven, filled the hearts of the females with songs of gratitude ; and the boat was hardly moored to the bank before they sprung upon the land, rejoiced once more to tread the solid earth, although it was the dreaded Indian shore. Bruce soon kindled a fire by the side of a large fallen tree, and setting up some forked sticks and poles, stretched some blankets across, in such a way as to make a rude tent. Beneath this shelter they spread their beds, choosing rather to risk the chance of an attack from Indians than to trust themselves on the water again that night. From the hunting camp of some white men, whose smoke the pilot had noticed just before the storm came on, he procured a fine fat saddle of venison, and the whole party feasted with cheerful hearts that evening on the nice steaks of this delicious meat. Some they broiled on the coals, while Bruce showed them how to roast it, hunter fashion, on a hickory skewer filled full of pieces and stuck up in the earth before the fire ; this, with a cup of hot coffee, furnished a very comfortable meal. They slept undisturbed that night ; though ever and anon, the sighing of the winds in the tops of the trees led the more timid of the females to fancy they heard the stealthy approach of Indians.

In the morning, the ground was covered with snow to the depth of several inches, which had fallen while they were asleep. The day following the storm was fine and pleasant, and the smooth, calm surface of the Ohio exhibited a striking contrast to the tumult and uproar which had agitated its bosom only a few hours before. From Fort McIntosh, at the mouth of the Beaver, to the new settlement at Muskingum, no white man had dared to plant himself on the Indian shore of the river, with the exception of a small blockhouse a few miles below Buffalo, which some hunters had built as a place to which they might retreat if attacked by their enemies, while out hunting in the region west of the river. Even here there was little or no clearing, and all else was unbroken wilderness. They embarked early in the morning and reached Buffalo that evening. In the course of the forenoon they found the pereauger of Bruce lodged on the shore and filled with water. It still contained the barrel of flour, meat, axe, etc., with all the traps but one. The buoyancy of the light poplar wood of which it was made, prevented it from sinking, and the ballast of the traps, axe, etc., from upsetting ; so that, quite unexpectedly, the old trapper recovered his boat and goods, which he had given up as utterly lost. At Buffalo, they were greeted with the loud laugh and boisterous welcome of Isaac, who, with Michael and Shaw, had been waiting one or two days with the horses for their arrival.

The women and children, still impressed with dread lest another storm should overtake them, concluded to lodge on shore, and accordingly took quarters for the night on the floor of a small log hut that stood at the extremity of the point of land at the mouth of Buffalo creek. In the morning Mrs. Devoll came near losing a part of her bedding. A gaily ornamented new woollen blanket had attracted the attention of Mrs. Riley, the mistress of the cabin, as it lay spread over the sleepers in the night, and in the hurry and bustle of rolling up the bed clothes, she adroitly managed to secrete it among her own bedding, stowed away in the corner of the room. Mrs. Devoll soon missed it, and after a careful but fruitless search among her own things, did not hesitate to accuse the woman of secreting it. She roundly denied any knowledge of the blanket. Being a resolute woman, and determined not to give it up in this way, Mrs. Devoll made an overhauling of Mrs. Riley's chattels, when much to the chagrin and disappointment of the border woman, she pulled out the lost article, rolled up in her dingy bedding. Thinking they had recovered all the missing goods, they hurried aboard their boat at the exciting call of Isaac, who was ready to depart, and in no very good humor with the hospitality of Mrs. Riley At Wheeling, where they stopped for some milk, they discovered, much to their vexation, that they had also lost a new two-quart measure, which they had brought all the way with them for the purpose of measuring the milk they should need to purchase on the road. In a few years after this adventure, during the Indian war, this family of Rileys, who still lived in the same spot, were all massacred by the savages.

At Grave creek they took on board a stout, hearty old man, as a passenger, by the name of Green. He assisted Bruce and their crew, each by taking turns at the oars and rowing all night, and with the music of Isaac and the old man, who proved an excellent singer, they made out to reach the mouth of Muskingum just at dark on Thursday evening, the fourth day after leaving Pittsburg. Ice had been making in the Ohio for the last twenty-four hours, and the travellers were fortunate in arriving as they did, for the following morning the Muskingum river was frozen over from shore to shore. Great was the consternation of Mrs. Rouse, who had an instinctive dread of Indians, at seeing the woods and side hill, back of Fort Harmer lighted up with a multitude of fires, when she was told that they were the camp fires of three hundred savages. They had come in to a treaty, which was held the ninth of January following. It was early in December, and the emigrants had been more than eight weeks on the road. The news of their arrival was soon carried to Campus Martius, the name of the new garrison. Capt. Devoll hurried on board, delighted once more to embrace his wife and children, from whom he had been absent more than a year. Their goods and chattels were put into the " Mayflower," which was used as a receiving boat for the emigrants, and with the women and children, landed at the Ohio company's wharf. Devoll had built a comfortable two-story house in one of the curtains of the garrison, to which all were removed that night, and his happy family slept once more under their own roof, in the far distant region of the Northwest Territory.

The following spring, a company or association was formed to commence the settlement fourteen miles below, on the right bank of the Ohio, afterwards called Belprie. Capt. Devoll, Mr. Rouse, Michael, Capt. Haskell and Isaac, joined this association. The latter returned to New England, and moved out his family in the fall of 1789. By the time the settlers were about to begin to reap a little of the fruits of their hard labor, in clearing land, building cabins, etc., the Indian war broke out, and they were all driven into garrison for some five years. Many were the dangers and hardships they here endured, suffering most from the small pox and scarlatina maligna.

In the summer of 1790, Bathsheba Rouse taught a school of young boys and girls at Belprie, which is believed to be the first school of white children ever assembled within the bounds of the present State of Ohio. The Moravian missionaries had Indian schools at Gnadenhutten and Schönbrunn, on the Tuscarawas, as early as the year 1779, eleven years before this time. She also taught for several successive summers within the walls of " Farmer's Castle," the name of the stout garrison built by the settlers sixteen miles below Marietta. After the close of the war the colonists moved out upon their farms. Mr. Rouse and his family remained in Belprie. Bathsheba married, soon after the close of the war, Richard, the son of Griffen Greene, one of the Ohio company's agents, and a leading man in all public affairs. Cynthia married the Hon. Paul Fearing, the first delegate to Congress from the Northwest Territory, and for many years a judge of the court. Elizabeth married Levi Barber, for many years receiver of public moneys, and member of Congress for this district during two sessions. The children of these emigrant females, for wealth and respectability, rank among the first of our citizens.

Thus closes this sketch of the early emigrants to Muskingum, whose adventures are only the counterpart of other families who crossed the Alleghany ranges in the year 1788. It is in fact a portion of the early history of Ohio, and should be preserved for the same reasons that Virgil has preserved the incidents of the voyage of Æneas from Troy to Italy—they were the founders of a new state. Those days of hardship cannot be reviewed with other than feelings of the highest respect for the individuals who dared to brave the difficulties and uncertainties of a pioneer life.*

* The foregoing memoir is much shortened from the original one by Dr Hildreth.

XII.

SARAH WHIPPLE SIBLEY.

SARAH W. SPROAT was born in Providence, Rhode Island, on the 28th of January, 1782. She was the only child of Col. Ebenezer Sproat, a gallant and accomplished officer of the Revolution, and the granddaughter of Commodore Abraham Whipple, who also repeatedly distinguished himself during that war by his activity and bravery. At the commencement of the struggle, Commodore Whipple was wealthy, but had impoverished himself by his advances to Government in fitting out vessels and men for the public service, for which he was never remunerated, and at its close he found he could no longer sustain the style of living befitting his position in society, and to which he was accustomed. His son-in-law, Col. Sproat, was in the same situation, and both being too proud and high-spirited to conform patiently to their change of circumstances, they determined to join a party of their companions-in-arms, who were about to seek a new home in the yet unexplored wilderness of the West.

They were of the advance party who landed in 1788 at the mouth of the Muskingum, and commenced the settlement of Marietta. Burnet says in his notes—"The early adventurers to the Northwestern Territory were generally men who had spent the prime of their lives in the war of Independence. Many of them had exhausted their fortunes in maintaining the desperate struggle, and

retired to tne wilderness to conceal their poverty, and avoid compari-
sons mortifying to their pride, while struggling to maintain their
families and improve their condition. Some were young men descended from Revolutionary patriots who had fallen in the contest, or
became too feeble to endure the fatigue of settling a wilderness.
Others were adventurous spirits, to whom any change might be for
the better."

The following year the new settlers were joined by their families.
It is difficult now to conceive the extent of the difficulties against
which these pioneers had to contend, besides the dangers that surrounded them. So great was the difficulty of transportation that
they were only able to bring the most simple necessaries of life with
them. After their cabins were built, some of them were for months
without other doors than blankets, and with no furniture but the
boxes and trunks they had brought, which were converted into seats,
beds, and tables as the occasion required; and just as they were becoming comfortable in their new homes, the fearful Indian war
broke out, and every day brought fresh accounts of horrible murders
committed in the immediate vicinity, almost at their doors. Col.
Sproat determined to remove his daughter to a place of safety, where
she might at the same time receive the necessary instruction which
during the existing disturbances she could not enjoy at home.

The Moravian school at Bethlehem then bore a high reputation,
and in 1792, when Miss Sproat was but ten years old, she accompanied her father over the mountains to Bethlehem, most of the way
on horseback; a journey that would be thought formidable at the
present day. She remained there three years, and then went to
Philadelphia to receive lessons in some accomplishments which she
had no opportunities for acquiring in Bethlehem. She resided while
in that city in the family of a friend of her father's, and became
strongly attached to its members. She made many warm friends
in Philadelphia, and left it with regret. But her father had become
impatient for her return, and went for her in the spring of 1797.
He at that time purchased a piano for her in Philadelphia, the first
taken west of the Alleghany mountains.

On her return, she found Marietta much changed and improved the inhabitants were no longer in fear of Indian incursions, and many new settlers had been added to their number. It had become quite a town, with a very pleasant society, and the danger they had shared in common had tended to strengthen the bond which already united the early colonists.

The years intervening between Miss Sproat's return and her marriage, passed away swiftly and happily. Being the only child, she was of course much caressed by her parents, and her natural gaiety and affectionate, generous disposition made her a favorite with her young friends. Her father had taken great pains to make her an accomplished horsewoman, and she was the constant companion of his rides. To this habit of exercise she was indebted for the ease with which she made the long and fatiguing journeys she was compelled to take in after life.

After the establishment of the Northwest Territorial Government the General Court had its sessions alternately at Cincinnati, Detroit, and Marietta. Mr. Sibley was a young lawyer of high standing, who had removed from Massachusetts to Ohio in 1797, and soon afterwards to Detroit. Judge Burnet says of him—"He possessed a sound mind, improved by a liberal education, and a stability and firmness of character which commanded general respect, and secured to him the confidence and esteem of his fellow members." He constantly attended the sessions of the Court, and was of course frequently in Marietta. It was there that he first became acquainted with Miss Sproat. They were married in October, 1802, but she did not go to Detroit until the following spring.

The way to Detroit at that time was by the Ohio river to Pittsburg, across to Erie, and thence by water to Detroit; the least fatiguing but a very tedious route. Being entirely at the mercy of wind and weather, travellers were often ten days crossing the lake, and in one instance a family was detained three weeks between Erie and the city of the straits.

Mrs. Sibley was warmly welcomed on her arrival by her husband's friends, and so kindly treated that she soon felt at home. The

10

society was delightful at that time. The fort was strongly garrisoned, and most of the officers were Southerners, possessing the warmth and ease of manner peculiar to the South. The inhabitants of the town and its vicinity were principally French. Some of these were descendants of noble families in France, and prided themselves upon their superior polish and refinement. For about six months in the year all communication with the rest of the world was cut off by ice and snow. At these seasons the people seemed determined to make up for their isolation by increased sociability among themselves, and every one kept open house. Some very agreeable persons resided on the opposite side of the river, families of British merchants who had formerly lived in Detroit, but on its cession to the Americans had removed to Canada. A constant intercourse had always been kept up, and they joined in all the gaieties of the place.

In August, 1804, Col. Sproat came to Detroit to take his daughter home to visit her mother. As public business required Mr. Sibley's attendance at Washington during the winter, it was arranged that Mrs. Sibley should return with her father to Marietta, and remain until the following spring. Their journey was made on horseback. The whole of the northern part of Ohio was at that time a dense wilderness, and travellers were obliged to camp out at night. Mrs. Sibley often spoke of an incident which occurred on this journey. The horse she rode was one which Col. Sproat had brought on expressly for his daughter's use, and was a great favorite. He was unfortunately taken sick on the way, and with difficulty they reached a spot suitable to encamp for the night. Everything possible was done for the relief of the poor animal, but all was in vain, and it was most distressing to hear his groans of agony. The woods around seemed to be swarming with wolves attracted by the cries of the horse, and they yelled and howled like so many demons. The fires around the camp were all that prevented them from rushing upon its inmates. Mrs. Sibley said she never spent such a fearful night. The poor horse died towards morning, and they left him with regret. Their journey was a long and fatiguing one, but they arrived in safety at Marietta.

It was providentially ordered that Mrs. Sibley should spend that winter at home, for she was thus enabled to cheer her father's last days by her presence. In February, without any previous warning, he was attacked by apoplexy, and died immediately. He was yet in the prime of life, being only fifty years old, and was generally regretted. His death was a heavy affliction to his daughter, for the tie had been unusually strong that existed between them; inheriting many of his traits of character, she had been his companion and had shared with him many daring adventures. He had almost idolized her, and she was equally devoted to him. Col. Sproat had many warm friends among his brother officers. The family still have in their possession a miniature of him painted by Kosciusko. They were intimate friends, and it was taken while they were together in winter-quarters during the Revolution. Burr, on his first visit to Ohio, is said to have shed tears over the grave of his old fellow-soldier.

Mrs. Sibley remained with her mother until the following summer, her husband having in the mean time returned from Washington to Detroit. In June, 1805, that city was entirely destroyed by fire. An extract from a letter written at that time by Mr. Sibley to his wife, will give an idea of the loss of property and the suffering that ensued. "June 16,—We are all, without a single exception, unhoused. The town of Detroit was on the 11th inst. in the course of three hours reduced to ashes. You can readily conceive the consternation and consequent confusion that prevailed. Much personal property, household furniture and merchandize fell a sacrifice to the devouring element. I had, from my situation, the good fortune to save our property from the fire, but from the bustle that prevailed, and the thefts committed, I have suffered considerably. We have been exerting ourselves since the fire to relieve the distressed. They are numerous, and demand every exertion we can make in their favor. The houses up and down the settlement are full, and for want of room many families still remain encamped in the open air.   The gentlemen from the other side have been liberal in furnishing provisions, which are still much wanted.

" My own loss, as compared with that of the citizens in general, is so trifling that I have scarcely thought seriously upon the subject.   The want of a house, added to the entire suspension of business, is the greatest inconvenience I experience.   I believe the present scene presents a phenomenon rarely to be met with ; a whole town burned with the exception of a single dwelling-house standing.   What measures will be adopted in rebuilding Detroit it is yet uncertain. A number of us are exerting ourselves in order that we may procure more room by widening the streets.   A meeting will be held at Mr. May's to-morrow, when the subject will be discussed ; the result will be uncertain.   What a gloomy prospect for our Governor, etc., when they arrive ! Not a single house for his reception or accommodation.   Our country was sufficiently poor before the late disaster— what will become of a number of poor persons I know not, unless some benevolent aid is offered from abroad.   This last resource appears doubtful.   We are not known in the States, therefore we have but little expectation that they will interest themselves for our relief."

Mr. Sibley fitted up an old house which was then considered quite a distance from town, a large open common intervening ; situated on the square opposite " the Biddle House," now in the very heart of the city.   He occupied the same house until 1835, a period of thirty years.   As soon as it was rendered comfortable he went to Marietta for his wife.   Michigan had only lately been organized into a territory, and upon the arrival of the newly appointed governor, Gen. Hull, Detroit was a perfect scene of desolation.   He was obliged to build a house immediately, for there was not one for him to live in.   The house he erected was considered a splendid one at that time, and was the same afterwards known as the American Hotel, which was burned in the fire of 1848.   On Mrs. Sibley's return, she again travelled on horseback, but only as far as Sandusky, from which place they came in a vessel.

But few events worthy of note occurred during the interval between her return and the war of 1812. She was then the mother of three children, and for their sake, even more than for her own, looked forward with dread to the prospect of another war. The events of that war, as connected with Detroit, are too well known to require a repetition here. Although exposed to so much danger, Mrs. Sibley remained with her husband, and in all the trials and horrors of that eventful time, bore herself most courageously.

At the time an attack upon the town was expected, it was thought advisable to place the women and children for greater security within the fort. During the terrible day of the cannonade, Mrs. Sibley said that not one woman gave way to fear ; that she never saw so much courage displayed. All seemed nerved by the exigencies of the time, and by the very danger to which they were exposed. They busied themselves in giving the only assistance in their power, making cartridges, and scraping lint for the wounded. Some dreadful scenes occurred on that day. In the room adjoining that in which the ladies were collected, four officers were shot by one ball. One of these was Mr. Sibley's cousin. When the news was announced of the surrender, the feeling of regret and indignation expressed was intense. They were all prepared for danger, but not for disgrace. As the American soldiers were marched out of the fort, Mrs. Dyson, the wife of an officer, collected all the clothing under the charge of the commissary, and threw it out of a window to the soldiers as they passed by, declaring that the British should not benefit by it.

After the surrender, Mr. Sibley applied to Gen. Proctor for permission to go on with his family to Ohio. It was denied at first, but afterwards granted, giving him only two days to make his preparations. Thus hastily they left their home, to remain until happier times. The vessel in which they embarked was a very small one, and exceedingly crowded, but there was no alternative ; and with heavy hearts they sailed for Erie. They remained with Mrs. Sibley's friends a year. As soon as Detroit was given up to the Americans they started on their return, but when they reached Cleveland found that it was rather late in the season, the few vessels then on the lake being laid up for the winter; and as it was impossible to go by land with a family of children they were obliged to remain there all winter. Cleveland was then but a small settlement, and separated by a dense wilderness from the southern towns of Ohio. During the time the lake was closed, the transportation of all articles was attended with great difficulty and expense, consequently every thing was enormously high. Mr. Sibley had expected to reach home before the winter, and was little prepared for such a detention. He had lost greatly by the war, and the utter cessation of all business for such a length of time with one who depended upon his profession for the support of his family, had so crippled his means that his inability to proceed homeward was excessively inconvenient to him. The family was treated with much kindness, but had to submit to great privation and discomfort, and they were heartily glad when the return of spring allowed them to return to Detroit.

Mrs. Sibley made but one more visit to Ohio, and that was in 1819. She then received intelligence of the deaths, within a short time of each other, of her aged grandparents, the venerable old Commodore and Mrs. Whipple. Mrs. Sproat being thus left entirely alone, as she had no other relatives in the west, she wrote to her daughter that if she could come for her she would return with her to Michigan.

Mrs. Sibley did not hesitate, but leaving her family under the charge of a faithful servant, set out on her journey. She went under the care of a gentleman from Detroit, and to save fatigue went as far as Sandusky in the new steamboat, "Walk in the Water," the first steamboat that ever ran on Lake Erie.

They sent their horses by a servant to meet them at Sandusky. This journey to Marietta was the last ever taken by Mrs. Sibley on horseback. She remained in Ohio only long enough to complete the preparations for Mrs. Sproat's removal. They returned by stage, as Mrs. Sproat was too old to undertake the journey on horseback. Mrs. Sproat remained with her daughter until her death, which took place in 1832.

The most eventful part of Mrs. Sibley's life was now past. Henceforth her time was principally occupied with the duties incumbent upon a wife and mother, and these were well and faithfully performed. A large family grew up around her, in whose minds it was ever her constant endeavor to instil such high principles as should make them true to themselves and useful members of society. To her most truly could the scriptural passage be applied, "Her children shall rise up and call her blessed."

It is difficult to convey an adequate idea of the actual condition of this portion of the great Mississippi valley in its transition state, or the important part in the formation of its daily life that fell to the lot of a pioneer matron. Of all these, there was not one better fitted by nature and education for the time and place than this noble woman. Blessed with a commanding person, a vigorous and cultivated intellect, undaunted courage, and an intuitive and clear perception of right and wrong, she exercised great influence upon the society in which she lived. Affectionate in disposition, frank in manner, and truly just as well as benevolent, she was during her whole married life the centre of an admiring circle of devoted friends. As age crept on, and disease confined her to the fireside, she still remained the object of profound and marked respect to the people of the city which had grown up around her, and when at length she was "gathered to her fathers," she died, as she had always lived, without one to cast a reproach upon her elevated and beautiful character.

A revolution like that of 1776—the surrender upon the altar of their country of the fortunes of the brave men who led the way to freedom—the poverty of the government and its consequent inability to repay these losses—the resulting necessity of making a home among the savages of a great wilderness, and reducing that wilderness to a state of law, order, and refinement; these were circumstances well fitted to develope the strong traits of character in the men and women of the great West. They cannot recur, and therefore we cannot expect again to see such a race. They have passed away, and henceforward we may expect what has always accompanied an age of refinement, the softening down of strong points of character, and in too many instances, enervation and effeminacy.

The husband of this honored lady, the Hon. Solomon Sibley, was for many years one of the judges of the Supreme Court of the territory of Michigan.   He lived to be not only the last relic of the ancient bar of Michigan proper, dating back to 1798, but also the last remaining link connecting the profession in that State of the present day with that of the Northwest Territory, of which he was a member previous to his removal to Detroit.

He was a native of Massachusetts, and was admitted to the bar in Virginia.   In 1797, he practised law with his friend Judge Burnet, of Cincinnati.   In 1799, having removed to Detroit, he was elected to the first territorial legislature of the Northwest Territory as representative for the county of Wayne, which then embraced the present State of Michigan.   This body held its sessions in Cincinnati.   In the records of the Historical Society of Ohio, Judge Sibley is mentioned as " among the most talented men of the House."   That he was held in the highest estimation by his fellow-citizens, is evinced by the fact, that as early as 1802 the electors of the town of Detroit voted him the freedom of the corporation " for his eminent services in behalf of the people of the territory."

In the uniform, quiet, and unostentatious devotion of his time and talents to the interests of his country, Judge Sibley continued to receive marked evidences of universal respect and confidence, till compelled by physical infirmity to retire from public life.   In his public relation of United States Commissioner—associated with Gen. Cass to negotiate the treaty by which the Indian title to a large part of the peninsula of Michigan was extinguished; as delegate representing the territory of Michigan in Congress; as District Attorney of the United States, and as Judge of the Supreme Court of Michigan, he won, as he well merited, the affection, respect and entire confidence of his contemporaries and associates.   All who were acquainted with him in private life cherished the highest respect and veneration for the character he had so justly acquired and sustained during a long and well spent life. In all private relations, he showed himself amiable, pure, and true to the various interests confided to him; in public ones, faithful, upright, and honorable; a sound and able lawyer, an impartial, honest, and discriminating judge.

For several years before his death, his health being too infirm for public duty, he gave himself up to the enjoyments of a happy home, where, surrounded by friends, he was gathered to his fathers, April 4th, 1846, aged seventy-seven. The members of the bar of Detroit, and officers of the respective courts assembled to express their regret, and esteem for his noble character, and wore mourning for the usual time.

XIII.

MARY DUNLEVY.

FEW among the pioneer mothers presented in their lives a more impressive example of the patient perseverance, courage, and energy of character which distinguished the matrons of that day, than the subject of the present brief sketch. The materials have been communicated by one of her family, whose recollections enable him to describe much of her experience in building a home in the wilderness.

Mary Craig was of Scottish parentage, and was born on the voyage from Scotland to America, about the year 1765. The family then came to settle in New York. At the commencement of the Revolutionary struggle, Mary was but ten years old, but she could understand that the people were unjustly oppressed, and her feelings were warmly interested in favor of the patriots. Her father had died soon after reaching the country, and she, with an elder sister and a younger brother, formed the little family under her mother's care. Their circumstances were comfortable, though they were not wealthy, and but for the outbreak of war, they would probably have remained together. The vicissitudes and dangers to which the inhabitants of the city were subjected by the approach of a hostile force, and the occupation of New York by British troops, caused no little alarm to Mrs Craig for the safety of herself and children ; she had few friends in the strange land, and it therefore can hardly be wondered at that, renewing acquaintance with a gentleman whom she had known in Scotland—now an officer in the British navy—she listened favorably to his addresses, and finally married him. Her husband, of course was a loyalist, and Mary had by this time become so thoroughly imbued with republican principles, that no kindness on the part of her stepfather could reconcile her to the restraints to which she was subjected in the family, in the expression of political opinions. It was not long before she left her home in the city, and went to reside at the house of Dr. Halstead, in Elizabethtown, New Jersey. This proved to be a final separation from the other members of her family. Her sister soon after married an Englishman, and went to England ; and when New York was evacuated by the British, her stepfather, with her mother, brother, and an infant half-sister, went with other refugees to Nova Scotia. Mary bore her part, meanwhile, in the apprehension and dangers to which the inhabitants of Elizabethtown were exposed during the war from the frequent incursions of the enemy. She repeatedly risked her life in endeavors to save the property of her friends from destruction, which she would do by earnest appeals to the invaders, trusting that her youth would ensure her own safety. On one occasion a sword was drawn upon her, with a threat that she should be killed if she did not leave the room ; but she persisted, and finally saved the property threatened. She was often occupied during the whole day or night in running bullets, or in attendance upon the wounded or dying. When the better time arrived, she witnessed the triumphal march of Gen. Washington on his way to New York, being one of a number of young girls who strewed the road with flowers as he passed. The disasters of a tedious war were soon forgotten in rejoicings for the establishment of liberty and peace ; but for Mary the anxious part of life's drama was but just commenced. In 1787 she was married to James Carpenter. The Northwest Territory, and especially the Miami country, was at that time much talked about, considerable excitement prevailing on the subject of emigration to the West, and Carpenter had recently returned from a visit of exploration to the Miami purchase in company with Judge Symmes and others. He was so much pleased with the new country that he determined to settle there, and Mary's inclination corresponded to his own. They left New Jersey with the first little colony of Judge Symmes, reached Limestone, now Maysville, Kentucky, late in the autumn of 1788, and the men, and a few of the stronger among the women, immediately repaired to Columbia, near the mouth of the Little Miami, five miles above the site of Cincinnati. Here they commenced building a log fort and cabins for the different families of the settlers, and laying out fields and gardens for cultivation the next spring, while the feebler members of the company remained in Kentucky during the winter.

In the spring, the fort being completed, all the settlers took up their residence at the locality selected. The families occupied the cabins built for them, but whenever there was an alarm of the approach of hostile Indians, they fled to the garrison, which was defended with all the strength of the colony, and the enemy chased away when not in large parties. Yet, notwithstanding the utmost precaution, the stealthy marauders sometimes succeeded in carrying off property and capturing prisoners, and even in killing several persons in the settlement. Mary, whose childhood had been familiar with the terrors of civil war, and whose heart was stout and resolute, was to be tried by the severest of sorrows. Carpenter's arduous labors during the first winter and spring in clearing the ground and assisting to raise the buildings, had caused a hemorrhage of the lungs, the effects of which brought on a decline, terminating in his death in less than two years. Mary was thus left with two young children, without a relative to protect her, in the midst of a wilderness, surrounded by savage foes ; but her courage and resolution did not falter under accumulated trials. She knew that her children had no dependence except on her care and labors, and trusting in the Providence whose kindness watches over the widow and the fatherless, she determined to lean, with her helpless babes, on His protection and guidance, and perform with untiring energy the duties that lay before her. She was urged to take up her residence in the fort, as she could not otherwise be safe from the frequent assaults of the savages ; but she persisted in remaining in her cabin, notwithstanding the remonstrances of her neighbors, and although her home was several hundred yards from the blockhouse. Her wounded heart preferred solitude to society ; the more so as in the promiscuous company frequently assembled in the garrison, the rough oaths of the soldiers might frequently be heard, and she resolved to risk living alone, rather than be distressed by associations repulsive to her delicate and sensitive nature. At the same time she planned the measures she would take in the event of danger, leaving the result with Him in whom her trust was placed. Beneath the puncheon floor laid in every cabin, there was generally dug a small cellar in which vegetables might be kept secure from frost. Every night she lifted one of these pieces of timber, and placed her children in a rough bed she had made in the cellar. As soon as they were asleep, the puncheon was laid down, and the mother took her position where she could see the Indians, when approaching, at a considerable distance. Here she would sit during the whole night, engaged, in the hours of wakefulness, in knitting or such housework as could be performed without any other light than from smothered embers not permitted to give out the slightest blaze. When the youngest child waked and required nursing, she would lift the puncheon, and sit on the edge of the opened floor till it was lulled to sleep, then deposit it once more in the secret bed and close the floor over it. Her resolution was taken, should the Indians attack one door, to make her escape by the opposite one to the fort, give the alarm, and bring the men to rescue her children before the foe could discover their hiding-place. Her fears were not groundless ; the Indians were often seen by her prowling about the little village, and on several occasions, when all was dark and still, they came to the door of her cabin, and attempted to enter. Finding the door barred, however, they did not, for some reason or other, attempt to force it ; so that the widow and her children remained undisturbed, while from other parts of the settlement property was stolen and prisoners taken, and one or two individuals were shot in close vicinity to the fort.

The emigrants who established themselves at Columbia, were men of energy and enterprise, and the little settlement for two or three years contained more inhabitants than any other in the Miami purchase. The second party destined for the Miami, was formed at Limestone; they landed the 24th of December, 1788, on the north bank of the Ohio, opposite the mouth of Licking river, and laid out a town, to which the name of Cincinnati was given the following year. The third party of adventurers to the purchase, under the immediate direction of Judge Symmes, established a station at 'North Bend,' the most northern bend in the Ohio below the mouth of the great Kanawha. The village has since become distinguished as the home of President Harrison, whose tomb, on one of its hills, can be seen from the river.

These three principal settlements of the Miami country had one general object, and were threatened by one common danger; yet, says Judge Burnet, there existed a strong spirit of rivalry among them, " each feeling a pride in the prosperity of the little colony to which he belonged. That spirit produced a strong influence on the feelings of the pioneers of the different villages, and an *esprit du corps* scarcely to be expected under circumstances so critical and dangerous as those which threatened them. For some time, it was matter of doubt which of the rivals, Columbia, Cincinnati, or North Bend, would eventually become the chief seat of business." The establishment of the garrison at Cincinnati, made it the head-quarters and depôt of the army. Fort Washington was the most extensive and important military work in the territory. It was said that the removal of the troops from the Bend, which was strenuously opposed by Judge Symmes, was caused by an attachment on the part of the officer in command, to a beautiful woman, whose departure to reside in Cincinnati opened the eyes of her admirer to its advantages for a military post, and thus made it the commercial emporium and the Queen City of the West.

I shall not hesitate to offer, in different memoirs, descriptions of pioneer life furnished by individuals whose recollections are entirely reliable. Although these may involve occasional repetition, they will enable us to perceive any difference of habits or manners in different parts of the country, and to appreciate more fully the spirit of enterprise and power of endurance which made the way so much easier to those who succeeded the early colonists. The densely wooded mountain ranges were a formidable barrier at that period between the old States and the new territories. The difficulties attending any communication can hardly be imagined by those who enjoy the facilities of travelling now, and made the work of the pioneer more arduous and hazardous than in more recent settlements, where the emigrant has the advantage of public conveyances, at least part of the way, and may find the necessaries of life within a distance readily accessible. It was no small undertaking to penetrate the unbroken forest, ascend or descend rivers that had never before been navigated, and carry to a home in the wilderness supplies for a household in a few chests. These usually held the clothing of the pioneer's family, while a few cooking utensils were added to the stock, and occasionally a table or bureau; though for such articles of furniture, as well as chairs and bedsteads, the settlers generally depended on the rough manufacture of the country. Shelves hewn by the axe supplied the place of bureaus and wardrobes, and two poles fastened in a corner of the cabin, the outer corner supported by a prop, answered the purpose of a bedstead, until better could be had. The pioneer's cabin was indeed a complete example of domestic economy. It was built of unhewn logs, sometimes in a single day, by the owner and eight or ten of the neighbors, who never refused their assistance. The floor was made of split slabs or puncheons, as they were called, dubbed with an adze, or where the resident was over nice, smoothed with the broad-axe on the upper side. The doors were made of boards riven from a tree of the proper length and thickness, and smoothed with a drawing-knife. The windows, in the earliest settlements, were made by cutting away the under and upper portions of two of the logs of the house, forming thus a square opening of suitable size, in which sometimes upright sticks were placed, covered with white paper, oiled with hog's fat or bear's oil, to admit the light in place of glass, a luxury not then to be procured The fire-place was usually very large, built up on three sides six or eight feet with stone, and then topped with "cat and clay," as it was termed. The cabin completed, the next thing was to clear a piece of ground for a cornpatch. A shovel-plow was generally used, as most convenient among the roots. The harness consisted mostly of leatherwood bark, except the collar, which was made of husks of corn plaited and sewed together.

Rough and uncouth in appearance as were these primitive cabins, they could be made very comfortable, and for health seemed preferable to many more civilized dwellings. One of them, sometimes containing but a single room, with a rude loft reached by a ladder, was the happy home of a numerous household; the children raised there growing up to usefulness and eminence among their fellow citizens. The children thus raised were generally of powerful frame, and possessed great physical strength; their height and proportions, it is said, being known, as a rule, to surpass those born after the erection of frame and brick dwellings. Sickness also was rare among them.

It is true that these rude habitations had some inconveniences, which might now be considered too formidable to contend with; and it may be thought strange how a female of cultivation and refinement could bring herself to live in one of them. Yet it is certain, that among the early pioneers who came to the Miami country, were some ladies of the highest consideration in New York and New Jersey; and it is no less certain that they readily and cheerfully accommodated themselves to the condition of things around them. The dressing-room and ornamental toilette were lacking; but they were dispensed with for such accommodations as necessity suggested. Each cabin usually contained two beds in the lower room, and these were separated from each other by full and flowing curtains around one at least, answering the purpose of a partition and dressing apartment.

The women of those times, it has been often observed, were of a sturdier nature than at the present day, and encountered both hardships and dangers with a philosophy and a grace which can now be hardly understood. Most of them undertook the labor of the household unassisted, requiring no help except when children were born, till the older ones grew old enough to be useful. There were but few single young women in the early settlement; if any came with friends from the east, they were very soon married and had their own household affairs to attend to. In the summer, besides the ordinary housework, the wife of the pioneer spun the wool which formed the winter's clothing for the male part of the family, as well as flannel for herself and the girls; in the winter was spun the flax of which clothing was made the ensuing summer. The buzz of the wheel, therefore, was heard at all seasons in the cabins of the early settlers, and often in the winter until the approach of midnight. Yet, with all these laborious duties, which were regularly and faithfully performed, the pioneer mothers found time to arrange their houses with the most scrupulous order and neatness, and were not without their social enjoyments. The afternoons of the long summer's day were frequently spent in visiting or receiving visits from neighbors within a few miles' distance. No motive could exist for a profession of friendship where the reality was not felt; and distress in any family never failed to elicit the sympathy and command the aid, so far as it could be rendered, of all the neighbors. Social intercourse was intimate, and the interchange of expressions of good feeling, sincere and constant; and never could one familiar with these associations forget the smooth winding foot paths which led through the deep forest and tall grass or underbrush from the house of one pioneer to that of another, traversed daily on errands of business or friendship, so that every family was kept acquainted with all the occurrences of the day throughout the settlement. If a fat bear or deer was killed by one it was generally divided, and the portions sent round as a token of kindly regard. Game was abundant, and the turkeys, venison and bear's meat which so frequently loaded the rustic tables, might well have been prized by the most fastidious epicures of advanced civilization.

On the whole the life of the pioneer, though one of hardship and danger, was one of stir and excitement, and a perfect freedom so agreeable to the enterprising rover, that it may be questioned whether it were not, for him at least, the happiest state of society. There was freshness and novelty in the scenery around him and in the adventurous experience of every day ; the keen invigorating air of the wildwood, and the constant exercise required, gave energy and activity to body and mind, and sustained and exhilarated the spirits ; no forms or ceremonious customs constrained or chilled social manners, and no jealousy or bitterness could arise out of difference in circumstances, distinctions growing out of condition being entirely unknown in those primitive communities. Good faith and honesty in business transactions were taken for granted on both sides, and the lack of them would have been punished by social outlawry. The general prevalence of good health was promoted by the constant exposure which hardened the pioneers to the sudden changes incident to a severe climate, and by their simplicity of diet. The cakes and preserves which nowadays take up so much of the attention of housekeepers in preparing, and are regarded as essential articles of provision in genteel houses, were almost unknown. The Kentucky "hoecake," or the "johnny" or "journey cake," of the Miami Valley, formed the favorite winter bread, and was used during a great part of the spring season. The corn was ground, before mills were erected, in a hand-mill, or pounded in a hominy-block, made by burning a hole in one end of a block of wood, the corn being pounded with a pestle made by driving an iron wedge into a stick of suitable size. When sufficiently pounded, it was sifted, and the finer portion made into bread and mush, the coarser being boiled for hominy. The meat was bear, venison, and wild turkey, as it was difficult to raise hogs or sheep on account of the wolves and bears.

The amusements of the men were such as developed physical strength and animated to cheerfulness. The chase, the principal one, served the purpose of an exciting and healthy exercise, while it furnished provision for the family. The women of course took no active part in this sport, except when the bear hunt roused the whole neighborhood, young and old, male and female, to partake in it with intense interest. A bear chase was usually commenced by the sounding of a peculiar note on the horn, which reverberated wildly among the hills and woods. Presently the distant howl of the hunter's dogs gave notice that the hunters were in pursuit of the enemy. Every man now seized his rifle and mounted his horse to join the chase, while those who could not do this, ran to see what was done. Sometimes the pursuit would continue all day, but generally it happened that in a few hours the bear was compelled to "tree," as it was called. As soon as the hunted animal had thus taken refuge, the hunter who chanced to be nearest the spot, summoned the others by a different note on his horn, and a few rifle shots usually either brought down the fugitive dead, or forced him to descend to escape the shower of bullets. When the bear found it necessary to leave his retreat, his practice generally was to roll himself into a ball-like shape by placing his head between his hind legs, and throw himself from the height. On striking the ground he would rebound several feet, and the instant he touched the ground again, his back was against the root of the tree, while, raising himself on his hind legs, he stood in an attitude of defiance, ready to do battle with the dogs who by that time were collected and eager for the assault. First with one fore paw and then with the other the bear would despatch the dogs as they rushed upon him. But though he could hold his ground thus bravely, it was not usually long before the fatal shot in the head from the hunter's rifle would lay the victim low, and end the chase for the day. The meat was then divided among the hunters, and they returned to their homes, weary and hungry, and perhaps wet with the falling rain or snow. At their cabins warm fires and comfortable suppers awaited them, and the incidents of the day afforded material for pleasant conversation during the evening. The excitement a chase of this kind always caused throughout the neighborhood can only be imagined by one who has witnessed such an occurrence.

The wolf made havoc with the few sheep introduced, and the wild deer ; the bear confined himself to hogs. His practice was to spring suddenly upon his victim, grasp him in his fore legs with irresistible force, erect himself upon his hind legs like a man, and make off in an instant with his load; the piercing squeal of the hog being the first warning to the owner. A large bear, meeting with no obstruction, would make his way through the woods in this manner, with a hog of good size, faster than a man on foot could follow.

The establishment of schools and places for stated religious meetings was coeval with the formation of every settlement, or at least attended to as soon as the pioneers had secured themselves from the savages and provided their families with the means of daily subsistence. The schoolhouses, like the primitive cabins, were roughly constructed, but in some of them men whose mental endowments and ripe scholarship have raised them to eminence in after life, received the first rudiments of education. It happened in some neighborhoods, it is true, that no schools were established; but the evil effects of such neglect were discernible long afterwards, and in some instances the want of general intelligence is still evident in those portions of the country. The privilege of hearing the gospel preached regularly every Sabbath, could not often be enjoyed, as different and distant neighborhoods had to be supplied, and there were but few pastors; but service was held, and sermons were read when no clergyman could attend, and the announcement that there was to be preaching would bring the settlers together from many miles around. The strength of their attachment to the Sabbath services is shown by the fact that they were not prevented, even when threatened with Indian incursions, from meeting in large numbers, to hear the word preached whenever an opportunity presented itself. While the danger was imminent it was usual for all the men to carry fire-arms and ammunition, as the law among them required every one to do; sentinels being placed on the watch while service was going on. It was not till after the peace which followed Wayne's treaty at Greenville that the necessity for carrying arms to religious meetings no longer existed, and in the outer settlements the custom was kept up for some years after. It was not an unusual sight to see a file of riflemen with their shot pouches, and arms at rest, stationed around the large congregations which in warm weather were accustomed to assemble in the woods for religious worship. When the necessity for this strict guard became less apparent, and the Indians had removed to a greater distance, these forest assemblages on the Sabbath were very large, different neighborhoods gathering in one place. It was not in the least uncommon for men and women to ride on horseback eight and ten miles to meeting, and the doing so was far from being considered a task or hardship.

One of the first schools established in the Northwestern Territory was in the settlement where Mrs. Carpenter lived. The young man who took charge of it, Francis Dunlevy, had served in many Indian campaigns, having, at the early age of fourteen, offered himself for military service, and been received in place of one of his neighbors who had been drafted, but who had a family dependent on him for support, and was unwilling to go. This was in 1777, and from that time to his coming to Columbia, he had been on service in occasional excursions against the savages. He served at the time of the disastrous defeat of Crawford at the Sandusky Plains in 1782, and after that time had travelled over those portions of the Northwest Territory which now constitute Ohio, Western Virginia, and the northern part of Kentucky. He was not only a man of great courage, spirit, and enterprise, but of such industry and perseverance, that in the midst of the labors and vicissitudes of numerous campaigns, and the privations to which he was subject in a forest life, he employed the intervals of leisure from military occupations in study, and acquired a classical education.

Having made up his mind to reside for the future in the Northwest Territory, he came to Columbia as teacher of the school in the latter part of the year 1792. He heard the story of Mrs. Carpenter's trials, and the fortitude with which she bore them; he sought her acquaintance, and finding in her a kindred spirit, in due time offered his hand and was accepted. They were married in January, 1793. Mr. Dunlevy was afterwards a highly respected member of the legislature of the North-west Territory, and of the convention which formed the constitution of Ohio. He also occupied, for fourteen years, the station of presiding judge in the Court of Common Pleas.

For many years after her removal, Mrs. Dunlevy heard not a word from any member of her mother's family. In 1804 she received a letter from her brother, directed to her " in the Miami country," by which she was informed of her mother's death, and that her brother had returned to the United States, and was then living near Lake Champlain. In 1806, her sister and her husband came from Liverpool to New York for the purpose of finding the scattered members of the family, but they learned on their arrival that the brother had died the same year, and that Mary was living in the " far west." A correspondence was held between the sisters, and a meeting appointed at Pittsburg, the elder sister insisting that she could not venture to encounter the dangers of entering an Indian country, as she considered Western Ohio ; but before she left New York to proceed that far, she was seized with yellow fever and died.

The two children of Mrs. Dunlevy by her first marriage attained to womanhood and were married. Besides these, she had three sons and three daughters, all of whom lived to maturity. The mother's affection for her children was one which absorbed every faculty of her nature. With a resolution that to the last would never give way before difficulties, she was delicate and susceptible in all her feelings, gentle, retiring, and affectionate, and clinging with absolute dependence to those in whom her devoted affections were centred. The death of her eldest daughter, therefore, though she had been married, and lived at a distance for some six years, was a blow from which she never recovered. Her life was afterwards secluded, and her social intercourse entirely confined to her children. A second daughter in five years followed the first to the grave, and four years afterwards, her youngest son having been called to a distant part of the country, was attacked by sudden illness and died far from home. Under these accumulated afflictions the spirit which had never faltered in the presence of danger, nor shrunk from trial in every other form, sank in the prostration of grief. Mrs. Dunlevy's health failed after the death of her eldest child, and slowly declined till 1828, when, without any particular disease, but a gradual failure of nervous energy, she departed this life, at Lebanon, Ohio, in the sixty-third year of her age. Judge Dunlevy survived her nearly twelve years, and was laid beside her in the burial-ground of the Baptist church, of which they had both long been members.

The following sketch of life in the woods is extracted from an article written by John S. Williams, the Editor of the American Pioneer:

"Emigrants poured in from different parts, cabins were put up in every direction, and women, children and goods tumbled into them. Every thing was bustle and confusion, and all at work that could work. Our cabin had been raised, covered, part of the cracks chinked, and part of the floor laid when we moved in, on Christmas day! We had intended an inside chimney, for we thought the chimney ought to be in the house. We had a log put across the whole width of the cabin for a mantel, but when the floor was in we found it so low as not to answer, and removed it. We got the rest of the floor laid in a very few days; the chinking of the cracks went on slowly, but the daubing could not proceed till weather more suitable, which happened in a few days; door-ways were sawed out and steps made of the logs, and the back of the chimney was raised up to the mantel, but the funnel of sticks and clay was delayèd until spring.

"In building our cabin it was set to front the north and south, my brother using my father's pocket compass on the occasion. We had no idea of living in a house that did not stand square with the earth itself. This argued our ignorance of the comforts and conveniences of a pioneer life. The position of the house, end to the hill, necessarily elevated the lower end, and the determination to have both a north and south door, added much to the airiness of the domicile, particularly after the green ash puncheons had shrunk so as to leave cracks in the floor and doors from one to two inches wide. At both the doors we had high, unsteady, and sometimes icy steps, made by piling up the logs cut out of the wall. We had a window, if it could be called a *window*, when perhaps it was the largest spot in the top, bottom or sides of the cabin at which the wind *could not* enter. It was made by sawing out a log, placing sticks across; and by pasting an old newspaper over the hole, and applying some hog's lard, we had a kind of glazing which shed a most beautiful and mellow light across the cabin when the sun shone on it. All other light entered at the doors, cracks and chimney.

"Our cabin was twenty-four by eighteen. The west end was occupied by two beds, the centre of each side by a door, and here our symmetry had to stop, for opposite the window, made of clapboards supported on pins driven into the logs, were our shelves. Upon these shelves my sister displayed in order a host of pewter plates, basins, dishes, and spoons, scoured and bright. A ladder of five rounds occupied the corner near the window. By this, when we got a floor above, we could ascend. Our chimney occupied most of the east end; pots and kettles were opposite the window under the shelves, a gun on hooks over the north door, four split-bottom chairs, three three-legged stools, and a small eight by ten looking-glass sloped from the wall over a large towel and combcase. These, with a clumsy shovel and a pair of tongs with one shank straight, completed our furniture, except a spinning-wheel and such things as were necessary to work with. It was absolutely necessary to have *three-legged* stools, as four legs of any thing could not all touch the floor at the same time.

"The completion of our cabin went on slowly. The season was inclement, and laborers were not to be had. We got our chimney up breast high as soon as we could, and our cabin daubed as high as the joists outside. It never was daubed on the inside, for my sister, who was very nice, could not consent to 'live right next to the mud.' My impression now is, that the window was not constructed till spring, for until the sticks and clay were put on the chimney we could possibly have no need of a window; the flood of light which always poured into the cabin from the fireplace would have extinguished our paper window, and rendered it as useless as the moon at noonday. We got a floor laid over head as soon as possible, perhaps in a month; but when it *was* laid, the reader will readily conceive of its imperviousness to wind or weather, when we mention that it was laid of loose clapboards split from a red oak, so twisting that each board lay on two diagonally opposite corners, and a cat might have shaken every board on our ceiling.

" The evenings of the first winter did not pass off as pleasantly as evenings afterwards. We had no corn to shell, no turnips to scrape, no tow to spin into rope-yarn, nor straw to plait for hats, and we had come so late we could get but few walnuts to crack. We had, however, the Bible, George Fox's Journal, Barkley's Apology, and to our stock was soon after added a borrowed copy of the Pilgrim's Progress, which we read twice through without stopping. The first winter our living was truly scanty and hard; but even this winter had its felicities. We had part of a barrel of flour which we had brought from Fredericktown. Besides this we had a part of a jar of hog's lard brought from old Carolina; not the tasteless stuff which now goes by that name, but pure leaf lard taken from hogs raised on pine roots and fattened on sweet potatoes, and into which, while trying, were immersed the boughs of the fragrant bay tree, that imparted to the lard a rich flavor. Of that flour, shortened with this lard, my sister every Sunday morning made short biscuit for breakfast.

" The winter was open, but windy. While the wind was of great use in driving the smoke and ashes out of our cabin, it shook terribly the timber standing almost over us. We were sometimes much and needlessly alarmed. We were surrounded by the tall giants of the forest, waving their boughs and knitting their brows over us, as if in defiance of our disturbing their repose, and usurping their long uncontested pre-emption rights. The beech on the left often shook his bushy head over us as if in absolute disapprobation of our settling there, threatening to crush us if we did not pack up and start. The walnut over the spring branch stood high and straight; no one could tell which way it inclined, but all concluded that if it had a preference it was in favor of quartering on our cabin. We got assistance to cut it down.

" The monotony of the time for several of the first years was enlivened by the howl of wild beasts. The wolves howling around us seemed to moan their inability to drive us from their long and undisputed domain. The bears, panthers and deer but seldom troubled us. When spring was fully come and our little patch of corn, three acres, put in among the beech roots, which at every step contended with the shovel-plough for the right of soil, and held it too, we enlarged our stock of conveniences. As soon as bark would peel off we could make ropes and bark boxes. These we stood in great need of, as such things as bureaus, stands, wardrobes, or even barrels were not to be had. Sometimes boxes made of slippery elm bark, shaved smooth, and the inside out, were ornamented with drawings of birds, trees, etc.

" We settled on beech land, which took much labor to clear. We could do no better than clear out the smaller stuff and burn the brush, &c., around the beeches which, in spite of the girdling and burning we could do to them, would leaf out the first year, and often a little the second. The land, however, was very rich, and would bring better corn than might be expected. We had to tend it principally with the hoe, that is, to chop down the nettles, the water-weed, and the touch-me-not. Grass, lamb's-quarter, and Spanish-needles were reserved to pester the better prepared farmer. We cleared a small turnip patch, which we got in about the 10th of August. We sowed timothy seed, which took well, and next year we had a little hay besides. The tops and blades of the corn were also carefully saved for our horse, cow, and the two sheep. The turnips were sweet and good, and in the fall we took care to gather walnuts and hickory nuts, which were very abundant. These, with the turnips which we scraped, supplied the place of fruit. I have always been partial to scraped turnips, and could now beat any three dandies at scraping them. Johnny-cake, also, when we had meal to make it of, helped to make up our evening's repast. The Sunday morning biscuit had all evaporated, but the loss was partially supplied by the nuts and turnips. Our regular supper was mush and milk, and by the time we had shelled our corn, stemmed tobacco, and plaited straw to make hats, etc., our appetites were sharp again. To relieve this difficulty, my brother and I would bake a thin johnny-cake, part of which we would eat, and leave the rest till morning. At daylight we would eat the rest as we walked from the house to work.

"The methods of eating mush and milk were various. Some would sit around the pot, every one taking therefrom for himself. Some would sit at table and have each his tin cup of milk, with a pewter spoon, taking just as much mush from the dish or the pot as he thought would fill his mouth, then lowering it into the milk and taking some to wash it down. This method kept the milk cool, and by frequent repetitions the pioneer would contract a faculty of correctly estimating the proper amount of each. Others would mix mush and milk together.

"To get grinding done was often a great difficulty, by reason of the scarcity of mills, the freezing in winter and the droughts in summer. We had often to manufacture meal in any way we could get the corn to pieces. We soaked and pounded it, we shaved it, we planed it, and, at the proper season, grated it. When one of our neighbors got a hand-mill, it was thought quite an acquisition to the neighborhood. In after years, when we could get grinding by waiting for our turn no more than one day and a night at a horse-mill, we thought ourselves happy. To save meal we often made pumpkin bread, in which, when meal was scarce, the pumpkin would so predominate as to render it next to impossible to tell our bread from that article, either by taste, looks, or the amount of nutriment it contained. Salt was five dollars per bushel, and we used none in our corn bread, which we soon liked as well without it. What meat we had at first was fresh, and but little of that, for had we been hunters we had no time for the chase.

"We had no candles, and cared but little about them except for summer use. My business was to ramble the woods every evening for seasoned sticks, or the bark of the shelly hickory, for light. 'Tis true that our light was not as good as candles, but we got along without fretting, for we depended more upon the goodness of our eyes than we did upon the brilliancy of the light."

Howe relates an anecdote of one Henry Perry, who in the fall of 1803, after getting up his cabin near Delhi, left his two sons and returned to Philadelphia for the remainder of his family, but finding his wife ill, and afterwards being ill himself, could not get back till the next June. These two little boys, Levi and Reuben, only eleven and nine years old, remained there alone, eight months, fifteen miles from any white family, and surrounded by Indians, with no food but the rabbits they could catch in hollow logs, the remainder of one deer that the wolves killed near them, and a little corn meal that they occasionally obtained of Thomas Cellar, by following down the "Indian trace." The winter was a severe one, and their cabin was open, having neither daubing, fire-place, nor chimney; they had no gun, and were wholly unaccustomed to forest life, being fresh from Wales, and yet these little fellows not only struggled through but actually made a considerable clearing! Jacob Fo st, at an early day, when his wife was sick and could obtain nothing to eat that she relished, procured a bushel of wheat, and throwing it upon his shoulders, carried it to Zanesville to get it ground, a distance of more than seventy-five miles by the tortuous path he had to traverse, and then shouldering his flour retraced his steps home, fording the streams and camping out nights."

Dr. Hildreth says that for many years after the first settlement of Ohio, salt had to be brought across the mountains on pack-horses. "Those immense fountains of brine that now are known to exist deep in the rocky beds below, were not then dreamed of; it was supposed that the west would always be dependent on the Atlantic coast for salt, and deeply deplored as a serious drawback on the prosperity of this beautiful region. Although springs of salt water were known in various places, they were of so poor and weak a quality as to require from four to six hundred gallons of the water to make a bushel of salt; and when made, it contained so much foreign matter as to render it a very inferior article. Yet as it could be used in place of the imported salt, and saved the borderer's money, at that day not very plenty, it was occasionally resorted to by the settlers, who, assembling in gangs of six or eight persons, with their domestic kettles, pack-horses and provisions, camped out for a week at a time in the vicinity of the saline. These springs were generally discovered by hunters, and were at remote points from the settlements."

XIV.

ANN BAILEY.

The account of the first settlement of Gallipolis, Ohio, forms a curious piece of pioneer history. When the disturbances of the French Revolution had driven many families from their native country, an office was opened in Paris for the sale of American lands owned by the "Scioto Company," and situated on the west bank of the Ohio river, above the mouth of the Big Scioto in the Northwest Territory. A general prospectus was issued, setting forth that the company owned a million of acres ; the advantages to the emigrant and ultimate value of the land, were glowingly painted, and hundreds rushed to the agents to purchase estates which might be acquired at a very moderate price. Some five or six hundred emigrants, including doctors, lawyers, officers, merchants, manufacturers, mechanics, farmers, gardeners, etc., with their deeds in their hands, and eager with hope and expectation, sailed in February, 1790, from Havre de Grace, five ships being chartered to convey them to Alexandria, Virginia. They were received with a warm and hospitable welcome by the inhabitants of that town, supplied with portions of their stores, and taught all that was necessary to learn as to the manner of living in the new country.*

---

* This account is abridged from one prepared by Gen. Lewis Newsom, one of the early residents of Gallipolis. He has also favored me with notices of Mrs. Bailey's life.

From a correspondence opened with the Secretary of the Treasury of the United States, the emigrants learned that the Scioto Company had failed in their engagements to government, and that the lands purchased from the Treasury Board had reverted and been sold in 1787 to the agents for the directors of the Ohio Company, pursuant to an act of Congress passed the July preceding. This was the first knowledge they had of their true situation, and the imposition practised on them. A general meeting was called, and a committee appointed to go to New York and demand indemnification of the acting agent for the Scioto Company, while another committee was to appeal to President Washington for a redress of their grievances. The result of the application to the agent of the Scioto Company was the promise that other lands should be secured to the emigrants in fulfilment of the engagements entered into, and that the site of Gallipolis should be surveyed into lots, houses erected, with defences against the Indians, and wagons and supplies provided to convey the colonists to Ohio. Notwithstanding this flattering report of their committee, many of them had no hope that the promises would be fulfilled, and removed to New York, Philadelphia, and elsewhere. As soon as wagons could be procured, the others left Alexandria and passed through Winchester to Brownsville on the Monongahela, where they were detained, as boats were not in readiness to proceed. They had shanties to lodge in, but the fall rains had set in, and they suffered many privations. Their voyage further was not a pleasant one, the river being low, and shoals frequent; but after a weary progress they reached the place of destination, in October, 1790, and landed with great joy. Surveyors had been sent to lay out the town, and workmen to build houses, and the first tree had been cut down on the 8th of June, by Col. Robert Safford. Four rows of twenty cabins, each with a door, windows, and wooden chimney, were put up, and as a better sort of habitation for those of the superior class, two rows of huts of hewn logs, a story and a half in height. Block-houses two stories high were also erected, with a high stockade fence, forming a sufficient fortification against attack. In one of the better cabins was a room

used for a ball-room and council chamber.   As soon as the quarters
of each family were assigned, their massive chests were opened and
relieved of the ponderous contents, which were distributed in the
community.

They entered upon the new mode of life with cheerfulness and a
social spirit; they had soirées, music, and dancing regularly; some
had mingled in the higher circles abroad and had cultivated literary
tastes, and there were scientific men who had spent years of study
in the first European institutions.   Few of them had ever wielded
an axe, but they did not shrink from severe labor; they cleared the
forest, prepared the soil for cultivation, and soon changed the wilderness to a land of more inviting aspect.   A corps of hunters
brought in regular supplies of game, and flour and grain were procured from Western Pennsylvania.   From the commencement of
the settlement service was performed by a Catholic priest, which was
regularly attended by the emigrants.   In a short time different
branches of business were commenced, retail stores opened, and
manufactures offered for sale and carried to other places.

In the spring of 1791, a party was sent out to explore the lands
from Gallipolis to the confluence of the Big Scioto with the Ohio.
A keel-boat was chartered and a crew obtained, with hunters, spies,
and scouts, making a formidable appearance with their camp
equipage and war accoutrements, while the colonists assembled to
bid them adieu.   They reached the mouth of the Big Scioto by the
aid of poles, pikes, &c., ascended it about a mile, and encamped near
the site of the court-house in Portsmouth.   The country was then
explored, and the lands examined along the banks of the river; the
hunters bringing in abundance of deer, turkeys, and other game.
On their return to Gallipolis, their report was joyfully received, and
hope was entertained that the Scioto company would yet put the
colonists in possession of the lands they had purchased.

It was now announced that a hostile band of Indians had been
prowling in the neighborhood; one emigrant was killed and two
were taken prisoners, while several horses and cattle were carried off.
A defensive force was organized, and on application to the Secretary

of War, assistance was sent. Few further depredations, however, were committed by the Indians, though they came occasionally to peep at the dances of the colonists, and the settlement continued for so long a time to enjoy immunity from attack, that it was supposed that the savages entertained unusually friendly feelings towards the French. After the victories of Gen. Wayne and the establishment of peace, a free intercourse was maintained between the residents at Gallipolis and the colonists from Massachussetts living at Marietta. The former soon became convinced that the agents of the Scioto Company could never secure them in the possession of their lands, and after some further endeavors to procure redress by prosecuting their claims, they were obliged to give up the hope of having their rights conceded. In a negotiation afterwards with the Ohio Company, many of the settlers were disappointed, and feeling themselves deceived, left the settlement, reducing the numbers of those remaining to about three hundred. A petition to Congress for an appropriation of lands for their benefit, presented by M. Gervais, resulted in the grant of twenty thousand acres, to be equally divided among the French emigrants living at Gallipolis at a certain time, under conditions that secured their settling there for some years. Other grants were afterwards made to other colonists opposite and below the mouth of Little Sandy River in Kentucky. Improvements in the lands went on: apple and peach orchards were planted, and the cider and brandy manufactured became a source of revenue. New emigrants came in, and in 1803, Gallia county was erected, Gallipolis being the county seat.

So interesting and romantic is the story of this settlement by the French, that no apology will be necessary for connecting the narrative with a brief notice of a remarkable woman, remembered by all the old inhabitants of Gallipolis, and throughout Western Virginia, and known by name to almost every child in the country. She was sometimes called "Mad Ann," and was a terror to refractory urchins. Her maiden name was Hennis. She was born at Liverpool, married Richard Trotter at the age of thirty, and came with him to the American colonies; both, on account of poverty, being "sold out" to service, according to custom, for the payment of the passage money, to a gentleman in Augusta county, Virginia. Having served him faithfully for the stipulated time, they became settlers.

The frontier having suffered much from Indian attacks, in the summer of 1774, Lord Dunmore, governor of Virginia, collected forces for an expedition against the Indian towns on the Scioto. Gen. Lewis, who had signalized himself in the field of Braddock's defeat, was ordered to march with his division to the junction of the Great Kanawha with the Ohio. Richard Trotter was a volunteer in his force. Lewis halted on the ground now occupied by the village of Point Pleasant, to await further communications from the commander-in-chief; but before his men could erect defences, except a few fallen trees, the scouts came into camp with intelligence that an army of Indian warriors was in their immediate vicinity. The troops were put in battle array, and in a very short time, on the morning of the 10th of October, a general engagement took place, in which the Virginians suffered great loss, though the Indians retreated. Among those engaged in this memorable battle, we find the names of Shelby, Sevier, and James Robertson.

Trotter was killed in this battle. From the period of his death, a strange and wild spirit seemed to possess the widow, who frequently expressed her hatred of the Indians, and her determination to have revenge. The opinion entertained by her neighbors that her intellects were somewhat disordered, was confirmed by her entire abandonment of all feminine employments. She no longer sewed, spun, or attended to household or garden concerns, but practised with the rifle, slung the tomahawk, and rode about the country attending every muster of soldiers. She even in part discarded female attire, and was seen clad in a hunting-shirt and moccasins, wearing her knife and tomahawk, and carrying her gun. Her manly spirit and resolve to avenge the death of her husband did not prevent her contracting a second alliance, and it was as Ann Bailey that, several years afterwards, she followed a body of soldiers sent to garrison a fort on the Great Kanawha, where Charleston is now located. The men often practised shooting at a target, and Ann, ambitious to dis-

11*

play her skill, would contend with the best marksmen and sometimes carry off the prize. At parade she handled fire-arms with the
expertness of a warrior, and the rifle was her constant companion.
Howe, in his historical work on Virginia, mentions that she
frequently acted as a messenger, carrying letters from the fort to
Point Pleasant, and that she generally rode on horseback, with a
rifle over her shoulder, and a knife and tomahawk in her belt. At
night she would encamp in the woods, letting her horse go free, and
then walking back some distance on the trail to escape discovery by
the vigilant savages.

Marauding parties of Indians were often seen in the valley of the
Kanawha, and the Virginians doubted not their intention of making
a desperate effort to dislodge them from this favorite hunting-ground.
A runner was sent from Capt. Arbuckle, at Point Pleasant, to Capt.
Clendenin, the commander of the garrison, with information that a
hundred or more Indian warriors had been seen the day previous
crossing the Ohio at Racoon Island, some ten miles below. It was
supposed their design was to attack the fort at Charleston, or at Big
Levels, in Greenbrier county. All the inhabitants around were immediately gathered into the fort.

At this crisis the terrible fact was announced that their ammunition was nearly exhausted. It was determined to send immediately
to Camp Union, now Lewisburg, for a supply ; but few men could
be spared from the fort, and none was willing to encounter, with a
small party, the perils of a hundred miles' journey through a trackless forest. Mrs. Bailey heard of the difficulty, and instantly offered
her services, saying she would go alone. Her acquaintance with the
country, her excellent horsemanship, her perseverance, and fearless
spirit, were well known, and the commander of the garrison at length
yielded to her solicitation. A good horse was furnished her, with a
stock of jerked venison and johnny-cake ; she set her face towards
Greenbrier, armed with rifle, etc., and resolutely overcoming every
obstacle in the ruggedness of the way through the woods, the mountains she had to cross, and the rivers to swim, undaunted by the
perils threatening from wild beasts and straggling parties of Indians,

she reached Camp Union in safety, delivered her orders, and being provided with a led horse fully laden, as well as her own, set forward on her return.

She used to relate how her trail was followed for hours together by wolves, watching for an opportunity to attack her horses. When night set in she was compelled to make large fires to keep the wild beasts at bay. To protect herself in slumber from the danger of rattlesnakes and copperheads, which infested the wilderness, she had to construct a pioneer bedstead every night, by driving into the ground four forked sticks about three feet high, adjust upon them other sticks to serve as bed rails and slats, and overlay them with a quantity of green boughs, her blanket serving as a musquito bar. Thus she would sleep amidst the howling of wolves, the screaming of panthers, and the buzzing of troublesome insects; at break of day replacing the loads on her horses, and resuming her journey, her simple breakfast being eaten on horseback. She arrived in safety with her supplies at the fort. It is said that the premeditated attack was made the very next day, and that the Indians were repulsed after a severe conflict. Mrs. Bailey was actively employed during the siege, and tradition says, fired several times upon the assailants. She always insisted that she had killed one Indian at least, and thus accomplished her revenge. The commandant has been heard to say that the fort could not have been saved without the timely supply of ammunition, thus giving the credit to Mrs. Bailey's exploit, which indeed is scarcely paralleled even among the many instances of heroism that abound in the history of the Revolutionary war.

After the troubles with the Indians were over, Mrs. Bailey still retained her singular habits. She spent much of her time in fishing and hunting, and would shoot deer and bears with the expertness of a backwoodsman. In person she was short and stout, and of coarse and masculine appearance, and she seldom wore a full woman's dress, having on usually a skirt with a man's coat over it, and buckskin leggins. The services she rendered in the war had greatly endeared her to the people, and her eccentricities were regarded with an in-

dulgence that would not have been extended to one who had no
such claims to gratitude.   She annually visited many of the people
of West Virginia, and received presents in clothing and other articles.
Gen. Newsom recollects seeing her in his boyhood, passing from the
Kanawha Valley to the counties near the Alleghanies, and returning
with her horse laden with gifts from those who remembered her
achievement.   Thus " Mad Ann " and her black horse, which she
called " Liverpool " in honor of her birthplace, were always greeted
with a smile of welcome wherever she chose to stop.   When her
son came to Ohio, where he owned a large body of land, she came
with him, and lived a few miles from Gallipolis.   'Here she was accustomed to wander about the country, received by all as a privileged
visitor, and supplied according to her need.   She seldom failed,
whenever there was a muster of the militia, to attend, armed like a
soldier, and march in the ranks.   " Not a man of them would have
put her out," said the General, in recounting the narrative.   She
loved solitude, and spent most of her time alone, but often gathered
the neighbors around her to relate the story of her adventures.   It
must be added that among her masculine habits she had that of
drinking occasionally, and that she sometimes exercised her skill in
boxing, an accomplishment in which she was well versed.   She
could read and write, and seems to have possessed an unusual share
of intelligence for one of her station in life.

A gentleman residing in Nashville, said he had seen her frequently
near Point Pleasant, about the year 1810 or 1811.   She called her
gun and canoe " Liverpool," as well as her horse.   She often took it
upon herself to enforce the keeping of the Sabbath by taking up such
boys as she found wandering about on that day, and compelling
them to sit around her in a cabin, while she opened school exercises
for their instruction, greatly to the terror of the delinquents.   The
gentleman referred to said he was chased by her some distance on
one of these occasions, and though lamed by a bruise on his foot,
ran as for dear life, having made his escape by jumping out of the
window of the hut where she had imprisoned a number of boys.

Mrs. Bailey's life was prolonged far beyond the ordinary limits;

according to her own account, she numbered several years over a century. Her death took place in 1825. The place of her burial is on a lonely hill near her son's residence, in the solitude of the woods, unmarked by a headstone. Gen. Newsom suggests that her remains should be removed by the citizens of Virginia to the spot where the fort stood in Charleston, and honored by a suitable monument.

XV.

ELIZABETH HARPER.

ELIZABETH BARTHOLOMEW, one of the pioneer band who made the earliest settlement in Northeastern Ohio, was born in Bethlehem, Hunterdon County, New Jersey, February 13th, 1749. She was the sixteenth child of her parents, and had still a younger sister. She was descended on the maternal side from the Huguenots of France, and her ancestors were persons of wealth and respectable rank, firmly attached to the principles they professed, and willing to surrender all, and yield themselves unto death, rather than give up their religious faith. They removed to Germany after the revocation of the edict of Nantes; and there is a family tradition that the grandmother of the subject of this sketch, then a child, was brought from Paris concealed in a chest. She married in Germany, and in an old age emigrated to America.

In 1771, Elizabeth was married to Alexander Harper, one of several brothers who had settled in Harpersfield, Delaware County, New York. At the outbreak of the Revolutionary war, these brothers immediately quitted their peaceful occupations to enter into the continental service, Alexander receiving a commission to act as captain of a company of rangers. The exposed situation of that portion of country, and the frequent visits of Indians and tories, made it necessary for the whig families to seek the protection of

Fort Schoharie. Mrs. Harper repaired thither with her family, including the aged parents of her husband. In time of comparative security, she lived at the distance of about a mile from the fort. Here, when there was a sudden alarm, she would herself harness her horses to the wagon, and placing in it her children and the old people, would drive with all speed to the fort, remaining within its walls until the danger was over, and then returning to her occupations on the farm. As peril became more frequent or imminent, the old people were removed to a place of greater security, while Mrs. Harper, with her four children and a lad they had taken to bring up, remained at home. One night they were startled by the sound of the alarm-gun. The mother took the youngest child in her arms, another on her back, and bidding the two elder hold fast to her clothes, set off to escape to the fort; the lad running closely behind her, and. calling to her in great terror not to leave him. The fugitives reached the fort in safety, and for the present Mrs. Harper concluded to take up her abode there. She would not, however, consent to live in idleness, supported by the labor of others, but undertook, as her special charge, the bread-baking for the whole garrison, which she did for six months. During her stay the fort sustained a siege from a party of tories and Indians, commanded by British officers. Messengers were despatched to the nearest posts for relief; but while this was slow in arriving, the commanding officer, in opposition to the wishes of all his men, determined on a capitulation, and ordered a flag of truce to be hoisted for that purpose. The announcement of his intention created a disaffection which soon amounted almost to rebellion. The women, among whom Mrs. Harper was a leading spirit, had on that day been busily occupied from early dawn in making cartridges, preparing ammunition, and serving rations to the wearied soldiers. They heartily sympathized in the determination expressed not to surrender without another effort to repel the besiegers.

One of the men declared his willingness to fire upon the flag which had been ordered to be hoisted, provided the women would conceal him. This they readily agreed to do, and as often as the flag was run up it was fired at, while the commander was unable to discover the author of this expression of contempt for his authority.   The delay consequent on this act of insubordination and the displeasure of the soldiers, prevented the capitulation being carried into effect, till the arrival of reinforcements caused the enemy to retreat.

In the spring of 1780, Capt. Harper availed himself of an interval in active service, to look after his property in Harpersfield.   While there with several of his friends, they were surprised by a party of Indians and tories under Brandt, and taken prisoners, an invalid brother-in-law being killed.   Harper and Brandt had been schoolfellows in boyhood, and the chief did not fail to show a remembrance of the days thus spent together.   The Indian captor of Harper treated him with great kindness, taking him, however, to Canada. Here his exchange was effected soon afterwards, but he was not released till peace was concluded ; being offered, meanwhile, large rewards by the British if he would enter into service on their side. Mrs. Harper remained in ignorance of his fate during the time of his absence, and supposing him killed, mourned for him, while she did not suffer grief to paralyze her efforts for the protection and support of her family.   All her characteristic energy was devoted to keeping them together, and doing what she could towards improving their shattered fortunes.

In the year 1797, a company was formed in Harpersfield, to purchase lands in the country then called " the far west."   Besides Alexander and Joseph Harper, the company consisted of William McFarland, Aaron Wheeler, and Roswell Hotchkiss ; others joining afterwards.   In June of that year these individuals entered into a contract with Oliver Phelps and Gideon Granger, members of the Connecticut Land Company, for six townships of land in what was then called New Connecticut, in the Northwestern Territory.   Three of these townships were to lie east and three west of the Cuyahoga river.   The Connecticut Land Company drew their lands in the same year, and the township now known as Harpersfield in Ashtabula County, was one of those which fell to the company formed at the town of that name in New York.

In September commissioners were sent out by them to explore the country. They were much pleased with the locality called Harpersfield, and selected it as the township most eligibly situated for the commencement of a settlement. On the 7th of March, 1798, Alexander Harper, William McFarland, and Ezra Gregory set out with their families on their journey to this land of promise. As the winter's snow was upon the ground, they came in sleighs as far as Rome, where they found further progress impracticable and were obliged to take up their quarters until the 1st of May. They then made another start in boats, and proceeded to Oswego, where they found a vessel which conveyed them to Queenstown. Thence they pursued their journey on the Canada side to Fort Erie, being obliged to take this circuitous route on account of there being no roads west of Genesee River, nor any inhabitants, except three families living at Buffalo, while a garrison was stationed at Erie, in Pennsylvania. At Fort Erie they found a small vessel which had been used for transporting military stores to the troops stationed at the West, and which was then ready to proceed up the lake with her usual lading of stores. This vessel was the only one owned on the American side, and the voyagers lost no time in securing passage in her for themselves and their families as far as the peninsula opposite Erie. As the boat, however, was small and already heavily laden, they were able to take with them but a slender stock of provisions. Having landed on the peninsula the party was obliged to stop for a week until they could procure boats in which to coast up the lake, at that time bordered by the primeval forest. After having spent nearly four months in performing a journey which now occupies but two or three days, they landed on the 28th of June at the mouth of Cunningham's Creek.

The cattle belonging to the pioneers had been sent through the wilderness, meeting them at the peninsula, whence they came up along the lake shore to the mouth of the stream. Here the men prepared sleds to transport the goods they had brought with them;

the whole party encamping that night on the beach. The next morning, Col. Harper, who was the oldest of the emigrants, and was then about fifty-five, set out on foot, accompanied by the women, comprising Mrs. Harper and two of her daughters, twelve and fourteen years of age, Mrs. Gregory and two daughters, Mrs. McFarland the Colonel's sister, and a girl whom she had brought up, named Parthena Mingus. Their new home was about four miles distant, and they followed up the boundary line of the township from the lake, each carrying articles of provisions or table furniture. Mrs. Harper carried a small copper tea-kettle, which she filled with water on the way to the place of destination. Their course lay through a forest unbroken except by the surveyor's lines, and the men who followed them were obliged to cut their way through for the passage of the sleds. About three in the afternoon they came to the corner of the township line, about half a mile north of the present site of Unionville, Ohio, where they were glad to halt, as they saw indications of a coming storm. The women busied themselves in striking a fire, and putting the tea-kettle over, while Col. Harper cut some forked poles and drove them in the ground, and then felled a large chestnut tree, from which he stripped the bark, and helped the women to stretch it across the poles so as to form a shelter, which they had just time to gather under when the storm burst upon them. It was not, however, of long continuance, and when the rest of the men arrived, they enlarged and enclosed the lodge, in which the whole company, consisting of twenty-five persons great and small, were obliged to take up their quarters. Their tea-table was then constructed in the same primitive fashion, and we may believe that the first meal was partaken of with excellent appetite, after the wanderings and labors of the day.

The lodge thus prepared was the common dwelling for three weeks, during which time some of the trees had been cut down, and a space cleared for a garden. The fourth of July was celebrated in the new Harpersfield by the planting of beans, corn and potatoes. The next thing was to build log cabins for the accommodation of the different families, and when this was done the company separated.

The location chosen by Col. Harper was where he first pitched his tent, while his brother-in-law took a piece of land about half a mile east of Unionville, near the spot now occupied by the Episcopal Church, and Mr. Gregory put up his dwelling close to the river where Clyde Furnace was afterwards built. The settlers suffered from the sickness peculiar to a new country when the season came. A hired man in Harper's service was taken ill in August, and soon after the Colonel himself was seized with the fever, of which he died on the tenth of September. They had been able to procure no medical aid, and a coffin was made by digging out the trunk of a tree and hewing a slab for the lid. This melancholy event was a peculiar and distressing affliction to the little band of pioneers, and its effect on them would have been paralysing, but that the firmness and energy exhibited by the widow, who now found her exertions necessary to sustain the rest, restored the confidence and hope which had nearly been extinguished by the loss of their leader. Although the principal sufferer by the dispensation, she would not for a moment listen favorably to the proposition made to abandon the enterprise. When an invitation came from friends in Pennsylvania for herself and daughters to spend the winter, both she and her eldest daughter, Elizabeth, declined, knowing how necessary was their presence to keep up the spirits of the little community, and that their departure would discourage many who had intended coming to join them in their forest home. The magnanimity of this resolution can be appreciated only in view of the hardships they knew it would be their lot to share.

In the fall, another small vessel was built for use on the American side of the lake, and two pioneers, one of whom was James Harper, were sent to Canada to procure provisions for the winter. They despatched four barrels of flour by this vessel, and waited some weeks for the other, the captain of which had agreed to bring provisions up the lake for them. Disappointed in this expectation, and hearing nothing of the vessel, they were compelled to return when the season was far advanced, without supplies; finding on their way home the remains of the vessel, which had been wrecked near Erie. They found also that the vessel which had on board the flour they had purchased had been driven into the basin, and was too fast locked in the ice to proceed. They were obliged therefore to remain till the ice became so strong that the flour could be removed in sleds. They at length arrived at home just in time to bring relief from absolute want to the settlers, who had lived six weeks without any kind of breadstuffs, substituting salt beef and turnips, the supply of which was just exhausted. Some grain had been raised at Elk Creek, in Pennsylvania, but there were no mills in that neighborhood, and the wheat afterwards procured there was brought in hand-sleds on the ice to Harpersfield. The records of the Historical Society state that the two sons of Mrs. Harper frequently brought bags of grain packed on their backs. It was ground in a hand-mill somewhat larger than a coffee-mill, which the pioneers had brought with them. By keeping this constantly in operation enough flour was obtained for daily use, mingled, of course, with the bran from which they had no means of separating it, but having a relish and sweetness which such necessity only could impart to the coarsest food.

There were no deer in the country at that time, but large droves of elk, the flesh of which resembled coarse beef, were frequently seen. The flesh of the bears was much more oily, and really very palatable; racoons also were abundant and easily obtained, and were much used by the settlers, although in after years of plenty they lost all relish for " coon meat." Hickory nuts were also abundant that year, and were found a valuable article of food when other provisions failed. It is worthy of notice, that in the severest straits to which the settlers were reduced, the utmost harmony and friendly feeling prevailed among them, and whatever game or provisions chanced to be obtained by any one family was freely shared with the other two.

Towards spring the men were again sent for a supply of wheat, but by that time the ice was growing tender, and the weather tended towards thawing, so that they were detained on the way much longer than they had expected, and on their arrival at home found the families reduced to the last extremity, having been without provisions for two days. In this time of distress, the fortitude and energy of Mrs. Harper aided in supporting the rest; she was fruitful in expedients, and for the last few days they had lived on the wild leeks she had gathered from the woods and boiled for them. Their troubles did not terminate with the severity of the winter. As soon as the lake opened, the men set out for Canada in boats to procure provisions, but found so much ice as they went down that they were unable to reach Buffalo without much detention. In the meantime new difficulties arose in the little settlement. The mill, on which all depended, was broken beyond hope of repair, and there appeared no way of grinding the wheat, which they could not pound so that bread could be made of it, and which, when prepared by boiling, proved unwholesome food. In this extremity some relief was afforded by the arrival, at the mouth of Cunningham's Creek, of Eliphalet Austin, who came to make preparations for a settlement at Austin-burgh, and gave the pioneers what they needed for immediate use from his supplies of provisions, thus preventing them from suffering till the return of their messengers.

Howe gives an anecdote of Mrs. John Austin, showing some of the troubles of the settlers. "Hearing, on one occasion, a bear among her hogs, she determined to defeat his purpose. First hurrying her little children up a ladder into her chamber, for safety, in case she was overcome by the animal, she seized a rifle, and rushing to the spot saw the bear only a few rods distant, carrying off a hog into the woods, while the prisoner sent forth deafening squeals, accompanied by the rest of the sty in full chorus. Nothing daunted, she rushed forward to the scene with her rifle ready cocked, on which the monster let go his prize, raised himself upon his haunches and faced her. Dropping upon her knees to obtain a steady aim, and resting her rifle on the fence, within six feet of the bear, the intrepid female pulled the trigger. Perhaps fortunately *for her*, the rifle missed fire. Again and again she snapped her piece, but with the same result. The bear, after keeping his position some time, dropped down on all fours, and leaving the hog behind, retreated to the forest and resigned the field to the woman."

About this time an accident not uncommon in this forest life occurred to Mrs. Harper. She went out one morning to find the cows, which had strayed away, but not having yet learned to tell the north side of a tree by the difference in the bark—a species of woodcraft with which she afterwards became familiar—she lost herself, and wandered all day along the banks of a stream that ran through the depths of the forest. Her family, of course, became alarmed at her lengthened absence and blew the horn repeatedly; but it was not until the shades of night had fallen that she heard the signal, when she managed to light upon the township line, and followed it to the clearing. In the summer following, her sons were obliged to watch closely the hogs they had brought from Canada, on account of the bears, which were very numerous and destructive to stock. The men being occupied in clearing and working the land, or procuring provisions, various out-door employments were cheerfully assumed by the women. One evening Mrs. Harper, with her eldest daughter, went out to look up the hogs, taking the path leading to the nearest neighbor's house. Presently they were startled by seeing a small bear's cub cross the path just in advance of them; it was followed by another, and the old bear composedly brought up the rear, taking no notice of the females, who made their way home with all speed. The pigs came to their quarters directly unharmed. So frequent were encounters with wild beasts, that the men never went beyond the clearing without fire-arms.

In July, 1799, Major Joseph Harper, the Colonel's brother, joined the colony with his family, while a relative of the same name, with some other families, made a settlement at Conneaut, "the Plymouth of the Western Reserve," some thirty miles down the lake. This year wheat, corn, etc., were raised sufficient for the consumption; but there was a scarcity of meat, the severity of the preceding winter having killed several of their cattle, and many of the hogs being devoured by the bears. The settlers were under the necessity, therefore, of depending on wild game, and the ease with which they secured it in traps, or by the unerring aim of their rifles, with their iron strength for the endurance of fatigue in ranging the forest, might well entitle them to be called "mighty hunters." But they were heavily laden with daily cares and laborious duties, which even the pleasures of the chase could not induce them to neglect; the clearing of the land and the culture of grain and vegetables demanded incessant attention, and the grinding of the grain was a matter requiring the exercise of some ingenuity. Corn they soon contrived to pound in mortars scooped in the top of oak stumps, with a pounder attached to a spring-pole; but they were obliged to send their wheat in boats down the lake as far as Walnut Creek, in Pennsylvania, where a mill was erected this year. The families of the new emigrants suffered considerably in the latter part of the summer from sickness, and Mrs. Harper went down to the settlement at Conneaut to offer assistance in attending to them. She remained some weeks occupied in her ministrations of kindness, and was not ready to return home till the last of November. Travelling in open boats and on horseback were the only modes practicable among the pioneers; the season was too far advanced for the first, and accompanied by her relative, James Harper, our benevolent heroine started on her homeward journey, the only road being along the lake shore. Fording the streams at their mouth, they had ridden some fifteen miles when they came to the mouth of Ashtabula Creek, across which a sand-bar had formed during the summer, but had now given way to the increased force of the waters flowing into the lake. Harper was not aware of the depth of the stream, into which he rode without hesitation, and presently found his horse swimming. He called out to warn his companion, but she was too anxious to reach home to heed his remonstrance, and followed him fearlessly. Both reached the other side with some difficulty, Mrs. Harper wet to the shoulders, and in this condition she rode the remainder of the way, arriving at home before midnight.

During the fall there were some accessions to the colony; Judge Wheeler, who had married a daughter of Col. Harper, came in October with his family, and Harper's eldest son, who had been out the year before and returned. For a year and a half after the settlement was commenced, they were not visited by Indians, though they frequently heard their dogs, and learned afterwards that they had not escaped the observation of their savage neighbors, who had counted them and noticed all their occupations and new arrivals. The winter of 1799-1800 was remarkable for the depth of snow upon the ground. In consequence of this, game could not be procured, and the Indians suffered severely. Some thirty of them, unable to procure anything to satisfy the cravings of hunger, came to the settlement to ask relief, and were treated with the most generous hospitality. They remained six weeks, sheltered and fed by the colonists, and when the snow was melted they found plenty of game in the forest, which they showed their gratitude by sharing with their white friends.

In March, 1800, Daniel Bartholomew brought out his family accompanied by that of Judge Griswold, whose destination was Windsor. They came on the ice from Buffalo, arriving only the day before the breaking up of the ice left the lake clear as far as the eye could reach. In the winter preceding, the whole Western Reserve had been erected into a county, which was called Trumbull, the part of it comprising Ashtabula being then included in one township, and called Richfield. In May there were still further accessions, in consequence of which a scarcity was experienced of provisions raised the previous year, and designed for the use of a much smaller number. The settlers were again compelled to send, in June, to Canada in an open boat, for fresh supplies. In August, an election was held for the purpose of sending a delegation to a convention appointed to be held at Chilicothe in the ensuing winter, for the purpose of taking measures preparatory to the admission of Ohio as a State into the Union. The winter of 1800-1801, passed without any remarkable occurrence, the country being healthy and provisions abundant. In the following June other families were added to the number of inhabitants, and the summer was signalized by the erection of a horse-mill, the first built in the country, and the only one for many miles round, till others were built in Austinburgh. The sufferings of the settlers from scarcity of food and other privations were now over, the advance of improvement developing the resources of the country · and the farmers were able to enlarge their cleared lands, and culti-vate the soil to better advantage. Their friends from the East con-tinued to join them, and Mrs. Harper had the satisfaction of seeing her elder children settled around her. In 1802, a school was estab-lished in the settlement; supposed to be the first on the Reserve. The scholars came from the distance of two miles and a half, and as the reputation of the institution extended, they were sent from Windsor and Burton, twenty and thirty miles distant. The same year regular meetings were established by the "Lovers of Good Order," and the year following saw numerous accessions.

In about three years after the commencement of the settlement, the Indians began to visit them periodically. They were chiefly Ojibways, and belonged to Lake Superior in the summer, but came down every fall in their bark canoes, and landing at the mouth of the streams, carried their canoes on their heads across the portage to Grand River, seven miles from the lake, where they took up their quarters for the winter, returning west in the spring. They mani-fested a friendly disposition towards the white men, and as the pio-neers gave them assistance in sickness and destitution, they endeav-ored to show their gratitude by bringing them portions of such large game as they killed. Many a choice piece of bear's or elk's meat, carefully wrapped in a blanket, has Mrs. Harper received from her savage friends. One day she saw a party of drunken Indians com-ing towards her house when the men were absent; and she had just time to conceal a small keg of liquor under the floor before they came in, demanding whiskey. They were told they could not have any, but insisting that they would, they commenced a search for it, and finding a barrel of vinegar, asked if that would "make drunk come," as if so, they would take it. Finding it not the right sort of stuff, they insisted, before leaving the house, on treating the women from a calabash of muddy whiskey which they carried with them.

During all the privations, trials and sufferings which Mrs. Harper was compelled to undergo, she was never known to yield to des-

23

pondency, but with untiring energy exerted herself to encourage all within the sphere of her influence, teaching them to bear up against misfortune, and make the best of the home where their lot was cast. Her own family knew not, until the hardships of pioneer life had been overcome, how much she had endured—how many hours of anxiety and sleepless nights she had passed in the days of darkness and disaster. She found her reward in the affection and usefulness of her children, several of whom filled important stations in their adopted State. During the war of 1812, the country was exposed to all the dangers of a frontier, liable, on every reverse of the American arms, to be overrun by hostile Indians. In time of danger, Mrs. Harper's advice was always eagerly sought, as one whose experience qualified her to decide on the best course in any emergency. Her grand-daughter well remembers seeing her one day engaged at the house of her son-in-law in showing a company of volunteers how to make cartridges.

Her life was prolonged to her eighty-fifth year, and she died on the 11th of June, 1833, retaining unimpaired until her last illness the characteristic strength of her remarkable mind.

" In May, 1799, Joel and Sarah Thorp moved with an ox-team from North Haven, Connecticut, to Millsford, in Ashtabula county, and were the first settlers in that region. They soon had a small clearing on and about an old beaver dam, which was very rich and mellow. Towards the first of June, the family being short of provisions, Mr. Thorp started off alone to procure some through the wilderness, with no guide but a pocket compass, to the nearest settlement, about twenty miles distant, in Pennsylvania. His family, consisting of Mrs. Thorp and three children—the oldest child, Basil, being but eight years of age—were before his return reduced to extremities for the want of food. They were compelled to dig for and in a measure subsist on roots, which yielded but little nourishment. The children in vain asked food, promising to be satisfied with the east possible portion. The boy Basil remembered to have seen some kernels of corn in a crack of one of the logs of the cabin, and passed hours in an unsuccessful search for them. Mrs. Thorp emptied the straw out of her bed, and picked it over to obtain the little wheat it contained, which she boiled and gave to her children. Her husband, it seems, had taught her to shoot at a mark, in which she acquired great skill. When all her means for procuring food were exhausted, she saw, as she stood in her cabin door, a wild turkey flying near. She took down her husband's rifle, and on looking for ammunition, was surprised to find only sufficient for a small charge. Carefully cleaning the barrel, so as not to lose any by its sticking to the sides as it went down, she set some apart for priming and loaded the piece with the remainder, and started in pursuit of the turkey, reflecting that on her success depended the lives of herself and children. Under the excitement of her feelings she came near defeating her object, by frightening the turkey, which flew a short distance and again alighted in a potatoe patch. Upon this, she returned to the house and waited until the fowl had begun to wallow in the loose earth. On her second approach, she acted with great caution and coolness, creeping slily on her hands and knees from log to log, until she had gained the last obstruction be-tween herself and the desired object. It was now a trying moment, and a crowd of emotions passed through her mind as she lifted the rifle to a level with her eye. She fired; the result was fortunate; the turkey was killed, and herself and family preserved from death by her skill. Mrs. Thorp married three times. Her first husband was killed in Canada in the war of 1812; her second was supposed to have been murdered. Her last husband's name was Gardiner. She died in Orange, in Cuyahoga county, Nov. 1st, 1846."*

The first surveying party of the Western Reserve landed at the mouth of Connèaut Creek, on the 4th of July, 1796. One of the company says—" We celebrated the day in the usual manner, so far as our means enabled us, by drinking patriotic toasts of pure lake

* Historical Collections of Ohio.

water from tin cups, and firing the usual number of salutes from two or three fowling-pieces."* The party numbered fifty two persons, including two women, Mrs. Gunn and Mrs. Stiles. The next day the laborers commenced building a house as the dwelling-place of the families and storehouse of their provisions. In their exploration the surveyors discovered a fine bee tree. " We encamped, cut down the tree, and ate to our satisfaction, each man filling his canteen ; and the residue was put into the bags of flour. Except for two or three days, while our honey lasted, we lived on bread alone. On our arrival at the lake we took the beach, and went east to our camp at Conneaut ; and what was remarkable, on our way we fell in with all three of the parties, who had each finished their lines and joined ours. During our absence the house had been completed, and Gen. Cleveland † had assembled there a small tribe of Indians residing a few miles up Conneaut Creek, had held a council with them, made them some presents, and established a friendly intercourse. The General had furnished himself with an Indian dress, and being of swarthy complexion, afforded an excellent likeness of an Indian chief, and was thereafter known in the party by the name of Pagua, the name of the chief of the tribe referred to."

The first permanent settlement was not commenced till two years afterwards. One of the early settlers, on his return from Erie, with corn, along the ice on the lake shore, fell into an " ice hole" some distance from the land, and after spending some time in vain efforts to extricate his horse, took the meal, saddle and bridle upon his shoulders, and made for the shore, with his clothes frozen stiff upon him. On the beach he kindled a fire, and after partially drying himself, proceeded on his journey. Some time after nightfall he came to a stream on the west bank of which stood an empty cabin ; to reach this and spend the night was his desire, but with the stream he was unacquainted. He built a large fire, and by the light of it ventured to ford it with his load ; fortunately the water

---

* MSS. in possession of John Barr, Esq., of Cleveland.

† Moses Cleveland, the Director of survey commenced by the Connecticut Land Company

was only about five feet deep, and after much danger and difficulty he succeeded in reaching the cabin, where, by building a fire, and running about to keep himself awake, he spent the night. The next day at night he reached home, almost exhausted by his load and want of food.

In the year 1798, small settlements, few and far between, sprinkled the Reserve, and a small illbuilt schooner constituted the American fleet on Lake Erie. Subsequently the Indian title to that part of the Reserve lying west of the Cuyahoga, was extinguished, and the lands were brought into market. An apology for a grist-mill had been erected near Cleveland, which had no competitor within a hundred miles, and gave general satisfaction, as few had any thing to grind. Five or six log cabins had been built in what was called "the city of Cleveland." Capt. Edward Paine made the first sleigh-track through the wilderness from Cataraugus to Erie, accompanied by his wife, her sister, and a female cousin, and encamped two nights in the snow. In the fall, business obliged James Kingsbury, the father of one of the families at Conneaut—the first, it is said, that wintered on the Reserve—to go to Connecticut; and it was the middle of November before he arrived at Buffalo on his return. The snow had fallen to the depth of two and a half feet, and the weather was extremely cold.

"From this point Mr. Kingsbury must leave the habitation of the white man, and make his way through a wilderness, one hundred and thirty miles, with no road to guide him except for a part of that distance the beach of the lake. He was sensible of the condition in which he had left his family; that they had but a scanty supply of provisions, and that his absence had already been longer than was expected. These circumstances, with the setting in of a winter so severe, filled his mind with the painful apprehension that his family might be suffering starvation. Having provided himself with such necessaries as he could procure, with which he loaded his horse, he set forth on foot, and leading his horse, pursued the beach of the lake. After a fatiguing march through the snow, he reached the Indian settlement on the Cataraugus. As from this place, on account of the bold projecting bluffs, he could no longer follow the beach, he procured an Indian, by the name of Seneca Billy, to guide him through the trackless forest, and took his course through the woods, leading his horse as before mentioned. In this manner he toiled through the deep snow, camping each night in the midst of it, for several days, when he reached Presqu' Isle. With much difficulty he was able at this place to procure a bag of corn, for which he paid three dollars a bushel. Here he dismissed his Indian guide, and again took to the lake, travelling upon the ice. He had proceeded in this manner as far as the fire spring, near the mouth of Elk Creek, when his horse broke through the ice, and though he extricated him, he was so badly injured that he was obliged to leave him ; and taking the bag of corn upon his own back, he reached his home, but not such a home as could afford him consolation after his excessive toil and suffering. He found a family perishing for want of food. His wife had given birth to a child, not only without any of those comforts which in such cases are usually deemed indispensable, but destitute of even the coarsest food, herself and family being in nearly a famishing state. The father soon after his arrival was doomed to see the child expire of starvation.

"The infant was, I believe, the first white child born on the Reserve. Some three or four months afterwards, Mrs. Stiles, of Cleveland, presented her husband with one more fortunate, not only as to life, but the means of sustaining it ; to wit—a donation of land by the Company—at least so said rumor.

"As the supply which Kingsbury had brought would last but a short time, it became necessary that he should procure more. The Connecticut Land Company had stored the provisions for the use of their surveyors at Cleveland, and Kingsbury knew that of this some barrels of salt beef still remained. Having lost his horse, as before mentioned, and being destitute of any other, it was fortunate that the severity of the season, which had contributed to the suffering of his family by making the ice excellent, facilitated at this time the means of supplying their wants. Taking advantage of this, he went

to Cleveland, (seventy miles) and procuring one of the barrels of
beef, drew it home upon the ice on a hand-sled, in which he was
assisted by a man then at Cleveland. When they arrived they
found the first shanty erected by the Company, occupied by Capt.
Hodge and family."

The wife of Hon. John Walworth, one of the earliest settlers of
Lake County, shared with him all the toils and privations attendant
upon a settlement in the wilderness. An old pioneer writes of her,
" In our pioneer days she went hand in hand with her husband
in all that was kind, hospitable, and generous ; and to her winning
and attractive manner, and her sprightliness and vivacity, we must
in part attribute the resort to their house of the polished and respectable part of the community. Twice has that lady travelled from this
country to the furthest part of Connecticut and back, on horseback :
I mention this to show her resolution and perseverance." Early in
1800, Mr. Walworth brought his family in a sleigh to Buffalo, where
they waited two weeks for a sleigh to come from Presqu' Isle, then
proceeded on the ice till they came opposite Cataraugus Creek.
Leaving the sleighs and horses some fifty or sixty roods out, the
party went to the shore and encamped under some hemlock trees,
and partook of a repast seasoned with hilarity and good feeling. The
next afternoon all arrived in safety at Presqu' Isle, whence Mr. Walworth went back to Buffalo for his goods. Mr. Walworth's nearest
neighbors east of his new purchase, were at Harpersfield, fifteen miles
distant. His family reached their new home April 7th, 1800, and lived
in a tent for two weeks, during which time the sun was not seen.*

On the 4th July, 1801, the first ball was given in Cleveland, at
Major Carter's log cabin under the hill. The company consisted of
a dozen ladies and from fifteen to twenty gentlemen. The dancers
kept time to Major Jones' violin, on the puncheon floor, and occasionally refreshed themselves with a glass of sling, made of maple
sugar and whiskey ; and never was the anniversary celebrated by
" a more joyful and harmonious company, than those who dance'

* MS. of J. Barr, Esq.

the scamperdown, double-shuffle, western swing, and half-moon" in that unostentatious place of assemblage.

The first school opened in the town was taught, in 1802, by Miss Anna Spafford, also in a room of Major Carter's cabin. This "thorough pioneer" appears to have been foremost in every advance of improvement. An incident in which his wife was concerned, showing something of the spirit of the times, I take from the MSS. referred to :—" In the summer of 1803, Mrs. Carter observed John Orric and another Indian lad in her garden, breaking some small fruit trees. Upon her reproving them, young Orric knocked her down with his war-club and seriously injured her. The lads fled immediately to the west side of the river to their fathers' lodges. Several days afterwards, Major Carter, who was on the watch, observed these lads, with others, amusing themselves with playing ball and swimming on the beach of the lake. He went there and took the lads prisoner, secured them with ropes, and took them to the Indian camp on the side hill, telling them he was going to hang them. Not finding Orric's father at the lodge, he released the other lad, and directed him to go and tell him he had John a prisoner and was going to hang him for striking his wife. The lad did the errand faithfully, for the Major soon heard the Indian whoop of alarm, followed speedily by the war-whoop from the different lodges on the west side of the river. John's father soon arrived, much excited, and with all the savageness of his nature depicted in his face, with his tomahawk uplifted ready for deadly revenge. He confronted the Major, giving him one of those fierce, gleaming stares, so significant in the Indian brave; but the eyes of the Major met his and did not quail. The injured husband and the enraged father stood and gazed long in silence, each glancing defiance at the other; at length the eye of the savage turned from the calm, fearless look of the white hunter, and he enquired the cause of his son's capture. Carter told him of John's assault upon his wife, and his determination to have him punished. By this time, traders and other Indians had arrived and proposed to arrange the matter. John's father sent him with twenty dollars to give to Mrs. Carter, and ask her forgiveness

for the injury he had done; the Major agreeing to nothing unless
Mrs. Carter was satisfied. Mrs. Carter indignantly refused the
proffered money, and ordered John out of the house; he returned
crestfallen to the council and reported the failure of his mission. By
this time Carter became much enraged, and notwithstanding he was
in the midst of over forty Indians, most of them well armed, it was
with great difficulty he could be prevailed upon not to kill John
upon the spot. After a long parley, however, he agreed that the
affair might rest for the present; but on this condition, that if John
was ever caught on the east side of the Cuyahoga River he should
certainly hang him."

XVI.

ELIZABETH TAPPEN.

ELIZABETH HARPER was the second daughter of Alexander and Elizabeth Harper, and was born February 24th, 1784, in Harpersfield, New York. She was in the fifteenth year of her age when she accompanied her parents to Ohio, in 1798, and was the oldest daughter who went with them, her elder sister having been married some years and remaining in their old home.

The labors and perils of commencing a settlement in an almost unbroken wilderness, encountered by all who took part in this adventurous enterprise, were shared without a murmur by the young girl, to whom fell, of course, no small part of the work of the household and the care of the younger children. The novelty of their mode of living, and the wild forest scenery, with incessant occupation, caused the time to pass speedily and pleasantly through the first summer; but with the approach of a more rigorous season, their hardships commenced, and the death of her beloved father brought before the bereaved family the realities of their situation, far from early friends, and isolated from the comforts of civilization. Elizabeth suffered much at this time of gloom and distrust, with a longing for home, and fears for the future; but the fortitude and resolution with which Mrs. Harper sustained herself under the pressure of calamity, had a due influence on the minds of her children, and the feeling of discontent was soon subdued.

During the absence of James, who went to Canada, as mentioned in the preceding sketch, to procure provisions, another son, William, broke his leg. The other boys were seven and nine years old, and as they could do nothing of consequence, the work of providing firewood for use in the house devolved entirely, for some four weeks, upon Elizabeth and her younger sister, Mary. It was no easy task to cut, split, and bring home all the fuel consumed, as the cabin was very open and large fires were required.

The prospects for the approaching winter were very dark, owing to the scarcity of provision and the want of comfortable quarters; and Mrs. Harper thought it best to send her younger daughter to stay with some friends at a settlement in Pennsylvania. She determined not to accept the invitation for herself, and Elizabeth decided to stay with her mother. The winter proved one of unusual severity, and the settlers suffered greatly from the want of provisions after the wreck of the only vessel on the southern shore of Lake Erie, their supplies having to be brought from Canada. Twice the little community was reduced almost to the point of starvation, having to relieve the cravings of hunger with strange substitutes for wholesome food. On the last occasion, when the men sent for supplies returned, they brought with them a small quantity of coarse Indian meal boiled, which was called samp. Mrs. Harper warmed a portion of this, and making some tea, called her family to partake of the simple meal, then a luxury privation had taught them to appreciate. Most of the children felt sick from absolute want, and disinclined to touch the food, but after tasting it, they were so eager for more that it required all the mother's firmness to restrain them from taking more than they could bear in so weakened a state.

It has been mentioned that a quantity of wheat raised in Pennsylvania, was brought on hand-sleds a distance of fifty miles on the ice to the settlement, and ground in a small mill belonging to one of the families. It was Elizabeth's work to grind that required for

her family.   She would take a peck of wheat and walk two miles
and a half to grind it, then carry home the meal and make it into
bread.   The mill would grind no more than a bushel of grain in
a day when constantly in use, and three families were to be supplied.   The men being occupied in bringing the wheat and attending to other necessary duties, the grinding was chiefly done by the
women.

Many of the cattle belonging to the settlers died this winter, and
some of the oxen disappeared, supposed to have been killed and
carried off by the Indians.   The disaster that caused so much inconvenience the following season—the breaking of the little mill
which had been so useful, set them upon the invention of a substitute.   A hole was burned and scraped in the top of an oak stump,
large enough to hold a quantity of corn which was then pounded as
fine as possible with a pounder attached to a spring pole resembling
a well-sweep, the heavy end being fastened to the ground.   This
contrivance was called a mortar.   Their ovens were equally primitive.   As neither brick nor stone was to be had, a stump was hewn
perfectly flat on the top, and a slab hewn out and laid upon it.   On
this the women spread a layer of clay, and placed upon it wood
heaped up in the form of an oven, covering the whole except a small
opening at one end, with a thick layer of clay.   It stood a short
time to dry, and then the wood was set on fire and burned out.
The oven thus manufactured proved an excellent one for use, and
served as a model for all the ovens in the country for some years
afterwards.

In the autumn of the second year of the settlement, Mrs.
Wheeler, Mrs. Harper's eldest daughter, came with her husband
and family, and they took up their residence in a cabin they built
half a mile from that of the widow.   They were joined by several
other families soon afterwards.

Some anecdotes of their encounters with the wild beasts of the
forest are remembered in family tradition.   One summer evening in
the third year, when William Harper was returning about dusk
from Judge Wheeler's, his attention was arrested by the sight of a

bear just in the path before him, engaged in devouring a hog he had just killed. William fired at the animal without apparent effect, and was hastily reloading his gun, when the bear desisted from his meal, and started in pursuit of the new enemy. Fortunately, a large tree was near at hand, which the young man ran round, the bear closely following and tearing off pieces of the bark in his fury. William contrived, while dodging him, to load his gun, and fired eleven times before the enraged animal fell to the ground; then, completely exhausted by the efforts he had made to keep the foe at bay, he hastened homeward, and met his brother, who alarmed by hearing reports in such rapid succession, had come to look for him. On going to the spot the next evening, they found the bear quite dead, with ten of the eleven balls in his body, the tree being entirely stripped of bark as high as he could reach.

It was not long after this that Elizabeth, while staying with her sister in the absence of her husband, was alarmed by an attack from one of these ferocious animals. A crazy woman belonging to the settlement had come to stay the night in the house. Late in the evening they heard a noise among some fowls roosting upon the projecting logs of the cabin, and going to the door they distinctly saw a large bear standing on his hind legs, trying to reach the fowls, that crowded together in their terror above the range of his paws. It required all Elizabeth's presence of mind and energy to prevent the lunatic from rushing out; but by alarming her fears she persuaded her to be quiet, and fastened the doors. A more severe encounter took place some years afterwards, in the house of her brother. A hungry bear broke into the yard and attempted to catch a goose wandering on the premises. Mrs. Harper, the sister-in-law, hastily called to her children to come in, and barred the door; but the fierce creature had heard the sound of her voice, and bent on securing his prey, sprang through the open window and attacked her. Her clothes were much torn, and her arm badly scratched; but her husband and a man who chanced to be with him coming to the rescue, they beat off the bear with clubs, and killed him. The

fright of Mrs. Harper had such an effect upon her that she suffered
n health for many years.

When the school was established in 1802, the earliest on the
Reserve, Elizabeth Harper was employed to teach it. The following winter Abraham Tappen was appointed to take charge of it,
and some of the scholars came from distant settlements. The
school was taught alternately by Tappen and Miss Harper during
the winter and summer, for some years. Religious meetings were
established about the same time.

In 1806, Elizabeth was married to Abraham Tappen, then
engaged as a surveyor, and employed in equalizing the claims of
land-holders. His duties compelled him to be absent from home
during a great part of the time, and after they were settled, the
labor of superintending the clearing of a new farm devolved upon
the wife. The work was done, however, with an energy and cheerful spirit worthy the daughter of such a mother ; and a substantial
foundation was thus laid for future comfort and prosperity. For a
few years the youthful couple lived in a small log hut containing
but one room, in which it was necessary very frequently to enter-
tain company, as Tappen's acquaintance and business associations
with land owners and land agents brought strangers continually to
his house, and the duties of hospitality were esteemed sacred in the
most primitive settlements. Mrs. Tappen was often obliged to
spread the floor with beds for the accommodation of her guests,
and the abundance of her table, and the excellent quality of her
cooking, could be attested by many who from time to time were the
chance inmates of her cheerful home. At that early period an unaf-
fected kindness of feeling, poorly replaced in a more advanced state
of society by the conventionalities of good breeding, prevailed among
the settlers, and some families were sincerely attached to each other.
Good offices were interchanged between neighbors every day, and a
friendly intercourse maintained by frequent visits. These were often
paid from one to another, even when a journey of fifteen miles on
horseback, occupying a whole day, had to be performed. The
alarms and accidents to which a new settlement is liable, tended

also to bind the emigrants together for mutual assistance and protection. One of a number of similar incidents which occurred in
1811, caused much trouble to the Harper family. A son of Mrs.
Wheeler, nine years of age, had gone out alone to gather chestnuts.
The afternoon was sultry, and he was thinly clad, but it was not
long before a terrible storm of wind and rain came on, prostrating
acres of the forest, and swelling the streams in a little while to
torrents. Just before dark, Mrs. Tappen received a hasty summons
to go to her sister, whom she found half frantic with fears for the
missing boy. The alarm quickly spread, the neighbors assembled,
and people came from a distance of fifteen and twenty miles to aid
in the search, which was continued through the next day and the
following one, without success, till near the close of the third day,
when the child was found in so exhausted a state that in attempting
to rise he fell upon his face. His limbs were torn and filled with
porcupine's quills.

Not very long afterwards, another boy belonging to the settlement was lost in the woods, and the members of his family, in the
search for him, called his name aloud repeatedly. It may not be
generally known that the panther, which at this time came frequently
near the dwellings of man, emits a cry resembling a human voice
in distress. The calling of the boy's name was several times
answered, as his friends supposed, and after following the sound and
hallooing some time, they discovered that the voice was not human.
In a state of torturing anxiety and apprehension, they were obliged
to wait for day-light, when the boy made his appearance. He had
wandered in an opposite direction from the panther's locality, and
had found shelter at a house, where he remained all night.

The experience of Mrs. Tappen during her residence in the backwoods was full of such incidents. But the forest around them
gradually receded before the axe of the enterprising emigrant, the
country became cleared and cultivated, and with the progress of
improvement the condition of the early settlers became more safe
and comfortable. Judge Tappen and Mrs. Tappen still reside on
the same farm which they first reduced to cultivation, about half a

mile from the spot where her father fixed his dwelling on his first removal to the country.   The little village of Unionville, in Lake County, Ohio, has been built partly on Judge Tappen's farm, and partly on the land formerly owned by his wife, the county line running through it.

XVII.

REBECCA HEALD.

It was the lot of this matron to have the story of her life associated with one of the most remarkable and melancholy events recorded in the annals of border warfare. She was the wife of Capt. Heald, commandant at Fort Dearborn, Chicago, and bore a part in the scenes of the massacre that took place there on the 15th August, 1812. A brief notice of her will be an appropriate introduction to an account of that memorable occurrence.

Rebecca Wells was the daughter of Col. Wells of Kentucky. Her uncle, with whom she resided in early life, was Capt. William Wells. The story of this brave man, who forms so conspicuous a figure in our frontier annals, was a singular romance. When a child he was captured by the Miami Indians, and became the adopted son of Little Turtle, the most eminent forest warrior and statesman between Pontiac and Tecumseh, and the leader of the confederated tribes. When old enough, the captive was compelled to do service, and took a distinguished part in the defeats of Harmar and St. Clair. It is said that his sagacity foresaw that the white men would be roused by these reverses to put forth their superior power in such a manner as to command success; and also that a desire to return to his own people influenced him to abandon the savages. "His mode of announcing this determination was in accordance with the simple and sententious habits of forest life. He was traversing the woods one morning with his adopted father, the Little Turtle, when pointing to the heavens, he said, ' When the sun reaches the meridian, I leave you for the whites ; and whenever you meet me in battle, you must kill me, as I shall endeavor to kill you.' The bonds of affection and respect which had bound these two singular and highly gifted men together were not severed or weakened by this abrupt declaration." Wells soon after joined the army of Gen. Wayne, who had taken command of the troops after the resignation of St. Clair, and by his knowledge of the forest, and of the Indian haunts, habits, and modes of warfare, became an invaluable auxiliary to the Americans. He commanded a very effective division of spies, of whom were the best woodsmen on the frontier, served faithfully and fought bravely through the campaign, and after Wayne's treaty at Greenville in 1795 had restored peace between the Indians and the whites, rejoined his foster father, Little Turtle, their friendship remaining uninterrupted till the death of the chief.

Gen. Hunt mentions an incident which may show the sanguinary spirit of the border warfare. Capt. Wells made an excursion with Lieut. McClenan and eleven men into the enemy's country, following a trail of Indians for two days. They came in sight of them just as they were about encamping for the night, and waited till it was dark to make their attack. Wells, having then assumed the dress of an Indian warrior, advanced with his men, who, on the first alarm given by the savages, threw themselves on the ground, while the Captain continued to approach. Supposing him a friend, the Indians met and took him into their camp, he taking the precaution to seat himself on the extreme right of the war-party, and within view of McClenan. He then announced himself as from the British fort Miami, and commenced giving the party, consisting of twenty-two Indians and a squaw, the news from their British allies. The squaw meanwhile placed over the fire a kettle full of hominy, and as it began to boil, stirred it with a ladle, when the party of white men, mistaking her motions for the concerted signal of attack, fired upon the savages. The poor squaw received a shot, and fell across the fire ; the Captain saw that his life depended on prompt action, and grasping his tomahawk, commenced the work of slaughter, while his men rushed into the midst. All the Indians were killed except three, who made their escape. Both the Captain and Lieutenant were wounded.

In consideration of his services, Capt. Wells was appointed Indian agent at Fort Wayne. At this post he continued until the war of 1812, soon after the outbreak of which he departed for the purpose of escorting the troops from Chicago to Fort Wayne.

The gentleman* to whom I am indebted for much of the information contained in this sketch, visited Capt. Wells at Fort Wayne in 1809, and there formed an acquaintance with his niece. One of his juvenile amusements was setting up a target for her to shoot at with a rifle. She and Capt. Heald were accustomed to go out with their rifles to shoot at the bunghole of a barrel at a distance of one hundred yards, and from continual practice Miss Wells had become extremely expert in that soldierlike exercise. The Captain was at that time evidently a candidate for the favor of the fair markswoman, and took great pleasure in instructing her in every species of military accomplishment which she took a fancy to learn. Shortly after this period they were married ; and in 1812 Capt. Heald was in command of the garrison at Chicago. This, it will be remembered, was at that time a remote outpost of the American frontier, scarcely to be called a settlement, as the only inhabitants without the garrison were a few Canadians and the family of a gentleman engaged in the fur trade, who had removed from St. Joseph's in 1804. He was a great favorite among the Indians, who called him by a name signifying "the Silverman," from the circumstance of his furnishing them with rings, brooches, and other ornaments of that metal. His influence with the tribes wherever his trading-posts were dispersed, made him an object of suspicion to the British, and being at length taken prisoner, he was detained in captivity till the close of the war.

The peninsula of Michigan was then a wilderness, peopled only

* Gen. John E. Hunt, of Maumee City, Ohio.

by savages; and intercourse between the posts of Fort Wayne, Detroit, and Chicago, was carried on by such hardy travellers as ventured occasionally to encounter the perils and fatigues of the journey, guided by a devious Indian trail, encamping at night beside a stream, or seeking shelter in some hospitable wigwam, or even lodging among the branches of the trees.* The fort at Chicago was constructed with two blockhouses on the southern side, and a sallyport or subterranean passage from the parade-ground to the river, designed either to facilitate an escape, or as a means of supplying the garrison with water during a siege. The chief officers at this time, besides Capt. Heald, were very young men; the command numbered about seventy-five men, not all of whom were able to do service. The garrison had maintained a constant and friendly intercourse with the neighboring Indians, and as the principal chiefs of all the bands in the vicinity seemed to be on the most amicable terms with the Americans, no interruption of their harmony was anticipated.

After the fatal event, however, many circumstances were recollected, which should have opened their eyes. One instance may be mentioned. In the spring previous, two Indians of the Calumet band came to the post, on a visit to the commanding officer. As they passed through the quarters, they saw Mrs. Heald and another lady playing at battledore, and one of the savages said to the interpreter, "The white chiefs' wives are amusing themselves; it will not be long before they are hoeing in our cornfields." This speech, then regarded as merely an idle threat, or an expression of jealous feeling at the contrast with the situation of their own women, was remembered mournfully some months afterwards.

The first alarm was given on the evening of the 7th of April, 1812. Near the junction of Chicago river with Lake Michigan, directly opposite the fort, from which it was separated by the river and a few rods of sloping green turf, stood the dwelling-house and trading establishment of Mr. Kinzie. This gentleman was at home,

---

* I have availed myself throughout this sketch, of a narrative of the massacre printed at Chicago in 1844; said to be written by an accomplished lady residing in that city.

playing the violin for the amusement of his children; they were dancing merrily, awaiting the return of their mother, who had gone a short distance up the river to visit a sick neighbor. Suddenly the door was thrown open, and Mrs. Kinzie rushed in, pale with affright, and hardly able to articulate—"The Indians! The Indians! They are up at Lee's place, killing and scalping!" This was a farm intersected by the river, about four miles from its mouth. Mrs. Kinzie, when she had breath enough to speak, informed her startled family that while she had been "at Burns', a man and boy were seen running down on the opposite side of the river; and that they had called across to Burns' family to save themselves, for the Indians were at Lee's place, from which they had just made their escape." The fugitives were on their way to the fort.

All was now consternation. The family were hurried into two old pirogues moored near the house, and paddled across the river to take refuge in the fort, where the man—a discharged soldier— and boy had already told their story. In the afternoon, a party of ten or twelve Indians, dressed and painted, had arrived at the house, and according to the custom among savages, entered and seated themselves without ceremony. Something in their appearance and manner had excited the suspicions of one of the family—a Frenchman—who observed, "I do not like the looks of these Indians; they are none of our folks. I know by their dress and paint that they are not Pottowattamies." Upon this the soldier bade the boy follow him, and walked leisurely towards the two canoes tied near the bank. Some of the Indians asked where he was going; on which he pointed to the cattle standing among the haystacks on the opposite bank and made signs that they must go and fodder them; and that they would return and get their supper. He got into one canoe and the boy into the other. When they had gained the other side of the narrow stream, they pulled some hay for the cattle, making a show of collecting them, and when they had gradually made a circuit, so that their movements were concealed by the haystacks, they took to the woods near, and made for the fort. They had run about a quarter of a mile, when they heard the discharge of two guns, and when they came opposite Burns' they called to warn the family of their danger and hastened on.

A party of five or six soldiers, commanded by Ronan, was sent from the fort to the rescue of Burns' family : they went up the river in a scow, took the mother with her infant scarcely a day old, on her bed to the boat, and conveyed her with the rest to the fort.

The same afternoon a corporal and six soldiers had gone up the river to fish. Fearing that they might encounter the savages, the commanding officer at the fort now ordered a cannon to be fired to warn them of danger. Hearing the signal, they put out their torches and dropped down the river in silence. It will be borne in mind that the unsettled state of the country since the battle of Tippecanoe the preceding November, caused every man to be on the alert, and the slightest alarm was sufficient to ensure vigilance. When the fishing party reached " Lee's place," it was proposed to stop and bid the inmates be on their guard, as the signal from the fort indicated danger. All was still around the house, but they groped their way, and as the corporal leaped the fence into the small enclosure, he placed his hand upon the dead body of a man, who he soon ascertained had been scalped. The faithful dog stood guarding the lifeless remains of his master. The soldiers retreated to their canoes, and reached the fort about eleven o'clock. The next morning a party of citizens and soldiers went to Lee's and found two dead bodies, which were buried near the fort. It was subsequently ascertained, from traders in the Indian country, that the perpetrators of this bloody deed were a party of Winnebagoes, who had come into the neighborhood determined to kill every white man without the walls of the fort. Hearing the report of the cannon, they set off on their retreat to their homes on Rock river.

The inhabitants of the place, consisting of a few discharged soldiers and some families of half-breeds, now entrenched themselves in the " agency house," a log building standing a few rods from the fort. It had piazzas in front and rear, which were planked up ; portholes were cut, and sentinels posted at night. The enemy was supposed to be still lurking in the neighborhood, and an order was issued forbidding any soldier or citizen to leave the vicinity of the garrison without a guard. One night a sergeant and private who were out on patrol, came suddenly upon a party of Indians in the pasture adjoining the esplanade, and fired upon them as they made good their retreat. The next morning traces of blood were found, extending some distance into the prairie. On another occasion the savages entered the esplanade to steal the horses, and not finding them in the stable, made themselves amends for their disappointment by stabbing the sheep and then turning them loose. The poor animals ran towards the fort; the alarm was given, and parties were sent out, but the marauders escaped.

These occurrences were enough to keep the inmates of the fort in a state of apprehension, but they were no further disturbed for many weeks. On the afternoon of August 7th, a Pottowattamie chief arrived at the post, bearing despatches from Gen. Hull, at Detroit, which announced the declaration of war between the United States and Great Britain; also that the island of Mackinaw had fallen into the hands of the British.

The orders to the commanding officer, Capt. Heald, were " to evacuate the post, if practicable, and in that event, to distribute all the United States' property contained in the fort and the United States' factory or agency, among the Indians in the neighborhood." After having delivered his despatches, the chief, Winnemeg, requested a private interview with Mr. Kinzie, who had taken up his residence within the garrison, stated that he was acquainted with the purport of the communications, and earnestly advised that the post should not be evacuated, since the garrison was well supplied with ammunition and provision for six months. It would be better to remain till a reinforcement could be sent to their assistance. In case, however, Capt. Heald should decide upon leaving the fort, it should be done immediately, as the Pottowattamies, through whose country they must pass, were ignorant of the object of Winnemeg's mission, and a forced march might be made before the hostile Indians were prepared to intercept them.

Capt. Heald was immediately informed of this advice, and replied that it was his intention to evacuate the fort; but that, inasmuch as he had received orders to distribute the United States' property, he would not leave till he had collected the Indians in the neighborhood and made an equitable division among them. Winnemeg then suggested the expediency of marching out and leaving all things standing, for while the savages were dividing the spoils the troops might possibly effect their retreat unmolested. This counsel, though strongly seconded, was not approved by the commanding officer.

The order for evacuating the post was read the next morning upon parade, and in the course of the day, as no council was called, the officers waited upon Capt. Heald, and urged him to relinquish his design on account of the improbability that the command would be permitted to pass in safety to Fort Wayne by the savages, whose thirst for slaughter could hardly be controlled by the few individuals who were supposed to have friendly feelings towards the Americans. Their march must of necessity be slow, as a number of women and children, with some invalid soldiers, would accompany the detachment. Their advice, therefore, was to remain, and fortify themselves as strongly as possible, in hopes that succor from the other side of the peninsula would arrive before they could be attacked by the British from Mackinaw. In reply to this remonstrance Capt. Heald urged that he should be censured for remaining when there appeared a prospect of a safe march, and that on the whole he deemed it most expedient to assemble the Indians, distribute the property among them, and then ask of them an escort to Fort Wayne, with the promise of a considerable reward upon their safe arrival, adding that he had full confidence in the friendly professions of the savages, from whom, as well as from the soldiers, the capture of Mackinaw had been kept a profound secret.

The project was considered a mad one, and much and increasing dissatisfaction prevailed among the officers and soldiers. The Indians became every day more unruly. Entering the fort in defiance of the sentinels, they often made their way without ceremony to the quarters of the officers. On one occasion a savage took up a rifle, and fired it in Mrs. Heald's parlor. Some supposed this a signal

for an attacк, as there was vehement agitation among the old chiefs
and squaws ; but the manifestation of hostile feeling was suppressed,
and the Captain continued to feel confidence in such an amicable disposition among the Indians, as would ensure the safety of his troops
on their march to Fort Wayne.

The inmates of the fort, meanwhile, suffered greatly from apprehension, scarcely daring to yield to sleep at night, and a general
gloom and distress prevailed. The Indians being assembled from
the neighboring villages, a council was held with them on the 12th,
Capt. Heald alone attending on the part of the military, as his officers refused to accompany him. Information had secretly been
brought to them that it was the intention of the young chiefs to fall
upon them and murder them while in council, but the Captain
could not be persuaded of the truth of this, and therefore left the
garrison, while the officers who remained took command of the
block-houses which overlooked the esplanade on which the council
was held, opened the port-holes, and pointed the cannon so as to
command the whole assembly.

" In council, the commanding officer informed the Indians of his
intention to distribute among them, the next day, not only the goods
lodged in the United States' Factory, but also the ammunition and
provisions with which the garrison was well supplied. He then
requested of the Pottowattamies an escort to Fort Wayne, promising
them a liberal reward upon their arrival there, in addition to the
presents they were now to receive. With many professions of
friendship and good-will the savages assented to all he proposed, and
promised all he required.

" After the council, Mr. Kinzie, who understood well, not only the
Indian character, but the present tone of feeling among them,
waited upon Capt. Heald, in the hope of opening his eyes to the
present posture of affairs. He reminded him that since the trouble
with the Indians upon the Wabash and its vicinity, there had
appeared a settled plan of hostilities towards the whites; in consequence of which, it had been the policy of the Americans to
withhold from them whatever would enable them to carry on their

13

warfare upon the defenceless settlers on the frontier. **Mr. Kinzie** recalled to Capt. Heald the fact that he had himself left home for Detroit the preceding autumn, and receiving, when he had proceeded as far as De Charme's,* the intelligence of the battle of Tippecanoe, he had immediately returned to Chicago, that he might despatch orders to his traders to furnish no ammunition to the Indians ; all that they had on hand was therefore secreted, and such of the traders as had not already started for their wintering-grounds, took neither powder nor shot with their outfit.

"Capt. Heald was struck with the impolicy of furnishing the enemy, (for such they must now consider their old neighbors,) with arms against himself, and determined to destroy all the ammunition, excepting what should be necessary for the use of his own troops. On the 13th, the goods, consisting of blankets, broadcloths, calicos, paints, etc., were distributed, as stipulated. The same evening, part of the ammunition and liquor was carried into the sally-port, and thrown into a well, which had been dug there to supply the garrison with water in case of emergency the remainder was transported as secretly as possible through the northern gate, and the heads of the barrels were knocked in, and the contents poured into the river. The same fate was shared by a large quantity of alcohol which had been deposited in a warehouse opposite the fort. The Indians suspected what was going on, and crept as near the scene of action as possible, but a vigilant watch was kept up, and no one was suffered to approach but those engaged in the affair. All the muskets not necessary for the march were broken up and thrown into the well, together with bags of shot, flints, gun-screws, etc.

"Some relief to the general despondency was afforded by the arrival, on the 14th of August, of Capt. Wells, with fifteen friendly Miamies. He had heard at Fort Wayne of the order for evacuating Fort Dearborn, and knowing the hostile determination of the Pottowattamies, had made a rapid march across the country to prevent the exposure of his relative, Capt. Heald, and his troops

* A trading establishment—now Ypsilanti.

to certain destruction. But he came too late. When he reached the post, he found that the ammunition had been destroyed, and the provisions given to the Indians. There was therefore no alternative, and every preparation was made for the march of the troops on the following morning.

"On the afternoon of the same day, a second council was held with the Indians. They expressed great indignation at the destruction of the ammunition and liquor. Notwithstanding the precautions that had been taken to preserve secrecy, the noise of knocking in the heads of the barrels had too plainly betrayed the operations of the preceding night; and so great was the quantity of liquor thrown into the river, that the taste of the water, the next morning, was, as one expressed it, 'strong grog.' Murmurs and threats were everywhere heard among the savages, and it was evident that the first moment of exposure would subject the troops to some manifestation of their disappointment and resentment.

"Among the chiefs were several who, although they shared the general hostile feeling of their tribe towards the Americans, yet retained a personal regard for the troops at this post, and for the few white citizens of the place. These exerted their utmost influence to allay the revengeful feelings of the young men, and to avert their sanguinary designs, but without effect. On the evening succeeding the last council, *Black Partridge*, a conspicuous chief, entered the quarters of the commanding officer. 'Father,' said he, 'I come to deliver up to you the medal I wear. It was given me by the Americans, and I have long worn it, in token of our mutual friendship. But our young men are resolved to imbrue their hands in the blood of the whites. I cannot restrain them, and I will not wear a token of peace while I am compelled to act as an enemy.' Had further evidence been wanting, this circumstance would have sufficiently proved to the devoted band the justice of their melancholy anticipations. Nevertheless, they went steadily on with the necessary preparations. Of the ammunition there had been reserved but twenty-five rounds, besides one box of cartridges, contained in the baggage-wagons. This must, under any circumstances o' danger, have proved an inadequate supply, but the prospect cf a fatiguing march forbade their embarrassing themselves with a larger quantity.

" The morning of the 15th arrived. All things were in readiness, and nine o'clock was the hour named for starting. Mr. Kinzie had volunteered to accompany the troops in their march, and had entrusted his family to the care of some friendly Indians, who had promised to convey them in a boat around the head of Lake Michigan, to a point* on the St. Joseph's river ; there to be joined by the troops, should the prosecution of their march be permitted them. Early in the morning he received a message from a chief of the St. Joseph's band, informing him that mischief was intended by the Pottowattamies who had promised to escort the detachment ; and urging him to relinquish his design of accompanying the troops by land, promising that the boat which should contain himself and family, should be permitted to pass in safety to St. Joseph's. Mr. Kinzie declined accepting this proposal, as he believed that his presence might operate as a restraint on the fury of the savages, so warmly were the greater part attached to himself and family. The party in the boat consisted of Mrs. Kinzie and her four younger children, a clerk, two servants, and the boatmen, besides the two Indians who acted as their protectors. The boat started, but had scarcely reached the mouth of the river, when another messenger from the chief arrived to detain them.

" In breathless expectation sat the wife and mother. She was a woman of uncommon energy and strength of character, yet her heart died within her as she folded her arms around her helpless infants, and gazed upon the march of her husband and eldest son to almost certain destruction.

" As the troops left the fort the band struck up the dead march.

---

* The spot now called *Bertrand*, then known by the name of *Parc aux Vaches*, from its having been a pasture-ground belonging to an old French fort in that neighborhood.

On they came in military array, Capt. Wells taking the lead, at the head of his little band of Miamies—his face blackened, in token of nis impending fate,* and took their route along the lake shore When they reached the point where commences the range of sand hill intervening between the prairie and the beach, the escort of Pottowattamies, in number about five hundred, kept the level of the prairie instead of continuing along the beach with the Americans and Miamies. They had marched perhaps a mile and a half, when Capt. Wells, who was somewhat in advance with his Miamies, came riding furiously back.

" 'They are about to attack us,' shouted he, 'form instantly, and charge upon them.'

" Scarcely were the words uttered when a volley was showered from among the sand-hills. The troops were hastily brought into line, and charged up the bank. One man, a veteran of seventy years, fell as they ascended. The remainder of the scene is best described in the words of an eye-witness and participator in the tragedy—Mrs. Helm, the wife of Lieut. Helm, and step-daughter of Mr. Kinzie.

" ' After we had left the bank and gained the prairie, the action became general. The Miamies fled at the outset. Their chief rode uy to the Pottowattamies, and said, ' You have deceived the Americans and us ; you have done a bad action, and (brandishing his tomahawk) I will be the first to head a party of Americans, and return to punish your treachery ;' so saying, he galloped after his companions, who were now scouring across the prairies.

" ' The troops behaved most gallantly. They were but a handful, but they resolved to sell their lives as dearly as possible. Our horses pranced and bounded, and could hardly be restrained, as the balls whistled among them. I drew off a little, and gazed upon my

* Col. Johnson says that Capt. Wells seeing all was lost, and not wishing to fall into the hands of the Indians, wetted powder and blacked his face in token of defiance, provoking the Indians, in the heat of the action, by taunts and jeers, to despatch him at once, instead of attempting to take him prisoner.

husband and father, who were yet unharmed. I felt that my hour was come, and endeavored to forget those I loved, and prepare myself for my approaching fate. While I was thus engaged, the surgeon came up. He was badly wounded. His horse had been shot under him, and he had received a ball in his leg. Every muscle of his countenance was quivering with the agony of terror. He said to me, ' Do you think they will take our lives ? I am badly wounded, but I think not mortally. Perhaps we might purchase our lives by promising them a large reward. Do you think there is any chance ?'

" ' Doctor,' said I, ' do not let us waste the few moments that yet remain to us, in such vain hopes. Our fate is inevitable. In a few moments we must appear before the bar of God. Let us endeavor to make what preparation is yet in our power.' ' Oh ! I cannot die !' exclaimed he, ' I am not fit to die—if I had but a short time to pre- pare—death is awful !' I pointed to Ensign Ronan, who, though mortally wounded, and nearly down, was still fighting with despera- tion upon one knee.

" ' Look at that man,' said I; ' he at least dies like a soldier !'

" ' Yes,' replied the unfortunate man, with a convulsive gasp, ' but he has no terrors for the future—he is an unbeliever !'

" ' At this moment, a young Indian raised his tomahawk at me. By springing aside, I avoided the blow which was intended for my skull, but which alighted on my shoulder. I seized him round the neck, and while exerting my utmost efforts to get possession of his scalping-knife, which hung in a scabbard over his breast, I was dragged from his grasp by an older Indian, who bore me, struggling and resisting, towards the lake. Notwithstanding the rapidity with which I was hurried along, I recognised, as I passed them, the lifeless remains of the unfortunate surgeon. Some murderous tom- ahawk had stretched him upon the very spot where I had last seen him.

" ' I was immediately plunged into the water, and held there with a forcible hand, notwithstanding my resistance. I soon perceived, however, that the object of my captor was not to drown me, as he held me firmly in such a position as to place my head above the water. This reassured me, and regarding him attentively, I soon recognised, in spite of the paint with which he was disguised, The Black Partridge.

"'When the firing had somewhat subsided, my preserver bore me from the water, and conducted me up the sand-banks. It was a burning August morning, and walking through the sand in my drenched condition, was inexpressibly painful and fatiguing. I stooped and took off my shoes, to free them from the sand with which they were nearly filled, when a squaw seized and carried them off, and I was obliged to proceed without them. When we had gained the prairie, I was met by my father, who told me that my husband was safe, and but slightly wounded. They led me gently back toward the Chicago river, along the southern bank of which was the Pottowattamie encampment. At one time, I was placed upon a horse without a saddle, but soon finding the motion insupportable, I sprang off. Supported partly by my kind conductor, and partly by another Indian, who held dangling in his hand the scalp of Capt. Wells, I dragged my fainting steps to one of the wigwams.'"

At the commencement of the action Capt. Wells was riding by the side of his niece. He said to her that he was satisfied there was not the least chance for his life, and that they must part to meet no more in this world, then started away to charge with the rest. It is said that Mrs. Heald saw him fall from his horse, struck by several rifle balls. Another account states that after the surrender, while an Indian was cruelly butchering some white children, Capt. Wells exclaimed, "then I will kill too," and set off towards the Indian camp near the fort, where their squaws and children had been left. Several pursued him, firing as he galloped along. He laid himself flat on the neck of his horse, loading and firing in that position, but was at length severely wounded, and his horse killed. Two friendly Indians who met him endeavored to save him from his enemies, and supported him after disengaging him from his horse, but he received his death-blow from one of his pursuers, who stabbed him in the back.

The charging of the troops drove back the Indians a considerable distance into the prairie, where the Captain ordered his men, diminished by more than two thirds of their number, to halt, and after a parley with the savages, agreed to surrender, stipulating that their lives should be spared, and that they should be delivered at one of the British posts, unless ransomed by traders in the Indian country. It appeared afterwards that the savages did not consider the wounded prisoners as included in the stipulation.

The lady whose narrative has been quoted, says, after she was taken to the wigwam, " the wife of a chief from the Illinois river was standing near, and seeing my exhausted condition, she seized a kettle, dipped up some water from a little stream that flowed near, threw into it some maple sugar, and stirring it up with her hand, gave it to me to drink. This act of kindness, in the midst of so many atrocities, touched me most sensibly, but my attention was soon diverted to other objects. An old squaw, infuriated by the loss of friends, or excited by the sanguinary scenes around her, seemed possessed by a demoniac ferocity. She seized a stable-fork, and assaulted one miserable victim, who lay groaning and writhing in the agony of his wounds, aggravated by the scorching beams of the sun. With a delicacy of feeling scarcely to have been expected under such circumstances, the chief stretched a mat across two poles, between me and this dreadful scene. I was thus spared, in some degree, a view of its horrors, although I could not entirely close my ears to the cries of the sufferer. The following night five more of the wounded prisoners were tomahawked.

" The heroic resolution of one of the soldiers' wives deserves to be recorded. She had from the first expressed a determination never to fall into the hands of the savages, believing that their prisoners were always subjected to tortures worse than death. When, therefore, a party came upon her, to make her prisoner, she fought with desperation, refusing to surrender, although assured of safe treatment;

and literally suffered herself to be cut to pieces, rather than become their captive.

"The horse Mrs. Heald rode was a fine, spirited animal, and the Indians were desirous to possess themselves of it unwounded. They therefore aimed their shots so as to disable the rider, without injuring her steed. This was at length accomplished, and her captor was in the act of disengaging her hat from her head, in order to scalp her, when young Chandonnai, a half-breed from St. Joseph's, ran up and offered for her ransom a mule he had just taken, adding the promise of ten bottles of whiskey, so soon as he should reach his village. The latter was a strong temptation. 'But,' said the Indian, 'she is badly wounded—she will die—will you give me the whiskey at all events?' Chandonnai promised that he would, and the bargain was concluded. Mrs. Heald was placed in the boat with Mrs. Kinzie and her children, covered with a buffalo robe, and enjoined silence as she valued her life. In this situation the heroic woman remained, without uttering a sound that could betray her to the savages, who were continually coming to the boat in search of prisoners, but who always retired peaceably when told that it contained only the family of *Shaw-ne-au-kee.* When the boat was at length permitted to return to the mansion of Mr. Kinzie, and Mrs. Heald was removed to the house for the purpose of dressing her wounds, Mr. Kinzie applied to an old chief who stood by, and who, like most of his tribe, possessed some skill in surgery, to extract a ball from the arm of the sufferer. 'No, father,' replied he, 'I cannot do it—it makes me sick here!' placing his hand upon his heart.

"From the Pottowattamie encampment, the family of Mr. Kinzie were conveyed across the river to their own mansion. There they were closely guarded by their Indian friends, whose intention it was to carry them to Detroit for security. The rest of the prisoners remained at the wigwams of their captors. The following morning, the work of plunder being completed, the Indians set fire to the fort. A very equitable distribution of the finery appeared to have been made, and shawls, ribbons, and feathers, were seen fluttering about in all directions The ludicrous appearance of one young

13*

fellow, who had arrayed himself in a muslin gown, and the bonnet of the commanding officer's lady, would under other circumstances have afforded matter of amusement.

" Black Partridge and Wau-ban-see, with three others of the tribe, having established themselves in the porch of the building as sentinels, to protect the family of Mr. Kinzie from any evil, all remained tranquil for a short space after the conflagration. Very soon, however, a party of Indians from the Wabash made their appearance. These were the most hostile and implacable of all the bands of the Pottowattamies. Being more remote, they had shared less than some of their brethren in the kindness of Mr. Kinzie and his family, and consequently their sentiments of regard for them were less powerful. Runners had been sent to the villages, to apprise them of the intended evacuation of the post, as well as the plan of the Indians assembled, to attack the troops. Thirsting to participate in such a scene, they hurried on, and great was their mortification, on arriving at the river Aux Plaines, to meet with a party of their friends, having their chief badly wounded, and to learn that the battle was over, the spoils divided, and the scalps all taken.

" On arriving at Chicago, they blackened their faces, and proceeded towards the residence of Mr. Kinzie. From his station on the piazza, Black Partridge had watched their approach, and his fears were particularly awakened for the safety of Mrs. Helm, who had recently come to the post, and was personally unknown to the more remote Indians. By his advice, she assumed the ordinary dress of a Frenchwoman of the country, a short gown and petticoat, with a blue cotton handkerchief wrapped around her head; and in this disguise she was conducted by Black Partridge to the house of Ouilmette, a Frenchman with a half-breed wife, who formed a part of the establishment of Mr. Kinzie, and whose dwelling was close at hand. It so happened that the Indians came first to this house in their search for prisoners. As they approached, the inmates, fearful that the fair complexion and general appearance of Mrs. Helm might betray her for an American raised the large feather bed and

placed her under the edge of it, upon the bedstead, with her face to
the wall. Mrs. Bisson, the sister of Ouilmette's wife, then seated
herself with her sewing upon the front of the bed. It was a hot day
in August, and the feverish excitement of fear and agitation,
together with her position, which was nearly suffocating, were so
painful, that Mrs. Helm at length entreated to be released and given
up to the Indians. ' I can but die,' said she, ' let them put an end
to my miseries at once.' Mrs. Bisson replied, ' Your death would
be the signal for the destruction of us all, for Black Partridge is
resolved, if one drop of the blood of your family is spilled, to take
the lives of all concerned in it, even his nearest friends, and if once
the work of murder commences, there will be no end of it, so long
as there remains one white person or half-breed in the country.'
This expostulation nerved Mrs. Helm with fresh resolution. The
Indians entered, and she could occasionally see them from her hiding-place, gliding about and inspecting every part of the room,
though without making any ostensible search, until, apparently
satisfied that there was no one concealed, they left the house. All
this time, Mrs. Bisson kept her seat upon the side of the bed, calmly
assorting and arranging the patchwork of the quilt on which she
was engaged, although she knew not but that the next moment she
might receive a tomahawk in her brain. Her self-command unquestionably saved the lives of all present.

" From Ouilmette's the savages proceeded to the dwelling of Mr.
Kinzie. They entered the parlor, in which were assembled the
family, with their faithful protectors, and seated themselves upon the
floor in profound silence. Black Partridge perceived, from their
moody and revengeful looks, what was passing in their minds, but
dared not remonstrate with them. He only observed in a low tone
to Wau-ban-see, ' We have endeavored to save our friends, but it
is in vain—nothing will save them now.' At this moment a friendly
whoop was heard from a party of new comers, on the opposite bank
of the river. Black Partridge sprang to meet their leader, as the
canoes in which they had hastily embarked touched the bank, and
bade him make all speed to the house. Billy Caldwell, for it was

he, entered the parlor with a calm step, and without a trace of agitation in his manner. He deliberately took off his accoutrements,
and placed them with his rifle behind the door; then saluted the
hostile savages.

" ' How now, my friends ! A good day to you. I was told
there were enemies here, but I am glad to find only friends. Why
have you blackened your faces ? Is it that you are mourning for
the friends you have lost in the battle? (purposely misunderstand-
ing this token of evil designs) or is it that you are fasting?
If so, ask our friend here, and he will give you to eat. He is the
Indians' friend, and never yet refused them what they had need of.'

" Thus taken by surprise, the savages were ashamed to acknowledge their bloody purpose; they therefore said modestly, that they
came to beg of their friend some white cotton, in which to wrap
their dead before interring them. This was given them, together
with some other presents, and they took their departure from the
premises.

"Little remains to be told. On the third day after the battle, the
family of Mr. Kinzie, with the clerks of the establishment, were
put in a boat, under the care of François, a half-breed interpreter,
and conveyed to St. Joseph's, where they remained until the following November. They were then carried to Detroit, under the
escort of Chandonnai and a trusty Indian friend, and together with
their negro servants, delivered up as prisoners of war to the British
commanding officer. It had been a stipulation at the surrender of
Detroit by Gen. Hull, that the American inhabitants should retain
the liberty of remaining undisturbed in their own dwellings, and
accordingly this family was permitted a quiet residence among their
friends at that place. Mr. Kinzie was not allowed to leave St.
Joseph's with his family, his Indian friends insisting upon his remaining to endeavor to secure some remnant of his scattered property, but anxiety for his family induced him to follow them in
January to Detroit, where he was received as a prisoner, and
paroled by Gen. Proctor.

"Of the other prisoners, Capt. and Mrs. Heald had been sent

across the Lake to St. Joseph's the day after the battle. Capt. Heald had received two wounds, and Mrs. Heald seven, the ball of one of which was cut out of her arm with a pen-knife by Mr. Kinzie, after the engagement.

"Capt. Heald was taken prisoner by an Indian from the Kankakee, who had a strong personal regard for him, and who, when he saw the wounded and enfeebled state of Mrs. Heald, released his prisoner, that he might accompany his wife to St. Joseph's. To the latter place they were accordingly carried by Chandonnai and his party. In the meantime, the Indian who had so nobly released his captive, returned to his village on the Kankakee, where he had the mortification of finding that his conduct had excited great dissatisfaction among his band. So great was the displeasure manifested that he resolved to make a journey to St. Joseph's and reclaim his prisoner. News of his intention being brought to the chiefs under whose care the prisoners were, they held a private council with Chandonnai and the principal men of the village, the result of which was a determination to send Capt. and Mrs. Heald to the island of Mackinaw, and deliver them up to the British. They were accordingly put in a bark canoe and paddled by the chief of the Pottowattamies, Robinson, and his wife, a distance of three hundred miles along the coast of Lake Michigan, and surrendered as prisoners of war to the commanding officer at Mackinaw.

"Lieut. Helm, who was likewise wounded, was carried by some friendly Indians to their village, on the *Au Sable* and thence to St. Louis, where he was liberated by the intervention of Thomas Forsyth, a trader among them. Mrs. Helm accompanied her father's family to Detroit. In the engagement she received a slight wound on the ancle, and had her horse shot under her.

"The soldiers, with their wives and children, were dispersed among the different villages of the Pottowattamies, upon the Illinois, Wabash, Rock River, and Milwaukie, until the following spring, when they were for the most part carried to Detroit, and ransomed. Some, however, were detained in captivity another year, during which

period they experienced more kindness than was to have been expected from an enemy in most cases so merciless."

Gen. Hunt adds, that some months after the massacre at Chicago,
he met Capt. and Mrs. Heald, walking in the street in Detroit.
They had just come from Mackinaw in a vessel, and were much
pleased to see their old friend. Mrs. Heald had recovered from her
wounds, and appeared to be as well as she had ever been. It is
probable that, after the termination of the war, her life was one of
quiet usefulness, like that of her sister pioneers; the occurrences in
which she had borne so prominent a part serving to relate as truth
more strange than fiction, to those whose fortunes had led them into
less stirring scenes.

MRS. HELM was the daughter of Col. McKillip, a British officer
attached to one of the companies who in 1794 were engaged in sustaining the Indian tribes in Northern Ohio against the government
of the United States. He lost his life at the fort at the Miami
Rapids, now Perrysburg. He had gone out at night to reconnoitre,
and returning in a stealthy manner, was mistaken for an enemy,
fired upon, and mortally wounded by his own sentinel. His widow
afterwards became the wife of John Kinzie, with whom, in 1803,
she removed to Chicago, then a mere trading post among the
Pottowattamies.

At the age of eighteen, the daughter was married to Lieut. Lina
J. Helm, of Kentucky. Her death took place at Watersville, in
Michigan, in 1844, and was very sudden. She had just risen from
the tea-table—one of the company having read to her a newspaper
paragraph relating to Henry Clay; and she said, "I hope I shall
live to see that man President." Scarcely were the words uttered,
than she fell backwards into the arms of an attendant and almost
instantly expired. Her interest in the great statesman is an evidence
of the patriotic feeling for which she was always remarkable. She
was generous, high-minded, and disinterested; possessing a calm
strength of nature, and was energetic and indefatigable in action. Her
piety was pure and ardent, yet wholly untinctured with fanaticism;
the faith and love by which the true Christian lifts his heart to God,

and with a sincerity and devotion rarely equalled, did she obey the precept, " thou shalt love thy neighbor as thyself."

Our wonder may well be excited at the heroism and the sufferings borne with such sturdy fortitude, of the pioneer women whose lot was cast in the midst of the troubles upon the frontier. Yet their attachment to this wild, unsettled life was still more remarkable ; for as the country became settled, they would encourage their husbands or sons to " sell out," and remove still further into the wilderness.

During the time of the possession of Detroit by the British, after the surrender of Gen. Hull, the frontier settlement suffered much from Indian depredation. The capture of the family of Mr. Snow, taken by the Ottawa Indians from their home on Cole Creek, in Huron County, may illustrate the experience of many unfortunates whose names tradition has not preserved. Mr. Snow chanced to be absent, when his house was surrounded by a hostile party, and his wife and nine children were made prisoners. The savages immediately started on their return, and had gone about five miles, travelling on foot, when it became evident that Mrs. Snow, whose health was delicate, could not drag herself much further. A brief council was held among the savages, and it was decided that she must be killed. Two young men were appointed to put the cruel sentence in execution, while the rest of the party moved forward ; the victim being ordered to keep her seat upon a log. Here her lifeless body was found by her husband and the men in pursuit. It is a somewhat curious circumstance, that one of the Indians who killed the unfortunate woman, afterwards expressed his remorse for the deed, and said he knew the Great Spirit was angry with him, for that the ground had trembled when she screamed, and his right arm had become completely withered by a rheumatic affection. His death might have been deemed also a judgment for the crime ; in a fit of intoxication he fell into the fire and burned himself so severely that he expired in a short time.

" On a beautiful Sunday morning in Detroit," continues my informant, " I heard the scalp whoop of a war party coming up the

river. When they came near, I discovered that they were carrying
a woman's scalp upon a pole, and that they had with them,
as prisoners, a family of nine children, from three years old up to
two girls full grown. These little captives had nothing on their
heads, and their clothes were torn into shreds by the brushwood and
the bushes in the way by which they had come. I went to meet
them, brought them into my house, gave them and their Indian
captors a meal, with a few loaves of bread for further use, and told
the children not to be frightened or uneasy, for that my brother
would buy them from the Indians when he should return from
Canada, whither he had gone to spend the Sabbath with his father-
in-law. The next day the prisoners came again, accompanied by
about five hundred Indians. My brother paid five hundred dollars
for their ransom, and sent them home. The girls informed me that
they had been treated by the Indians with kindness and respect.
Indeed, it may be recorded, to the praise of the Indian character,
and in extenuation of their cruelties, that an instance has not been
known of improper conduct towards a captive white woman. Their
apology for the murder of Mrs. Snow was, that they feared her
release might lead to their discovery by the whites in pursuit."

The Rev. J. M. Peck of Illinois mentions the name of Catharine
Lemen, as a pioneer who came to that region as early as 1786, with
her husband and two children. The family were exposed to Indian
depredations during the whole period of the border troubles; and
many instances are remembered in which she exhibited a heroic and
Christian spirit. She had ten children, four of whom became
ministers of the gospel. Mrs. Edwards, the wife of Governor
Edwards, is also mentioned as a matron distinguished for lofty and
heroic traits of character. She sustained her husband through his
public life, having the entire management of his large estate and its
settlement after his death.

XVIII.

ABIGAIL SNELLING.

THOMAS HUNT, the father of the subject of the present memoir was a Revolutionary officer, and a native of Watertown, Massachusetts. He entered the American army as a volunteer, and was soon, commissioned in the regular service; was in the expedition against Ticonderoga commanded by Ethan Allen, and one of the party who made themselves masters of Crown Point. He was with Gen. Wayne at Stoney Point, among the volunteers of the "forlorn hope," and was there wounded in the ankle. In 1794, he joined the army under Wayne against the Indians, and served out the campaign, returning then to his family residence at Watertown. In 1798, he was promoted to the rank of Lieutenant-Colonel of the first regiment of infantry, and ordered to Fort Wayne, where he remained until the death of Col. Hamtramack at Detroit, when he became Colonel, and took the command of that post, remained there some time, and afterwards went to Mackinaw.

Our heroine was but six weeks old when the family left Water town, and was carried on a pillow in such a vehicle as was then used for stages, over very rough roads, for many miles only rendered passable by logs placed side by side, forming what are termed corduroy roads. The severity of the exercise, as may be remembered b · those who have travelled over such roads in a new country, always caused an outcry on approaching them, from man, woman, and child, with petitions to get out and walk; frequently at the risk of being bitten by rattlesnakes which were often concealed between the logs. When they arrived at Mackinaw, they went to the Government House, which they were to occupy. The English commander had left it with the furniture, even the window curtains suspended from the windows, and there was an air of comfort in and about the house. The Fort stood on the height, the town was small, the streets were very narrow, the houses built in the old French style, and the town was enclosed with pickets, with a gate at each end.

One of the little girl's earliest recollections was visiting in the family of a Scotch gentleman, Dr. Mitchell, who had married an Indian wife. She dressed herself in silks and satins when at home, but resumed her native dress when among the Chippewas, her own people. She would sometimes be absent many months, purchasing furs to send to Montreal, for her agent there to sell; and in this way she amassed a large fortune for her husband. At one time, after she had been absent more than six months, it was reported that she had been killed by some rival trader. She heard on her way home that such news had been received, and when her flotilla appeared in sight, threw herself on the bottom of her birch canoe. Her husband, with spy-glass in hand, was on the beach, eagerly looking to see if indeed his wife was not there, and was about turning away with a heavy heart, when she leaped from her bark exclaiming, " Not dead yet!" Her two daughters were sent to Montreal to be educated, and returned home highly accomplished and very beautiful women. One of them afterwards married an officer.

Abigail was about seven years old when her parents left Mackinaw to return to Detroit, on their way to St. Louis. The troops had left Detroit but a short time when the town was burned to ashes, in 1805. The little party reached Fort Wayne, where they rested for a week, at which time Col. Hunt's eldest daughter, not quite fifteen, was married to the surgeon of the post, Dr. Edwards. She was left behind when the family resumed their journey, and they proceeded in a flat-bottomed boat, called an "ark," which could only be used in descending with the current. Col. Hunt had one of these boats partitioned off into rooms, making a parlor, bed-rooms, and kitchen; bedsteads were put up, and each apartment arranged in the same order as in a house. This was a slow mode of travelling, but extremely comfortable, and little apprehension was felt at that time of the Indians, although they frequently surrounded the boat, begging for bread and some of their "father's milk" (whiskey). At Vincennes, the voyagers were hospitably received at the house of Gen. W. H. Harrison, but their stay was short, and they proceeded to St. Louis. Gen. Wilkinson was there at that time, and ordered Col. Hunt to take command of the garrison at the mouth of the Missouri, eighteen miles above St. Louis. This was about the time of Burr's conspiracy, and a court martial was immediately held to try a Major Bruff, who was suspected of being one of his adherents. He was acquitted. Then arrived at the gar-rison Lewis and Clark, from their exploring expedition; and the peculiar appearance of their dress, made of deerskins, the outer garment fringed and worked with porcupine quills, something be tween a military undress frock coat and Indian shirt, with their leggins and moccasins, three-cornered cocked hats and long beards, caused no small wonder among the younger members of the family.

Gen. Pike was at this time a captain in Col. Hunt's regiment, and was selected by the government to explore the Upper Missis sippi. He left his wife and little daughter under the protection of Col. Hunt, on his departure in the following year. His absence was prolonged nearly two years, during which time his friend was re-moved from this world. Col. Hunt died after a protracted illness, in 1809. The dispensation was a heart-breaking one to the devoted wife. She did not, could not, shed a tear, but would sigh continu-ally, and sometimes exclaim, "Oh! that I could weep—what a relief it would be!" Ere long she was unable to swallow solid food, and even liquids without difficulty. Some friends thought visiting the grave would have the effect of making her weep, but it threw her into spasms, after which no further effort was made, and she gradually sank, until she died in six months after the death of her husband.

Mrs. Hunt's eldest son, twenty-two years of age, was then just established in business as a merchant in Detroit. When he heard of his father's death, he prepared immediately to meet the family at St. Louis, and on the journey tidings reached him that his mother also was no more. This double bereavement, with the responsibility of a large family depending upon his care, was too heavy a burden for his anxious mind. He became ill of a fever, which reduced him so much, that on arriving at St. Louis he could scarcely reach the house of a friend where the family were awaiting his arrival. For the first time in her life, his little sister felt a dreary sense of desolation—a knowledge that she was homeless, and an orphan. No tender mother now called her child to her in the evening to say her prayers; no longer were the children assembled together on the Sabbath afternoon to be instructed from the Bible and catechism. This feeling of loneliness added to the poignancy of grief for her departed parents; the first of the sorrows by which that young, gentle, loving heart was to be tried—the first experience of the universal lot of humanity. The young mourner was led, in that time of suffering, to turn to the Bible for consolation, and was consoled in the promise there found, "I will be a father to the fatherless."

As soon as her brother had recovered his strength, the family commenced their journey, their destination being Waltham, Massachusetts, where their maternal grandfather, Mr. Samuel Wellington, resided. When they reached Vincennes, they were again received into the family of Gen. Harrison, and stayed two weeks to recruit. The mode of conveyance at that time was in an open barge, with an awning stretched over it. The crew were soldiers for a part of the way, afterwards Frenchmen, "voyageurs," as they were called. Tents were pitched every night, and the evening was spent in preparing food for the following day. The party was often supplied with game by the Indians, who frequently spread their blankets around their fires to sleep for the night; yet though the savages were friendly, the children could not divest themselves of fear which often drove away sleep at night, to be made up by sleeping all the next day in the boat. The next stopping place was Fort Wayne, where the eldest sister, Mrs. Edwards, had been left six years before. The meeting was an affecting one. The travellers did not remain long, as Mr. Hunt's business demanded his presence in Detroit. One of the brothers, John E. Hunt, was left with Dr. Edwards, and the youngest but one of the sisters (now married to Mr. Wendell, of Detroit); and as soon as Mr. Hunt had arranged his business, the rest resumed their journey, another brother, Thomas, being left in Detroit in his brother's store as clerk. Afterwards, in 1812, he was commissioned in the army as captain.

After a tedious journey of months, the travellers arrived at their grand-father's in Waltham. Abby was sent to a boarding school in Salem, under the charge of Mrs. Cranch, and there remained until some time in 1811. Col. Henry J. Hunt of Detroit, who was then married to Miss Ann Mackintosh of Moy, Canada, then came, in company with his wife, to take his sister, and she returned with them to Detroit.

The following year, war was declared with Great Britain. The first intimation had of it in Detroit was seeing the ferry boat hauled up, and the ferryman taken prisoner and sent to Malden. This caused a dreadful sensation in the town, especially in the house of Col. Hunt, his wife being deprived of the privilege of communication with her father's family, and plunged into deep distress on that account. There were many other families in the same situation; and brothers seemed arrayed against each other. The only Protestant church near enough to be attended every Sunday, was at Sandwich, nearly opposite Detroit, and the Hunt family had always crossed the river on Saturday, spending Sunday at Mr. Mackintosh's in order to attend the Episcopal service. It was the first Protestant church Miss Hunt had ever attended, and she was there baptised and received the communion. The privation of such privileges was deeply felt by her.

Before long, intelligence was brought of the approach and the arrival of Gen. Hull's army at the Maumee on the 30th of June. The troops had collected at Dayton to the number of about two thousand drafted men and volunteers from Ohio; the regular force comprising about three hundred soldiers. They had cut their way through the wilderness and endured many hardships. The 4th regiment, commanded by Col. James Miller, had acquired a good reputation in the battle of Tippecanoe under Gen. Harrison on the 6th of November, 1811. None of the officers had distinguished themselves more than Capt. Snelling. He was one of the gallant band that made a successful charge, and drove the enemy into the swamp, putting an end to the conflict. An incident of this battle gave occasion for the exercise of his benevolence. At dawn of day a lad fourteen years old, was seen bending over the lifeless body of his father, which lay weltering in blood, and proved to be that of Capt. Spencer of the militia. The lad had been seen fighting by his father's side during the engagement, and even after his death, at one moment weeping for his parent, the next loading his rifle and firing upon the enemy. Capt. Snelling was much interested in the boy, took charge of him, and afterwards petitioned for a cadet's warrant, which he received, and sent him to West Point. From that institution he graduated at the termination of four years with honor, and while there sent every month half his pay to his widowed mother, then in Kentucky. He received a commission in the army and many years afterwards died, having the rank of major.

Before leaving the Maumee, Gen. Hull sent a vessel to Detroit, in which were placed his sick and most of his goods, sending with it his instructions and army roll. The British at Malden having information of the declaration of war, captured the vessel and unsuspecting crew, and from them received the first intelligence of the war. Capt. Gooding, of the 4th regiment, and his wife were on board. She related afterwards an exploit of her's while at Malden, which showed the tenderness of female nature combined with manly perseverance and courage. The prisoners were confined below deck, and very much crowded, as it was a small vessel; the weather was very warm, they were fed with salt meat, without sugar, tea or

coffee, and many fell sick. When Mrs. Gooding was told by the
Captain of their situation, she set her wits to work to contrive how
to relieve them. She knew they were soon to be sent in the same
vessel to Montreal, and no time was to be lost. She obtained leave
from one in authority to visit a family up the river with whom she
had formerly been acquainted, and walked on a mile or more alone,
without exactly knowing what she was about to do, when she observed a large house on a farm which seemed blessed with abundance. She entered, introduced herself to the lady of the house, and
told her, in a very pathetic narrative, who she was, the situation of
the sick prisoners, and her desire to awaken sympathy in the hearts
f those who had it in their power to relieve them. The lady hesitated a moment and then said, " What can I do in this matter? If
I listen to the dictates of my own heart, I could easily fill you
a basket with coffee, tea and sugar, rice, etc., but I dare not send
it." " Listen to the dictates of that heart," cried Mrs. Gooding, " I
myself will carry the basket, and if you have fresh meat for soup I
can conceal it in the bushes until I can convey it to the vessel."
The lady immediately had a lamb killed ; Mrs. Gooding herself hid
it ; managed to carry the basket on board that afternoon, and in
the evening, before nine o'clock, the four quarters of lamb.

Gen. Hull arrived with his army at Detroit early in July. Dr.
Edwards joined the army at Dayton, as Major of one of the regi-
ments, and had John E. Hunt with him, so that amidst the din of
war their young sister was rejoiced to see them again. In a few
days Capt. Snelling was introduced to Miss Hunt, as one of the
heroes of Tippecanoe, by Maj. Edwards ; and soon after the young
officer asked the brother's permission to address her. In due time
they were engaged.

On the 12th July, Gen. Hull crossed the river to Sandwich, and
established his forces there, with a view to the attack on Malden.
Many of the officers urged him immediately to storm that place,
which was twelve miles below his encampment, and then very weakly
garrisoned, as was made known to the officers by deserters who
came thence after they heard Gen. Hull had crossed. Captain

Snelling said, "Give me permission, and with my company and those who will volunteer, I will make the attempt." Colonels Cass and Miller, by an attack on the advanced party, on La Riviere Canard, showed that the men were able and willing to push their conquest if the chance were given; but they were suddenly recalled, and the enterprize was abandoned. On the 7th of August Gen. Hull returned to Detroit, much to the disappointment of the whole army, who now had lost all confidence in him, since he had lost, by refusing to listen to his eager officers, the opportunity of obtaining possession of the key to the Canadian provinces, when it might have been taken with scarce the firing of a gun.

Col. Proctor soon after arrived at Malden, attempted to cut off supplies from Ohio, and succeeded in stopping some stores on their way to Detroit, at the river Raisin, thirty-six miles distant, defeating Van Horn, who had been sent by Gen. Hull to escort them. On receiving this intelligence, Gen. Hull sent three hundred regulars, the 4th Regiment and two hundred militia, under the command of Col. James Miller, to open the communication. The British had thrown up a breastwork four miles from Brownstown, at a place called Monguagon, behind which a great number of the Indians under Tecumseh lay concealed. On the 9th of August, while on its march, the detachment drew near the ambuscade. The advanced guard, commanded by Capt. Snelling, was considerably in advance of the main body when suddenly the attack was made on him. His party sustained themselves until Gen. Miller, with the utmost speed and coolness, drew up his men, opened a brisk fire and then charged. The British regulars gave way, but the Indians under Tecumseh betaking themselves to the woods on each side, did much execution. The British again rallied, and were again repulsed; and Majors Muir and Tecumseh both being wounded, were compelled to yield, retiring slowly before the bayonets to Brownstown. They would all have been taken prisoners had they not had boats in readiness to cross the river. During the engagement a mounted officer delayed charging as he was ordered; Capt. Snelling directed him to dismount, and himself sprung upon the horse. The officer being a tall man, he found the stirrups much too long, but there was no time to be lost; he therefore clung to the horse with his knees, and in this ludicrous predicament performed the duty which belonged to another. His brother officers often laughed at the recollection of his appearance at that time.

Meanwhile his friends in Detroit hearing the roar of the cannon knew there was fighting. Thomas Hunt was then a volunteer, and the feelings of the young girl, whose brother and betrothed lover were in danger, may be imagined. Young Hunt had rode a white horse, which returned and stood at the stable door, the saddle pulled away and covered with blood; and the conclusion was inevitable that he had fallen from his horse, either killed or wounded. As cart after cart came in with the wounded, Miss Hunt heard it whispered, "It must be Capt. Snelling," and on enquiry was informed that an officer answering the description of him had been mortally wounded. In the agony of her feelings she was about rushing by all to the cart when she was forcibly detained, and some one went to ascertain if it indeed was so; but soon returned with a bright countenance, saying, " it is not Snelling, it is Peters, and he is only slightly wounded." On further inquiry she learned that Mr. Hunt was safe, having given up his horse for the use of a wounded man who had fainted and fallen off. The next day the absentees returned. In this engagement Capt. Snelling had his hat knocked off by a ball, and the hilt of his sword grazed. At one time he observed an Indian from behind a tree very near him raise his rifle to shoot him; he sprang forward, knocked the gun from his grasp, and plunged the point of his sword through his neck, when he fell lifeless. The Captain supposed from the situation of the Indian that he had been previously wounded.

On the 13th of August, Miss Hunt, then only fifteen years old, was married to Capt. Snelling by the Chaplain of Gen. Hull's army. General Hull and several other officers were present, with a few ladies. The ceremony had been performed but a few moments when the drum beat to arms; and Capt. Snelling instantly started up to go in search of his sword. All rushed to the door except

14

Gen. Hull, who laying his hand on the young officer's shoulder as he was about leaving the house, said, "Snelling, you need not go, I will excuse you." "By no means," was the reply, "I feel more like doing my duty now than ever." "Stay, it is a false alarm by my order," said the General.

About this time, Gen. Brock reached Malden with reinforcements, and immediately planted batteries opposite the fort of Detroit. From Col. Hunt's house the family could distinctly see the men at work, by the aid of a spy glass. Then were seen two British officers with a white flag of truce, crossing at the ferry; they were met at the wharf and blindfolded, and were conducted to the first house, which happened to be that of Col. Hunt. The youthful bride saw them enter the parlor with Gen. Hull, his aid, who was his son, and some others; and the door was locked. They demanded, in the name of Gen. Brock, a surrender, stating that he should otherwise be unable to restrain the fury of the savages, but were answered by a spirited refusal. The British officers returned to the boat in the same manner, and presently the firing commenced from their bat-teries, and continued without much effect until the next morning.

About this time Michilimackinac was captured, and Lieut. Hanks, who commanded, was sent on parole to Detroit; his wife being with him. His command consisted of but fifty men, the enemy numbered over one thousand, including Indians; and Lieut. Hanks had received no information of the declaration of war! Being on parole, he was of course bound to remain neutral, and it happened that he was in a room with some others, when a shell from the enemy passed into the room, scattering death and destruction. Mrs. Hanks was with the other ladies in an adjoining room, where all were employed in making flannel bags to put powder in for the cannon. When they heard the report and the groans, all rushed to the door, for it was but a narrow entry that divided the two rooms. Mrs. Hanks was in advance, when the door was opened by one of the wounded, and Lieut. Hanks was seen with his bowels torn open and dreadfully dis-figured. A blanket was immediately thrown over him by one who came in. Three others had been badly wounded and two killed by that single bomb-shell. Mrs. Hanks saw at a glance the condition of her husband, and that there was no hope of life, and for a time she was bereft of reason.

It having been reported by some Frenchmen, that the British were preparing to cross the river opposite Spring Wells, Capt. Snelling was sent to watch their movements and report. He left Detroit about nine o'clock in the evening, with a detachment of men, and returning next morning before daylight, he reported to the General that from appearances, they would cross the river at that point, three miles from Detroit, that morning. The alarm of Gen. Hull now became extreme, and his appearance that morning was pitiable. The balls were flying very fast over the fort, and several men were killed; the chimney of the room in which the ladies were at work, was struck and fell with some of the roof into the apartment. The ladies were then advised to go into an empty bombproof magazine for safety, and took Mrs. Hanks with them, she being quite frantic. In passing the parade ground several shells burst over them, but they escaped injury, and reaching the magazine found it filled with women and children from the town; some fainting, and some in convulsions with fear. The picture of woe was complete when Mrs. Hanks was placed among the sufferers. Presently, Mrs. Snelling heard herself called by name, and going to the door, found it was her husband. He said, " My dear wife, I know not what moment I may be shot down; I have come to say farewell, and ask you to make me a promise, that in case I fall you will *never marry an Englishman.*" His weeping bride assented without being able to speak, and they parted.

While the British were crossing the river, Gen. Hull was entreated by the officers to prevent their landing, which they insisted could be done; at least, they might sink every other boat; but he would not allow a gun to be fired. The field officers, suspecting he intended to surrender, determined on his arrest; this, however, was prevented, in consequence of the absence of Colonels Cass and McArthur, who had been detached with four hundred men on a third expedition to the river Raisin. Had they been present, there is no doubt the project would have been carried into effect. On that morning Gen. Miller was very ill of chill and fever.

The morning of the 16th (three days after the marriage of our fair friend) the British landed at Spring Wells, and marched up in solid column along the river bank. The American troops now eagerly waited for orders; they were strongly fortified, and cannon loaded with grape stood on a commanding eminence, ready to sweep the advancing columns. At this crisis, what was their mortification and disappointment, when orders were given them to retire within the fort! When there, Capt. Snelling saw Gen. Hull's aid trying to plant a white flag: "Snelling," said he, "come and help me fix this flag." "No, sir; I will not soil my hands with that flag," was the indignant answer.

Gen Hull, panic-stricken, surrendered the fortress without even stipulating the terms; even Colonels Cass and McArthur's detachment was included. Language cannot adequately describe or express the emotions that filled the hearts of those brave soldiers, as they stacked their arms to be conveyed away by the British soldiers. Mrs. Snelling now returned to her brother's house, and for the first time saw Tecumseh. He was a noble looking warrior, on horseback at the head of his band of Indians, who had fired off their guns before they were permitted to enter the town; they passed by the door in good order, being evidently under restraint; but how long would it last! It was felt to be a relief when Capt. Snelling informed his wife the vessels were in sight in which all the prisoners were to embark. Col. H. I. Hunt was permitted to remain on parole, Detroit being his home, and John E. Hunt stayed with him; but Thomas, afterwards a captain in the army, and the brother-in-law, Maj. Edwards, accompanied the prisoners. They were put on board the Queen Charlotte, where they found Gen. Hull and staff, with several other officers and their wives. They were very much crowded, the state-rooms being occupied by the General and his staff, while the rest made pallets on the cabin floor. It may be supposed that no one slept much that night. Gen. Hull's conduct was freely discussed within his hearing; and bitter, bitter indeed, were the feelings expressed against him. The next day, much to the satisfaction of Mrs. Snelling, her party, with others, was put on board the vessel commanded by Captain Mackintosh, at his request. He gave her up his own stateroom, and handed her the key of the box that contained his preserves and other niceties. He told the prisoners that if the army had marched to Malden at the time they crossed the river, that post would have been taken without the cost of a life.

When they arrived at Erie, the British guards took charge of the captive troops, and each American captain was placed at the head of his company, surrounded by a British guard, and marched to Fort George, eighteen miles, where vessels were in readiness to proceed to Kingston. Gen. Hull and his staff were placed in carriages. Mackintosh promised Capt. Snelling he would place his young wife in the hands of a friend, who would see that she had a conveyance to join him at Fort George. He did so, but was obliged to return to his vessel; however, Mr. Warren promised to send her the same afternoon. Soon after she was joined by the wife of Capt. Fuller, of the 4th regiment. When Capt. Snelling then bade a brief adieu to his wife, "You may have need of money," said he, and gave her a half eagle.

With much impatience the ladies waited for Mr. Warren to make his appearance with a carriage. When tea was ready he came, but said all the carriages in the place were gone, and he could furnish nothing better than a lumber wagon. They eagerly exclaimed, "That will do, let us have it!" "But you must not go on to-night, it is too late," he persisted; "the roads are filled with straggling Indians; it will not do—it would be rashness to venture. I will have everything ready by daylight to-morrow morning." The ladies remonstrated against delay. "They have all gone; the troops will embark, and sail without us, and we shall be left behind." "Oh, no!" replied Warren; "unless the wind changes they cannot leave."

His involuntary guests passed a sleepless night in his house. They were up two hours before daylight, and endeavored in various ways to rouse their host, but in vain. Day dawned; they opened the window, to see if the wind had changed; it blew from the same direction, and they were more calm. When the sun rose, they went to Mr. Warren immediately, and begged the fulfilment of his promise. He went out, and expecting him back every moment, they got their luggage ready in the hall, every moment seeming an age. At length, a negro man drove up to the door about nine o'clock, in a large lumber wagon; their hearts sank within them, for they had supposed that Mr. Warren would accompany them. The man came into the hall, and asked, " Is this the luggage? Heavy load!—take all day to get there!" " And is not Mr. Warren going with us?" " No, marm; cannot go; told me to go." Thus the wedding tour of our fair bride promised to be an adventurous one! Their fears were divided between the negro man and the Indians who were straggling on the roads. They had a great deal of baggage, and were completely in the power of the driver. Mrs. Snelling said to him imploringly, " If you will make haste, and take us safely through, I will give you this gold piece, and our husbands, who are both Captains in the American army, will pay you well besides." The man answered that he would do his best.

When he stopped to water the horses at a tavern, there were a number of Indians about the house, and the ladies begged the driver not to let them know they were prisoners. They remained in the wagon while he went for water, watching him narrowly however, and not suffering him to delay a moment. When he resumed his seat, they breathed more freely. At noon some crackers and cheese were purchased, and they prevailed upon the driver to be satisfied with it for his dinner. Often they met three or four Indians, who sometimes stopped the driver to talk to him, and were inquisitive to know who the women were, what was in the trunks, &c., &c. During such times, although the prisoners trembled in every nerve, they appeared in a very merry mood, signifying to them and the driver that they were in a hurry. He cracked his whip, and as they went on, leaving the Indians behind, they set up a frightful yell, enough to chill the blood with fear.

As they drew near Fort George, they became still more anxious, for as nearly as they could judge the wind had changed, or was changing. It was late in the afternoon, and still they had some distance to go. Within a few miles of the fort, they met a foot traveller from there, who told them all the vessels had gone except one. In that one Capt. Snelling and Capt. Fuller were pacing the deck, sometimes looking with eagerness towards the shore, then beseeching the Captain of the sloop, who was a kind-hearted man, to delay only a little longer, notwithstanding orders had been sent him to proceed. Just as the words, " I can wait no longer, I must obey orders," passed his lips, handkerchiefs were seen waving from the shore ; a boat was sent, and the travellers were soon in their husbands' arms. Even the rough but kind-hearted sailor witnessing the scene, wiped his eyes ; and as the good Captain approached, the tears rolled down his cheeks. It was a joyous, though a tearful meeting.

The next thought was for the baggage. Where was it ? It had been left in the lumber wagon, for no one had bestowed a thought upon it, and the vessel was already miles from shore. The negro probably carried it home as a prize, for the owners never heard of it again, though for some time they entertained a hope that the trunks would be forwarded to them. The Captain seemed to take quite an interest in Mrs. Snelling, having learned she was a bride of but two weeks, and so young ; and his kind feeling was manifested by giving up to her his own stateroom, and sometimes sending nice things from his table to her. Such kindness, at such a time, was sensibly felt and appreciated. Capt. Snelling told his wife he had a little difficulty while on the march with one of the British officers who was with the guard. It was a very warm day, and almost choked with dust and thirst, he stepped on the grass, a very short distance from where he was marching, when the officer rudely pushed him back. Pale with rage, " Sir," said Snelling, " had I my sword by my side, you would not thus dare to lay hands upon me. I trust the day may come when I shall be able to show you how a gentleman ought to behave under similar circum

14*

stances." It was not a little singular that this same officer was after-wards taken prisoner by the Americans, and fell into the hands of Capt. Snelling, to be conducted to Fort Erie. He was a married man, and expected to have been detained a long time from his family. But his generous foe, then Inspector-General, used his in fluence to effect his exchange. They parted with expressions of sincere friendship.

The stay of the prisoners at Kingston was only sufficiently long to remove them from the vessels to the large barges or batteaux which were in readiness for the descent of the St. Lawrence. The lot of our party fell again to the same boat in which were Gen. Hull and staff. The journey was without much incident. At night they stopped at some small village, where lodging in bed-rooms could not be had for all who applied; and several times the high-spirited Capt. Snelling would rebel and give expression to his feelings, when a room for which he had spoken, would be given to a British officer.

On arriving at St. John's, four or five miles from Montreal, the prisoners were ordered to be arranged by companies, with their officers, and marched under guard to the city. Gen. Hull and staff, with an escort of British officers, went in carriages; the officers' ladies two and two in gigs, and then the troops in the rear, with a guard on each side, completed the procession. When they reached the city, a full band of music went in advance of Gen. Hull's carriage, and began to play Yankee Doodle. The General having said in his proclamation " I will go through Montreal with Yankee Doodle," they were determined to make good his promise.

It was evening, and the streets were illuminated, every window in every house being filled with lights, and when the procession came opposite Nelson's Monument, there were cheers given, and a cry " hats off!" An attempt was made to compel all to the act of reverence, by knocking off the prisoners' hats or caps. A militia officer tried it with Capt. Snelling, " At your peril, Sir, touch me ;" was the quick warning, and before he could do anything rash, a regular officer rode up and rebuked the militia officer. At this moment a lady made her way through the crowd and guard towards the prisoners, and fell, overcome by emotion. She was lifted up, and the Captain recognized Mrs. Gooding. His party was conducted to a hotel, where they met Capt. Gooding also.

During the evening, after they had taken possession of their room, a tap was heard at the door, and a servant brought in a tray, on which were glasses and a decanter of wine, placed it on the table, and said—" Capt. F— will be here to see you, Capt. Snelling." He entered soon after, and Capt. Snelling saw in him the gentleman who had insisted on knocking off his cap ; he came to apologize for his conduct, and requested permission to drink a glass of wine with him. In a few days the married officers were paroled, and left Montreal on their way to Boston. Here Captain and Mrs. Snelling remained until he was exchanged, at which time he was ordered to Plattsburg to join Gen. Hampton's army. The admirable wife, who had shared his dangers, remained in Boston. The separation lasted some months, when unexpectedly the Captain made his appearance, informing Mrs. Snelling that he was going to Washington city, having an extremely unpleasant duty to perform, that of taking a man into custody that very night while in bed, one of a party who supplied the enemy with provisions, and must be taken to Washington. He left his wife about twelve o'clock at night, saying he should have assistance, and she must not be uneasy, for that if he succeeded in securing the man, he would stop in the carriage and let her know of his safety. In two hours he returned, told her they had succeeded, and that the prisoner was in irons in the carriage, with a guard. " I pity his poor wife," added he, " I wish you to take a carriage to-morrow, drive to No. ——, Water Street, ask for the lady of the house, and say to her that her husband will be in Washington, for a few days, and then return to her in safety." In two weeks Capt. Snelling came back ; the man had turned States' evidence against others, and had been dismissed.

About this time Mrs. Snelling's eldest child was born—she being only sixteen years of age. Her little daughter Mary beguiled many an anxious hour of separation from her father ; that father being in

constant peril. He passed through many dangers while in Plattsburg and its vicinity, and rose rapidly in rank, Generals Izard and
Macomb being in command. Mrs. Snelling joined him there. Before long Gen. Izard's division was ordered to Fort Erie, and Capt.
Snelling belonged to that division. His wife remained in Burlington, on the other side of Lake Champlain, and was there when
Commodore McDonough gained his victory, hearing distinctly the
roar of the artillery, and relieved beyond measure when the news
came of the victory. It was shouted from mouth to mouth, and
from door to door, "Victory! Victory!"

The details of the siege of Fort Erie may be found in historical
works. At this time Snelling was in the staff of Gen. Izard, and
was Inspector-general, with the rank of Colonel. Gen. Brown commanded at Fort Erie. When the troops went into winter quarters
at Buffalo, Mrs. Snelling again joined him at Buffalo with her little
daughter. She had travelled forty-one miles on horse-back, over the
very same corduroy roads she had been carried over eighteen years
before. Her brother, Capt. Hunt, met her at Batavia and carried
little Mary on a pillow before him; she had been very ill, and the
journey restored her to health.

After peace was proclaimed, Col. Snelling and his family, accompanied by his wife's brother, left Buffalo to visit friends in Detroit.
They embarked in a small vessel with a favorable wind, but the next
day there were indications of a storm; the wind veered round and they
beat about the lake several days. When the storm began to rage
with fury, there were no safe harbors near, and they made but little
progress—and were out of provisions and fuel. A few potatoes were
found, but no fire to cook them. Mrs. Snelling was very sea-sick,
and did not require food, but her little Mary lay by her side gnaw-
ing a raw potatoe. The storm still increased, but the captain of the
vessel hoped to reach Cleveland with the side wind, and at daylight
the third day they found themselves opposite that place, though
they dared not approach the wharf. Guns of distress were fired
but with little hope, for men could not be found to risk their own lives
to save them. The captain then announced that his anchor dragged

and he feared would not hold the vessel. Soon were seen preparations to man a boat; it pushed off from shore and approached the shoals; then was the greatest danger; it passed over and reached the vessel. Capt. Hunt came to his sister and said, " Abby, what will you do; remain here in so much peril, or go in the boat, where there is perhaps greater?" She replied, "I will go." She was taken upon deck; the waves were terrific; the boat would now rise on the summit of a huge billow, now plunge into a deep abyss, and it seemed impossible that the lady and her child could be placed in the boat. But in spite of peril, she hardly knew how, she was seated in the boat with her child and her brother, and after a few minutes gained courage to look back towards the vessel, of which she could only see the top of the mast. At the moment they reached the shoals, a huge wave broke over them and half filled the boat. Some of the men bailed while others plied the oars with renewed energy. When they touched land Mrs. Snelling was taken fainting from the boat and conveyed to an inn; and it was several days before she recovered from the terrors of that storm.

Great was the joy that prevailed in the heart of every wife at the return of peace. In the following spring, Snelling under the peace organization, was Lieut. Colonel of the 6th infantry, and ordered to Governor's Island, Col. Atkinson commanding. He remained there with his family over a year, when the regiment was ordered to Plattsburg, where they had resided about four years when an order came for St. Louis, *en route* for the Upper Mississippi or Missouri! Mrs. Snelling had then three children, and her youngest sister and one of her brothers, a graduate from West Point—Lieut. Wellington Hunt, then a married man—were with her family.

The troops went up to the barracks at Bellefountain, where she visited the graves of her parents, finding them in good order with the exception of the railing which enclosed the mounds. Her youngest child, fifteen months old, was then very ill; he had been named Thomas, after his grandfather. He died and was buried beside his brave ancestor. During the winter of their stay there, the sis ter, Eliza M. Hunt, was married to Mr. Soulard, a French gentleman of great worth.

In the following summer, Snelling was promoted Colonel of the 5th regiment, and ordered up the Mississippi, to relieve Lieut. Colo nel Leavenworth, who was also promoted to another regiment. He had conducted the 5th regiment from Detroit to within eight miles of the Falls of St. Anthony. The journey was exceedingly tedious and disagreeable, in a keel boat laboriously propelled by men with long poles, placed against their shoulders, along a gangway on each side of the boat. The weather was very warm and the musquitoes numerous day and night. The cabin was very low, confined, and uncomfortable. It was three weeks or more before they arrived at Prairie du Chien, during which time very little sound sleep was obtained by the young mother, from fear of the Indians, the Sac and Fox, the most savage looking and ferocious she had ever seen. They seemed to be very fond of dress, and their faces were painted of all colors ; the hair cut close to within an inch of the top of the head, and that decorated with a variety of ribbons and feathers, and often a small looking-glass suspended from the neck. Many of them were certainly great beaux, but they looked hideous, and were terrific objects to a timid woman.

When the voyagers arrived at Prairie du Chien, they found Gov. Cass and his party ; he held councils with the Indians, for the purpose of bringing about a peace between the Sac and Fox tribes, Chippewas and Sioux. Our friends were detained there several weeks by court-martial, of which Col. Snelling was President. They had till three hundred miles to go before they reached the encampment of the 5th regiment, and there were several Indian villages on the route. The magnificent scenery of this river has been often described. Lake Pepin is a beautiful expansion about twenty-four miles in length, and from two to four broad. At length they arrived safe through many fatigues to the end of their journey, and received a hearty welcome from friends they had never seen before, and from Capt. Gooding and his wife, whom they were again delighted to meet.

Their daughter had been married a few days previous to the Adjutant of the regiment.

Great solicitude was felt to have a temporary garrison erected with such defences as could be then made, before the long and severe winter set in. The traders brought news that the Indians were very insolent, and it was said a white man had been killed on the St. Peter's river. A council was called and the murderers were demanded, hostages being taken from the council until they were delivered. They were confined in the guard room, and narrowly watched. All felt that the little community was exposed and almost at the mercy of an enemy, and great exertions were made to complete the temporary barracks for the winter with blockhouses and other defences. Indians meanwhile were collecting in great numbers, and would sometimes show themselves at a distance. The traders in the vicinity often came in, and said the friendly Indians had gone in pursuit of the murderers, and no doubt would succeed in taking them; but if they did not, the friends of the hostages would attempt to rescue them. Scouts were accordingly kept out every night, and the troops slept on their arms. For the mother—trembling for her little ones more than herself, no sooner would she close her eyes at night, than she would start, thinking she heard the war whoop of the savages. The wolves too, half-starved, were extremely daring, and if the cook happened to leave a bucket of swill at the back door, they were sure to empty it of its contents.

As soon as the log barracks were finished, the families moved into them. They were built in four rows forming a square, a blockhouse on either side; and situated where the village of Mendota now stands. The Indian hostages were now put in greater security. They were evidently becoming impatient of restraint, and perhaps had doubts as to the result. One morning as usual, they were taken a short distance into the woods under guard, when suddenly one of them (there were three) started and ran for his life. Those behind set up a yell and the guard fired at him, but he was beyond reach. The others were immediately taken back to the guard-house, and an interpreter sent for, who enquired of them if it was a preconcerted plan of the whole; they declared it was not, and that until the fugitive started to run, they were ignorant of his design, and supposed it merely a sudden desire for freedom.   They said further that he would no doubt urge the immediate surrender of the guilty parties, and laughingly said the lad was so fat, from being so well fed, they were surprised to see him run so fast!

Col. Snelling and the Indian agent thought it advisable to send the murderers to the agent at St. Louis, as soon as they should be brought in and before navigation closed.   At length they came, conducted by a large number of their own tribe.   There were two, but only one was sent to St. Louis, as there was but one white man killed.   It was represented to the Indians in council, that when one white man killed another, his life paid the penalty ; and since one of their people had killed a white man his life must pay the forfeit, unless their great father in Washington should pardon him.   The savages signified assent by a " ugh !"   As soon as the criminal was gone quiet was restored among the Indians for the winter.

In September, 1819, Mrs. Snelling's fifth child was born.   Her sick room was papered and carpeted with buffalo robes, and made quite warm and comfortable.   There were three ladies besides her in the garrison, and they were like one family, spending their time instructing their children, and receiving instruction in the French language from a soldier who it was said had been an officer in Buonaparte's army.   Mrs. Snelling, Mrs. Clark and an officer, comprised the class.   During the winter, parties of men were sent off to cut down trees, hew timber, &c., for the permanent fort, which was to be built on the high point of land between the mouth of the St. Peter's and Mississippi, a point selected by Gen. Pike when he explored the river, as a good site for a fort, and on which Col. Snelling at once decided it should be built.   There was a tree standing at the extreme point, with the name of Pike carved on it by his own hand.   Strict orders were given " to spare that tree;" for it was looked upon by the officers as sacred to his memory, and was carefully guarded, but the care was in vain.   One morning it was found cut down, and great was the lamentation.   It never was known who had done the deed; there was a mystery about it that was never solved.

The first row of barracks that were put up, were of hewn logs, the others of stone. The fort was built in a diamond shape, to suit the ground at the extreme point. Where the tree had stood, was a half-moon battery, and inside this was the officers' quarters, a very neat stone building, the front of cut stone ; at the opposite point a tower. The fort was enclosed by a high stone wall, and is well represented in the drawings of it.

At the expiration of two years, the regiment moved into the fort, although not completed. The families of the officers occupied quarters in the row assigned to them. It was just before this time that Mrs. Snelling lost her youngest child—thirteen months old. In June, 1823, the first steamboat made its appearance at the fort, much to the astonishment of the savages, who placed their hands over their mouths—their usual way of expressing astonishment, and called it a " fire-boat." A salute was fired from the fort, as it was expected that the Inspector general was on board ; and it was returned from the boat. The Indians knew not what to make of it, and they were greatly alarmed, until all was explained. Additions were made to the society of the garrison ; several officers, who had been absent, returned to their regiment, bringing wives and sisters, so that at one time the company numbered ten ladies. There were six companies, which fully officered, would have given eighteen or twenty officers, but there were seldom or never that number present at one time. An Italian gentleman came on the boat, who professed to be travelling for the purpose of writing a book, and brought letters of introduction from Mrs. Snelling's friends in St. Louis. The Colonel invited him to his house to remain as long as he pleased, and he was with them several months. He could not speak English, but spoke French fluently, and seemed much pleased when he found his fair hostess could speak the language, she having learned it when a child at St. Louis. A French school was the first she ever attended, and she thus early acquired a perfectly correct pronunciation. She lamented on one occasion to Mr. Beltrami, that her teacher had received his discharge, and was about leaving, and he politely offered his services in that capacity. She was then translating the life of Cæsar in an abridged form, and from the emotion betrayed by the foreigner at a portion of the reading, it was concluded he had been banished from the Pope's dominions at Rome, and that the lesson reminded him of his misfortunes. The passport he showed, gave him the title of " Le Chevalier Count Beltrami."

About this time, Major Long's expedition arrived, to explore the St. Peter's river, and when they left Beltrami accompanied them. When his book was published at New Orleans, he sent Mrs. Snelling a copy. While at the fort he was busy in collecting Indian curiosities. One day he brought a Sioux chief into Mrs. Snelling's room, who had on his neck a necklace of bears' claws highly polished, saying, " I cannot tempt this chief to part with his necklace, pray see what you can do with him, he will not refuse you." " He wears it," answered the lady, " as a trophy of his prowess, and a badge of honor; however, I will try." After some time, Wanata said, " On one condition I will consent; if you will cut off your hair, braid it, and let it take the place of mine you may have the necklace." All laughed heartily at his contrivance to get rid of further importunity.

One day a call was heard from a sentinel on the river bank, to the corporal of the guard, that a child had fallen into the river, and several ran in the direction the sentinel pointed. The gardener who was at work at a short distance, cried out, " It is the Colonel's son, Henry! Save him!" His mother heard the cry, " A child is drowning!" and ran out upon the battery to see and hear what was the matter. She saw them draw the boy out, place him on a blanket, and hasten up the hill; they approached her house, when the Colonel hastened towards her saying, " We came near losing our child!" and she saw it was indeed her own. He was pale as death, but soon recovered, and lives to tell the story of an immense catfish dragging him into the river while fishing.

In 1823, news was brought by the traders that two white children were with a party of Sioux, on the St. I eter's. It appeared from what they could learn, that a family from Red River—Selkirk's settlement—had been on their way to the Fort, when a war party of Sioux met them, murdered the parents and an infant, and made the boys prisoner. Col. Snelling sent an officer with a party of soldiers to rescue the children. After some delay in the ransom, they were finally brought. An old squaw, who had the youngest, was very unwilling to give him up, and indeed the child did not wish to leave her. The oldest, about eight years old, said his name was John Tully, and his brother, five years old, Abraham. His mother had an infant, but he saw the Indians dash its brains out against a tree, then kill his father and mother. Because he cried, they took him by his hair, and cut a small piece from his head, which was a running sore when he was re-taken. Col. Snelling took John into his family, Major Clark the other, but he was afterwards sent to an orphan asylum in New York. The eldest died of lockjaw, occasioned by a cut in the ankle while using an axe. His deathbed conversion was affecting and remarkable. One day, after he had been ill several weeks, he said, " Mrs. Snelling, I have been a very wicked boy ; I once tried to poison my father because he said he would whip me. I stole a ring from you, which you valued much, and sold it to a soldier, and then I told you a lie about it. I have given you a great deal of trouble. I have been very wicked. I am going to die the day after to-morrow, and don't know where I shall go. Oh, pray for me."

His benefactress answered, " John, God will forgive you, if you repent ; but you must pray, too, for yourself. God is more willing to hear than we are to pray. Christ died to save just such a sinner as you are, and you must call upon that Saviour to save you." All his sins appeared to rise before him as he confessed them, and he seemed to feel that he was too great a sinner to hope for pardon. Mrs. Snelling read to him, and instructed him. He never had received any religious instruction, except in the Sunday school taught by Mrs. Clark and herself, and being accustomed to say his prayers with her children, and always to be present when she read the church service on Sundays. The next morning after the above con versation, when she asked him how he had rested during the night, he said, " I prayed very often in the night ; I shall die to-morrow, and I know not what will become of me." For several hours he remained tranquil, with his eyes closed, but would answer whenever spoken to ; then suddenly he exclaimed, " Glory ! glory !" His friend said, " John, what do you mean by that word ?" " Oh ! Mrs. Snelling, I feel so good—I feel so good ! Oh ! I cannot tell you how good I feel." She knew not that he ever heard that word unless from her prayer-book. He lost all consciousness on the day he said he should die, and expired at the succeeding dawn.

During this year the commandant was visited by Gen. Scott anc. suite, and the fort was completed. Heretofore it had been called Fort St. Anthony, but Gen. Scott issued an order giving it the name of Fort Snelling. He expressed his approbation of the construction and site of the fort, etc., spent a week with his friends, and visited the falls and a chain of lakes where they were used to amuse them- selves fishing, and where the water was so clear they could see the fish playing about the hook. One of the lakes Mrs. Snelling named Scott Lake.

Another of her amusements was riding on horseback. When a child she had been accustomed to ride every morning with her father, and acquired great confidence in the management of a horse. Her husband seldom would ride with her, but Capt. Martin Scott was in the regiment, and often accompanied her. One day they saw a wolf; the dogs gave chase, and they followed until they ran down the poor creature, the bonnet of the fair huntress having fallen back, and her hair streaming loose in the wind.

In 1825, the family left Fort Snelling to visit their friends in Detroit. It was late in the season, October, before they set out homeward, by the way of Green Bay, where Mrs. Snelling's brother, Lieut. Wellington Hunt, was stationed. They spent a week in his family, and when they reached Lake Pepin the ice was running so rapidly they were compelled to stop ; the ice had cut through the cabin so that it leaked. A small log cabin was put up, and an

express sent to the fort, one hundred miles, for sleighs to convey
them thither, and provisions, as they had nothing but corn, which
they boiled in ash-water with a little salt. Fears were entertained
by Col. Snelling that the express might not reach the fort, and
another was sent a week after. One day, after two weeks, there was
a sound of sleigh bells, and Henry, who was the first to hear, ran to
meet them, and soon returned with two loaves of bread, which he
threw into his mother's lap, crying, " eat, mother, eat." The children ate bread as if famished, and even the little Marion, but eight
months old, partook of the general joy. They had seen no Indians,
who had all gone to their winter grounds. Some of the officers
came to meet the Colonel's family, and they were soon on the move
again. They were welcomed back joyfully by all their friends, and
many of their favorite Indians came to see them. One poor savage,
who always furnished them with game, came leaning on his staff, looking pale and emaciated ; he was very sick, he said, and came to see
them once more before he died. He could scarcely crawl back to his
lodge, and the next day expired.

At this time a party of the Chippewas and Sioux held a council with
the Indian agent. There had been war between the two nations for
a long time ; the agent desired to act as mediator between them, and
sent for them to meet him. After the council the two parties smoked
the pipe of peace. The Chippewas killed a dog, made a feast, and
invited the Sioux to their lodges, which were under the guns of the
fort. In the evening, about nine o'clock, the firing of guns was
heard ; the sentinel called " corporal of the guard" repeatedly, in
quick succession. The wild cries of women and children were heard,
for the Chippewas had their families with them, and several Indians
came rushing into the hall of the commanding officer, trying to tell
what was the matter. The officer of the day reported that the
Sioux, after partaking of the hospitalities of the Chippewas, and
being apparently good friends, had some of them returned, placed
their guns under the wigwams, and fired, killing some and wounding others. The wounded were conveyed into the hospital to have
their wounds dressed. Other particulars of this occurrence, with

the determination of the Chippewas to have vengeance, the action of the commanding officer, and the surrender and punishment of the perpetrators of the deed, are related in another memoir. The traders said the Sioux were perfectly satisfied, much more so than if the offenders had been imprisoned and sent to St. Louis.

In 1826, Capt. Thomas Hunt, who was residing at Washington, wrote to his sister, urging her and the Colonel to send their two eldest children to him to be educated. Their daughter Mary was now fourteen, and as Capt. Plympton and his wife were going, her parents got her in readiness to accompany them. Her mother thought not it would cost so many tears to part with her child; but when she returned home from the boat, she told Mrs. Clark it " seemed like a death in the family." Soon an opportunity offered, and they sent Henry also.

In 1827 the Indians began to show signs of hostility near Prairie du Chien; they murdered two white men and a young girl, the daughter of one of them, and attacked two boats with supplies for Fort Snelling, killing and wounding several of the crew. Col. Snelling ordered out as many of his command as could be spared from the fort, and with his officers descended the river to the relief of Fort Crawford, or to attack any hostile force of Indians he might meet. There were two large villages of Indians between the two forts, and it was expected, when they approached, they would be attacked, but there was not an Indian to be seen. When they reached Prairie du Chien, they ascertained that the outrage had been committed by Winnebagoes and not Sioux. When Gen. Atkinson heard this at St. Louis, he sent and seized the chief, Red Bird, and one or two others, who were tried, convicted, and executed. After an absence of six weeks, the party returned without being obliged to fire a gun.

One day soon after his return, the Colonel came in to tell his wife the express had brought them a mail, holding in his hand a letter sealed with black. She exclaimed, " My Mary is dead." " No," said her husband, " the letter is from Detroit." It brought the intelligence of her much loved brother Henry's death. He was much loved and respected by all who knew him; was mayor of the city and colonel of the militia, and his funeral was the largest ever known in Michigan. After the massacre at Frenchtown by the Indians, in 1813, he had spent a great deal of money in ransoming prisoners, many of whom still affectionately cherish his memory. He had proved a father to his sister and family, and was mourned by them deeply and long.

In the fall of 1827, the regiment was ordered to Jefferson Barracks. When the family arrived at St. Louis, they took lodgings for the winter, Colonel Snelling having obtained leave to go to Washington to settle some public accounts and to bring home his daughter. He wrote to her mother in glowing terms of her improvement in person and mind, and that she received much attention for one of her age, not yet sixteen. " As Mary will not again," he concluded, "have so good an opportunity, I have encouraged her to accept invitations to the different soirées; she has had cards for the season from all." Mary wrote, "I have attended many parties, but I do not enjoy them, for my dear mother is not with me, and I am so impatient to embrace her." Alas! the All Wise Disposer of events had ordered it otherwise. One more letter her mother received from her, and hoped before many weeks to see her, but at the time she was expecting her arrival, a letter was written to her sister, Mrs. Soulard, that Mary was dead!

Col. Snelling wrote afterwards, that on the 2d of February she had been at Mrs. Clay's party and danced, and had taken cold while standing to wait for the carriage; the cold terminating in a brain fever. Mrs. Adams, the wife of the President, showed great interest in the young stranger, as did many others, and every attention was paid her that could be desired; but there was no solace for the deep wound in the mother's heart. She had felt a presentiment that she should never more see her daughter, and was in some measure prepared for the stroke which almost crushed her: she was enabled to look with faith to Him from whose hand it came, to feel that He was too wise to err—too good to afflict willingly, and to bow in humble submission to the most painful dispensation of his Providence. Her husband wrote that he should be obliged to remain still longer in Washington ; it would improve her health to travel, and she must join him without delay. In May she left St. Louis with her three children and nurse, found her husband and son well, the latter much grown, and received a cordial welcome from her brother and sister-in-law.

Her cup of affliction was not yet full ; in two months her husband was seized with inflammation of the brain and died in three weeks. In communicating the sad event to the army, the General-in-Chief thought it but an act of justice to make a public acknowledgment of his services.[*]

At this period of distress Mrs. Snelling's youngest child, Josiah, was not expected to live. She resigned him willingly ; but he was spared to her, and lived to be her great comfort. In a month she was on her way to Detroit. A farm three miles up the river belonged to her, and thither she took her children. Her brother, George Hunt, took charge of the farm and lived in her family. After residing two years upon it, Mrs. Snelling found it necessary to remove into the city, where she took a few boarders, and rented her farm. In 1835 she sold it for nine thousand dollars, purchased a lot in the city and built a brick house. Her son Henry, who had gone to New York on business, became acquainted with Miss Putnam, the sister of the publisher, a lady of high literary ability and intelligence, and they were soon afterwards married. Capt. Thomas Hunt was at this time residing in Detroit. He died very suddenly in consequence of a fall, leaving a very interesting family. Gov. Mason offered Mrs. Snelling a high rent for her house, and she consented to let it, provided he would purchase her new furniture, which he did. She then accepted an invitation from her brother,

* " Colonel Snelling joined the army in early youth. In the battle of Tippecanoe, he was distinguished for gallantry and good conduct. Subsequently and during the whole of the late war with Great Britain, from the battle of Brownstown to the termination of the contest, he was actively employed in he field, with credit to himself and honor to his country.—*Letter written by vrder of Major-General Macomb, dated August 21st,* 1828.

Gen. Hunt, at Maumee city, to reside in his family, having now only her daughter Marion (afterwards Mrs. Hazard) and her youngest son with her. Her son James had gone to West Point.

In 1841 Mrs. Snelling was married to the Rev. J. E. Chaplin, the grandson of President Edwards. He was appointed principal to one of the branches of the Michigan State Institution, and they removed to White Pigeon in Michigan, where Mr. Chaplin died in 1846, much beloved and lamented. For five years his wife had lived with him in great happiness, and she felt that he had only gone home a little before her.

In 1844 her son James graduated, and was ordered to Texas in Gen. Worth's regiment. He was at the battle of Palo Alto and Reseca, in all the battles with Gen. Taylor excepting Buena Vista. At that time Gen. Worth's regiment was with Gen. Scott's division. He was at the siege of Vera Cruz and Cherubusco, at which time Gen. Scott mentions him in his dispatches. At Molino del Rey he was severely wounded; the ball entering the left breast passed under his arm, and was cut out from his back. He received two brevets, making him *passed* captain. Although his father had been in eleven skirmishes and battles he had never lost a drop of blood, but the son was less fortunate, and at twenty-three nearly lost his life. It was six weeks after seeing his name published among those who were severely wounded before his mother heard from him direct, and during that time, her state of suspense was terrible. One day as she left home for a walk, she noticed the stage approaching her house, and as it was passing, Mr. Hazard put his head out and said, " You had better go back, there is some one here you would like to see." She turned to go back, saw the stage stop, and her son get out, and sank on her knees returning thanks to God that her eyes again beheld him. He afterwards went to Texas with his regiment.

In 1849 Mrs. Chaplin travelled with her nephew, Major Hunt, and her two nieces up the Mississippi to Fort Snelling. She found twenty-one years had made great changes and great improvements; the party went in a splendid steamboat, beautifully furnished, with table sumptuously supplied, and either side of the river was dotted with cultivated fields and large towns—the transformation seemed almost magical. When they arrived at the Fort, she met an old friend in Col. Loomis, who was very polite in taking her about the country that she might see all she could in the short time they had to stay. She visited the grave of her little daughter, and could decipher the name on the stone although much defaced. The Colonel promised to have a new one put up. An old Indian woman recognized her, saying she had seen her a long time ago, and she was much delighted to find she had been remembered. She also went over the house so long occupied by her family. On their return they stopped at St. Paul's, where the governor of the territory resides, and there found a niece who had married Mr. Welsh of Michigan.

One of the passengers taken in at that place, in conversation with one of the ladies, related the story of the murder of the Chippewas by the Sioux after the treaty, and the punishment of the guilty persons, with some fanciful embellishment, by way of exemplifying the Indian traits of generosity and self-devotion, stating that the friend of one of the culprits had offered himself a voluntary victim in his place, the other being a married man, and that the innocent substitute had been delivered up to the Chippewas by the commanding officer. His strictures on the conduct of Col. Snelling were interrupted by a mild rebuke from Mrs. Chaplin, who informed him the account he had given of the transaction was incorrect. " You seem to speak knowingly on the subject, madam," said the stranger. " I should be happy to get the right story. " I was the wife of that commanding officer," she replied, "and remember well all the circumstances ;" which she then related, and was told by the gentleman that he was writing a book, " and had received the story from a trader." His experience in this instance might be a lesson to those who rely on floating traditions unsupported by competent authority.

Mrs. Chaplin is now happily at home with her daughter, Mrs. Hazard, and resides in Cincinnati. Her life has been a chequered and eventful one, and many sorrows have fallen to her lot; but these have

been borne with resignation and submission to the will of her
Heavenly Father, to whose guidance she committed her youth, and
who has blessed her with the enjoyment of the peace and prosperity
won through a period of hardship and distress. Her family connections are numerous, and a very large circle of friends and
acquaintances admire her talents and love her virtues.

XIX.

MARY McMILLAN.

Lanman, the author of a pleasing History of Michigan, says it embraces three epochs; the first a romantic one, extending to 1760, when the dominion over the small portion of inhabited territory passed from France to Great Britain. The earliest gleam of civilization at that period had scarcely penetrated its forests, and the boat-songs of the French furtraders, as they swept its lakes, alone awoke the echoes. The second epoch may be called a military one. It commenced with the Pontiac war, and extends through the struggles of the British, Indians, and Americans to obtain undisputed possession of the country; terminating with the victory of Commodore Perry, the defeat of Proctor, etc. The third and last period comprises the enterprising, mechanical, and working age of Michigan, commencing with the introduction of the public lands into market; it is the epoch of agriculture, manufactures, and commerce; the day of harbors, cities, canals, and railroads, in which forests have been surveyed and cleared, streams and lakes covered with sails, States founded, and their internal resources developed.

A few small settlements were made along the lakes at a very early period. Sault Ste. Marie, like the other French posts, had a fort and chapel in 1688, and was a favorite resort for traders and savages on their way to the forests of Lake Superior, its settlers being a few Indians, called the Salteurs, who lived by fishing in the rapids. A goldsmith, who went there afterwards, wrought from the pure copper found in that region, bracelets, candlesticks, crosses, and censers, for sale among the savages. From time to time Jesuit missionaries were sent from Quebec and Montreal to these distant posts, but they remained without any organized colonial government, or any connected history, forming a part of the Canadian domain, inhabited only by wandering Indians or migrating traders, whose headquarters were at Montreal or Quebec. The vast tracts extending from the St. Lawrence to the Mississippi, fertile, and watered by noble streams, with inland seas offering facilities for commerce, were thus wandered over by herds of deer, elk, and buffalo, or tribes as wild as the beasts of the forest.

Baron La Hontan, who came at a very early period, says, describing Lake Erie, " It is assuredly the finest on earth ; its banks decked with oak trees, elms, and chestnuts, entwined with vines bearing rich clusters to their tops, and its forests abounding with turkeys, deer, and wild beeves, frequented too by warlike hunters." The French scattered along the lake border, were there for the purpose of pushing the fur trade into the Indian territory, and except the commandants at the posts, were chiefly merchants engaged in this traffic. The coureurs des bois, or rangers of the woods, were often half-breeds, and were hardy and skilled in propelling the canoe, fishing, hunting, or sending a rifle-ball to the "right eye" of the buffalo. They procured cargoes of furs from the Indians, and carried large packs of goods across portages in the interior, by straps suspended from their foreheads or shoulders. They were familiar with every rock and island, bay and shoal, of the western waters. The ordinary dress of a Canadian furtrader, was a cloth fastened about the middle, a loose shirt, a " molton" or blanket-coat, a red worsted or leathern cap, and sometimes a surtout of coarse blue cloth, and cap of the same material ; elk-skin trowsers, with seams adorned with fringe ; a scarlet woollen sash tied round the waist, in which a broad hunting-knife was stuck, and buck-skin moccasins. In later years they wore a shirt of striped cotton, trowsers of cloth or leather, leggins like the Indians, deer-skin moccasins, colored belt of worsted, with knife and tobacco-pouch, and blue woollen cap with red feather. The half-breeds were demi-savage, and were employed as guides or rangers, to manage the canoes in remote trading excursions. European goods were exchanged for peltries, which were taken to the depôts on the lakes, and thence transported eastward. The individuals who devoted their attention to agriculture usually wore a long surtout and sash, with red cap and deer-skin moccasins, while the gentlemen visiting the country preserved the garb in vogue in the days of Louis XIV. Agriculture was then limited to a few patches of corn and wheat, the grain being ground in wind-mills. The French soldiers, with their blue coats turned up with white facings, and short-clothes, and the priests with their long gowns and black bands, who had their stations near the forts, formed a strong contrast in their appearance to the Indians who loitered around the posts.*

The women made coarse cotton and woollen garments for the Indian traders. The amusements were chiefly dancing to the violin, and hunting in the forests; to which may be added the observance of the festivals enjoined by the church. Fishing was a constant occupation; canoes passed in every direction over the streams and bays, and the varieties of fish now esteemed so delicious, were taken in great abundance, and formed a principal article of food. The social condition of these primitive inhabitants was not as civilized as in the larger colonial settlements; the humble emigrants went out with their tents, their axes, their hoes, their stores of ammunition and provisions, and their cattle, to win a subsistence by hard labor, and had little regard to the amenities which are the growth of a settled community. The priests had much influence, and frequently was the lonely altar, with its rude candlesticks and censers carved from native copper, erected under the forest boughs, surrounded by savages in the wild costume of their tribes, deer or buffalo skins, with the cincture of the war eagle on their heads, their necklaces

* Lanman's History.

of bear's claws, and moccasins embroidered with porcupine's quills. The solemn chant went up amidst the distant howling of wild beasts, and the solitary bark chapels, adorned by no sculptured marble or golden lamps, but surmounted by the rudely framed cross, looked out on a domain of prairie, lake, and unbroken forest; yet was the wealth of art surpassed:

> " Iris all hues; roses and jessamines
> Reared high their flourished heads between, and wrought
> Mosaic; under foot the violet,
> Crocus, and hyacinth, with rich inlay,
> Broidered the ground, more colored than with stones
> Of costliest emblem."

A volume might be written upon the Indian mythology of the lakes. Each rock, island, lake, river, wood and cataract along the shores of Michigan, had its presiding genius, good or evil; legends peopled the earth and air, spirits floated through the forests and danced along the streams; manitous of darkness performed their orgies in the storms, and the islands abounded with golden sands watched like the fleece of old, by serpents, birds of prey, and mighty giants. To these, sacrifices of tobacco pipes and other offerings were continually presented. In 1721, Charlevoix was informed that Michabout was the manitou of the lakes, and the island of Michili-mackinac his birth-place. The name of this island signifies " a great turtle," from its resemblance to one, or in the Chippewa speech, " the place of giant fairies." This deity, it is said, created Lake Superior that his Indians might catch beaver; and the savages believe the fragments of rock at the Sault and other rapids are remains of the causeway constructed by him to dam up the waters.

The social condition of the settlers of Michigan was not much improved by the transfer of the country from the French to the British government. By the capitulation of Montreal, the French subjects were permitted to remain, and the fur trade was prosecuted by their agency under English companies. Till 1762 the peninsula remained quiet, while war raged at a distance; but the war of the Pontiac confederacy soon carried disturbance to its borders. The details of this period belong to history. It is proper merely to mention the plot by which this famous Indian chief aimed to destroy the fort of Detroit. He had ordered his Indians to saw off their rifles, conceal them under their blankets, and gain admission to the fort under pretence of holding a peaceable council. On a signal given by his delivering a belt of wampum in a specified manner, the savages were to rush on the soldiers, and fling open the gates to the body of warriors on the outside. Word was then sent to Major Gladwyn that Pontiac would hold a council with the English commander on the 9th of May, 1763. The evening before, an Indian woman employed by the Major to make some elk-skin moccasins, brought them to the fort. Gladwyn, pleased with her work, bespoke more, and having paid her for the first, sent a servant to see her safely through the gates. Here she lingered, looking wistfully at the river, and her behavior appearing singular, the servant asked the cause of her delay, but received no answer. The commanding officer then called her in, and asked why she hesitated, when, calling to mind his former kindness, the woman said she would not take away the skin, as she would not be able to bring it back. This remark exciting suspicion, she was induced by promises of safety and reward, to reveal the whole plot. The officers thought it a trick, but the night was spent in preparation; guards were placed on the ramparts, and every man was ready for defence. Their suspicions were confirmed by the distant sounds heard of the war-songs and dances of the Indians. In the morning Pontiac came with his chiefs and braves to the council-house, and was received by the Major and officers. The appearance of warlike preparation could not escape the Indians, and when they were seated on the skins, Pontiac asked the cause, which he was told was the necessity of military discipline. He professed much friendship for the English in his speech, but his gestures became violent as he approached the point when he was to give the concerted signal. The officers drew their swords, the soldiers at the doors clattered their arms, and as the chief presented the belt in his usual manner, thus failing to give the signal, the Major accused him of being a traitor, and pulling aside his blanket, showed his rifle. The Indians were ordered to quit the fort instantly, being assured of safety beyond the pickets, and were received by the warriors without with yells and firing, and other demonstrations of hostility towards the garrison, the more fierce on account of the failure of the enterprise.

During the Revolutionary struggle the peninsula remained in comparative quiet. Although constituting a part of the Canadian territory, a magazine of arms for the savage allies of the loyalists, and a mart where scalps were bought and sold, it can boast no prominent events to give interest to its history, because not made the theatre of action. A mere outpost of Canada, it was a magnificent extent of wilderness, in which the axe had scarcely felled a tree; trackless, save where Indian trails wound through the dense forests and flowery oaklands; unbroken, except by scattered Indian villages and corn-fields studding the prairies, or the solitary posts of fur traders. The treaty of 1783 included the peninsula within the bounds of American territory. At this time its sparse white population consisted chiefly of French and English, whose settlements were confined to the vicinity of trading posts along the lakes and the banks of the principal rivers. When the ravages of the savage tribes on the frontier were terminated by the victories of Gen. Wayne and the treaty in 1795, the tide of emigration began to flow more steadily westward. Michigan was erected into a separate territory in 1805, but the progress of settlement was slow, and the principal business carried on was still the fur trade.

In 1810 the island of Mackinaw, a romantic point, rising like an altar from the realm of waters, was the central mart of traffic, and the lakes were sprinkled with canoes of traders and Indians; the merry Canadian voyageur bartering his trinkets at booths scattered along the shores, and the red warrior with his fantastic ornaments, his silver armlets and embroidered moccasins, coming to exchange his treasures, or on fishing and hunting excursions. The fur merchants went up the lakes in large canoes, manned by Canadians, to meet their agents returning from the remote wilderness at Fort William, one of the principal pioneer posts of the northwest country.

The council house was a large wooden building, hung with trophies of the chase, and Indian implements of war or peaceful employment. Thus the romantic aspect of the country had not yet disappeared, though the post was crowded with traders, and the epoch of mercantile enterprise was in its meridian. The semi-barbarous dominion exercised for a century over the lakes and the region on their borders, had not yet been swept away even by the wings of commerce.

The war of 1812 was a crisis which brought renewed devastations upon the frontier, and the borders were overrun by the British and their savage allies. Although, by act of Congress in May of this year, two millions of acres were ordered to be surveyed, little inducement was held out to emigrants to penetrate a remote wilderness, through which there were no roads, and as late as 1820 Detroit, Frenchtown, Mackinaw, and Sault Ste. Marie, were the chief settlements within the present limits of the State. When, some time afterwards, expeditions were projected for exploring the country, the interior was yet a ranging ground for savages and wild beasts, intersected by Indian trails, with here and there, by the lakes or streams, a few clusters of log houses, or the huts of Frenchmen; the roads constructed in 1823 scarcely passable in the most favorable season. Gradually, however, the forest began to resound with the huntsman's axe, and the log tenements of the hardy pioneers to stud the wilderness. The social progress of the territory was not marked by any stirring events. The advance of emigration along its rivers was solitary and silent; the cannon and bayonet had long since given place to the plough and the woodman's axe, and the subjugation of the wild forest was achieved without the necessity of disputing possession of the soil with human foes. The emigrants scattered themselves by degrees over the interior, finding a dry and fertile soil, well adapted for culture, and a country rich in varied and picturesque scenery. The lake-like and rolling prairies, with their wooded islands and forest borders, were beautiful beyond description; the white oak openings were like stately parks enamelled with flowers, and the burr-oak groves like orchards studded with large pear trees. The mounds rose from thirty or forty to two hundred feet, and hill and dale, secluded lake and forest tract, with its dense growth of beech, black walnut, elm, maple, hickory, oaks of different kinds, etc., its luxuriant wild grape vines and rich underwood, presented scenes that might well captivate the new comers. One by one, or in small numbers, wagons bearing the families of the pioneers, with their furniture, might be seen winding over the rough roads or along the shores ; then smoke rose curling through the woods from the prostrate trunks of smouldering trees; the settler having cleared a small space, built his log house, while his cattle fed on the luxuriant herbage in the vicinity ; the labors of the plough followed those of the axe, the winter was weathered through, and the succeeding year saw him an independent freeholder, with a market at his door for the produce of his farm.

Mrs. McMillan was among the early settlers of the eastern portion of Michigan. Her removal with husband and children from a populous and cultivated region, was a laborious journey, performed in the manner above mentioned, in a small wagon, laden with a few necessary articles of comfort for their new home ; by slow and toilsome stages—their nights being passed under some temporary shelter, insufficiently protected from the attacks of wild beasts, and subject to inconvenience from night dews, cold winds, and troublesome insects. Their establishment was attended with the same circumstances of labor and hardship, which have been described in numerous other cases. We pass to some incidents that may serve to illustrate the times, as well as show the courage and energy of this strong-hearted matron.

In 1813 she was living on the Canada side, in a small house on the banks of the Thames, a beautiful little river whose bright waters were often skimmed by canoes of savages intent on plunder or slaughter, the shrill war-whoop often resounding from the depths of the woods. McMillan had left his family to enter into active military service, and their home was two miles distant from the nearest neighbor. The country had been kept in a continual state of alarm by marauding parties of Indians, who did not hesitate to kill and capture, as well as rob the defenceless settlers. Mrs. McMillan suf-

15*

fered the more from anxiety at this critical period, as in the absence of her husband the care of their young children devolved entirely upon her, and her sole protection was her own prudence and energy. One day having heard rumors of the approach of a hostile party, and being apprehensive of a sudden attack, she took her infant and walked to the nearest house in search of information.   There she was startled with the intelligence that savages had been seen in the vicinity, and that they had gone in the direction of her dwelling, where they would probably stop during the day.   The matron thought of the little ones she had left at home unprotected, and a sickening terror entered her heart.   She stayed to hear no more, but hastened homeward, bearing in her arms the unconscious babe who might now be all that remained to her.   As she came near, her eyes were eagerly strained for a sight of those beloved ones who were accustomed to run to meet her; all was silence; and when she dashed open the door and stood within the dwelling, a scene of desolation met her view !   Every article of furniture had disappeared; the floor was dusty with the track of footsteps, and not one of her children was anywhere on the premises.

. The alarm and anguish of the mother may be better imagined than described.   The fatal idea had flashed at once on her mind, that her little ones had been either murdered or carried away captive by the merciless Indians.   In this terrible emergency she lost none of her self-possession, nor her usual sagacity of judgment. The savages could not have gone far, and her only course was to cross the river and seek aid immediately.   But there was no canoe, nor mode of conveyance; she could not swim, nor could she leave her helpless infant behind her.   She was not long in discovering a way to overcome the difficulty.   Hastily rolling some logs into the water, she placed two boards across them, forming a kind of raft, on which she stepped cautiously, carrying her babe, managed to hold the frail craft together while she guided its course, and reached the opposite shore in safety.   Here her terror and anguish were suddenly changed into joy; the children had heard of the near approach of Indians immediately after their mother's departure, and having taken the precaution to put the furniture in the cellar, out of the intruders' way, they had crossed the river to seek protection from the neighbors on the other side.

On another occasion Mrs. McMillan suffered from Indian depredation. A large party from the different tribes was on the way to Toronto, and in the course of a single day some two hundred of them stopped at her house, plundering it of all it contained. McMillan was still absent, and the mother did not dare to interfere for the rescue of any portion of her property, lest she should draw down vengeance upon herself and her innocent children. The work of spoiling went on, therefore, while they stood quietly aloof. A fine flock of geese, which she had raised with care, was on the grass before the door, and the Indians soon commenced execution among them. Mrs. McMillan started forward to save her favorites; but a gun was instantly levelled at her, with the threat of shooting, if she ventured to interrupt the sport. Like many other matrons of that day, she prided herself on a handsome set of pewter dishes and plates, which her industrious scouring kept as bright as silver. Their polish and beauty pleased the Indians, who tried them by biting, to ascertain' if they were real silver, and the whole stock speedily passed into the possession of the depredators, who left only a knife and a tin cup in the house. When the last of the enemy had passed over the river, the terrified family found themselves in safety, but exhausted with hunger, while nothing in the shape of food was left about the place. They were compelled to fast till supplies could be brought from a distance of several miles.

When the war was over, and comparative quiet established, McMillan and his family, with two or three others, removed to Detroit, ascending the river on a large raft. The trials of the wife were not ended. Straggling bands of savages were still lurking in the neighborhood of the city, ready for any deed of robbery or bloodshed. One evening when McMillan had left his home for a short time, the silence was broken by the report of a gun, which caused some alarm to his wife and children, though they were far

from anticipating the extent of their calamity.   The father's prolonged absence caused apprehension, which was terminated by fata.
certainty; during the night his lifeless body was brought home.
This blow was severely felt by the bereaved wife, but a sense of
duty to the loved ones dependent on her, prevented her from being
utterly overwhelmed.   It may be imagined, after this sad tragedy,
how anxiously passed the nights in her lonely dwelling.   In the
middle of one dark night, the roar of the alarm guns was again
heard.   The affrighted mother sprang up, gathered her children
hastily together, and knowing well there was no safety within
doors, hurried with them from the house.   The house of a friend
at a considerable distance, offered shelter, but the darkness was
intense; the fugitives lost their way, and ere long found themselves
in the midst of the deep mire for which the roads of Detroit were
formerly so celebrated.   More urgent peril, however, was behind
them; they struggled on, leaving their shoes in the mud, and managed to escape to the house of their friend, where they were received
with kindness.   The mother's quick eye, scanning her rescued
group, now discovered that her son, eleven years of age, was
missing!   The alarm was given, and the next day men were sent
in every direction about the country to search for him; but all in
vain.   It was too certain that he had been captured, and the dis-
tracted mother feared he had been murdered by the relentless
savages.   For four long months she endured the tortures of suspense.   She then learned that her boy had been taken prisoner, and
was still held in captivity at some distance from the city.   The sum
demanded for his ransom was speedily sent, and he was restored to
the arms of his mother.   During his captivity he had fared hardly,
subsisting chiefly on buds and roots, and never having even a piece
of bread.   This son is now living at Jackson, Michigan.

    After the termination of the Indian troubles, Mrs. McMillan
maintained her family by her exertions, giving each of her children
a substantial education, with such training as to fit them for every
duty and vicissitude of life.   She made enough to purchase a valu
able piece of land near the Presbyterian church, with a large framed

house, which is now known as the Temperance or Purdy's Hotel. Mrs. McMillan resides in the city with one of her sons, and is often solicited by those who have heard something of her romantic history, to relate her adventures in detail, and describe the life led by many who like her, encountered the perils of war in a new country.

XX.

CHARLOTTE A. CLARK.

THIS lady accompanied her husband, who was commissary to the United States troops, in November, 1819, to a military station on the Upper Mississippi, situated on the St. Peter's side of the river. Several persons went with them from Prairie du Chien; the voyage being made in keel-boats, and the waters so low that the men were obliged frequently to wade in the river and draw them through the sand. Six weeks were occupied in passing over the distance of three hundred miles, one week of which was spent at Lake Pepin.

Having reached the place of destination, the company were obliged to live in their boats till pickets could be erected for their protection against the Indians, who not understanding the object of this invasion of the wild, or the display of arms and ammunition, might fall upon them in some unguarded moment. Huts also had to be built, though in the rudest manner, to serve as a shelter during the winter from the rigors of a severe climate. After living with her family in the boat for a month, it was a highly appreciated luxury for Mrs. Clark to find herself at home in a log hut, plastered with clay, and "chinked" for her reception. It was December before they got into winter quarters, and the fierce winds of that exposed region, with terrific storms now and then, were enough to make them wish to keep within doors as much as possible. Once, in a violent tempest, the roof of their dwelling was raised by the wind, and partially slid off; there was no protection for the inmates, but the baby in the cradle was pushed under the bed for safety. Notwithstanding these discomforts and perils, the inconveniences they had to encounter, and their isolated situation, the little party of emigrants were not without their social enjoyments. They were nearly all young married persons, cheerful and fond of gaiety, and had their dancing assemblages once a fortnight. An instance of the kindness of the commanding officer, Col. Leavenworth, deserves mention. One of the other officers having been attacked with symptoms of scurvy, and great alarm prevailing on that account, the Colonel took a sleigh, and accompanied by a few friends, set off on a journey through the country inhabited by Indians, not knowing what dangers he might encounter from their hostility, or the perils of the way, for the purpose of procuring medicinal roots. The party was absent several days, and in the meantime collected a supply of hemlock and spignet, which they used with excellent effect in curing the disease.

In the ensuing summer, when Col. Snelling had the command, Fort Snelling was begun. St. Louis, distant nine hundred miles, was at that time the nearest town of any importance. After the erection of the fort, Mrs. Clark says—" we made the first clearing at the Falls of St. Anthony, and built a grist-mill." The wife of Capt. George Gooding, of the 5th regiment, was the first white woman who ever visited those beautiful falls. She afterwards married Col. Johnson, and went to reside in St. Louis. The daughter of Mrs. Clark, now Mrs. Van Cleve of Ann Arbor, was born while the troops were stationed at Prairie du Chien. At that time Col. Leavenworth received orders to go up to the place where, in the following summer, Fort Snelling was built. He went, though he had at this time no wholesome provisions; even the bread, it was said, was "two inches in the barrels thick with mould;" no vegetables were to be had, and several of the men were perishing with scurvy. The Sioux Indians were in the vicinity, and they were mutually suspicious of each other, so that no game could be bought; nor was there a prospect of matters being mended till more amicable rela tions could be established. The prices of such fresh edibles as could be procured at Prairie du Chien were enormous ; a small and lean chicken procured for a sick lady cost a dollar ; beets as large as the finger, one dollar a dozen ; and onions were ten dollars a bushel. The cold is described as so intense that the soldiers called out merely while they could answer to the roll, often had their faces frost-bitten ; the thermometer at seven in the morning being known to stand thirty-five degrees below zero.

Mrs. Clark remained at Fort Snelling, with the exception of about a year, till 1827. The only young lady in the company was married when about fifteen years of age, to a Mr. Dennis, also of the army. The wedding took place in the winter, and the bridal party was obliged to descend the river, three hundred miles, on the ice, to Prairie du Chien, to have the ceremony performed. The monotony of their life was varied by continual alarms and excitements, from the encounters of the hostile tribes of Sioux and Chippewas, who came frequently into their close neighborhood, and were not scrupulous as to deeds of violence and treachery towards each other. The incidents we shall mention, illustrative of other experiences, are alluded to in a preceding memoir.

The quarters within the fort were crowded, and Mrs. Clark's house, a substantial stone building, stood without the walls a few rods distant, on the military land adjoining. After the conclusion of the amicable treaty already mentioned, the Chippewas had pitched their camp at the foot of a hill not far from this house. About nine o'clock in the evening, the family was alarmed by an unusual noise in that direction, and the discharge of firearms. A gentleman who was at that time the guest of Mr. Clark, entered in haste and some trepidation, saying that a bullet had just whistled past his head, and that there must be some difficulty " below." The seclusion of the dwelling was thought of with terror whenever there was any alarm at night, though the sight of the fort close at hand gave courage to all in the daytime. Protection and aid, however, were promptly invoked, and the troops aroused. It appeared that some of the Sioux, after having sat in the wigwams of the Chippewas, smoked the pipe of peace, and bid them good night, had deliberately turned about and fired upon them. The confusion that ensued may be imagined; the Chippewas flew to arms, and the treacherous Sioux made their escape. The commanding officer of the garrison had the wounded taken to the hospital, and attended to as well as the circumstances permitted. Among them was an aged chief and his little daughter, only ten years of age, in whom the ladies were deeply interested. She was much injured, and survived but a short time. The Indians called upon the commander, as the representative of their "great father," to compel the Sioux to render satisfaction for this cruel outrage; and in pursuance of the instructions of government to commanders on the out-posts, to maintain peace as far as possible between the hostile tribes without interfering in their affairs, he sent an order to the chiefs requiring the surrender of the young men who had been guilty.

Not long after this, a large party of Sioux was seen approaching the fort. " We could see them," said Mrs. Clark, " for a long way on the hills by which Fort Snelling is surrounded, and it was easy to perceive at once that they were disposed to resist the summons. The interpreter, who was a thorough fellow, and knew how important was an aspect of courage and determination in dealing with savages, went out to meet them, and informed them what would be the consequence of their refusal to comply with the just demand; their great father, the President, would send into the country as many warriors as there were leaves on the trees, or blades of grass under their feet, and these would kill and burn until not a Sioux should be left. A hurried council was held by the chiefs, and at length it was decided that the criminals should be given up." They were accordingly delivered, and put in durance to await the pleasure of the injured tribe. Meanwhile the old chief who had been wounded and bereaved of his child, was rapidly sinking to the grave, and true to his warrior nature, desired only to live long enough to see just vengeance overtake the murderers. They were appointed to suffer the Indian punishment of running the gauntlet.

An enclosed piece of ground was selected, not far from the fort, lined with men and women of both tribes, the soldiers of the garrison being also spectators of the scene. The dying chief appeared, borne on the shoulders of his young men; and all was soon in readiness. If the condemned could reach the further side of the fence, where their friends were stationed, their lives were safe. Again to quote Mrs. Clark: " A gentleman who chanced to be in company with several Chippewa braves who had just come from the fort, and were walking towards the ground, told me they were laughing and talking as if perfectly indifferent to what was going on, till they reached the place where the deadly work was about to commence. Then their countenances underwent a fearful change almost instantaneously, expressing the darkest passion and the most ferocious hatred."

The scene was one of intense and terrible interest. It lasted but a few moments, amid cheers from both sides, and yells that were absolutely deafening. The children of the white residents who witnessed it, partook of the wild excitement. " My brother Malcolm," says Mrs. Clark's daughter, " a little fellow, threw up his cap, and shouted with the rest. One young Indian— 'Young Six' he was called—had petted us frequently, and was a great favorite; we were anxious he should escape, and watched his fearful race with breathless eagerness. He reached the fence, and sprang upon it; a moment more and he would have been safe among his friends, who were ready to receive and welcome him, when suddenly he bounded high in air and fell, pierced by a shower of bullets." Women and men then rushed frantically upon the bodies of the slain; the scalps were torn off, and the corpses horribly mutilated with hatchets, the squaws even thrusting their fingers into the bullet-holes, and licking the blood as it flowed! When the savage avengers supposed they had done their duty to their lost friends, the scene was closed with their scalp-dance, the fearful orgies being prolonged several hours.

Perhaps, in the exposed and perilous situation of the garrison, the commandant could not venture to interfere with the execution of savage vengeance; for the mangled bodies of the slain were suffered to lie a long time unburied. The old chief, feeling now that his time was come for departure to the spirit-land, caused himself to be painted according to Indian custom, and the scalps to be hung round his neck, sang his own death-song, and expired with the calmness of a hero or a philosopher.

The daughter of Mrs. Clark was married to Mr. Van Cleve while her parents were at Fort Winnebago. They were obliged to send one hundred miles for the clergyman—Rev. Dr. Gregory, then missionary to the Indians near Green Bay. It was said that when he arrived, it was well he was familiar with the service, being so snow-blind from his long drive, that he could not have read it.

Mrs. Clark is described as still a very handsome woman, with grey hair neatly arranged over a classic head, and a countenance lighted up with intelligence and spirit when in conversation, with great sweetness of expression at all times. She interests every one who forms her acquaintance, and often delights her friends by a narration of the incidents of her pioneer experience, delineating the scenes at Fort Snelling with so much graphic and vivid power that they seem to pass before the auditor. Her children inherit her talent, with her agreeable person and manners, and are ornaments of the polished society in which they move. Mrs. Van Cleve resides at Ann Arbor, Michigan; Mrs. Clark, Miss Clark and Mrs. Lincoln, in Cincinnati, and another married daughter on the other side of the river in Kentucky. Malcolm Clark has spent many years at a distance from civilization among the aboriginal tribes, and is now a trader near Fort Benton in Oregon, married to a woman of the "Black Foot" Indians. He is highly respected by them, and called "Lesokin," or "four bears," because he killed four of those animals one morning before breakfast. In 1850 he returned to "the settlements," on a visit to his family, bringing his two elder children to his sister to be educated at Ann Arbor. The girl—Pistapowaca—had been christened before her arrival by a Roman Catholic priest, but the boy—Natiena—was baptized in St. Andrew's church in that village—the grandmother herself leading him to the font, and appearing as the only sponsor. The father had a Spanish boy with him, bound to his service by a tie of grati tude, whose duty it was to attend the children.   Mr. Clark wore his Indian dress—the leggins ornamented with human hair—as far east as St. Louis—and so much had his complexion changed, that his sisters would scarcely have recognized him.   The mother had cheerfully consented to part with her children for their good, for she had a stout heart, and knew they ought to be taught many things. Her boy, she said, would certainly return ; he was to be a great chief, as her father had been ; and so, when the canoe was ready for the departure of her husband and children, she accompanied them to the river side, and as the bark pushed off, threw herself upon the ground, concealing her face in her dress.   When, after rounding a point, they again caught sight of her, she was still lying motionless, absorbed in grief.   When the father left his children to return to his distant home, the little girl, taught to subdue the expression of emotion, would not suffer herself to cry out ; but clasped her throat with her hands to choke down her feelings.

One incident in Clark's early life is characteristic.   When a mere lad, the men at the fort had trapped a wolf, and were debating how they could manage to muzzle him, before taking him out. Malcolm passing by, inquired what they were about, and imme- diately offered to hold the animal.   Suiting the action to the word, he clapped his hands on either side the creature's jaws, and held them forcibly together, while the soldiers slipped on the cords. Clark was at West Point when the Texan difficulties with Mexico broke out, and departed to join the service ; working his way after- wards to his present home, where the traders have established a garrison of their own, for protection against the hostile Indians. Nearly all of them have married Indian women, who, proud of the alliance, have become the " exclusives" of the country, refusing to hold intercourse with other squaws.   The boy aforementioned was the son of a Spaniard by an Indian wife, and had been captured by a party of Indians who had come unexpectedly upon the garrison, seized him while others escaped, and were about to satiate their revenge by torturing him.   Watching his opportunity, with won- derful address, Clark rushed out at the gate of the fort into the midst of the savages, caught the boy, and was again safe within the walls before the Indians had recovered from their surprise. The poor lad was wounded severely by the hatchets thrown at him, the scars of which he bore ever afterwards. He became so much attached to his deliverer, that he could not be induced at any time to separate from him.

Hezekiah Geer was one of the most enterprising among the pioneers of Illinois. His residence is now at Galena, where he is one of the largest lead dealers in that region; and his present prosperity, nobly earned as it has been, is doubly enjoyed from the remembrance of the hardship, privation, and actual suffering endured on their first migration into the country, when the means of the new settler were inadequate without incessant toil to the wants of a large family; when for years they scarcely saw the face of a clergyman, except at distant intervals an itinerant missionary. The reward of these labors, which Mr. Geer's children share in peace and abundance, she who partook all his cares, and practised every self-denial to lighten them, did not live to enjoy. They removed from Massachusetts to the southern part of Illinois some time about 1820, when the portions of country now covered with smiling villages and thriving farms were a wilderness untrodden save by the roving hunter, the surveyor, or the savages who receded before the footsteps of civilization. Her experience is much the same with that of many others who left home and kindred to seek better fortune in the forest, and found themselves obliged to struggle with difficulties they had never, or but faintly imagined.

During the Black Hawk war a large part of Michigan and the neighboring territories suffered much from apprehension of danger, kept up by floating rumors that the Indians were intent on depredations and incited to attack the whites by the occurrences that had taken place in Illinois. Mr. Geer and his family had then been living at Galena some years. The inhabitants of the place and neighborhood were in a state of excitement from continual alarms, and prepared to take refuge in the fort, in case of the appearance of the dreaded enemy. It was an object with the commander to assure himself that he might depend on the promptitude and courage of his troops and the citizen volunteers in case of sudden attack, and he adopted a singular method of testing these qualities. One dark and stormy night he caused a select number to march off silently to a hill not far distant, where they raised the Indian war whoop. The ruse was but too successful in creating a general panic; the soldiers of the garrison and men of the village were instantly on the alert and ready for action ; but the terror and confusion that prevailed among the helpless women and children, were beyond the power of language to describe. Mrs. Geer was at that time the mother of a young infant, with twins not more than two years old. Springing out of bed and hastily throwing on a few articles of clothing, she caught in her arms her babe and one of the twins—her eldest daughter—and followed by the other children, rushed forth, hurrying to the shelter and protection of the fort. Mr. Geer was at that time holding a command, having been on duty since the breaking out of the war. The effects of this cruel experiment were fatal to some of the children who were borne into the cold night air and storm by their terrified mothers. Both those Mrs. Geer carried in her arms died from the effects of the exposure. Yet in the midst of the general consternation occasioned by the alarm, some of the women found time to laugh; for one man who in his fear had hid himself in a corner of the room where they were gathered in the fort, was discovered by some of them, and driven out with a flourish of broomsticks.

Mrs. Clark said that while her husband was at Fort Winnebago, it was no uncommon thing to test the courage of the soldiers by getting up a false alarm. The lead mines were then attracting considerable attention, and desertions to them were so common among the soldiers in the winter of 1819, that orders were often given to beat the long roll at dead of night, that it might be ascertained who was missing. The commanding officer, just before this signal

sounded, would go round to the beds of those soldiers in whose
fidelity he had confidence to notify them of the object of the alarm.
But the women even of his own family, though warned, could not
hear the dismal note of the drum without a thrill of terror. It may
be supposed that experiments of this kind could not be frequently
repeated with the intended effect.

At the time of Mrs. Geer's last illness and death, her husband
sent two hundred miles for an Episcopal clergyman to administer
the sacrament and baptize his children ; but the spirit could not
linger for the "slow arrival," and had already gone to sit at the heavenly table of Him on whom her hopes of everlasting life were
fixed. Her last resting place is near the great Mississippi.

Mrs. Geer's name was Charlotte Clark. She was the sister of
Rev. William A. Clark, D.D., Rector of All Saints' Church, New
York, Rev. Orin Clark, D.D., formerly Rector at Geneva, New
York, and Rev. John A. Clark, D.D., of Philadelphia. Mrs. William A. Clark should be numbered among the Western female pioneers. When a young and gay girl, she removed with her god-
parents, Mr. and Mrs. TenEyck, and the Vredenburghs to Skeneateles, then almost a wilderness. At the time of her marriage, Mr.
Clark was one of the first missionaries of the Episcopal church in
Western New York ; and to him she proved a true co-worker in his
duties, conforming cheerfully to the circumstances in which she was
placed, and giving up her own inclinations at all times. She became
the mother of nine children. The family removed to Buffalo about
1817, and to Michigan in the spring of 1837, after which Mrs.
Clark suffered every year from the fevers of the country, which
undermined a constitution naturally strong. She is retiring in
manner and domestic in her habits, yet fond of society at home, and
charming all who approach her. The habit acquired through years
of self-denial of sacrificing her own inclinations, has caused her to
think less of the merely ornamental than the useful in life. In the
first year after her marriage, she was accustomed to wear white muslin dresses ; but "some of the congregation" in the country village
where her husband officiated, decided that she was "too much

dressed," and finding that the matter was commented on, she laid aside the obnoxious garments and never afterwards wore white. The corner stone of the first Episcopal church in Buffalo was laid by Mr. Clark. He lived but three years after leaving the city of New York for Michigan, and lies buried in a beautiful opening near the village of Brighton, Livingston County. His children owe the cultivation of their talents, and their usefulness in life, to the judicious training of their parents, and most affectionately do they acknowledge the obligation. They have truly risen up to call their mother blessed. Two of them, Chloe and Mary H. Clark, now reside in Ann Arbor, Michigan, and one is a minister of an Episcopal church n Cincinnati.

XXI.

SARAH BRYAN.

In the severe labors peculiar to pioneers in a new country, the trials
and privations they were compelled to encounter from day to day,
Mrs. Bryan was as conspicuous as any of the early settlers of Michigan. She came with John Bryan her husband, to Ypsilanti, taking
up their residence on a small farm at what is now called " Woodruff's Grove." Her journal says : " We left Geneseo October 7th,
1823, for our new home—arrived in Detroit in ten days ; put up at
the Widow Hubbard's, who kept a sort of boarding house, and deposited our goods in the cellar till my husband could go out to the
" Grove" (as the settlement was then called) and procure a team to
move us through. He returned in three days with a man, two yoke
of oxen, and a wagon, which we found was not sufficient to contain
all our goods and the family. This consisted of five children, besides
myself and husband. Fortunately for us, however, we found a young
man who was going out with but half a load, and persuaded him to
take the remainder of ours. After a wearisome and almost indescribable journey of four days through thick woods, my husband cutting
the road before us with an axe, we came, the night of October 23rd,
to the beautiful Huron shore. We had the privilege of staying in
a log cabin till we could build one of our own, which we moved
into the last day of December. Eight weeks after this, February
27th, 1824, Alpha was born ; we called him Alpha Washtenaw

16

the latter name being given in honor of the county, and the former
on account of his being the first white child born in the county."
Allen and Ramsay, the first settlers of Ann Arbor, agreed to mark
the auspicious event by presenting the infant with a lot of land at
the county seat.

" It was amusing that first fall and winter to hear the corn mills
in operation every morning before daylight. There were but two
in the settlement, made by burning a hole in the top of a sound
oak stump, large enough to hold a peck or more. After scraping
the coal clean from the stump, one end of a stick, some six feet
long and eight inches in diameter, was rounded, and it was suspended from a spring-pole so that the rounded end would clear the
stump when hanging loosely. A hole was bored through this pestle
and a stick driven through projecting on each side for handles, and
the mill was finished. One man would pound a peck of dry corn
in half an hour so that half of it would pass through a sieve for
bread ; the coarser part being either ground again or boiled for
hominy. Very little bread of any other kind was used in the settlement for the first two years. But as regards my own experience,
the autumn of 1824 was the most trying. Thus far we had en
countered few more inconveniences than we anticipated in the wilderness, and I was prepared for them, prepared to bear all without
a murmur. In October Mr. Bryan accepted an offer to finish a
building at Maumee city, and shipped his tools at Detroit, where he
had been doing an eight months' job. He came home and stayed
a few days to provide some wood, and told me if he was likely to
be more than three weeks absent, he would return at the end of
that time and put up more provisions, as our small stock would
be then exhausted. No person had then attempted to penetrate
the forest from our place to Monroe, but rather than go round by
Brownstown, he determined to take the risk of finding his way
through the woods alone. My heart sank within me to think of
what would be my fate and that of my six children, if any evil
should befal him alone in the forest; I however summoned my
fortitude and resolved not to be faint-hearted."

An attack of illness followed. "The three weeks passed; a good supply of potatoes was nearly all the provisions we had left, and I began to look with great anxiety for my husband. A felon on my right hand deprived me entirely of the use of it for more than three weeks. With the pain, fatigue, and want of sleep I was ready to despair, but for my children's sake I kept up my resolution; still no tidings came from Mr. Bryan, and my fears for his safety became more and more painful. Two months passed, and brought cold December for me and my little ones, but brought no news from him whose duty it was to provide for us. My sufferings became extreme. I tried to get some one to go in search of him, and ascertain at least if he ever got through the woods alive, but I had no money even to bear expenses, and all told me they 'guessed' he was safe and would soon return. How myself and babes were to live meanwhile . knew not. We had eaten nothing but potatoes for several weeks; the neighbors were nearly as destitute and had nothing to lend, even if I could have borrowed when I could not expect to pay again. For a temporary change in diet from potatoes alone, I ventured to borrow a few ears of corn, promising to pay if Mr. Bryan ever returned; this I shelled and boiled to jelly, which we relished very much while it lasted.

"It was now the 23d of December; I had been all day trying to induce some one to go to Maumee for tidings, and had succeeded in obtaining a promise from a young man that he would go in two or three days if I would get a horse. Alas! horses were as scarce as bread, and I knew it would be impossible to procure one. I returned home and stood in our log cabin door, thinking what to do next, when my husband rode up, and put an end to my fears. He had written several letters, which were delayed in Detroit, and never reached me. Finding wages high, and the roads very bad, he had concluded to remain, supposing I was well provided for. Our sufferings for five or six years after this were even greater, if possible, than before, but it would take a volume to describe them."

These difficulties passed over. Mr. and Mrs. Bryan had what served for a competence in those days, and were of excellent charac-

ter and industrious habits ; being of respectable stock, and training
up their children to become useful members of the community
Their care and efforts were required for a large family ; and those
who live within reach of all the advantages of civilization, can hardly
understand the difficulties in the way of improvement which existed
in a pioneer settlement.   There were no public schools, no churches,
nor did there seem to be any Sabbaths, judging from observation of
the habits of some of the backwoodsmen.   The first Sabbath school
gathered together in this place, was in the summer of 1828.   That
same year a small school was kept in a log room some twelve or
fourteen feet square, by a young woman whose education hardly
fitted her for the employment.   Mrs. Bryan, with a few other
women of the settlement, took a great interest in the Sunday school,
and some other efficient plans for benevolent effort were set on foot
through her active agency and coöperation.   She was directress of
the first benevolent society in that part of the country.   The new
emigrants at that time suffered much from sickness peculiar to the
region, and often whole families were prostrated at once by the
fever of the country.   Mrs. Bryan did not spare herself when her
aid or nursing was required by her neighbors ; day and night found
her at the bedside of the suffering, or in the shanties of the poor,
and many an invalid who had no comfortable shelter has been taken
to her own home, provided with everything requisite, and waited
upon with all the tenderness and care of a mother.

As the children grew older, the want of a good school was more
sensibly felt ; and as there was none in the vicinity, Mrs. Bryan
appropriated to the purpose the best room in her house, and engaged
a young man of good education, who was in want of a comfortable
home, to teach her children, with others in the village who were
permitted to join them.   Thus was a good foundation laid for the
advantages afterwards enjoyed, and each member of their large family
received a substantial English education.   Some of them have since
attained to distinguished excellence in the higher departments of
literature.   The eldest daughter, now residing in Illinois, was equalled
by few scholars of the time in various branches of study, particularly

mathematics; and the second daughter is now Mrs. Lois B. Adams, with whose high reputation as a poet and prose writer many American readers are acquainted. Her first poetical effusions appeared in the Kalamazoo Telegraph, in which paper Mr. Adams had an interest at the time of her marriage. She now resides in the southern part of Kentucky, where she has charge of a female seminary.

In 1835 or '6 Mr. and Mrs. Bryan removed from Ypsilanti, and at present are living in Constantine, Michigan. They had eight children at the time of their removal, and all have grown up to respectability and usefulness, having in early life had the judicious training of a religious mother, who watched over them in love, guiding them by precept and example, and by her affectionate and cheerful spirit diffusing perpetual sunshine in her home.

A lady whose family lived in Livingston county, one of the most recently settled in Michigan, and inhabited generally by poor people, says their range of what might be called society was limited to less than half a dozen families, the nearest distant about four miles, and some ten or more from each other. They had left a large circle of friends in the city of New York, and as it may be supposed, felt the change to the wild country; yet were they contented and cheerful, pining only when prevented by inclement weather from wandering through the woods or fields in summer, plucking the wild flowers which grow in such profusion and beauty in the openings. The annual fires kindled by the Indians and first settlers to destroy the old grass, and prepare for an early and abundant crop in spring, are said to have produced many of the openings, the flames extending often beyond the marshes or prairies. The farmers were in the habit of ploughing trenches round the outside of their fences to ensure their safety; yet sometimes the fire did serious damage among haystacks, wheat or barns, to which the wind carried it. In consequence of this danger, severe legal penalties were attached to the act of setting fire to marshes, yet it continued to be practised for years till they became private property, sadly marring the beauty of the view, destroying the trees, and preventing the growth of the young oaks. The bushes which sprang in a season from their roots, called "oak grubs," are difficult to remove from the soil. A poor man whose means just sufficed to remove his family, and perhaps keep one cow, had often to work out many days before he could afford to hire a " breaking up team," which was a plough constructed for the purpose, and from five to seven yoke of oxen. The wife picked and dried berries in the fall, often in marshes so wet that she was obliged to wear her husband's boots. By the sale of cranberries, she furnished herself with many little comforts she could not otherwise have procured. Flour could always be had at the mills in exchange for this article. By such industry and patient perseverance was the way prepared for the occupation of those lands by an intelligent, enterprising, and now prosperous people. Not the least of the sufferings of the primitive settlers arose from sickness, whole families having to pass through the terrible acclimating, often at the same time, and the ravages of disease sometimes leaving desolate the widow and the orphan, far distant from kindred or early friends. At such time the sympathy and kind offices of neighbors were never withheld, even though they might also be suffering and almost destitute. Physicians were few and far apart in the inland counties, and even when their attendance could be had, their want of knowledge of the local fevers was often the source of mischief rather than good.

A change nas now passed over the face of the country. How progressive has been the expression " the far West !" Many years since it might have meant the western part of New York, as a resident of its metropolis once said she had been " out west" to visit her sister, who lived at Pennyan, in Yates County ! A young woman of Skeneateles was engaged many years—her friends being unwilling to let her marry and go so far away as the Ohio ; and when finally the knot was tied, she remained three years under the parental roof before she could be permitted to take so long and perilous a journey. From the Ohio the foot of emigration bore " the far West" farther ; it settled for a while in Indiana, Illinois and Michigan, then passed to Iowa and Wisconsin, and now is wavering beyond the Mississippi in Minnesota, with the cry for Oregon and

California. And not long since, we noticed a jocular proposition to erect a tollgate at the boundary of the domain of the United States, in the middle of the Pacific Ocean.

Sylvia Chapin, the wife of Dr. Cyrenius Chapin, was the oldest pioneer among the first settlers of Buffalo. In all the vicissitudes she experienced, she well and faithfully discharged the duties that lay before her, as wife, mother, neighbor, and Christian woman ; exhibiting, with the high qualities of firmness and energy, a quiet dignity, gentleness and kindliness which won the affection of those who knew her best, as well as commanded the respect of her acquaintances. Her " patient continuance in well doing," has met its reward in the comfort and respectability of her advanced age, passed among her children and descendants.

Dr. Chapin came to Buffalo with his family in 1805. It is stated in Turner's "Pioneer History of the Holland Purchase of Western New York, etc.," that in 1806 there were but sixteen houses in the place, and those located on what is now called Main Street. It will be remembered that in December 1813 the town was burnt by the British, who had crossed near Black Rock. On hearing their firing, Chapin, who commanded a portion of the citizen soldiery, went to meet the enemy, and holding up his cane, with a white handkerchief fastened to the end, obtained a parley, and finally a promise that the town should be spared. Mrs. Chapin at this period of anxiety was compelled to leave home to assist in the care of her daughter's sick husband, but before her departure instructed her two other little girls to sleep always with a bundle of necessary clothing under their heads, and in case of alarm, to go off with the rest of the citizens if necessary. The agreement not to molest the town was violated. Dr. Chapin was on duty, and of course unable to attend to his children. Louisa related how they were waked at dead of night with the noise and confusion in the streets.

hurriedly made their simple preparations, and stepped out of doors to join the crowd. In the darkness, amid the severity of winter, women and children took up their doleful march. The first glimmering of day mingled with the lurid glare from their burning dwellings, and at almost every step those who fled from their homes encountered the wounded and fugitives from the action below. In the pressure and confusion of the crowd hurrying onward, mothers were separated from their children, and lost sight of each other, being in many cases for days ignorant of the fate of their beloved relatives. On, on our fugitives went through the dark deep woods, continually within hearing of the savage yells around them, and trembling with fear, for they could not tell where the Indians were, and they seemed to be coming upon them. Finally, after a travel of some hours, the little girls halted with the rest, and were refreshed with a drink of milk at a farmhouse. In the mean time, while this was going on in the neighborhood of Buffalo, Mrs. Chapin was overwhelmed with anxiety about her husband and children. The sick man she nursed had died, and she was for weeks uncertain of the fate of her children, and for some days of that of her husband, for she knew there had been an engagement.

One woman of masculine bearing, Mrs. St. John, persisted notwithstanding the general alarm, in staying with her young daughters to protect their property, and succeeded in obtaining the favor of having the house she occupied exempted from destruction. It was the only building saved except the stone jail, which resisted the efforts to set it on fire. The house was afterwards presented to Mrs. St. John by the authorities. A neighbor on the opposite side of the street, a Mrs. Lovejoy, was less fortunate. It was supposed that fear had driven her into temporary insanity; she made no attempt to solicit mercy or protection, but barricaded her doors and windows, and thus awaited the intruders. For a while she was unmolested, till an Indian, bent on plunder, effected his entrance; then, instead of submitting to what was inevitable, the loss of her goods, Mrs. Lovejoy attempted to rescue them, and defended herself with a large carving knife. In a contest for a red merino 'ong shawl she wounded the savage, nearly severing his thumb from his hand. The Indian ran across the way to Mrs. St. John, whom he ordered to bind it up; then hurried back, she knew too well for the purpose of vengeance. The next thing she heard was a scream, and presently the savage appeared again, a scalp with a woman's long hair hanging from his belt.

Mrs. Chapin preserved several pieces of plate which were at that time in her possession. A silver pitcher in her house bears the inscription :—"Presented by the citizens of Buffalo to Colonel Cyrenius Chapin, the brave soldier, the good citizen, the honest man."

Tradition says that Tecumseh often caused much annoyance to one lady in Detroit, by cutting the air with his tomahawk close to her daughters' heads; also that her ingenuity devised a scheme of revenge on one occasion, when her children had the measles, and the chief had laid himself on her floor to sleep. She gave him the pillow from under the heads of the sick ones, hoping he would take the disease and lose his life by following the Indian practice of jumping into the water in case of fever. There was no time to test the success of her plan, for shortly after this occurred the battle of the Thames, in which Tecumseh lost his life.

A woman in one of the remote counties of Michigan told one of her neighbors, that after her removal to her new house, when the few provisions they had been able to bring were exhausted, and the roads so wretched through the heavily timbered land that it was scarcely possible to bring supplies from Detroit, her family had lived on potato tops, boiled with a little salt, till something better could be raised. In the early settlement of Wayne county a family having succeeded in getting a pig, penned it up and began to fatten it for slaughter, when the matron one day, at home alone with her children, was alarmed by the sight of a huge bear helping himself without ceremony at her out-of-door larder. Fortunately, she was acquainted with the use of a rifle, and having wounded, succeeded in driving away the bear; he was afterwards tracked by the men, and his thieving career ended with his life.

16*

The story of Lucy Chapin—no relative of those mentioned—is mentioned among the reminiscences of this period. A New England family, sensible, well-educated, and accustomed to all the advantages found in long established communities, from a flaw in the deed securing their farm, found themselves suddenly homeless. One of the brothers, who had learned the carpenter's trade, went with his sister Lucy to Hamburg, near Buffalo, and purchased land, which he set about clearing to make a home for his mother and the rest of the family. He built a rough log hut, which was for some time without a window, the opening being closed when it was cold or stormy, and the room left in darkness. The brother was obliged to work out at his trade, for means to carry on improvements at his own place, and meanwhile the sister was often left alone for three weeks at a time. She became so nervously sensitive, that the slightest noise would alarm her, and but for a determined spirit, and her brother's cheerful temperament, she thought her reason would have given way. On one occasion, a weary old man called at the house to ask for a cup of water; Lucy, terrified she knew not at what, ran off, and was found by her brother on his return after one of his long absences, sitting on a stump weeping. He encouraged her, and both returned home, where they found the stranger waiting quietly. Their neighbors lived at a considerable distance, and were all poor and illiterate; they found no congenial society, avoided all association with others except what necessity and civility required, and led a life of hermit-like seclusion, Lucy assisting to provide necessaries by sewing whenever she could get any work to do. It was not long before a family by the name of Russell, agreeable, intelligent, and kind-hearted, came to live in their vicinity; they had been banished by change of fortune from their early home, but were cultivated, and had books, and their arrival was joyfully welcomed by the emigrants. Miss Chapin afterwards kept house in Buffalo for her brother Roswell, who was engaged in the practice of law, and many anecdotes are told of her economy, industry, and ingenuity. She described, among her experiences in the backwoods, her sufferings during an illness when the snow-wreaths often lay upon the coverlet of her bed; their only security for the door, till it could be hung, being to push the wash-tub against it. She would never allow her friends at home in New England to know the trials she endured. "They can never know the half," she used to say. The loneliness, anxieties, and hardships she suffered so long, seriously impaired her health in after life.

An anecdote illustrative of female quickness of apprehension and presence of mind, is related of the housekeeper of Gen. Porter, at Black Rock. Early one morning, before the General had risen, a party of Indians in the British service, who had crossed from the Canada side, came to the door, demanding to see him. The house-keeper, without betraying the least surprise or alarm, informed them that the General had just gone up to Buffalo, pointing to the road which led thither by the most circuitous course. As the savages hurried away, in hopes of overtaking the object of their pursuit, she gave the alarm to the General, who lost no time in mounting his horse and riding by the shortest way to the town, where he arrived in time to make preparation for the enemy.

Mr. Turner relates a story of " a night with the wolves," which is worth mentioning as an incident of pioneer life. One of the early settlers of Niagara County had just finished building a log hut—the door only wanting—in the woods, for the occupancy of his family. It was so far to go to mill, that when it was necessary to fetch a supply of flour, he was always obliged to be a night away from home. One night, in his absence, the wife heard wolves snarling just at the door, which was only defended by a blanket. Terrified for the safety of her young children, she forgot all fears for herself, and stood with axe in hand at the opening, keeping guard during the long hours of that night, till the howling died away in the distance, and she was satisfied the fierce creatures would return no more.

"The early settlers in Farmershill, Cataraugus, drew up a code of rules for their mutual advantage, from which the following curious section is extracted : ' If any single woman over fourteen years of age shall come to reside in our village, and no one of this confederacy shall offer her his company within a fortnight thereafter, then in such case our board shall be called together, and some one shall be appointed to make her a visit, whose duty it shall be to perform the same, or forfeit the approbation of the company and pay a fine sufficiently large to buy the lady thus neglected a new dress.' Few towns," continues Turner, " in the Purchase have been more prosperous; and it is quite likely that this early regulation aided essentially in the work of founding a new settlement and speeding its progress

As an offset to the above, the same writer gives an account of a bachelor's settlement in Orleans County, which, as might be ex pected, turned out a failure. A cotemporary says : " They began in a year or two to go east and get them wives." This broke up the establishment, and most of its bachelor founders became Benedicts and heads of families.

" By perseverance I succeeded early one morning in getting to the old burial place of the Senecas. The Indian church—now used as a stable, with hay protruding from the windows and ma- nure heaps outside—arrested my attention, and I stopped opposite the lane leading from the main road to the spot I sought. At the end of this lane, leaping over a broken rail fence, and following a little foot-path running by the side of a potato patch, a few steps brought me to one of the most beautiful and quiet nooks in the world; a pleasant opening, rather more elevated than the rest of the field with which it was enclosed, and shaded here and there by large oaks, the branches of which were now swaying in the wind, and sighing a requiem to the memory of the red man. Graves were thickly sown around—some marked by boards, others only by the swelling of the turf. There were four marble slabs ; two in a picketed enclosure were monuments of white children ; one of the daughter of a clergyman, probably the local missionary. The most prominent, which was not enclosed, bore the inscription, ' In memory of the white woman, Mary Jemison, daughter of Thomas Jemison and Jane Irwin, born on the ocean between Ireland and Philadelphia in 1742 or '3, taken captive at Marsh Creek, Pa. in

1755, carried down the Ohio, adopted into an Indian family in 1759, removed to Genesee River, naturalized in 1817, removed to this place in 1831. Having survived two husbands and five children, leaving three still alive, she died Sept. 19th, 1833, aged about ninety-one years, having a few weeks before expressed a hope of pardon, etc.' A little beyond Mary Jemison's grave, was that of Red Jacket, the celebrated orator and chief." The stone was much mutilated, being broken off so as to deface the inscription.

———

Mrs. Anderson, whose house was visited by depredators, boldly faced them for the protection of her property. Seating herself on a trunk they were about to carry off, she told them they might shoot her, but should never possess it while she lived. The Indians, with a significant " ugh" left her, saying she was too much of a man to be robbed. One of the early settlers in Plymouth, Wayne County, Michigan, showed a more timid spirit and fared worse, it being her practice at first to yield implicitly to their demands. Once she was compelled to hand out of the oven the rolls she had just baked for supper. One evening, her husband having gone to a neighbor's a quarter of a mile distant, her child lying asleep in the bed, and she occupied in sewing, the door was softly opened, and an Indian entered, " with the stealthy tread peculiar to the moccasined foot." He made signs that he wanted whiskey. After going around the house as if in search of the article, followed by the savage, she took up her child, and making him understand that it was to be had at the neighbor's house, motioned him to follow her, and walked the whole distance through the woods with him to the place of safety, where she arrived breathless with terror and agitation.

ELIZA BULL, afterwards Mrs. Sinclair, visited the capital of Wis-consin in 1846 or '47, and describes the country as very new, and the society extremely limited. The scenery of the locality was wild and picturesque, and from the window of her room at the inn Mrs. Bull could frequently see as many as thirty-six prairie fowls going to roost in a single tree. Every evening in the winter the sound of men stunning fish by striking on the ice was plainly to be heard. One large room in the capitol was appropriated to public gatherings of all descriptions, and in the course of a single week would be used for dancing assemblies, public lectures, funeral services, and preach-ing by the Methodist congregation. At the balls, the belle of the company was usually the chambermaid of the tavern which was the place of entertainment, a young lady of ash-colored complexion, and locks of similar hue, whose fairy feet were graced with red morocco boots. The party was often enlivened by the presence of members of the legislature. These, with a respectable attendance of their constituents, shuffled around the room with great energy, having cigars in their mouths, and for the most part wearing their hats. If their boots or shoes were found inconvenient in their Terpsicho-rean evolutions, they were kicked off without ceremony, and the figures completed in stocking-feet. When supper was ready, the company rushed pell-mell through a dark passage to the "pro-vender," on which they fell to work without mincing.

Near Madison are four small lakes, beside one of which, on "Sauk Prairie," then quite removed from the neighborhood of civilized residents, stood the dwelling of an Austrian named Haraz-thy. He was said to be a count, and his wife's manners indicated that they had been accustomed to cultivated society. It was rumored that his voluntary banishment from his country had been caused by political difficulties, and that he wished to seclude himself from the sight and society of men, having been made misanthropic by disappointed ambition. His father—who was called a general, and always wore his military dress, came out with the family. The elder Mrs. Harazthy did not long survive her removal, but died of very home sickness. The younger used to relate how many years before, a gipsey fortune-teller had foretold that they would remove to a far country, and that the count's mother would die in their new home. Mrs. Sinclair described this foreigner as a fine, tall and "rosy-faced" woman, with very pleasing manners, and conversation made the more interesting by her foreign accent and imperfect command of English. For months after her removal she refused to receive visitors, but often at twilight would sit at her window looking out upon the wild and strange scenery, watching sometimes whole droves of wolves coming down to the lake to drink. Her family was once startled in the night by piercing cries, and found at their door a poor woman with a child in her arms ; she had been terrified by what she took for signs of a meditated Indian attack, and had run twelve miles barefoot through the snow to seek protection, her husband being absent. Her alarm proved groundless, but she had endured as much as if flying from a troop of enemies. The Austrian mentioned kept a variety store for the Indians and the few settlers who lived in that portion of country. His log dwelling-house was picturesquely situated on the margin of the lake and the forest.

XXII.

MARY ANN RUMSEY.

THE perils and privations incident to the occupation of the lands, in Michigan by the first settlers were not, indeed, so terrible or so romantic as those encountered at an earlier period, when the adventurous few who penetrated the wilderness were exposed to the fury of a savage foe, and assaults far more to be dreaded than those of the wild beasts of the forest. Yet the later pioneers, if they had not to dispute the possession of the soil at the risk of their lives, had their trials and sufferings—their dangers too—not the less difficult to endure because the narration is rather amusing than thrilling. They had also to struggle with that feeling of isolation and loneliness which presses heavily on those who have severed all the endearing ties of home, where cluster those fond attachments only formed in youth. Many a sad hour was passed in remembrance and regret by the young wife in the absence of her husband, when she had no sympathizing friend in whose bosom she could pour her griefs. Little given to repining as she might be, faithful to her duties, and disposed to make the best of everything, still thoughts of the loved ones from whom she had parted for life would weigh on her spirits, and fill her eyes with tears, brushed hastily away while she busied herself about her household employments. A touching instance of the heart's yearning for companionship occurs to memory, mentioned by one of the female pioneers, who had been three weeks in their new home without having seen the face of another woman. "One Sunday," she said, "I told my husband that beyond the thick wood, just in the rear of our dwelling, I could see from the upper window another log house. I wanted him to go there with me; we went, and as we approached I saw the woman come out, appearing to be busy about something at the back door. *That was enough;* I did not care to go any further; we went home; I had seen her, and that satisfied me."

Ann Arbor is the county seat of Washtenaw County. The Indian name, *Washtenong,* signifies "grand" or "beautiful," and Grand River takes its name from the same word. It was called "Arbor," on account of the noble aspect of the original site of the village, which was a burr oak opening, resembling an arbor laid out and cultivated by the hand of taste. For the prefix of "Ann," it was indebted, according to undeniable tradition, to two prominent women whose husbands were the first purchasers and settlers in the vicinity. Some have maintained that the place owed its entire name to them, from the fact that they lived, until houses could be built, in a kind of rude arbor made by poles covered with boughs. However that may be, it is certain that John Allen and Walter Rumsey gave the name to the new settlement, afterwards confirmed by State authority, and ever since retained. Their first garden was the ground now occupied as the public square; and here Allen, who had considerable skill in these matters, planted and raised a fine stock of vegetables, enabling them to supply the neighbors whom their persuasions had induced to join their little community. The two leaders above mentioned came in February, 1824, Rumsey being accompanied by his wife. This couple emigrated from some part of the State of New York, which has furnished so many enterprising families among the inhabitants of Michigan. Some of the New England stock, who were a little proud of their land of the pilgrims, were accustomed to say they "had *stopped* some years in the State of New York on their way to the West."

The arbor, or tent, which formed the first shelter for this little party, and served them as such for two weeks, was made of their sleigh-box, with a rag carpet spread over boughs of trees, which were of course denuded of leaves; for there grew not an evergreen within miles, except a few cedars on a hill some two miles from the locality.   They had brought with them a few barrels of provisions; and as there were no regular roads all the way to Detroit, and the travelling was tedious and difficult, they lost no time in making a treaty with the roving Indians, who agreed to furnish them with regular supplies of corn and venison.   On this they subsisted while they industriously prepared the ground and planted grain and vegetables to serve them for the coming summer and winter.   " Ann Arbor" had been the favorite dancing ground of the Pottawattomies, many families of whom lived in the neighborhood.   Their place of council was in the light "opening" selected by Allen for his garden, on which at this time there was scarcely a tree.   Those that now adorn the square, have been since planted; most of them more than ten years afterwards.

The visits of the Indians were peaceable enough, and generally welcome, for they brought deer and wild turkeys to exchange for other articles, game being then abundant in the woods.   Sometimes, indeed, when they found none but women at home, they showed themselves a little disposed to encroach upon hospitality. Mrs. Rumsey confessed being frightened at one time by their wild behavior; but assuming a stern and commanding air, she bade them begone, flourishing a broom at the same time; and though they could not have been said to be afraid of her weapon, they did not hesitate to obey.   All the cotemporaries of Mrs. Rumsey agree in describing her as a woman of remarkable beauty and distinguished appearance, and of energetic character, singularly fitted to be a useful pioneer in a new country where difficulties and discouragements must be met with unflinching courage, fortitude, and patient perseverance.   Her commanding aspect—whether natural or the result of a habit of being foremost in enterprise—was well suited to her qualities of determination and strength of purpose.   Her cheerful disposition, disregard of hardships, and resolute way of

" making the best of everything," have often been mentioned with admiration. " When we had been out land-hunting," said Mr. Allen, " or otherwise engaged through the day, so that we returned late and tired out, she was always ready for us with good humor and *a good supper*." By such aid and encouragement is it that woman—a true help-meet—can hold up man's hands and strengthen his heart when disquieted by care and vexation. To be enabled to appreciate the worth of such a household companion, one must have spent a year at least in the backwoods. Experience and necessity here furnished the best kind of education, fitting for the endurance of every trial, and the thorough enjoyment of the labor-bought pleasures which are relished most keenly when alternated with privations.

In the course of a few months other families moved into the neighborhood; and on the succeeding Fourth of July (1824), there was a joyous celebration of the nation's birthday. The anniversary falling on a Sunday, it was kept on Monday, having been celebrated the Saturday before at " Woodruff's Grove," near the site of the present village of Ypsilanti. About forty guests, among whom were the women of course, sat down to partake of the rustic dinner. It was either on this occasion, or on the anniversary following, celebrated also at Ann Arbor, that the family of Mr. White, one of the " neighbors," were put to much inconvenience by the escape of their oxen; which calamity imposed on them the necessity of walking home in terror, for the distant howling of wolves could be heard all the way. At the assemblage on the Fourth of July, 1825, the white inhabitants of the county were present in mass—forty or fifty in all.

The howling of wolves was a species of nocturnal music often listened to by the pioneers of Michigan. A lady who removed there many years later, says that on moonlight evenings they often stood to hear their howling, some three miles distant, answered by the barking of their dogs. The sound was distinct, and appeared to be much nearer. In the early settlement of the country, a woman going one day to the spring for water, saw as she sup posed, the dog belonging to the family drinking, and finding that he did not get out of the way as she came up, struck him with her pail, which she then filled and carried back to the house. There she saw the dog lying quietly under the bed, and a sudden flash of recollection convinced her that she had seen a wolf at the spring. She roused the men, and the animal was pursued and killed. Notwithstanding the cowardice of the gray wolf, it was always, especially in packs, a terror to the women of the country. Other wild beasts were disposed to dispute with man the possession of their forest domain. A young woman in Livingston County, standing one day outside her " shanty," fancied she heard a crackling in the boughs of the tree above her, and looking up, caught the eyes of a panther glaring upon her, as the animal was preparing for a fatal spring. With a presence of mind which the habit of looking danger in the face alone could give, she stepped cautiously backward, still keeping her eyes steadily fixed on the creature, and slipping behind the blanket which served for a door, took down her husband's rifle, which was kept loaded and ready for use. Lifting a corner of the blanket, she deliberately took aim and fired ; the shot took effect, and the panther fell to the ground in the death-struggle.

In the eyes of her neighbors, Mrs. Rumsey was a prominent female member of the community ; for such qualities of mind, in a primitive state of society, never fail to exercise a controlling influence. Something of romance, too, was added to the interest surrounding her. It was said—though it might have been mere gossip—that her early life had been clouded by unhappiness consequent upon an ill-assorted marriage, and that she had little to regret in the years passed in her former home. Little was known of her story, for she never showed herself inclined to be communicative on the subject, and the intuitive delicacy of her associates forbade their scrutiny into what plainly did not concern them. Those were not the days withal when news travelled on the wings of the wind, or with the flash of the lightning ; and if there had been aught in the experience of former years which she did not wish to recall, Mrs. Rumsey was in no danger of having it snatched from the friendly keeping of the past, and paraded before the curious gaze of the public. So the mystery about her remained unfathomed, as she did not choose to explain it. Her circumstances at that time were comfortable, and happy in her round of duties, it did not appear that she suffered her thoughts to dwell on the past, though once, in a moment of great distress, on the occasion of the sudden death of a beloved child, she let fall expressions which set afloat the conjectures of her neighbors, and awakened curiosity which was never fully satisfied. She was not, however, the less respected on that account. In the first stages of society, when no artificial distinctions are recognized, and social intercourse is unrestricted by form, the standing of individuals is seldom questioned if they prove useful and agreeable. Mr. Rumsey died at Ann Arbor, and his widow afterwards married a Mr. Van Fossen, and removed to Indiana, where she died.

The first sleighs used by these primitive settlers were made by bending two poles, which served for runners, a crate for the box surmounting them. The large double sleigh was an improvement pertaining to a more advanced stage. Before grain could be raised it was often necessary, notwithstanding the aid of their Indian allies, to go to Detroit to procure flour—a journey which usually consumed a week. Whenever it had to be performed, the labor of every man in the settlement was in requisition to put the roads in order. In one case, when the head of a family was detained two or three weeks by some accident at the mill, the wife dug ground-nuts and picked up every other edible thing that could furnish food for herself and children. Another woman who was reduced to her last biscuit, declared laughingly that she would not have it said they ever were out of bread in her western home, and had the biscuit placed every day on the table for a fortnight, till new supplies came. Game, particularly venison, was plenty in those days, and some of the settlers, who were excellent hunters, killed enough for the use of their families and for the demands of hospitality.

The second "Ann," who gave the village of Ann Arbor its name, came to Michigan in October, 1824, with the parents of her husband, and his brother, James Turner Allen, who has ever since resided there and raised a large family. The Allens were from Augusta county in Virginia, and well to do in the world; they brought several horses and other stock with them, a useful accession to the means of the little settlement. The women performed nearly all the journey on horseback, Ann Allen carrying her infant child in her arms. This child is now the wife of Dr. Waddell, and is living in Virginia. Mrs. Allen entered with a ready spirit of enterprise into the laborious duties required of the wife of a settler. As the community increased, her husband was called to fill official stations of importance. He was afterwards twice elected Senator to the legislature, but the roving habits of his early life, like those of Daniel Boone, were in the way of his living contented in a settlement that could no longer be termed "wild," when lands further west were yet unexplored. He went to California when the gold fever was at its height, and died there.

His widow returned to Virginia. Her bearing and manners were those of a well-bred lady; uniformly gentle and quiet, and marked by the ease and refinement which evince habitual acquaintance with good society. Her maiden name was Barry; she was left an orphan at an early age, and sent to Ireland to be reared under the care of a maiden aunt. Her education was completed at Baltimore, under the charge of her maternal uncle, Mr. Keim. She was quite an heiress, and was married first to Dr. McCue, of Virginia. Her many admirable qualities and winning traits of character, are remembered by all her former neighbors in the village.

Elizabeth Allen, her mother-in-law, still lives at Ann Arbor. The character of this excellent matron, who is often described as the ideal of a pioneer, is so remarkable as to call for a brief notice. Coming so early to the backwoods, she had to encounter not a few dangers as well as inconveniencies from the frequent visits of savages, as yet not used to the sight of civilization. In her youth she was eminently handsome, and even at the age of seventy-six retains a most prepossessing appearance, having a tall and symmetrical figure, but slightly bent, with a complexion showing the freshness of habitual health. Hers was a proud and happy bridal in the Old Dominion, and she was fondly attached to the country where her best years had been spent ; but she murmured not when it became her duty to follow her husband to a distant land. He now lies buried near the spot he chose for his home, with many relatives around him ; and by the widow's direction, a place beside him is reserved for her. Her religious faith, always sound and bright—for she had made it the staff and guide of life—has been strengthened by the chastening sorrow she has been called to endure ; and the humility with which she has submitted to every painful dispensation, offers a salutary lesson both to the afflicted and the prosperous. She has always been noted for the strong practical sense which fits its possessor for every event and vicissitude, in every station of life ; yet is her heart open and kind, her benevolent impulses withal being regulated at all times by sterling judgment. She is one of those persons of whom it can be said, "Place her in any situation, and she will appear well."

In her reminiscences of those early days, Mrs. Allen often speaks of two young women in particular, who did much to enliven the society of the place. One of them, Miss Hopy Johnson, undertook the charge of the school kept in a small log house, to which she was frequently obliged to walk quite a distance from down the river. The exposure in all weathers, and with but indifferent protection against the cold and wet, injured her health, and one evening she informed the school she should not be able to teach any longer. James, one of Mrs. Allen's grandchildren, then under her care, came running home, so out of breath that he could hardly speak, and entreated his grandmamma to take the teacher to live in her house. She promised to decide after consulting her husband, who was then busily engaged in making "Michigan bedsteads" of tamarack poles stripped of the bark. Plenty of beds had been brought from Virginia ; but some arrangement might be necessary for the accommodation of another inmate. However, the child's entreaty was so urgent for an answer before Miss Johnson should have dismissed her pupils and gone home, that his grandmother bade him "tell her she may come and take us as she finds us." He ran back delighted, and presently returned with the teacher, so grateful for the offer of a home which enabled her to continue her beloved occupation, that when the little boy led her in with—"Grandmamma, here is Miss Johnson," she sank upon a seat and wept for joy. This little incident throws an interesting light on the manners of that day. When asked how they enjoyed life in the privation of so many comforts and of the society of old friends, Mrs. Allen would reply : "We were all brothers and sisters then. When my son Turner was married, he said, 'You have always given the other children a good wedding; I want you to do as well by me ;' and so we invited everybody in the village, and had as good a supper as could be got up."

True to the habits of a matron of the olden time, Mrs. Allen has always shown a delicate sense of propriety in her deportment and conversation. She looks back with some pride to the days of her bellehood, and speaks occasionally of the sixteen offers received before she was eighteen ; but with her characteristic regard for decorum, tells of the reproof she once administered to one over forward suitor. In the mountainous parts of Virginia, where carriages were but little used, the men and women were accustomed to travel altogether on horseback. Miss Tate (afterwards Mrs. Allen) was one day in attendance at a funeral, after the conclusion of which the newly bereaved widower rode up to the side of her horse, and to her extreme surprise, expressed a wish that she might be induced to consent to fill the place of the dear departed one whose mortal remains had just been laid in the grave. The young lady regarded him with astonishment and displeasure, and sternly forbade him to name that subject to her again under a year. Just a year from that day he proposed in due form, and was rejected !

Mrs. Allen is accustomed to express herself at all times in a manner so forcible and decisive, and at the same time with so much dignity, as to evince talent of no ordinary kind. Frequently her language rises almost to the poetical, without the least design of ornamental expression. Speaking of a grandchild who was extremely cold in her manner, she said, " I loved her much, that is, all she would let me get at to love." At another time, when a young mother, showing her little daughter, apologized for the dirt on her hands, as she had been playing in a sand heap, the matron replied, " It will do her no harm ; there is always rain enough in the heavens to wash such clean ;" thus unconsciously using a phrase nearly identical with the words of Shakspeare, a poet with whom she was by no means familiar. Being once asked if she had not reared a large family, she answered, " Oh, no, I have only had seven children. I laid out to have no less than a dozen ; but the grandchildren left motherless whom I have brought up, perhaps make out the number." She has reared five of these, and has lived to see the third generation.

There was a single piano in the settlement, owned by a Miss Clark, now Mrs. Kingsley ; and seldom did she touch the keys without unexpected listeners. Often, as a shadow darkened the window, could she observe the form of a Pottawattomie Indian, accompanied perhaps by two or three squaws with their papooses. This patriarch of pianos is still extant, and stands as prim as ever upon its thin legs, a type amongst the scores that have succeeded it, of a bygone age, and representing something of the stately politeness and formal breeding of the ladies and gentlemen of its own date.

Some, with an obstinately rustic taste, seemed to prefer the rudest articles of furniture used in the infancy of the settlement, to the modern improvements afterwards introduced. A housewife in Michigan, finding the men of her establishment too busy *clearing* to lend her much aid, set about contriving a press in which she could make cheese. She succeeded in making one in the corner of a rail fence ; and it was observed that, thrifty as she was, she could not be induced without great reluctance, to exchange this press of her own contrivance for one of more pretension, though adopted and praised by all her neighbors.

17

Among the privations of the early settlers, not the least was the difficulty of hearing from the friends they had left at "the East." Not only were the mails slow and uncertain, but the postage of a letter was twenty-five cents; a fourth of a man's pay for a hard day's work. So expensive a treat could not be often indulged in, and accordingly it seldom happened that more than one or two letters were exchanged in the course of a 'year by a single emigrant family.

The burning of the marshes often running far into the upland, which was done every year by the Indians and old hunters, was sometimes attended by accidents, the fire extending to the opening and overrunning the land to the destruction of oak-grubs and tall trees. An enterprising and industrious young emigrant had built a comfortable house in a pleasant opening for himself and his sisters, one of whom had charge of it. One day while she was alone, the brother being absent on business, she discovered that the grass was on fire, and that the devouring element was rapidly approaching. All her efforts were bent to keep it from the premises; but finding she could do nothing to check its progress, and that the outhouses were in imminent danger, she ran to the door of her dwelling for her bonnet, threw in her apron which she pulled off hastily from a woman's instinctive impulse of neatness, and without looking back, hurried to the nearest neighbor's, some three miles off, for assistance. As soon as possible she returned with help; but they were greeted by a melancholy sight. The burning of the grass, it was evident, had not extended to the house; but the building was in flames, and past the hope of saving even an article of furniture. The poor girl then discovered that the fire must have originated from her apron, which probably concealed a spark when she threw it in; and thus she had the chagrin of knowing that her very eagerness had been the means of depriving herself and family of the only shelter they could call their own.

The mention of fire reminds us of another curious anecdote recorded in the annals of Detroit. There was at one time a town ordinance that every house should be provided with a butt of water for use in case of fire, the owner being subject to a fine in case of disobedience. A widow whose neglect had been passed over several times by the inspectors, one day saw them coming on their usual errand, and resolved that they should not have it to say they had found her cask *empty*, jumped into it herself. The stratagem so pleased the men that, laughing heartily, they fetched water and filled the butt for her.

Some other incidents illustrative of the times, are mentioned by the old settlers. One tells how a large sleighing party went at night to Dexter, and how Judge Dexter figured as a seer, and told the fortunes of the company. They were very merry returning, though it was near morning, and intensely cold. A sudden breakdown took place, and one of the gentlemen was obliged to go back some distance to borrow an axe to repair the damage. Those left waiting, fearing that without some precaution they should perish with cold, spread the buffalo skins on the hard snow, and had a lively dance upon them; till the sleigh being mended, they returned to Ann Arbor without further hindrance.

The inhabitants of Detroit may remember a remarkable old woman, Mrs. Chappel by name, a true "Betty O'Flanagan," who followed in the rear of Wayne's army, and afterwards kept pushing away from civilization. At the time my informant knew her, she kept a small tavern on the Pontiac turnpike, much resorted to by the young men of the town, it being just distant enough for a pleasant ride. As the hostess was very homely, they were accustomed to call her in jest "Old Mother Handsome;" listening often to the reminiscences with which she was wont to interlard her preparations for supper. When grumbling at the trouble given her, she would declare that she should have been better off had "Mad Anthony" lived. She would have been a fine character for a romance, and deserves more than a mere mention, as a representative of the spirit of her day among the ruder class of settlers.

XXIII.

HARRIET L. NOBLE.

IN 1824 there was almost as great an excitement in Western New York about going to Michigan as there has been recently in regard to California. One of those enterprising settlers, the wife of Nathaniel Noble, has favored me with some of her recollections, which present a graphic picture of early times in this State. No language cou be so appropriate as her own.

" My husband was seized with the mania, and accordingly made preparation to start in January with his brother. They took the Ohio route, and were nearly a month in getting through; coming by way of Monroe, and thence to Ypsilanti and Ann Arbor. Mr. John Allen and Walter Rumsey with his wife and two men had been there some four or five weeks, had built a small house, moved into it the day my husband and his brother arrived, and were just preparing their first meal, which the newcomers had the pleasure of partaking. They spent a few days here, located a farm a little above the town on the river Huron, and returned through Canada. They had been so much pleased with the country, that they immediately commenced preparing to emigrate; and as near as I can recollect, we started about the 20th of September, 1824, for Michigan. We travelled from our house in Geneva to Buffalo in wagons. The roads were bad, and we were obliged to wait in

Buffalo four days for a boat, as the steamboat ' Michigan' was the only one on the lake. After waiting so long we found she had put into Erie for repairs, and had no prospect of being able to run again for some time. The next step was to take passage in a schooner, which was considered a terrible undertaking for so dangerous a voyage as it was then thought to be. At length we went on board ' the Prudence,' of Cleveland, Capt. Johnson. A more inconvenient little bark could not well be imagined. We were seven days on Lake Erie, and so entirely prostrated with seasickness, as scarcely to be able to attend to the wants of our little ones. I had a little girl of three years, and a babe some months old, and Sister Noble had six children, one an infant. It was a tedious voyage ; the lake was very rough most of the time, and I thought f we were only on land again, I should be satisfied, if it was a wilderness. I could not then realize what it would be to live without a comfortable house through the winter, but sad experience afterwards taught me a lesson not to be forgotten.

" We came into the Detroit river ; it was beautiful then as now ; on the Canada side, in particular, you will scarce perceive any change. As we approached Detroit, the ' Cantonment' with the American flag floating on its walls, was decidedly the most interesting of any part of the town ; for a city it was certainly the most filthy, irregular place I had ever seen ; the streets were filled with Indians and low French, and at that time I could not tell the difference between them. We spent two days in making preparations for going out to Ann Arbor, and during that time I never saw a genteelly-dressed person in the streets. There were no carriages ; the most wealthy families rode in French carts, sitting on the bottom upon some kind of mat ; and the streets were so muddy these were the only vehicles convenient for getting about. I said to myself, ' if this be a Western city, give me a home in the woods.' I think it was on the 3d of October we started from Detroit, with a pair of oxen and a wagon, a few articles for cooking, and such necessaries as we could not do without. It was necessary that they should be few as possible, for our families were a full load for this mode of travelling. After travelling all day we found ourselves but ten miles from Detroit (at what is now Dearborn); here we spent the night at a kind of tavern, the only one west of the city. Our lodging was the floor, and the other entertainment was to match. The next day we set out as early as possible, in hopes to get through the woods before dark, but night found us about half way through, and there remained no other resource but to camp out, and make ourselves contented. The men built a large fire and prepared our supper. My sister and myself could assist but little, so fatigued were we with walking and carrying our infants. There were fifteen in our company. Two gentlemen going to Ypsilanti had travelled with us from Buffalo; the rest were our own families. We were all pretty cheerful, until we began to think of lying down for the night. The men did not seem to dread it, however, and were soon fast asleep, but sleep was not for me in such a wilderness. I could think of nothing but wild beasts, or something as bad; so that I had the pleasure of watching while the others slept. It seemed a long, long night, and never in my life did I feel more grateful for the blessing of returning day. We started again as early as possible, all who could walk moving on a little in advance of the wagon; the small children were the only ones who thought of riding. Every few rods it would take two or three men to pry the wagon out of the mud, while those who walked were obliged to force their way over fallen timber, brush, &c. Thus passed the day; at night we found ourselves on the plains, three miles from Ypsilanti. My feet were so swollen I could walk no further. We got into the wagon and rode as far as Woodruff's grove, a little below Ypsilanti. There were some four or five families at this place. The next day we left for Ann Arbor. We were delighted with the country before us; it was beautiful in its natural state; and I have sometimes thought that cultivation has marred its loveliness. Where Ypsilanti now stands, there was but one building—an old trading-house on the west side of the river; the situation was fine—there were scattering oaks and no brushwood. Here we met a large number of Indians; and one old squaw followed us some distance with her papoose, determined to swap babies. At last she gave it up, and for one I felt relieved.

" We passed two log houses between this and Ann Arbor About the middle of the afternoon we found ourselves at our journey's end—but what a prospect? There were some six or seven log huts occupied by as many inmates as could be crowded into them. It was too much to think of asking strangers to give us a place to stay in even for one night under such circumstances. Mr. John Allen himself made us the offer of sharing with him the comfort of a shelter from storm, if not from cold. His house was large for a log one, but quite unfinished ; there was a ground floor and a small piece above. When we got our things stored in this place, we found the number sheltered to be twenty-one women and children, and fourteen men. There were but two bedsteads in the house, and those who could not occupy these, slept on feather beds upon the floor. When the children were put in bed you could not set a foot down without stepping on a foot or hand ; the consequence was we had music most of the time.

" We cooked our meals in the open air, there being no fire in the house but a small box-stove. The fall winds were not very favorable to such business ; we would frequently find our clothes on fire, but fortunately we did not often get burned. When one meal was over, however, we dreaded preparing the next. We lived in this way until our husbands got a log house raised and the roof on ; this took them about six weeks, at the end of which time we went into it, without door, floor, chimney, or anything but logs and roof. There were no means of getting boards for a floor, as everything must be brought from Detroit, and we could not think of drawing lumber over such a road. The only alternative was to split slabs of oak with an axe. My husband was not a mechanic, but he managed to make a floor in this way that kept us from the ground. I was most anxious for a door, as the wolves would come about in the evening, and sometimes stay all night and keep up a serenade that would almost chill the blood in my veins. Of all noises I think the howling of wolves and the yell of Indians the most fearful ; at

least it appeared so to me then, when I was not able to close the
door against them.   I had the greatest terror of Indians ; for I had
never seen any before I came to Michigan but Oneidas, and they
were very different, being partially civilized.

"We had our house comfortable as such a rude building could
be, by the first of February.   It was a mild winter; there was
snow enough to cover the ground only four days, a fortunate
circumstance for us.   We enjoyed uninterrupted health, but in the
spring the ague with its accompaniments gave us a call, and by
the middle of August there were but four out of fourteen who could
call themselves well.   We then fancied we were too near the river
for health.   We sold out and bought again ten miles west of Ann
Arbor, a place which suited us better ; and just a year from the
day we came to Ann Arbor, moved out of it to Dexter.   There
was one house here, Judge Dexter's ; he was building a saw-
mill, and had a number of men at work at the time ; besides these
there was not a white family west of Ann Arbor in Michigan territory.   Our log house was just raised, forming only the square log
pen.   Of course it did not look very inviting, but it was our home,
and we must make the best of it.   I helped to raise the rafters and
put on the roof, but it was the last of November before our roof was
completed.   We were obliged to wait for the mill to run in order
to get boards for making it.   The doorway I had no means of
closing except by hanging up a blanket, and frequently when I
would raise it to step out, there would be two or three of our dusky
neighbors peeping in to see what was there.   It would always give
me such a start, I could not suppress a scream, to which they would
reply with ' Ugh !' and a hearty laugh.   They knew I was afraid,
and liked to torment me.   Sometimes they would throng the house
and stay two or three hours.   If I was alone they would help themselves to what they liked.   The only way in which I could restrain
them at all, was to threaten that I would tell Cass ; he was governor
of the territory, and they stood in great fear of him.   At last we got
a door.   The next thing wanted was a chimney ; winter was close
at hand and the stone was not drawn.   I said to my husband, ' I

think I can drive the oxen and draw the stones, while you dig them from the ground and load them.' He thought I could not, but consented to let me try. He loaded them on a kind of sled; I drove to the house, rolled them off, and drove back for another load. I succeeded so well that we got enough in this way to build our chimney. My husband and myself were four days building it. I suppose most of my lady friends would think a woman quite out of ' her legitimate sphere' in turning mason, but I was not at all particular what kind of labor I performed, so we were only comfortable and provided with the necessaries of life. Many times I had been obliged to take my children, put on their cloaks, and sit on the south side of the house in the sun to keep them warm ; anything was preferable to smoke. When we had a chimney and floor, and a door to close up our little log cabin, I have often thought it the most comfortable little place that could possibly be built in so new a country ; and but for the want of provisions of almost every kind, we should have enjoyed it much. The roads had been so bad all the fall that we had waited until this time, and I think it was December when my husband went to Detroit for supplies. Fifteen days were consumed in going and coming. We had been without flour for three weeks or more, and it was hard to manage with young children thus. After being without bread three or four days, my little boy, two years old, looked me in the face and said, ' Ma, why don't you make bread ; don't you like it ? I do.' His innocent complaint brought forth the first tears I had shed in Michigan on account of any privations I had to suffer, and they were about the last. I am not of a desponding disposition, nor often low-spirited, and having left New York to make Michigan my home, I had no idea of going back, or being very unhappy. Yet the want of society, of church privileges, and in fact almost every thing that makes life desirable, would often make me sad in spite of all effort to the contrary. I had no ladies' society for one year after coming to Dexter, except that of sister Noble and a Mrs. Taylor, and was more lonely than either of them, my family being so small.

" The winter passed rather gloomily, but when spring came, every·

17*

thing looked delightful. We thought our hardships nearly at an end, when early in the summer my husband was taken with the ague. He had not been sick at all the first year; of course he must be acclimated. He had never suffered from ague or fever of any kind before, and it was a severe trial for him, with so much to do and no help to be had. He would break the ague and work for a few days, when it would return. In this way he made his garden, planted his corn, and thought he was quite well. About August he harvested his wheat and cut his hay, but could get no help to draw it, and was again taken with ague. I had it myself, and both my children. Sometimes we would all be ill at a time. Mr. Noble and I had it every other day. He was almost discouraged, and said he should have to sell his cattle or let them starve. I said to him, 'to-morrow we shall neither of us have the ague, and I believe I can load and stack the hay, if my strength permits.' As soon as breakfast was over, I prepared to go into the meadow, where I loaded and stacked seven loads that day. The next day my husband had the ague more severely than common, but not so with me; the exercise broke the chills, and I was able to assist him whenever he was well enough, until our hay was all secured. In the fall we had several added to our circle. We were more healthy then, and began to flatter ourselves that we could live very comfortably through the winter of 1826; but we were not destined to enjoy that blessing, for in November my husband had his left hand blown to pieces by the accidental discharge of a gun, which confined him to the house until April. The hay I had stacked during the summer I had to feed out to the cattle with my own hands in the winter, and often cut the wood for three days at a time. The logs which I alone rolled in, would surprise any one who has never been put to the test of necessity, which compels people to do what under other circumstances they would not have thought possible. This third winter in Michigan was decidedly the hardest I had yet encountered. In the spring, Mr. Noble could go out by carrying his hand in a sling. He commenced ploughing to prepare for planting his corn. Being weak from his wound, the ague returned again, but he worked every other day until his corn was planted. He then went to New York, came back in July, and brought a nephew with him, who relieved me from helping him in the work out of doors. Although I was obliged to stack the hay this third fall, I believe it was the last labor of the kind I ever performed. At this time we began to have quite a little society; we were fortunate in having good neighbors, and for some years were almost like one family, our interests being the same, and envy, jealousy, and all bitter feelings unknown among us. We cannot speak so favorably of the present time.

"When I look back upon my life, and see the ups and downs, the hardships and privations I have been called upon to endure, I feel no wish to be young again. I was in the prime of life when I came to Michigan—only twenty-one, and my husband was thirty-three. Neither of us knew the reality of hardship. Could we have known what it was to be pioneers in a new country, we should never have had the courage to come; but I am satisfied that with all the disadvantages of raising a family in a new country, there is a consolation in knowing that our children are prepared to brave the ills of life, I believe, far better than they would have been had we never left New York."

In view of the formidable journey described by Mrs. Noble from Detroit to Ypsilanti, it should be mentioned that it is thirty miles by railroad, and ten miles thence to Ann Arbor; Dexter being still ten miles further. As a confirmation of her remark about the awe in which the Indians stood of Cass, an incident may be mentioned. One summer's day, accompanied by his negro man, he rode up, on his way from the West, to the door of one of the early settlers in this county, to get a draught of water from the well. As he was about going on, a party of a hundred Indians on their way from Detroit, stopped also, and began stacking their guns by the side of the house, evidently intending to make a long stay. The woman, who chanced to be alone, was very much frightened, and as the savages paid no attention to her request that they would go on, she begged Gov. Cass to interfere. He spoke a few words to them in their own language, and as soon as they knew him, they should ered their weapons and were "marching off in double quick time."

The old picturesque looking windmill on the American side of the Detroit river, is the one to which all the people in western Michigan, some thirty years ago, were obliged to come for their grinding. It is now dismantled of its wings, and the tower in a ruinous state.

The lady whose narrative is quoted is, it will be acknowledged, "a pioneer indeed." She is, moreover, an interesting and charming woman, and admirable in all the relations she has filled. Her manner is described as being remarkably attractive, and her portraiture in conversation of the hardships and peculiarities of pioneer life, as being vivid and thrilling. "She talks with so much spirit," says one of her friends, "that I know she can make a more sprightly narrative than any I have read." Her children have prospered and are most highly respected, and neither they nor their descendants will be likely to forget how deeply they are indebted to a mother so enterprising and energetic, and so affectionately mindful of their interests.

———

The village of Dixboro' in Washtenaw County, Michigan, was first laid out by Mr. Dix of Massachusetts, and was once somewhat flourishing, though now a miserable looking place, owning scarce a dwelling that is not in a state of dilapidation. The inhabitants are not remarkable for superstition; yet it is curious to notice how strong is the current belief even to the present day, in an old ghost story. "To doubt it," says a resident, "is to offer a personal insult." The tale ran briefly thus: A new settler by the name of Van Wart, a relative of one of the captors of André, who had taken up his quarters in a house recently occupied by a widow then deceased, testified to the nocturnal visits of an apparition, whom the neighbors supposed to be no other than the woman's ghost. From what transpired during these visitations, it was supposed she had been murdered by her brother-in-law for the sake of concealing some crime committed years before. The matter was made the subject of legal investigation, and Van Wart's testimony taken in full, under oath, by the magistrate before a jury. The grave was opened and the body examined to ascertain if her death had been caused by poison; probably the only instance in this century at least of a corpse being disinterred upon the evidence of a ghost! The appearance of the dead was startlingly like the description given by the ghost seer, who had never seen her living; but nothing was found to justify condemnation of the accused, who was accordingly released and left the country. The Scotch physician who attended the woman in her last illness, and was supposed to be implicated in the deed, also quitted the community. The old log house is still standing, with the room called Tophet, because appropriated to the use of the sick as a hospital—now in a sadly tumbledown condition, but once the seat of cheerful hospitality. In the olden time, many a merry company from Ann Arbor was wont to resort there, spending the evening in dancing and festivity. Ypsilanti and Dexter were also favorite places of resort for sleighing and pic-nic parties. The latter village was laid out by Judge Dexter, brother to the celebrated lawyer of that name in Boston.

Miss Frances Trask was a cousin of Mrs. Dix, and figured prominently at that day in the little community as a belle somewhat on the Amazon order. She had much talent, with a degree of cultivation that caused her to be looked up to with respect as a person of unusual accomplishments; she possessed, moreover, real worth and good qualities of heart; but her eccentricities and unfeminine defiance of general opinion in many trifling matters, often startled her quiet neighbors, and made it necessary for those who loved her most to defend her from censure. She was much admired by the men; her piquancy of wit, force and decision of character, and a sort of happy audacity, setting off to advantage her personal attractions. Yet she was not wanting in fitness for the usefulness peculiar to woman; in cases of sickness she could do more than any one else, and would watch for many nights together, bearing fatigues under which an ordinary constitution must have sunk. In emergencies that required prompt action, her energy was praised with enthusiasm by her own sex. Finally, when pecuniary embarrassments made it necessary for Dix and his family to leave their home, and the wife, a gentle, ladylike creature, was overpowered with grief, and could do little to expedite preparations, Frances was the *nerve* of them all. She packed up everything, dressed the children one by one the last morning, placing each on a chair when in readiness, with orders not to move, and with cheerful alacrity arranged everything for their departure. She had accustomed herself to firing at a mark, and was considered one of the best shots in the country, besides being able to ride a horse with any racer. It was said she could cut off a chicken's head at an almost incredible number of rods, and that she often went out deer hunting; but this last tradition does not vouch for. She was the life of pic-nics or pleasure parties, and seldom let pass an opportunity of making a smart or satirical speech, sometimes at the expense of delicate regard for the feelings of others. A certain Judge Thompson, who had held office at Batavia at the time of Morgan's abduction, as sheriff of the county, and had earned a notoriety in no wise enviable, chanced to be helping her at a pic-nic on one occasion, and began to rally her on her penchant for meat; "Yes," she retorted, "I am fond of flesh; you of blood;" a rejoinder which was keenly felt by the mortified official.

On another occasion the lady seems to have met her match, being excessively annoyed by a gallant who chose to vex her by pretending to mistake her name, calling her "Miss Trash," and then correcting himself with an apparently confused apology. She used to laugh heartily in mentioning a speech meant to be particularly ill-natured, levelled at her at a dinner party at Ypsilanti by a lady of her own stamp, who had become irritated beyond forbearance by some of her sallies. Looking significantly at Miss Trask, she gave her toast, saying, "When Boston next takes an emetic, I hope it will turn its head towards the ocean."

It may well be imagined that those to whom Miss Trask chose to be amiable, liked her much, while she was thoroughly detested by those who had suffered from the arrows of her wit. Strange as it may seem, she was held in high esteem by many of her own sex, notwithstanding her boldness of carriage, from which it may be inferred that she affected to be more lawless than she was in reality. She accompanied Mr. Dix and his family when they removed to Texas. Some two years since, when she returned on a visit to Michigan, the manifest change and improvement in her bearing and manners were the subject of general remark. She had grown absolutely quiet and dignified; so that those who had heard only of her early fame, expressed some disappointment at not finding her the dashing, sprightly creature she had been represented. Time and the trials and labors incident to life in a new country had tamed her wild spirit; she had mourned the loss of a brother in the Texan service, and had undergone a second term of the difficulties and privations of pioneer life. The government of Texas, however, had shown that they appreciated her services by voting her a large tract of land in compliment to her opening the first seminary for young ladies in that State. This possession, with the portion of land assigned to her deceased brother, made her a wealthy woman. Among the curiosities she brought from her new home, her Mexican blanket attracted great attention from its novelty, elegance and richness. Some said it had been valued in Boston at a thousand dollars. A story had gone about, the details of which were denied by the heroine, that during the struggle in Texas, a Mexican attempting to force his way into the house at a time when Mr. Dix was too ill to act on the defensive, had been shot by the intrepid sister-in-law.

It may be conjectured that Miss Trask had many admirers. She had been engaged at Dixboro' to Sherman Dix, a relative of her brother-in-law, and somewhat her junior; but they quarrelled, it was said, upon one occasion when she was suffering from an attack of ague—about some trifling matter, and the suitor was peremptorily dismissed. When the family removed to Texas some years afterwards, the young man followed, and remained a bachelor; whether on account of a lingering attachment to the fair inconstant, or some other reason, it has not been recorded. Miss Trask's matrimonial destiny at length overtook her ; she married at Austin a Mr. Thompson, and was left a widow in a few months. Her nephew by marriage is Secretary of State in Texas, and a son and daughter of Mr. Thompson reside at Chicago.

Among the early settlers of Michigan who deserve a notice, should be numbered Mrs. Hector Scott, the daughter of Luther Martin, the lawyer who so ably and successfully defended Aaron Burr. She came to the State before 1837, and is still residing in Detroit. She has passed through many severe reverses and trials ; but her intellectual ability, energy, and firmness of character, have sustained her, constraining the admiration and respect of all who enjoy her acquaintance. Like her, Mrs. Talbot, once a celebrated beauty, retains the dignified manners of the olden time. She was the daughter of Commodore Truxton. She still resides on her farm near Pontiac ; the ancient log house embowered in eglantine, and showing evidence within doors of a refinement of taste which can invest with elegance the homeliest materials.

At Union City, in the southern part of Michigan, lives Mrs. Mosely, daughter of the missionary, Bingham, and the first white child born in the Sandwich Islands. The first child born at the Falls of St. Anthony was Mrs. Horatio Van Cleve, the daughter of Maj. Nathan Clark. Orren and Ann White, descendants of the New England pilgrims, came to Ann Arbor the second year after its settlement, and still reside on the place they purchased, about two miles from the village.

Mrs. Goodrich, one of the pioneers, who came with her husband and family to Michigan as early as 1827, prides herself somewhat on a thrifty grape vine which ornaments her beautiful garden, brought by her from New England, and a shoot from those vines at " Bloody Brook," the tempting clusters of which enticed the unfortunate young men whose massacre gave name to the locality

Miss Hoit, who lived in the northern part of Livingston County, when the country was covered with thick forests, wandered one day so far, while gathering wild flowers, that she entirely lost her way. In her distress she heard the tinkling of cow-bells, and following the sound, remained with the cattle till evening, when she went home in safety under their escort.

The wife of a pioneer who had lived in " the bush " nearly three years without seeing another white female face, has spoken of the delight with which she found a dandelion in bloom near her door-step. Probably the seed of the golden flower had been brought with that of the "tame grass," as they called "timothy" in dis-tinction from the native marsh grass ; and its unexpected ap-pearance brought back so vividly her old home associations and remembrance of the beloved ones there, that she could not resist the impulse to " sit down and have a good cry." " I felt less lonely," she said, " all that day, and ever since.   My dandelions are the only ones in the settlement, and I take care that they and the white clover, which has since made its appearance, shall not run out." Another in Illinois, who had for a long time lived without windows, found herself at last able to indulge in the luxury of glass panes, and had a small window set, so that she could see to sew in the day-time in winter.   All the first day, while plying her needle, she found herself continually looking off, to wonder at the novelty of what she had been formerly used to regard as an indispensable conve-nience.   The dwellers on the heavily timbered land, which unlike the pleasant " openings " where the sunshine falls, afforded no relief except the "clearing" marked with blackened stumps, were sub-jected to dangers as well as inconvenience.   Mrs. Comstock, de-scribing her primitive home in Shiwasse County, says,—" We had previously had a log house erected in the woods, but we came up in a boat by the river, and when we reached the spot, were obliged to have a road cut before we could get to our home.   Here for a long time I never dared trust our children outside the enclosure for fear of the bears ; for those animals would often come close about us, even to the fence."

Many of the families who had removed to Detroit before the war of 1812, returned east previous to its outbreak, being in dread of attacks from the Indians in the neighborhood, who were known to be in British pay, and made frequent demonstrations of hostility; sometimes encamping near the houses of residents in numbers of three or four hundred. Captives brought to Detroit by the savages, were often purchased there to save them from a more terrible fate. A young girl who had been thus taken into a family, one day seeing a party of Indians pass by, uttered a piercing shriek, and fell senseless to the floor. On recovering consciousness, she declared that she had seen her mother's scalp in possession of one of the savages, recognizing it by the long light braid of hair. Her story was confirmed by a person who had seen the mother and daughter brought with other prisoners from near Sandusky, Ohio. The mother being in feeble health, and unable to travel as fast as was required, was tomahawked, her daughter being hurried on in ignorance of the cruel murder.

At the time of Hull's surrender, the women expressed much indignation. A Mrs. Woodward, since well known in Detroit, mentions a hairbreadth escape. One morning during the war, she had risen, dressed herself as usual, and was sitting by an open window which looked upon the Canada side; suddenly a cannon-ball whizzed past her face and buried itself in the side of the house. She avers that it actually straightened the curls of her hair.

The preceding notices may serve to show something of the privations and perils encountered by female pioneers in Michigan, and the heroism, patience, and energy with which they were met, as well as afford a glimpse into the peculiar character which, marking the early settlers, has in some degree been transmitted to their children.

XXIV.

EVEN as late as 1835, the emigrants who poured into Michigan, often building their homes in the dense forest or on wild prairie land, are entitled to be called pioneers. An idea of the scenery of portions of the peninsula at that period, and the mode of living among the early settlers, may be given best in the language of one who has had opportunity of observing them. For this purpose, I am permitted to make a few extracts from a manuscript journal kept by a highly gifted and accomplished lady, now residing in the western part of New York, who travelled in that year on horseback through the lower peninsula:

"Bronson (now Kalamazoo), May 28th, 1835. Owing to the uniform progress of journeying day after day from Jacksonburgh to Marshall, a distance of thirty-six, and from Marshall hence, of thirty-seven miles, 'the little lines of yesterday' have well-nigh faded without being noticed. The memory of the beautiful, and of such beauty—a forest in its wildness—is so much more powerful than distinct, and having the same characteristics, presents so much uniformity that but little record can be made. On our route we passed over some twenty miles through the wild woods, without seeing a human being. The foliage was just bursting from its numberless sheaths into rich drapery our pathway was literally strewn with flowers, the horses pressing them at every step, while the birds in their leafy homes, deluged the otherwise unbroken stillness with wild and delicious melody.   The silence of the deep forest, during the brief intervals of these untaught lays, seems strangely oppressive ; yet ere you can analyze its unwonted power, earth's lyre, with its myriad tones, is struck again, and you are roused to the liveliest sympathy.   I had somewhat the feeling of Milton's Eve, differently applied.   She asked, ' Wherefore all night long *shine* these ?'   My heart-query was, ' Wherefore all this wealth of varied note and strain ?'   But the same heart answered, ' These feathered songsters know of home, and love, and sweet companionship, and joyously give thanks for the gift of being, telling to each other, and to Him who made them, of the blessing of life.'

" This day we first saw the Kalamazoo River—a narrow, dark stream.   We stopped at a small log cabin, which on its shingle sign advertised ' Entertainment for man and beast ;' doubtless after the fashion of the settlements the proprietors had left, and we were grateful for any shelter from the noonday sun.   I noticed, while sitting in an inner room, to which, as a lady traveller, I was ceremoniously conducted, that the landlord eyed my husband with singular, yet irresolute attention.   I did not fancy, however, that he had ever seen him before.   He was an odd-looking personage ; rather slight in his general proportions, and short in stature ; he had large, prominent features, overshadowed by a shock of coarse yellow hair, faded and worn, that gave him a wild and savage aspect, particularly as this hair and his complexion seemed scarcely to vary a shade in tint.   After repeated advances, accompanied with stolen and hurried glances at my husband, he rushed out from his so-called bar, and broke out into a sort of earnest thanksgiving, blessing him for having ejected him from one of the small pieces of land contracted to settlers in western New York.   He went on to say that he did not at first recognize him, but he did now, and could tell him that sending him from that farm was one of the best things that ever happened to him ; that after he was sent away because he could not pay a cent on his land, he came to this place, and would not give ten acres of it for fifty like that he left in the State of New York. Setting aside the intrinsic value so earnestly put forth, this new and much-prized possession was truly a beautiful spot. The dark current of the river was rushing with arrowy swiftness past the trail on which he had piled his log dwelling. A fine piece of rising ground formed the back-ground, which was imperfectly subdued by cultivation, while a little to the west a scene lay revealed that might do for a glimpse of fairy-land. A small lake, with its sparkling waters, reposed like a jewel in its dark green setting. The forest, on the one side, was enlivened with the luxuriance of the dog-wood, now in full blossom as far as the eye could reach. The large white flowers dispensed in such profusion, gave more the aspect of a boundless garden of lilies, than the unsuspected treasures of an uncultivated wilderness. There were clear openings on the other side, the meadow-like ground being just sprinkled with trees, as if arrayed for picturesque landscape beauty, affording wider vistas from the foliage only making itself seen in delicate tracery, not being yet quite unfolded.

> ' Many an elf and many a fay
> Here might hold their pastime gay.'

" Our landlady for the hour seemed to share fully her husband's feelings of self-gratulation, though she told me it was pretty hard times when they had to live in and under their ox-wagon during the early spring days, while the logs were felled and put up for their home. This log house would be quite an object of interest to persons unaccustomed to the pristine dwellings of the western territories. It seemed to consist of three distinct buildings, probably put up at different periods, to meet the increasing demands of ambition as prosperity more abounded. What was evidently the first pile of logs, was used as a bar-room of the roughest construction. This also served as a counter for the ready-change business of this much frequented inn. The boards, or rather planks of the floor, were hewn, and laid down so unequally as to be perilous to

an unwary or even rapid step. Directly in the rear was the
kitchen, in which the culinary implements and table necessaries
were arranged, evidently with an attempt at order without the recognized law thereunto of anything in heaven or earth. The cooking apparatus was so simple, and the vessels for various uses so few
in number, as to excite my wonder and admiration at woman's
homely tact and skill; and wayworn traveller though I was, the
preparation for our noonday meal was almost as engrossing as the
partaking thereof after it was prepared. A third division of the
house served as a *parlor* for our hostess, and as an occasional bedroom for ' special people'—a phrase which I found quite current as
a designation for the more fastidious class of travellers, who now
began to pass through this hitherto almost unknown territory.
Above the main part of these buildings extended a sort of garret,
lighted by a window of four small panes in one end, and the opening of the ladder-way—the only mode of entrance. This was the
dormitory of India-rubber like capacity for the multitudes who in
this season of land-speculation, did here nightly congregate.

" On the fifth of June, we pursued our journey toward the south-
eastern part of the territory, intending to take a look at Lake Michigan from the mouth of the St. Joseph's River. Our way lay
through forests and openings similar to those through which we
had passed for days, but afterwards we struck into the more heavily
timbered land, which the growth of the advancing season had clad
with cumbrous garments of foliage, closing up the vistas of beauty
and light; in places denying the summer sun its right to rest upon
the flowers and shrubs it had but lately warmed into being. At
nearly noon, we came upon the edge of a large prairie, the
largest in the Territory, which although much smaller than those
spread farther westward, had still all the distinctive features of those
vast and undulating plains. The landscape was expanded and beautiful, and yet one can scarcely make intelligible the penetrating sentiment of its beauty. Perhaps the first influence consisted in the
sense of relief from the pent up feeling we had experienced in the
close pressure as it were, of the deep, **dark** forest from which we

emerged. In the centre of this plain was a collection of 'innumerous boughs' like an island in the midst of circling waters. The prairie was begirt by a belt of timbered land, though the outline was so dim in the distance, as rather to look like a lazy cloud resting for support upon the verge of the horizon. We gave our horses the reins, and they cantered merrily across the rich plain, the whole covered in this early summer with short and close grass. Innumerable flowers raised their variegated heads between the tiny meshes of network woven by the wild pea, while the butterflies, with their bright tints and quick fluttering wings, were perpetually upspringing, startled by our approach. After crossing the prairie we again struck into the forest, having previously stopped at the island inn for some refreshment.

"Towards evening, as was our wont, we felt that we must look along our way for some lodging for the night. Our custom had been, except in the villages, not to seek accommodation at the inns scattered at irregular distances along the road. The new settlers continually moving in toward their purchases, and the number of speculators in pursuit of locations on which to raise, not dwellings, but future fortunes, so completely filled them up, as to render it an impossibility to find for a lady even momentary seclusion, much less repose. Our practice was as soon as we found the shadows beginning to lengthen, to stop at the first decent log house and ask for a drink of water. Getting the water afforded time and opportunity for reconnoitering; and if the tin cup or basin in which the draught was offered looked clean, and the premises in any way inviting by comparison, we made the request that we could be accommodated for the night. We had not on this evening seen any houses, the tract of country through which we had been passing for some hours being without settlement.

"On coming up to some woodmen whose gleaming axes told that their whereabouts was near at hand, we stopped, and after exchanging mutual glances of inquiry, my husband asked if they could tell us where we could find a tavern? They looked at each other and then askance at us. The question was repeated again; they looked bewildered, when my husband thoughtfully changed his phrase and said—' Where can I stay to-night, and have good care taken of my horses ?' The answer then came quickly—' Oh, at Nicholas B—'s, the Hooshier's, he has a first-rate place, and takes in every night a great many folks.' We made two or three further inquiries and passed on, with our expectations considerably raised in prospect of the promised accommodation.

"Just after sunset, we reached the place designated by the wood-man, and peering through the gloaming, I espied a good-sized frame barn, with an enclosure, and all the appearance of a well stocked barn and rick. I fairly screamed with delight, so important to our further journey was the welfare of our horses, and so certain did the indication seem of a comfortable resting place for my own wearied limbs. We soon came out of the forest, upon the edge of a small prairie; there stood the barn in very truth, but I looked around in vain for the house which I had pictured in such glowing colors to myself, as presenting some comparison in size and comfort to the barn. A sudden chill of loneliness came over us. There lay the prairie, about three hundred acres in extent, shrubless and bare, except the patches of recent cultivation, which, however, in the dim light, gave but little indication of richness or growth. The trees shut us in completely, and after traversing the deep forest as we had been for hours, we could not even let imagination picture a livelier or brighter scene beyond. Night came rapidly on, while we stood baffled, without a present sign of human existence. Our horses had for a mile or two been lagging, perhaps in memory of the morning scamper and noon-day refreshment; and now the whole group seemed peculiarly sensible of the influence of solitude, which in us soon resolved itself into utter dreariness. A fresh glance of scrutiny, however, enabled us to descry a very small hut jutting into the woods, as uninviting a log house as we had seen in all our wanderings. We both looked at it for some moments without speaking, so completely paralyzed were all our high raised expectations. I then exclaimed, ' We cannot stay in that hovel.' But fastidiousness was soon displaced by eagerness with me, when my husband calmly said—'We must find shelter there or in the barn, for no further can we go to-night.' We urged our horses to the door; a well stood directly in front of it, a rare and great treasure in a new settlement, and after grateful notice of this, my husband entered the dwelling. He asked the woman civilly, 'if she could accommodate us for the night.' Her answer came quick in utterance and shrill in tone. 'I suppose I shall have to, any way.' Such was our welcome. But necessity here giving no scope to pride, or even wonted self-respect, obliged me to dismount and receive the favor so grudgingly bestowed. The woman was perhaps about thirty years of age, plain in feature, and old-fashioned beyond my memory in attire. Her dress was a thick striped material, woven to defy time and its ravages. It was unlike any fabric to which I had been accustomed. It fitted the figure almost closely, low in the neck, with sleeves just coming below the elbow. The dress was extremely short-waisted, without a particle of fulness in the skirt, save the ordinary plaiting just behind essential to convenience. She had on no shoes or stockings, and a faded bandana handkerchief was tied in a loose knot around her neck. Her hair was bound straight about her head, and fastened with some sort of a metal comb, just large enough to perform its office.

"On my entrance a wooden chair was handed me, after being hurriedly dusted; it was low and rickety, but it instantly bestowed the promise of rest, which I so much craved after sitting so many hours in the saddle. My husband, without entering the hut, went on the woman's vague direction to find the landlord, that our horses, whose prospects of accommodation were so far beyond ours, might speedily receive attention. As soon as he was gone, I essayed an acquaintance with my hostess, and soon believed that her want of courtesy at our reception proceeded more from a fear of not being able to make us comfortable, than from vexation at the present trouble. Two children, the eldest of them not more than two years of age, divided her care with the present bustle of preparing a meal and entertaining me by rapid talking. Her face became almost pleasant with the interest it soon showed in transforming

18

me into a newspaper, from which she could extract without much trouble the information desired by woman, let her nook of the world be ever so obscure, or her connection with the things without ever so slight. I had in my daily progress become quite used to this sort of questioning, and in some instances had to make my tarrying a lasting memorial of usefulness, by drawing patterns of certain garments, collars, caps, etc., with a coal on the floor or table, where paper could not be had, so that when cloth could be procured the latest mode might be used in its fashioning. While thus engaged in conversation, growing in self-importance every moment, and quite forgetting that I was an unwished-for guest, I took a survey of the house. It was, of course, built of logs, fourteen feet by sixteen; its sides five feet six inches in height, and the roof covered with strips of bark. A few scattering boards made the floor. It had not the ordinary stick and round chimney common to log houses, but a sort of box was made of split logs at one end of the room; this was filled in with dirt and ashes, and the fire built in the centre of it. An opening in the ill-made roof permitted the smoke to find egress, though occasional puffs during the process of getting supper, advised us of its loitering presence. After my survey of the room itself, I began to take notice of the furniture, and more especially of its sleeping facilities. Two bedsteads, each sustained by *one* post—quite an anomaly in my previous experience of cabinet furniture; a large chest, which had evidently borne journeying when the essay at house-keeping was made away from the paternal home; a small box of home manufacture, and some other absolute essentials to the wants of even the poorest dwelling, constituted its wealth. I must add a note of description of the bedsteads. Two sides were formed by the projection of the logs of which the hut was made into the room; the *one* post supported the other two pieces, which were on the other ends inserted into the sides of the house. Feather-beds were heaped high upon them, and these were covered with blue and white woollen coverlids, doubtless part of the portion brought by the young wife to her husband. Small pillows, with clean-looking cotton pillow-cases, completed their decoration.

"I had noticed that my hostess, during her bustle and constant chat with me, had gone frequently to the door, and looked anxiously into the increasing darkness, I of course supposed from no other motive than a desire to find out whether my husband had found hers, and secured attention for our horses. But not so interested was she in her stranger guests. At another visit to the low door, her anxiety could not be restrained, and she exclaimed, 'I wonder where my children can be! They ought to have been here more than an hour ago; they are always out of the way when I want them.' I looked aghast. More children! How many—how old! What could be done with them! I had been puzzling myself to know how *six* of us could be accommodated in the two beds, and in this tiny room; and now an indefinite number to be expected, how could we be made even tolerably comfortable? Speculation—quiet though it was—was soon to be ended by more precise apprehension, when *four* children, three boys and a girl, came rushing from the woods into the house, animated by all the buoyancy of hungry little mortals just liberated from a day's confinement and control. It being quite dark without, the light, small as it was within the dwelling, formed a strong contrast, and the little urchins were so suddenly arrested upon perceiving a stranger, that they stood like so many statues, incapable of thought or movement The remonstrance of the mother quickly restored them, and then began importunate demands for something to eat. Thus there were six children, the father and mother, with ourselves, to be stowed away for the night. It was in vain for me to speculate upon the probable disposition of these numbers, so trusting as I had often done before to the elastic capabilities of these log houses, I determined to bide my time.

" Our host came in with my husband, both bending low in passing through the door. My husband gave a wistful glance at me, and seemed reassured when a *widened* rather than a *lengthened* face was turned upon him. Truth to tell, I was almost convulsed with laughter at some of the previous proceedings of my hostess The ill-jointed planks which served for our floor, were quickly brushed hither and thither with an Indian broom (made of wood finely splintered); the flying dust seeming to have no particular destination, save to seek new places of deposit. The children were repeatedly hushed and pushed into sundry nooks and corners, while the cooking of the supper went on. The little urchins peered at the stranger, and anon played tricks with each other, when a sudden burst, caused by outbreaking mischief, would occasion a new effort at quieting. In process of time our supper was served, and ere long we gathered to the meal. The table was an oaken plank, supported by three stout sticks put into bored holes, for legs. A table-cloth being altogether a superfluous luxury, we dispensed with it; some bread, baked in an open kettle, pork fried in the same utensil, and tea with maple sugar, formed the variety presented to us. Neither milk nor butter were afforded, and yet we were at a regular house of entertainment, kept by a large landed proprietor. Strange to say, the meal was quite palatable, eaten with a healthful appetite after a day's ride on horseback of some thirty-five miles. Soon after tea, the children being fed by pieces put into their hands during the time we were supping, I ventured to hint, that as I was very tired I should like to go to bed. The woman went to the chest which I had before noticed, took out two clean sheets, spread them upon one of the feather beds, and again put on the woollen coverlet, although it was a June night, a fire burning briskly, and ten persons were to inhabit the small apartment. Immediately after the bed was prepared, the hostess said in an authoritative tone to her husband, 'Nicholas, the lady wishes to go to bed; turn your face to the wall.' Nicholas, as if accustomed to this nightly drill, wheeled swiftly about, and stood as still as if suddenly become one of the scanty articles of furniture.

" This said Nicholas looked somewhat like a barbarian, his bushy head and unshaven beard presenting quite a wild appearance. He however seemed intelligent enough for his locality and business, and took most excellent care of our horses. My toilet for the night was very speedily made, and I threw myself on the bed, having first removed the odious coverlet. Still no new developements were made in reference to the accommodation of the youthful group ; ere long, however, sundry signs of sleepiness appeared, betokened by fretfulness and some quarrelling, and then the mother proceeded to lift out two trundle beds made of pieces of board nailed together. The absence of rollers made the operation rather laborious, but the husband and father vouchsafed not his aid. It was finally done by the woman alone, and into these five of the little ones were speedily placed. Very soon after, the dim, flickering light was put out, and we were left utterly abandoned, as I feared, to suffocation. I remonstrated decidedly against the shutting of the door, but was told there was fear of the wolves; and indeed before morning our ears were saluted with the shrill, though somewhat smothered howl of these prowlers of the forest. I bore the heat and bad air for several hours, and then in desperation for want of a pure breath, I commenced picking the chinking out from between the logs at the side of the bed, and in this way secured for myself a breathing place, amid the enjoyment of which I fell asleep, and awaked not until the broad sunbeams were laughing in my face.

* * * * * * *

"During the last week we have made an excursion into the upper part of the lower peninsula of Michigan. Early in the morning of Monday, we left the village and crossed the Ke-Kalamazoo in a miserably constructed scow, and soon after receiving a wrong direction, lost our way. Pursuing, however, a trail for some distance, not knowing whither it would lead us, we came to an Indian trader's house, pleasantly located upon the banks of the river. We met before we reached this place, some Indians curiously and fantastically dressed with feathers, ribbons, &c. They were mounted on ponies, and seemed bound on some official expedition. They all appeared happy and good-natured. The trader gave us very vague directions for our onward way, but perhaps as definite as a route through an uninhabited forest could be made. The direction was after this fashion :—Take the right hand trail, then the left, and afterwards strike across the woods to the right of the sun, with some intimation that at certain distances lakes would be seen, and openings which would give us fresh energy and perseverance. Making practical these suggestions as far as we might, aided by a pocket compass and the extra bestowment of shrewdness with which my husband is endowed, we reached a prairie where there was a small settlement, and stopped for a few moments to avail ourselves of the intelligence, if so be we could find any, of a man loitering by the side of the trail, in hopes of further direction, and then passed into the dense wilderness. Our destination was an Indian village at a distance of twenty-six miles. The interval had no human habitation, and we were carefully charged to follow without deviation the particular trail to the village. Here and there were traces of a recent Indian encampment, and in one or two places we saw the smoke ascending from their unextinguished fires. The country had the same beauty with which we had become so familiar. The few clouds were motionless, the water in the many lakes we passed sparkled, but scarcely showed the tiniest ripple. As before nature's deep repose was broken, when the many birds swelled out their rich choruses, and every little trill met our ears with peculiar distinctness. We passed over a number of small but beautiful prairies, like g rden spots covered in wild luxuriance with flowers of every form and hue emitting delicate and delicious perfume. This last seemed rather peculiar to this part of the country, for in spite of what philosophers tell us, wild flowers have ordinarily no fragrance to common perception. In some districts we rode through dark and tangled forest, the straggling, yet by its heavy masses closely plaited foliage, bounding our vision to a few feet on either side, and then almost before we felt the confinement we passed out into an opening, where the bright sunbeams darting quick lines of light left the shadowed portion darker from the contrast. Again we would ride among the trees on the smooth turf, not a shrub or a brush marring the velvet surface, while the lofty trees overarching in their rich foliage, canopied our pathway.

" The hours of the day seemed long in passing, from the necessity of carefully watching the trail, and not having any incident linked to humanity to enliven us. About half an hour before the summer sun was to sink to his rest, we came upon the edge of a wet prairie or marsh about half a mile in extent. I shrank from crossing it, as the uncertain tread of my horse's feet upon the yielding turf made my seat unsteady, and altogether annoyed and repelled me. But there was no alternative ; the trail wound across it in its zigzag line, and we dared not at that hour run the risk of delay, lest we should lose in the deepening twilight its uncertain guidance. We pressed on, feeling at every step that our horses at the next might sink their hoofs too deeply for extrication. The peculiarity of this marsh was in the fact that there was not the slightest appearance of mud ; all was a bright green sward, or would have been in the glowing sunshine, but this was resting on a watery bed, into which it sank at every pressure. We however at last safely crossed the marsh after some toil, when lo, a new anxiety awaited me. A dark stream intervened between us and the solid ground, and as the spot where we stood was evidently the ford, cross it we must. The pool, or creek, or whatever might be its appropriate designation, was black as Erebus, with sloping banks, and though narrow, looked so deep in the uncertainty, that I quite feared it would engulph us. My husband bade me tarry until he had crossed it, and I felt quite sick with fear for him when I saw him plunge in. The struggling of his large and powerful horse tended not to reassure me, but when safely across, he said he would return and exchange horses with me. I could not think of permitting him to do so, and this gave me a momentary spasm of courage, trusting to the agility, if not strength of my own animal. The moment of descent into the pool was the last of distinct consciousness, and I was borne through I know not how. When I recovered I found myself sitting upon the ground, the muddy water streaming down my face, where it had been thrown in profusion by my terrified husband. He had expected to see me fall from my horse into the stream. I had not been well for a day or two, and this descent into the turbid waters quite unnerved me.

" To our dismay we perceived our horses had strayed, and already it was almost too dark to see the trail, our sole guide. I immediately anticipated an unguarded night in the wild wood before us; but a kind Providence induced our steeds to regard my husband's well known whistle, and both returned to our eager grasp. Ere it was quite night we heard the cheering sound of a woodman's axe, and guided by its repeated stroke, soon perceived a dim light in the distance. On coming up to the man, who seemed to be cutting wood for culinary purposes of the night, we asked for the trader; the man said he was about home, and could accommodate us and our horses for the night. We passed on. I entered the dwelling; it was laid up with logs, some fifty or sixty feet square, and but very recently erected. It had neither door, window, nor division between earth and roof. There was no floor laid, except for a small part of it, which formed a sort of dais, on which were two bedsteads and beds. A large pleasant-looking Frenchwoman met me, and in imperfect English gave me a cheerful welcome. I believe she was really delighted to greet me, so seldom did a woman find her way to her far-off dwelling. I was utterly weary, but the large, bare, unfurnished room gave but little promise of seclusion or quiet. Supper was soon served, venison, cranberries and bread, with a good cup of tea, sweetened with maple sugar, forming our meal. I soon found that eleven men, with the trader and his wife, and her maid of all work, were to occupy the same sleeping apartment with my husband and myself. I was too much jaded, however, to regard the absence of even such proprieties of life with much sensibility, and begged to go to bed, as my only prospective comfort on earth. In this I was gratified, and within an hour after my arrival I had taken possession of one of the two visible beds. My fellow-lodgers I believe rested on buffalo skins strewn at their will about the earth enclosed by the logs.

" Soon after going to bed I discovered what my husband had carefully kept from me—that we were surrounded by some two hundred Indians, who were now sheltered in the hut the trader had abandoned for this new one, and were preparing to hold, this night, one of their peculiar festivals. Soon after they commenced their hideous singing and dancing, accompanied by the beating of sticks upon something that resembled a gong, altogether forming a combination of sound and movement as revolting as any thing I ever saw or heard. In the intervals when they paused for rest, the night hawks, wheeling close to our low hut, by their wild shrill cries effectually set sleep at defiance. Never amid earth's varied experiences shall I forget that night.

"Feverish and ill, I arose the next morning, with scarcely purpose enough to link thought with plan, but on the suggestion that if we proceeded on our journey to the Grand River country, I must suffer myself to be paddled across the Thornapple river by an Indian, alone with him in his canoe, while our horses should swim under the guidance of my husband, I decided that it was not possible, and soon after got ready to retrace our steps. To avoid the re-crossing of the marsh, and the discomforts of the evening before, the Indian trader, at our suggestion, indeed solicitation, promised to be our guide by a more circuitous route. To be our companion it was necessary to catch one of the many Indian ponies that were feeding in a drove not far from the hut. The process amazed me much. A rope was fastened to the side of the house, some four feet from the ground, and two or three of the Indians held the line firmly at the other end, while others drove the horses up towards the house, and when sufficiently near, quietly enclosed them with the circling cord, which as soon as the horses perceived, they yielded quietly, and the one selected even bowed his head to the halter. Experience had evidently taught them that resistance was vain.

*   *   *   *   *   *

"Late on Saturday afternoon we arrived at the village of ———, where we proposed spending the Sabbath. Externally the inn promised well, as it was large, well ventilated, and apparently comfortably furnished. We soon tested the truth of the ever applicable maxim, that 'appearances often deceive.' Our supper was one of the worst prepared and most uncomfortable meals that had been offered in all our journey. The utter want of cleanliness was absolutely

18*

disgusting, and no part of the house seemed in its arrangement to recognize the fact that human comfort and health required as indispensable the use of fresh water and soap. I was shown with some parade into my room, which was a large one, furnished barely with the things required, and soon retired after a serious conflict between weariness and the revulsion of feeling occasioned by the appearance of the bed. However, fatigue triumphed ; and protecting myself from contact with sheets and pillow-cases as best I might, I threw myself upon the bed. Almost immediately after I was informed in a sort of apologetic way, that my room was the thoroughfare of the sleeping loft above ; and as there was no other ingress or egress, I was compelled to acquiesce in the arrangement, as if it were a matter of course. Some twenty men passed thus to their repose ; but as they were sad laggards on the beautiful Sabbath, I was able to get up, and take such time as I pleased for my toilet, without fear of being disturbed.

" The evening before I had asked the little handmaid of the inn to bring me in the morning a basin of water and a towel, having provided myself with the latter article in case of need on my journey, but not thinking of using my own in a large inn, and that in one of the chief villages in Michigan. In the morning I again demanded of the girl the indispensable convenience, which she speedily brought in the form of an earthen *pint* bowl of water, and a coarse towel, not quite half a yard square. I however received it gratefully, and determined to make the best of it until I could find pump, cistern, or spring, when to my amazement and amusement too, in a few moments the girl returned with the request that I would *lend* my towel to the Judge (the Circuit Court was holding a session there), and she would *return* it in a few moments.

" After a breakfast which was but a slight improvement upon the evening meal, we asked if there was any religious service held in the place, and were told that there was, at the usual hour, in a certain school-house to which we were directed, and which we reached after a disagreeable walk across a marsh. The school-house resem bled in proportions a ten-pin alley, rude and incomplete in construction, and exhibited marks (such as broken windows, etc.) of physical energy ill directed, rather than the practical effects of any mental skill. When we reached the house about a dozen were assembled, which number increased in about twenty-five minutes to as many persons. I became weary and impatient, but the audience contented themselves while awaiting the arrival of their minister who was regularly employed to preach twice on the Sabbath, with conversation one with another. After a while, when the delay even to the villagers seemed unreasonable and unaccountable, and possibly the 'on dits' of the past week had been thoroughly gone over, there was a visible stir in the congregation, and as if with one consent they evinced a disposition to inquire into the matter. At last one man arose, observed that there must be something the matter with their minister, and inquired if any one present had heard of his having left town. No one seemed to know anything respecting him, and then a proposition was made to disperse. A hymn was given out by some one who commenced without delay in a powerful and rather pleasant voice, and sang manfully through six verses of a hymn unknown I presume to the rest of the audience, and which was entirely inappropriate to both time and circumstances.

"Before this was quite ended the people began to go out, and at its close there was a general movement. Suddenly this seemed to be arrested, and we all stopped at the whisper, 'He has come—he is here!' We again took our seats, and the clergyman walked in and up to the desk with calm unruffled mien, as if the ordinary hour for his duty had but just arrived. After sitting a moment, with due solemnity he arose, and instead of offering prayer, or any religious sentiment, said coolly, 'My friends, I did not hear the bell when it was rung this morning, and forgot to look at my watch; I was waiting for the bell when one of the young men came up for me. As there are so few left here of the congregation, I think we will wait for service until the afternoon.' And then, without a prayer, benediction, or reminder of any sort that this was holy time, we were allowed to depart.

"That afternoon my husband and myself preferred to worship in the glorious temple of the adjoining forest, where we found

"'Neath cloistered boughs the floral bell that swingeth,
  And tolls its perfume on the passing air,
Makes Sabbath in the woods, and ever ringeth
  A call to prayer.' "

A few extracts from another journal of a lady residing in Michigan, whose family removed thither in 1837, and as usual occupied a log cabin till their house was ready, will further illustrate our subject.

"The house stood on a plain which had once been covered with beautiful trees, of which now remained only the stumps—for every thing like a tree which could possibly cast its longest shadow within range of the dwelling had been hewn down; and there, as an old woman said to me, 'the sun could shine in nicely all day long, looking so *improvement* like;' and there the tenement stood, not with bare walls, for the native bark had not left the logs. A small door gave entrance to its one room, eighteen or twenty feet square; one little window with four panes of glass made darkness, dust, and cobwebs visible; a huge 'Dutch chimney' occupied the opposite side, and as time had been busy with its untempered clay, having broken away one half its hearth and left many of its ribs bare, added greatly to the dust and litter covering the black oaken boards of the floor. These boards had been laid down without planing or nailing to the beams on which they rested, and it behoved one to step daintily in approaching their extremities. I giddily wished to be first to set foot within our new home, and had jumped from the carriage and rushed to the latch-string, exclaiming 'now on your patron lady call,' when I found myself landed in the cellar. Fortunately it was not very deep, and on my ascension, mamma's rueful face warned me to make merry of it all. New rough boards were laid about half way across the beams overhead, and these ur 'landlord' called the 'chamber floor.' The ascent was by a ladder of most primitive construction."   *   *   *

" We have knelt together in prayer for the first time in our new home, and have gathered around the family board to our first meal in our own wilderness. This family board was two boards resting at either end on barrels, and we sat on our trunks, as we have no chairs; our furniture cannot be brought from Detroit until the mud assuages and the dry land begins to appear. Seventeen of us sat down, and my dear father looked quite patriarchal, dispensing food to such a multitude. Such artificial distinctions as servant and master not eating together, are not to be known among us."   *   *

" We have tacked sheets against the edges of the boards consti- tuting the 'chamber floor,' which are to be drawn up during the day, and at night let down to form a sleeping room for what our helps call the 'females.' We have made a bedstead for papa and mamma, by putting together six large trunks, which during the day- time serve us for seats, and fortunately we brought a feather bed in the baggage-wagon. For the rest we have filled straw ticks with the sweet smelling marsh hay.

" *May* 24*th.*—Last night just as sleep had pressed his heaviest seal upon our eyelids, the fearful cry of ' fire,' dispelled his poppy charm. We waked to a startling consciousness of danger, at the red glare and roaring crackling flames. Then dash went the cold water, darkness followed, and then came running little rivulets of the extinguishing element, making deposits around our beds upon the floor. We were half frozen for the rest of the night, and this morn- ing they are building a new chimney. The logs are sawn out, and large cobble stones piled one upon another—the chinks filled in with clay—then from among the trees of the forest are sought out a couple of bent boughs with exactly the right curve—these are the jams, and are fastened—the upper ends from ten to twelve feet apart—in the beams that support the second floor. They are set from five to six feet from the logs of the nouse side, into which their lower ends are securely fastened. A quantity of green wood is then split up into slats, nailed across these and also laid up above them as children build pens with corn cobs, gradually lessening as they approach the roof, from which they rise some two feet; the whole is finally plastered over with new clay, and the chimney is now ready for use; the blue smoke begins to curl from its top; and there will be no danger of this one's taking fire for some years, being made of such green materials.   It was a good thing that mamma with her New York notions about fires, refused to go to sleep last night without two pails of water in the house, although the men had to go a quarter of a mile to the creek for it.   This perseverance in an old habit saved us our present home, as the fire never could have been extinguished if the water had not been on the spot.

" Our carpenter is making us some seats and a table.   The latter consists of two wooden horses with a moveable top, made of four boards nicely planed and joined together: the seats are slabs about four feet long, with four sticks driven for legs.   They are one and all to go out of doors at nights, to let the beds come in—the latter take day board on the fence.   Some wooden pins have been driven into the logs on one side of the house, and boards placed upon them for shelves, and on these must repose the milk-pans, dishes, &c.   When we would go into the cellar we take up an entire board and jump down about four feet.   But what are a few trifling inconveniences in the midst of a world so robed in beauty, so garlanded with flowers !

" *May 25th.*—Papa inquired yesterday at dinner of our landlord if he could find us a washerwoman.   His characteristic reply was, that he presumed the widow Lewis would willingly come and help us wash, if she was sure of being ' treated like a human.'   ' And how shall that be ?' asked papa.   ' Oh, if the young ladies will call on her.   You know the folks round here think you are all so proud.'   Papa looked at me, and I said I would call if it was not too far.   ' Oh they live just over the hill, not more than half a mile. Mrs. Lewis is the daughter of old Mr. Dean, who was here this morning—she has five children—there are two married sons with their wives and two children each, also living with them in the house, and then there is another daughter, Jenny Deans, as they call her, quite an old girl.' My ideas brightened at the charmed name of ' Jenny Deans,' and I began to fancy it would be pleasant to call—and so call we did—but the Deans were all gone for the cows. We went in and had a little chat with old Mrs. Deans, whose pale grey hair neatly folded beneath the plain cap, looked quite beautiful. It was a very comfortable new log house, with its clean and stationary floor—its two doors opening opposite each other—its large sash window, home-made chairs and bedsteads too. ' Your house is much better than Mr. B—'s,' observed I, in reply to some inquiry of the old dame, as to how we liked living in a log house. ' Ah yes,' said she, ' but it will do you good to learn how poor people live.' It seems to give the people here indescribable happiness to know we are worse off than themselves.

" About an hour after our return, the whole missing population of the Dean mansion returned our call. We arranged with them the preliminaries for ' the great wash,' which is to come off to-morrow. Mamma could not coax them to take it to themselves although, because of the scarcity of water in our own immediate neighborhood, the clothes are all to be taken to their own washing ground on the banks of a beautiful lake, a little back from their house. The widow Lewis would have one of us to help her, although offered double the amount to do it alone. And so I shall attend upon her ladyship to-morrow, although mamma will not believe that I know anything about washing. Papa came to our aid with the observation, ' the children must all learn to work, and the sooner they begin the better.'

" *May* 27th.—Yesterday was one of those glorious days when earth, sky and sunshine, seem to have met in gala mood to celebrate the carnival of time. At an early hour the requisites for the grand washing were placed in our oxen chariot, and the children, who looked upon the whole as a fine frolic, mounted on top of the load. How beautiful looked the world as we slowly wended our way beneath those stately old oaks which, shading the flow ery lawns, deserve the name of oak orchards. The birds were singing and the sun was shining, and not yet were the dewdrops exhaled. Those pert little children of spring, the anemones and violets, were everywhere opening their blue eyes. On one side of a growing wheatfield, a soft green sward sloped gently to the shore of a little gem of a lake, bordered by a stately growth of park-like trees on all sides but one, where a heavy growth of tamarack cast a deep shadow, beautiful from the contrast of cheerful light. In the most picturesque spot on the borders of this lake was built our gipsy fire—and around it were gathered such a group! The beau of the morning was the man who owns our log tenement, and acts in the double capacity of landlord and laborer ; beside him sat upon the same log Jenny Deans. Oh, with what a broken pinion came fancy from her dreamland flight—and yet she seems a character in her way—dressed in a gown of many colors, from the oft application of a new piece to the old garment. Her ugliness, however, faded to a thing of naught beside the Lewis family—the whole of whom, six in number, were present with us for the entire day.   *   *   *   *

"Mamma is beginning to look almost worn out with her many cares, and constant watching and anxiety about papa, who suffers continually. It seems as if those who sit beside the sick and suffering endure half their agony, feel every pain that racks the anguished nerves, and almost lose their identity in the strong sympathy that hour after hour binds frail woman to the side of the weary couch, through long nights suspending every breath and motion of the tired frame, longing to hush the very beatings of her heart, lest she disturb the light half slumber of the invalid. Ah, these are the hours that take large drafts from life, that dim the flush of youth, that drink the dew of the morning. But they give the soul its beauty and perfection, and therefore should we rejoice that they are woman's allotted task."   *   *

"*May 29th.*—Mrs. B—— was telling us to-day that many people lived for weeks last winter on boiled acorns. It is almost

impossible to get seed for planting—potatoes after the eyes were cut
out, it is said, have sold for ten dollars a bushel."

" *June 1st.*—A barrel of white fish is spoiled to-day. The field
mice have got into the milk pans and committed suicide."

" *June 2nd.*—Returning with little Jessie from a visit, as the twilight was beginning to grow shadowy, we crossed the desert marsh
and came in sight of a lonely house on its verge. On the height
that overlooked our way, stood a woman locking weird as any
Meg Merrilies that ever haunted "Ellengowan." Her form was tall,
straight and very lank, a closely clinging, scanty garment of a
gloomy gray material added, if possible, to her height ; her head
was covered with a red bandanna, pinned cornerwise beneath her
chin, in her hand she held an oaken stick, and just as we came near
she was lifting up her voice to cry aloud. The shriek formed itself
into the words, " have you seen Mary ? have you seen Mary or the
cow ?" I had not seen Mary or the cow, and went on my way
wondering. It seems the tall woman is no common person. According to the heraldry of the wild woods the Winchel's are quite
a distinguished family. Such distinction would have suited the
leader of a bandit horde in the dark forests of old Germany, or have
given renown to one of the fierce barons of feudal times. Uncle
Jake, as the head of the house is called, inhabits the lonely log cabin
by the marsh-side, and exercises his taste for cruelty at the expense
of his cattle instead of the lives of his fellow creatures, so we call
him an old savage, and probably his name will die with him, as die
yearly many of his flocks and herds from the effects of his blows.
Strange to say, however, this rude, fierce man, with all his uncurbed
passions and taste for club discipline, has never been known to ill-
treat his wife. It is said she commands his respect in an extraor-
dinary degree by her quiet dignity of manner and womanly reserve,
never noticing his violent outbursts of rage, nor interfering in the
least with his proceedings, though he has during the few years of
their sojourn here, beaten two cows to death and several oxen.
Their food is of the coarsest kind, but she asks no luxuries ; the social
tea-kettle finds no place on their hearth, no chicken scratches in the

desolate barnyard, no soft-furred pussy purrs beside the door, no dog could live upon the premises; corn, bread, potatoes, and milk when the cow gets leave to live, constitute their bill of fare the year round.   Only one child and that a daughter has come to the desolate home of these people, the Mary who was missing to-night.

"*June 3rd.*—We had another visitor this afternoon.   A pleasant, kind looking man, of a most excellent countenance, rode up to the door and claimed papa as a cousin, and was recognised at once though they had not met for twenty years.   He has a house full of daughters with whom we are to be excellent friends, although they live some fifteen miles hence, and he promises us some chickens and a kitten, a necessary kind of domestics that we have not yet seen in the region round about.   A good old woman, too, has sent for the washing, which she will perform at her own house, without any of us acting as laundry maids.   The drove of calves is increasing, and they begin to talk about sacrificing the two oldest, but Liney and Niagara shall not want for petitioners before the house of Lords."

"*June 10th.*—Rain! rain! rain!   For three days the windows of heaven have been opened, and torrents of water have fallen over the earth, and some few cataracts have found their way through our roof, which, by the way, is not shielded by shingles, but covered with long slabs held down by poles of tamarack or willow.

" When the door is open the rain beats in, and when it is closed the chimney smokes.   The cattle, on social thoughts intent, have gathered round the house, from which no fence excludes them, and thus increase the mud every body is bringing in on their feet.   The beds are piled up in one corner; the table seems more huge than ever; the topheavy slab seats are continually tumbling over; papa's rheumatism is horrible; the baby cries because of the smoke; the men, under shadow of the ladder, are mending nets and making hoe handles, ox bows, and whip stocks, and of course increasing the general litter with their whittling; the children are building play-houses under the table, and of course greatly facilitating the motion of the pen essaying to write above.   The four little panes of glass just make darkness visible, and around them those who would read or write congregate—a solemn looking assemblage, and as ruminating as those chewing the cud without. But the children are coming from under the table asking for a story; the babe consents to go to sleep; the shavings are swept into the fire, which therefore concludes to blaze more and smoke less; our good father is falling into a doze, and so the owl's eyes shall be laid aside with madam goose's fragment, and pleasant fairy-dom come with its gorgeous dreams at the juvenile bidding. It will not take much imagination after this week's experience for them to believe that whole nations of people could live in a nut-shell, or more magnificent still, inhabit gorgeous palaces within the cup of the lily."

XXV.

ELIZABETH KENTON.*

THE name of Simon Kenton has a conspicuous place in the annals of the early pioneers, second only to that of the renowned woodsman, Daniel Boone. One of the counties of Kentucky is named after him, and the incidents of his life are related in the history of that State and in many biographical sketches, forming a narrative more thrilling in interest than any romance ever written. Such instances of desperate and mortal encounter, such hairbreadth escapes from imminent peril, such hours of fearful suspense and sudden alternations from hope to despair, from the very grasp of death to unexpected deliverance, were surely never pictured by pure imagination. Born in Virginia, he was involved when scarcely grown to manhood in a romantic adventure growing out of rivalry in love, which came near to having a fatal termination, and launched him into life with no protection but a resolute spirit and a robust frame. Leaving his home, he plunged into the wilderness of the Alleghany mountains, and joining parties of explorers and traders, spent two or three years

* The papers relating to Mrs. Kenton were received after the volume was stereotyped, which accident causes the appearance of the memoir thus out of its proper place. It should be read next to that of Rebecca Boone. I am indebted to the kindness of B. Henkle, Esq., of Rensselaer, Indiana, to whom the materials were furnished by the daughter of Gen. Kenton.

in hunting and trapping in the neighbourhood of the Kanawha river, till the breaking out of the war between the Indian tribes and the colonies in 1774, in which campaign he did service as a spy. With two companions he afterwards penetrated the wilds of Kentucky and built a cabin on the spot where now stands the town of Washington, aiding the other settlers in their struggles with the Indians, and meeting with many adventures. The most remarkable of these—unparalleled in the history of the West—is the succession of incidents that followed his capture by the Indians when carrying off some of their horses. For weeks his fate vibrated between life and death, the gleams of sunshine quickly followed by deepest gloom, no efforts or wisdom of his own availing aught to save him at any time, but the changes in his fortune wrought by seeming accidents. He was tied, Mazeppa-like, on the back of an unbroken horse; was eight times exposed to the gauntlet, and three times bound to the stake, with no prospect of rescue from a terrible death. Once he was saved by the interference of Simon Girty, who, learning his name, discovered in him an old companion and friend; once the celebrated Mingo chief, Logan, interceded in his behalf, and he was rescued by an Indian agent. These experiences, and his after services with Gen. George Rogers Clarke, and in other campaigns to the close of Wayne's decisive one, are fully related in recent biographies.

The first wife of Gen. Kenton was Martha Dowden, to whom he was married about 1785, in Mason County, Kentucky. They lived together ten years, when she died, leaving him four children, all of whom lived to maturity. The only survivor among them is the wife of John McCord, of Urbana, Ohio.

Elizabeth, the second wife, was the youngest daughter of Stephen Jarboe, a native of France, who settled first in Maryland, where he married Elizabeth, the daughter of Thomas Clelland. She was a well educated woman, and a deeply spiritual Christian, in membership with the Presbyterian Church. The family removed to Mason County, Kentucky, about the year 1796, at which time Elizabeth, the daughter, was seventeen years old. Her opportunities of education had been such as were usual in that early day, when the acquirements of women were generally confined to reading, writing, and the elements of arithmetic.

Not long after the removal to Kentucky, Mr. Jarboe was obliged to go to Maryland, whence he was prevented from returning to his family by ill health, for seven or eight years. It will be borne in mind that travelling, in those days, was no light undertaking. Within that time Mrs. Jarboe with her children had removed into what is now Clarke County in Ohio. Her home was with her youngest son, Philip Jarboe, about four miles north of Springfield, where she died in the spring of 1808. Shortly after her death Mr. Jarboe was enabled to return, and in the same year, at the same house, he also closed his earthly pilgrimage. His acquaintances remember his arrival—a feeble old man, sadly emaciated, coming, as he said, to lay his bones by the side of her who was the companion of his youth. After a life of many sorrows they sleep in a quiet spot within sight of the Mad River and Lake Erie Railroad, near their last home on earth.

Their daughter Elizabeth was a young woman of rare attractions of person and manner, and as it may be supposed, had numerous admirers. Among these a Mr. Reuben Clark had found favor in her eyes, and it was expected that she would marry him. But the sagacious pioneer and hero of Indian encounters had seen and loved her, and moreover had lost none of his early aversion to a rival. He gave young Clark some employment which took him to Virginia, and would oblige him to be absent a considerable length of time. Having removed him from the scene of action, he laid siege presently to the heart of the fair lady, and brought the citadel, ere long, to terms of capitulation. They were married in the year 1798, at Kenton's Station, the Rev. William Wood of the Baptist Church officiating; nor did the wife ever again see her former lover

A few months after the marriage, General and Mrs. Kenton re moved to Cincinnati, where they resided six or eight months, and removed in the spring of 1799, to what was then called the Mad River country. Their first residence was near a trading house kept

by a Frenchman named De Baw, about four miles north of Spring
field. The whole region, at that period, was an almost unbroken
wilderness, traversed continually by parties of Indians, who, though
not openly hostile, were exceedingly troublesome. Often when in-
toxicated they would visit the cabins of the settlers, and finding the
men absent, by threats extort provisions and whiskey from the
women. On one occasion, when there were no men on the premises,
and all was quiet in Mrs. Kenton's cabin, the door was suddenly
burst open, and a drunken Indian, entirely naked, came in and demanded whiskey, threatening to kill her, with furious gestures, in
case of refusal. When he found his menaces were likely to be of
no avail, he snatched up the child, her eldest daughter, out of the
cradle, and made for the camp of the savages as fast as his feet could
carry him. The feelings of the terrified mother cannot easily be
described; but her agony of suspense was soon over; the rest of
the party immediately brought back the child, and called upon Mrs.
Kenton to say what punishment should be inflicted on the delinquent.
She required nothing, however, but to be protected against such
outrages in future.

The home of the forest warrior consisted of two roughly constructed log cabins, with the usual accompaniment of puncheon
floors, mud chimneys, clapboard doors, etc. Here were established
Kenton's family, composed of himself and wife with five children,
and his two mothers-in-law with their families, besides some black
people. Their experiences of privation and suffering during the
earliest years of the settlement may be understood in some measure
by those already described; but there were circumstances which
added much to the trials that fell to the lot of Mrs. Kenton. The
General, it will be remembered, being one of the earliest pioneers
of Kentucky, besides defending the first settlers against their Indian
foes, had located their pre-emptions, traversing with them the rugged
mountains and rich valleys in search of the best lands. The latch-
string of Kenton's cabin always hung outside the door, and a
welcome was ready for all who sought his hospitality. His
generosity and habitual kindness to strangers had contributed

as much as that of any other man in Kentucky to stamp the character for liberal hospitality, since proverbially attached to the State. He was extensively known, and had the reputation of wealth ; his wealth, however, consisted wholly in Kentucky land claims, which were totally unproductive, while his cabin was the resort of every shelterless emigrant, land hunter, or soldier, and even the wandering Indian had liberty at any time to claim the supply of his wants. The readers of Gen. Kenton's life will recollect the incident of an Indian at old Chilicothe seizing an axe and breaking his arm with it. The name of this savage was Boner, and it was afterwards his custom to come frequently to his house, and after eating and drinking, amuse the company by acting out a pantomime representing his own outbreak of fury, and the terror and grief of Mrs. Kenton on that occasion.

With this continual influx of visitors, for whom provision was necessary as well as for the wants of a large family, with means of procuring none of the luxuries and but few of the comforts of life, and without congenial society, the first ten years of Mrs. Kenton's residence in Ohio were passed in incessant toil and privation, relieved by little of the quiet so necessary to one like her, and so ardently desired. But she was a seeker of " a better country," and the firm faith of a Christian sustained her in every difficulty. In 1808 she became a member of the Methodist Episcopal Church. In 1810, Gen. Kenton removed to Urbana, in Champaign County, where the family lived eight years. Here their privations were less, but Mrs. Kenton suffered from incessant mental anxiety caused by the injustice done her husband, and the loss he sustained in endeavoring to recover something of his extensive land claims in Kentucky. Being wholly uneducated, he was obliged to entrust the management of his business to agents who proved dishonest, and involved him in inextricable lawsuits in which he was mulcted in heavy costs. Nay more, truth compels the record which is a stain upon the national honor—the barbarous laws then in force, sanctioning these wrongs, permitted the imprisonment of the brave pioneer, and his confinement within " prison bounds," for several of the best years of his life. Thus was he reduced from a supposed condition of opulence to abject poverty, and even pursued like a felon, his free spirit harassed by more than the deprivation of liberty to the limbs, the sense of cruel injustice and oppression.

Mrs. Kenton possessed a disposition peculiarly sensitive, and these wrongs and sorrows embittered what should have been the happiest years of her life. In 1818, having procured a small portion of wild land in what is now Logan County, they took up their residence upon it, obtaining from it a meagre living, far from those who had thronged around them in the days of their prosperity. In 1836, after enduring much suffering, Gen. Kenton departed this life, rejoicing in the prospect of one where his portion could not be taken from him. His faithful wife attended him in his painful illness with the assiduous tenderness and care bestowed by a mother on her child. Her spirits, already weighed down by calamity, were broken, and her strong constitution impaired by the exertions necessary in this labor of love, and after her husband's death she never recovered her health or cheerfulness. In the same year she removed to Indiana. Her strength gradually declined until the autumn of 1842, when she became almost helpless. Having long looked on approaching death with calmness and Christian hope, she quietly made a disposition of her remaining effects, leaving to each of her children and grand-children a small bequest, in token of affectionate remembrance. To the sons of her eldest daughter, Mrs. Parkison she left quilts on which she had wrought their names with her own hand. Her faculties were retained perfectly to the last, though she spoke not for some hours before the final moment. Her sufferings terminated at the residence of J. G. Parkison, her son in-law, in Jasper County, Indiana, Nov. 27th, 1842.

Mrs. Kenton was rather tall, and had a very graceful figure; her complexion was extremely fair, and she had blue eyes and dark hair. Her daughter, Mrs. Parkison, describes her appearance on one occasion, on returning from Dayton, thirty miles distant, where she had been to acknowledge a deed. She wore a dark calico dress made in the fashion then called a habit; long-waisted, and the

19

skirt plaited full all around ; over this a "joseph," or short riding dress of brown cassimere, with green spots, and a green silk or satin bonnet differing little from the late fashion, without a cap.

This lady remembers, among the visitors at her father's house, old Isaac Zane, who had an Indian wife. He brought his half breed daughter to be instructed by Mrs. Kenton in the knowledge and manners of the white ladies. Ebenezer Zane, his son, was also a frequent visitor, and told Miss Kenton he had named his little daughter—Matilda—after her. The child received the customary present, and some twenty years afterwards Mrs. Parkison was surprised at being shown a piece of the new dress given her little namesake by the General. Mrs. Parkison still resides in Indiana.

INDEX

www.ingramcontent.com/pod-product-compliance
Lightning Source LLC
Chambersburg PA
CBHW070239290326
41929CB00046B/1919